SHAKESPEARE AND THE TRADITIONS OF COMEDY

LEO SALINGAR

Fellow of Trinity College, Cambridge

CAMBRIDGE UNIVERSITY PRESS

Published by the Syndics of the Cambridge University Press
Bentley House, 200 Euston Road, London NW1 2DB
American Branch: 32 East 57th Street, New York, N.Y. 10022

© Cambridge University Press 1974

Library of Congress Catalogue Card Number: 73–91617

ISBN: 0 521 20384 8

First published 1974

Printed in Great Britain
by W & J Mackay Limited, Chatham

TO JEAN

CONTENTS

vii

PREFACE

I began work for this book a long time ago with the intention of writing a study of Shakespeare's comedies introduced by some account in outline of the earlier dramatic forms and traditions that influenced him. A study following these lines could, I thought, throw fresh light on the conventions he uses or the ideas associated with them, as well as on his position in the drama of his time and possibly on the course of his personal development. But I found that if my historical outline was to be of use or interest for my purpose I could not make it brief enough to fit the whole undertaking conveniently into one pair of covers. Consequently, I have divided my undertaking into two. A sequel to this book will discuss Shakespeare's comedies more directly and continuously; the present book is largely historical and my discussion here of details from Shakespeare's plays is selective (without, I trust, being arbitrary). My object is to indicate what seem to me his points of departure: his choice of narrative and dramatic conventions from the medieval traditions of stage romance; his far-reaching but independent application of classico-renaissance conceptions of comedy; and finally some of the innovations connected with his position as an Elizabethan actor–dramatist writing in the first period of the commercial theatre in Europe, or with his personal interest in Italian short stories.

A reader can soon see that I have depended extensively on Professor Geoffrey Bullough's invaluable examination of Shakespeare's sources. My concern, however, is less with particular sources than with general traditions or underlying conventions. In describing medieval influences I have had to use indirect evidence and inference because although the continuity of stage romance from Chaucer's time to Shakespeare's seems to me demonstrable and important, the direct evidence for it from English sources is only fragmentary. In describing the classical legacy to Shakespeare and the Italian additions to it, on the other hand, it has been necessary to select and compress. In both cases, I have ventured into ground where I cannot claim a specialist's familiar knowledge or insight. Such an enterprise, I am aware, carries particular risks. But a restricted approach to Shakespeare's antecedents would be false to the subject, and the risks have seemed worth accepting for the sake of a comparative survey which tries to take account, as I believe it must, of contrasts and variations in the long traditions of comedy as well as inheritances and resemblances.

I have concentrated on the history of comedy as a dramatic form, rather than 'the comic spirit'. I have not followed a chronological order. For the sequence of the argument, however, I have discussed the medieval traditions behind Shakespeare's comedies in chapter 2 before turning to the classical and then the renaissance traditions in chapters 3 to 5.

I have confined the footnotes to references and have tried to make each entry as short as clarity will allow. Fuller references to the books and articles cited will be found in the bibliography.

Parts of this book are based on material in articles of mine in *Shakespeare Quarterly* and *Renaissance Drama* and in a contribution to the collection on *Dramaturgie et Société* published by the Centre National de la Recherche Scientifique; I am grateful for the editors' permission to use this material again. I owe a number of ideas to the give-and-take of supervisions with my students at Cambridge; and I am grateful for the opportunities I have had to try out my opinions in lectures for the Cambridge Board of Extra-Mural Studies, for M. Jean Jacquot's research seminar on the theatre at the C.N.R.S. in Paris and for the English departments at Rouen and other universities abroad, as well as for the English Faculty at Cambridge. I owe more suggestions than can be adequately pointed out in footnotes to the work of M. Jacquot, and a general and long-standing debt to Professor M. C. Bradbrook, who supervised my first post-graduate research. Professors Bradbrook, M. I. Finley and D. H. Green and Mr H. A. Mason have kindly read parts or all of my typescript and I should like to thank them for their criticism and comment. Mr Mason has also helped me most generously in the preparation of the index. I am grateful to Dr and Mrs C. E. Baron for their kindness in helping to check the proofs. And not the least of my gratitude is due to my wife for her help in preparing the bibliography and for many practical suggestions.

Leo Salingar

March 1974

I

THE UNFAITHFUL MIRROR

'O Muse, banish wars and dance with me, your friend, celebrating the weddings of the gods, the banquets of men, and the festivals of the blessed' – for these are the themes that have always been your care.

Aristophanes

Comedy is a game played to throw reflections upon social life, and it deals with human nature in the drawing-room of civilised men and women.

Meredith

Comedy has usually meant one thing in theory and another in practice. In the mainstream of critical theory the prime task allotted to it has been the representation of typical characters and probable incidents from common life; according to the definition attributed to Cicero, which renaissance humanists and their successors never tired of repeating, it was 'the imitation of life, the mirror of custom, the image of truth'. This definition can be taken in two senses, as a mirror can be used either to reflect one's appearance or to correct it; but in its most direct sense the definition simply ignores or even contradicts the evidence that many of the plays it refers to are fantastic or remote from ordinary life and that most, if not all, of them contain situations that strain probability. And, for similar reasons, the argument that a comedy is essentially an instrument for moral correction remains, on the face of it, special pleading or else a pious aspiration. The interpretation of Shakespeare's comedies, in particular, has suffered from the discrepancy between critical theory and the practice of his art.

From the Greeks to Shakespeare's time and beyond, comedy has kept the signs of its origins in, and association with, seasonal festivities; the plot conventions which renaissance playwrights inherited from the New Comedy of Plautus and Terence were not imitations of common events but schematic episodes from romance or domesticated myth, or else stylised versions of practical jokes. The central figure in Old Comedy was a masked buffoon; and, with or without the assistance of a clown, the writers of comedy since Aristophanes have exalted high spirits and a primitive desire for life-renewal, instead of seeking merely to reflect life as it stands. They have loaded their dice in favour of youth, luck and mother-wit, as against such civilising virtues as prudence, sobriety and discretion. It is hardly surprising, therefore, that many renaissance moralists, in spite of their reverence for Latin culture, attacked comedy fiercely, and that some of them, like Ascham, only countenanced the academic study of Plautus and Terence under caution. As to the Comic Muse on the early Elizabethan stage, even Sidney, defending the drama, felt bound to concede that 'naughty Play-makers and Stage-keepers have justly made [her] odious'. The typical humanist apology for comedy, which Sidney adopted, consisted of reiterating the notion of the art-form as a mirror in one sense while restricting it in another: in the first place, the 'right use' of comedy, as 'an imitation of the common errors of our life', was to serve as a signal against the traps of experience; and secondly, Sidney would admit to the stage such laughter as conveys 'delightful teaching', but not 'such scornful matters as stirreth laughter only'. Similarly Ben Jonson, among others following Sidney's lead, appeals to the Ciceronian definition of comedy only to limit it right away to 'a thing throughout pleasant and ridiculous, and accommodated to the correction of manners'. Instead of admitting that their time-honoured analogy of the mirror is either false or insufficient, theorists in this dominant neo-classical vein try to take advantage of its ambiguity; under pretence of describing what comedy is like they are recommending how it ought to be read and how it ought to be written. In the meantime, they tacitly accept the second inherited but logically unrelated principle about comedy, that – far from reproducing the miscellaneous sequence of real life – the incidents in a comic play should follow a route predetermined, at least in general terms, as a passage from distress to a happy ending. There is no necessary connection between the principle of the happy ending and the principle of the mirror (however inter-preted), even though writers of comedy have habitually obliged them to coincide.

Shakespeare too acknowledges that 'the purpose of playing' – not limited to comedy, indeed – 'was and is to hold, as 'twere, the mirror up to nature', with the function of illuminating and correcting moral behaviour; at least, he acknowledges the force of this theory to the extent of making Hamlet expound it. But there is nothing in his text to show whether Shakespeare himself considers this statement as an apology for his own comedies already acted, or as a critique of his own comedies (both of which seem unlikely), or as the strongest theory available, or the one most in character for the scholarly prince. However this may be, those later critics, Meredith for example, who have sought in comedy for a picture of manners as free as possible from stage convention, have taken their standards not from Shakespeare but from Molière or Jonson or Terence. Yet at bottom there is little to choose between Shakespeare and the other dramatists with respect to their faithfulness to common reality. Terence's *Brothers*, for example, contains a study in character and manners, it is true, but the plot depends on the conventional bases of coincidence, dissimulation and a sudden change of heart. Possibly *Le Misanthrope* is the only traditional comic masterpiece in which the impression of artifice resides only in the manners of the characters portrayed, and theatrical devices such as coincidence or mistakes of identity seem to contribute nothing of importance. But one masterpiece does not make a genre. And it can hardly be maintained that here Molière has dropped his usual methods for the sake of an untrammelled essay in realism; on the contrary, the brilliance of *Le Misanthrope* lies in the way the poet has identified psychological realism with the festive conventions of the comic stage by setting his protagonist in opposition to a pleasure-loving, artificial society whose members try to live their daily lives as a ceremony of *complaisance*. As for the difference between the 'realistic' Ben Jonson and Shakespeare the 'romantic', the former's criticisms of the latter are certainly significant. But considered barely as portraits of manners and recitals of imaginary events, Jonson's comedies are no more credible than Shakespeare's. And Jonson, plainly, had no intention of severing comedy from festivity; witness *Bartholomew Fair*.

In *Love's Labour's Lost* Rosaline says of Berowne that

> His eye begets occasion for his wit,
> For every object that the one doth catch
> The other turns to a mirth-loving jest,
> Which his fair tongue, conceit's expositor,
> Delivers in such apt and gracious words
> That aged ears play truant at his tales
> And younger hearings are quite ravished;
> So sweet and voluble is his discourse.

This speech, with its nice distinction between the appeal of mirth to Youth and Age, recalls Sidney's praise of the poet as story-teller – 'with a tale forsooth he cometh unto you, with a tale which holdeth children from play, and old men from the chimney corner'; it could easily have

3

furnished hints for Coleridge's remarkable chapter on the characteristics of Shakespeare's early verse, or have sprung from a moment of
self-analysis by the dramatist. For Shakespeare is fond of describing
'wit' in terms of quick-ranging observation and the rapid yet harmon-
ious interconnection of ideas. It is a kind of verbal dance, a voluntary
animation of the ordinary course of thought. And Shakespeare's 'wit'
is so diffused through his comedies that we are given a heightened
sense of life, which is still true to, or continuous with, normal experience, in spite of the implausibility of much of the supporting
fiction. Presumably this is near to what Dr Johnson had in mind when,
after conventional praise to Shakespeare for upholding 'a faithful mirror
of manners and of life', he stressed the breadth of the dramatist's
outlook and the ease and flow of his dialogue:

In the writings of other poets a character is too often an individual; in those
of Shakespeare it is commonly a species...Yet his real power is not shown in
the splendour of particular passages, but by the progress of his fable, and the
tenour of his dialogue;...the dialogue of this author is often so evidently
determined by the incident which produces it, and is pursued with so much
ease and simplicity, that it seems scarcely to claim the merit of fiction, but
to have been gleaned by diligent selection out of common conversation, and
common occurrences.

While Dr Johnson's enthusiasm – not too strong a word here – seems
admirable, and justified, it may be questioned how far the dialogues in
Shakespeare's comedies really resemble 'common conversation', or
whether he could have distilled them from common conversation by a
process of 'selection' that was nothing other than 'diligent': Johnson
here is surely trimming his response to the text to fit the demands of
criticism and his age. Yet conversely (but inconsistently – at least, on
a literal reading of the doctrine of the stage as a mirror), he complains
that Shakespeare neglects poetic justice 'and is so much more careful
to please than to instruct, that he seems to write without any moral
purpose'; that the poet is carried away by his love of 'a quibble'; and
that he is often careless in plot construction, especially towards the
end of his play. Thus Johnson comments that at the end of *As You Like It*
Shakespeare 'lost an opportunity of exhibiting a moral lesson' (by
omitting to show the interview between Duke Frederick and the
hermit); that towards the end of *The Shrew* 'the arrival of the real
father, perhaps, produces more perplexity than pleasure'; and, on the
ending of *Twelfth Night*, that

4

the marriage of Olivia, and the succeeding perplexity, though well enough contrived to divert on the stage, wants credibility, and fails to produce the proper instruction required in the drama, as it exhibits no just picture of life.

In these cases, especially the last, it seems to be precisely the speed and gaiety of Shakespeare's invention that displease Johnson or leave him dissatisfied.

Much of Johnson's criticism of Shakespeare for distorting a 'just picture of life' in his comedies has, of course, outlived the neoclassical formulas in which it is couched. Shaw, looking down from a more-than-Augustan height on the provincial snob he takes the Elizabethan to be, distinguishes firmly between Shakespeare's hackneyed falsehoods, his incomparable word-music, and those wry insights into character which, from this viewpoint, made him a genuine forerunner of Ibsen, even though he failed to invent the technique of dénouement through discussion; for Shaw, 'Shakespeare survives by what he has in common with Ibsen'.[1] And some commentators today still find themselves trying to explain away the pleasure the comedies give, or can give, in the theatre, as if under a rule of aesthetic self-denial. For example, Derek Traversi, a critic very attentive to the figurative dimension of Shakespeare's verse, has restated the realistic objection to his comedies with more gravity than Johnson. The underlying experience of Shakespeare's comedies, Traversi writes, is 'not finally dissimilar in kind' from that in the tragedies or histories; but it is harder to reach, because the comedies contain more of 'an important element of convention, which has to be mastered before the human content of the plays...can begin to make itself felt'.[2] Now, it is true that conventions change and that what gave pleasure to one age – or would not have fixed itself as convention – may become obtrusive or irritating to another. But, equally, a stage convention, such as a familiar twist in a plot, is an expressive sign, a means of communication, between the playwrights who use it and the audiences who enjoy or at least accept it – until time has reduced it to a dead convention, or a bad habit. A writer who allows convention to obstruct the human content of his plays either has little human content to communicate or should not be writing for the stage. Yet this is exactly Mr Traversi's preliminary view of Shakespeare in his comedies:

---

[1] Shaw, *Ibsenism*, p. 198. (*Note*: footnote references to books and articles will be given in an abbreviated form; see the Bibliography at the end of this book).

[2] Traversi, *Shakespeare: The Early Comedies*, p. 7.

5

Artificial situations, contrived marriages, elaborate happy endings, all set in countries of the imagination, frequently act, even while they exercise their magic upon us, as impediments to full and direct participation in the dramatist's intention: impediments which, without doubt, it is well worth overcoming, but which call for a special effort, a particular kind of attention, before the necessary fullness of response can be achieved.

To be sure, the critic has allowed that these 'artificial situations' work a kind of 'magic' on us; and he goes on to argue that as Shakespeare developed he learned to put them to 'more distinctively human use'. Yet he is urging that, in order to attain 'the necessary fullness of response' to the plays, we must deliberately resist and disregard what Shakespeare wrote. The critic claims to know 'the dramatist's intention' (or else, what it should have been) more positively than the dramatist. And it seems clear that what this intention should have been is a realistic unfolding of personal complications – something very like Dr Johnson's 'just picture of life', or perhaps like Shaw's definition of 'an interesting play', one in which there is discussion of 'problems of conduct and character of personal importance to the audience'.[1] The objection that Traversi raises once again cannot simply be brushed aside. But in his argument, the possibility that Shakespeare enjoyed the 'magic' transmitted through stage contrivances is not fairly discussed; still less, the possibility that he valued them also as expressive devices, as means of shaping and crystallising his reaction to life.

The apparent opposition in discussions of Shakespeare's comedies between the critics' pleasure and the critics' judgment must stem very largely from the long-established assumption that a comedy should be intended as a *reflection* of something else. Along this line of thinking, reservations about Shakespeare must always come back to blaming him, not simply for deficiencies in human insight or occasional lapses, but for submitting to the conditions of the theatre as he knew it; except that all other writers of comedy should surely find themselves in the same boat. It cannot be shown, moreover, that Shakespeare accepted the theatrical, non-realistic elements in his art reluctantly, or that his interest in these things diminished as his thought and experience matured. On the contrary, he was from the beginning an experimenter and innovator in dramatic artifice, to a greater extent than is often supposed; and his later work shows him, not abandoning, but readapting and refining upon, the artificial devices

[1] Shaw, *Ibsenism*, p. 190.

of dramatic construction he had used in his early plays.

Nevertheless, it would be hard to imagine that Shakespeare compared the stage to a mirror without any belief in the comparison at
all. And, of course, the critical problem with regard to his comedies
would not have remained active if his sense of human reality was not
omnipresent and so powerful. We seem to be left with the paradox
that Shakespeare, in his abounding vitality, constantly reflects, or
rather illuminates, the world outside the theatre, constantly imagines
lifelike feelings and impulses in his characters and yet as constantly
mixes reality with convention or artifice; in brief, real people in unreal
situations.

A partial way out from this difficulty would seem to be to interpret
the non-realistic elements in his comedies and romances figuratively
or symbolically – a procedure which could find support in the
fondness of the Elizabethans for allegory and emblem. But with many
passages, even entire plays, a critical search for hidden meanings
can only be imposed by force.[1] And any symbolic interpretation
must take into account the whole of a playwright's dramatic
language, his idiom of action and staging as well as his poetic
imagery.

A more general solution would be to admit that a comedy can be
read, as it is instinctively received by an audience, on two planes at
once. It is a representation of life outside the theatre, partly by way of
explicit comment, mainly by way of an imitation of speech and action,
more or less literal, more or less figurative. At the same time, it is the
text for a performance which is to exist, for the time being, as an end
in itself. It provides for a series of gestures, physical and verbal. On
this plane, a comedy may approximate to ritual or to pastime,
celebration or entertainment; but it draws its meaning from its
occasion, as a performance by actors before an audience, and ultimately from the general tradition of similar occasions, rather than
from the particular story, the imaginary life-situation, of the characters
the performers are impersonating. The two planes of meaning are
perceived together, generic and particular, acting types and acted
characters, comedy as performance and as representation. And in a
successful comedy the two planes correspond to and reinforce one
another. But they must still be felt to be independent to some extent
(for otherwise it is doubtful whether we should experience the
satisfaction that comes from a complex and yet unified work of art).

[1] See Leavis, 'The Criticism of Shakespeare's Last Plays', in *The Common Pursuit*.

Never wholly independent, however. A performance without some continuous thread of representation could form a revue, but not a comedy. On the other hand, the characters and actions in a comedy never have the air of having been chosen quite freely from the author's observation of life, but always seem to emerge from, or return towards, the tradition of performance. Representation and performance are distinguishable but inseparable.

In Shakespeare's plays the sense of comedy as performance is most evident in those passages of clowning, dancing, music and the like which at first seem little more than interludes or embellishments, inessential to the plot. But the influence of the same tradition is at work, at a further remove, in the artificial-seeming conventions of his plots as well.

COMEDY AS CELEBRATION

'Is not a comonty' (or comedy), asks Christopher Sly, 'a Christmas gambold or a tumbling-trick?' No, he is told, 'it is a kind of history' (a kind recommended as a cure for 'melancholy'). But the play shows he is partly correct, since it consists largely of knockabout, practical jokes and disguises, of a kind appropriate to the Tudor Christmas holidays, the season of Misrule; the same spirit is released in the trick played on Malvolio in *Twelfth Night*. Similarly, in *Love's Labour's Lost*, when the lords' stratagem of a masked wooing has been turned to their ridicule, Berowne guesses that the ladies, 'Knowing aforehand of our merriment', had determined 'To dash it like a Christmas comedy'. At the end of the scenes of complication in *A Midsummer Night's Dream*, Theseus, out for a morning's hunting and finding the four lovers incongruously asleep in the wood, can only account for their presence by supposing that

> No doubt they rose up early to observe
> The rite of May; and, hearing our intent,
> Came here in grace of our solemnity.

These passages compare the comic action of the plays to holiday customs. Elsewhere in Elizabethan drama comedy is associated with special moments of triumph, or preparations for triumph, at court; for example, in *Edward II* Gaveston plans to confirm his hold on the king by means of 'Italian masks by night,|Sweet speeches, comedies, and pleasing shows', and at the end of *3 Henry VI*, Edward IV will mark his victory with 'stately triumphs' and 'mirthful comic shows,| Such as befits the pleasure of the court'. As C. L. Barber has emphasised in his book on *Shakespeare's Festive Comedy*, there is more than a passing or surface connection in Shakespeare's time between the idea of comedy and the ideas of holiday pastime and courtly revels.

Pastime and revelry constituted a kind of borderland between everyday life and the stage; and several episodes and structural motifs in Shakespeare's comedies are situated, as it were, in this borderland. The tricks practised on Sly and Malvolio are both described as 'pastime'; so is the lords' plan to woo the ladies in disguise in *Love's Labour's Lost*:

> In the afternoon
> We will with some strange pastime solace them,
> Such as the shortness of the time can shape;
> For revels, dances, masks, and merry hours,
> Forerun fair Love, strewing her way with flowers.

Each of these episodes forms an impromptu social game or entertainment, though it has seasonal precedents. Likewise, the deception played on Beatrice and Benedick to bring them together in *Much Ado* is a 'sport' devised by Don Pedro and his friends so that 'the time shall not go dully by us' in the interval before Claudio's wedding. At other times the revelling is more ceremonious, as with the masquerade held to celebrate Don Pedro's visit to Leonato's house after his successful campaign, or the masque before Bassanio's wooing voyage to Belmont, or the wedding masques mounted at short notice (by magical aid) in *As You Like It* and *The Tempest*. In *Love's Labour's Lost* and again in *A Midsummer Night's Dream* the whole framework of the action is contrived to resemble a courtly fête. In the former, in spite of the King of Navarre's initial inhospitality, the Princess of France is received, after all, like a royal visitor – like Elizabeth on progress at a noble household, as in the 'Princely Pleasures' at Kenilworth in 1575: she is regaled with a shoot, a masked dance with gifts, and a pageant followed by a song. Here the main plot, such as it is, turns on the welcoming of the Princess. In *A Midsummer Night's Dream* – where Oberon associates his love-inducing flower with the water-pageants and fireworks prominent at courtly festivals, and where Theseus recalls royal visits on progress[1] – the plots which

---

[1] *Midsummer Night's Dream*, II.i.148ff; V.i.44ff; (all line-references to Shakespeare

9

frame the central action arise from the preparations of the fairies and the mechanicals to honour Theseus' wedding celebrations, on which they converge, while the central plot dealing with the lovers comes to rest at the same goal. The general shaping of these two plays seems to be Shakespeare's invention; that is, they are exceptions to his usual method of adapting the broad lines of a comic plot from some previous play or narrative – as are also the plots of 'sport' directed against Malvolio and against Beatrice and Benedick. In *Love's Labour's Lost* and *A Midsummer Night's Dream* he appears to be aiming at a balance between formal ceremony and episodes of sudden impulse or sheer confusion, which yet fall, as if in spite of the actors' intentions, into patterns of custom and revelry. The masque of Russians which forms the centrepiece of the reception for the Princess in *Love's Labour's Lost* is not, in fact, a ceremony prepared in advance to seem like a surprise, as courtesy and fashion would have enjoined, but an improvisation which misfires – and thereby comes to resemble 'a Christmas comedy' after all. (Here Shakespeare was probably taking hints from actuality, for at the Gray's Inn Christmas revels of 1594, where his own *Comedy of Errors* made part of the entertainment, the Prince of Purpoole – or master of ceremonies – solemnly received an embassy of 'Russians', in other words, the 'Lord Ambassador' from the Inner Temple with his train; but the reception of these envoys was thrown into 'confusion and errors', to the 'utter discredit' of the 'Prince' of Gray's Inn. Nevertheless, the 'Prince' was invited to give a masque before Queen Elizabeth at Shrove-tide, following a pretended return visit to Russia, so that the chronicler of Gray's Inn recorded, 'Our Christmas would not leave us till such time as Lent was ready to entertain us.')[1] In the *Dream*, again, the lovers' flight from Athens, which threatens to clash with the royal solemnities, falls into place after all as a seeming 'rite of May'. Conversely, in each of these two comedies the prepared play-within-the-play turns into a fiasco, entertaining the spectators through the players' blunders. In each comedy, the spirit of revelry is invoked, disturbed and reaffirmed; and the characters comply with it most observantly when they are caught off their guard.

Beneath the pattern of a courtly entertainment in *Love's Labour's Lost* there is also a strong sense of the rhythm of the seasons. The guiding theme is the opposition between Carnival and Lent. By

refer to Alexander's edition of his *Works* unless otherwise specified). See John Dover Wilson, *Shakespeare's Happy Comedies*, pp. 191–207.

1 David (ed.), *Love's Labour's Lost*, p. xxxi; Bullough, *Sources*, vol. I, pp. 431–2, 438–41.

swearing to withdraw for three years, 'Not to see ladies, study, fast, not sleep', the King and his lords are in effect forming an untimely lenten vow; they break it in a carnival masquerade for love; but the ladies will not accept these 'perjur'd' suitors until after they have observed a kind of Lent in earnest for a year, the King in 'some forlorn and naked hermitage' and Berowne in a hospital, comforting the sick. Here again, it seems plausible to conjecture that Shakespeare was utilising recent history (or gossip), for in some ways his fictitious King of Navarre, with his ill-timed 'Academe', resembles Henry III of France, who really founded an academy, and who was notorious for his intemperance, in pleasure and penitence alike.[1] (According to the English ambassador, 'if he had a foolish toy in his head, or a monk's weed to make, or an *Ave Maria* to say, he would let his state go to wrack'; after the Carnival of 1587, a Parisian lawyer noted in his diary:

Aux jours gras, le roi fait mascarades, ballets et festins aux dames, selon sa mode accoutumée, et se donne du plaisir et du bon temps tout son saoul; et persévérant en ses dévotions (que beaucoup appelaient hypocrisie), le premier jour de carême se renferma aux capucins, faisant ou feignant y faire pénitence avec ses mignons.)

At the same time, whatever Shakespeare's use of French history (which in any case is garbled, probably by intention), his scenario has affinities with the folk-game of the 'Fight between Carnival and Lent'; at least, with the manner in which it is interpreted in Bruegel's painting, where one set of followers is shown dancing in masks, making love, watching plays or crowding into taverns, while the others are attending church or giving charity to cripples and the poor. Shakespeare, too, emphasises a moral cycle in his play, which he identifies with the cycle of the seasons. When Berowne protests against his companions' inappropriate vow to study, he explains:

> At Christmas I no more desire a rose
> Than wish a snow in May's new-fangled shows;
> But like of each thing that in season grows;

but when he smoothes away their scruples against breaking their oath for love, he provides the witty casuistry that

> It is religion to be thus forsworn;

[1] Yates, *French Academies*; Black, *Elizabeth*, p. 316; de L'Estoile, *Journal*, p. 221 (*cf ibid.*, pp. 111, 120, 134, 190).

> For charity itself fulfils the law,
> And who can sever love from charity?

– and then he urges them to action with the double-edged encouragement,

> Allons! allons! Sow'd cockle reap'd no corn,
> And justice always whirls in equal measure.
> Light wenches may prove plagues to men forsworn;
> If so, our copper buys no better treasure.

It is 'in equal measure' for such trifling that the ladies impose their penance and withhold their conditional consent to marry

> until the twelve celestial signs
> Have brought about the annual reckoning;

and the same 'equal measure' is heard in the closing song, a debate on medieval lines between the Owl and the Cuckoo, pitting the 'fear' belonging to Spring against the 'merry note' of Winter.

In several of his comedies, Shakespeare brings festivity into contact with natural magic. The fugitive Athenian lovers are saved by the fairies' magic in the wood, and at the end of the *Dream* the fairies, their own quarrels reconciled, come to bless the marriages and avert 'the blots of Nature's hand' from their offspring with ritual dance and song. By the conclusion of *The Merry Wives* (as Northrop Frye remarks), 'Falstaff must have felt that, after being thrown into the water, dressed up as a witch and beaten out of a house with curses, and finally supplied with a beast's head and singed with candles, he had done about all that could reasonably be asked of any fertility spirit';[1] the story of the stag-headed Herne the Hunter haunting Windsor Forest, which provides the opportunity for the final episode of 'public sport' and quasi-ritual purgation at Falstaff's expense, sounds convincingly like an 'old tale' from folklore, though it seems most likely that Shakespeare made it up. When Perdita greets Polixenes with flowers at the sheep-shearing feast in *The Winter's Tale*, she expresses a keen, even superstitious, reverence for the magical personality of the year through its changing phases:

> Sir, the year growing ancient,
> Not yet on summer's death nor on the birth
> Of trembling winter, the fairest flow'rs o' th' season
> Are our carnations and streak'd gillyvors,

---

[1] Frye, *Anatomy of Criticism*, p. 183.

Which some call nature's bastards. Of that kind
Our rustic garden's barren; and I care not
To get slips of them.
                    Wherefore, gentle maiden,
Do you neglect them?
                    For I have heard it said
There is an art which in their piedness shares
With great creating nature.

In reply, Polixenes argues that the gardener's interference with nature is itself 'an art | That nature makes'. Dramatically, their dialogue is highly ambiguous; but, ambiguous though it is, both speakers acknowledge the potency of a natural cycle. Through this scene as a whole, with its blend of folklore and mythology, there runs a strong suggestion that this festive moment is to coincide with a change in the direction of the story; Perdita herself has been introduced like 'Flora | Peering in April's front'.

The association between comedy and festivity and magic was, of course, latent in popular tradition, in the ancient tradition of rejoicing so as to usher in a fresh season and also purging away evil so as to begin the year anew or warding off the threatening spirits set loose at a turning-point of the year.[1] But, among the Elizabethans, Shakespeare seems to have been exceptionally sensitive to this tradition, as is suggested by the very choice of such titles as *A Midsummer Night's Dream* and *Twelfth Night*. True, he makes free with the calendar (which was not exacting, however, where popular customs were concerned): he brings 'the rite of May' into his 'midsummer' comedy and describes the behaviour of Malvolio and Sir Andrew in his 'Christmas' play as 'midsummer madness' and then as 'more matter for a May morning'; the title of the play stands for a mood rather than a date. (Similarly, there is little more than a marginal overlap between title and plot in Chapman's comedy, *May-Day*.) What counts in these Shakespearean titles is the suggestion of a festive but yet critical passage of time, when the characters are swept out of their previous selves and brought into a fresh harmony with a natural order and sequence in life. The marriages at the end of a Shakespearean comedy (or the conditional consent in *Love's Labour's Lost*) usually carry a feeling of integration and the promise of a new beginning in life for the leading characters. This kind of ending is conventional in comedy, of course – though it is not universal; what is strongly or distinctively Shakespearean

[1] See Chambers, *Mediaeval Stage*, vol. I, bk II; Toschi, *Origini*; Gaster, *Thespis*.

13

is the accompanying suggestion of harmonisation with the natural order. In this sense, his comedies are celebrations; and their hilarity and horseplay and music and dancing and hints of ritual or magic, which seem to interfere with their function as straightforward reflections of common life, contribute to their quality as celebrations.

They usually end with a promise of fresh happiness. But usually, as well, they bring about a return in some form to the original state of affairs. 'Our wooing doth not end like an old play', Berowne complains; but the ordeal of austerity takes the lords back to their original self-denial with a fresh purpose. In *A Midsummer Night's Dream* the lovers come back to Athens, Hermia is reconciled with her father, Demetrius has returned to Helena. By the end of *As You Like It*, Orlando is friends with Oliver and Rosalind is reunited with her father and both are about to be restored to court. The plots seem to accomplish a circular movement in bringing the main characters back to their rightful or natural position.

As C. L. Barber argues, the mood in these 'idyllic' comedies is a mood of holiday, or '*release*', 'making the whole experience of the play like that of a revel'; the leading characters are set free from some of their previous social or psychological constraints. But from their point of view this freedom comes inadvertently; it is 'events' that place them 'in the position of festive celebrants'.[1] In other words, the movement of the plot, which ends by restoring the gifts of nature, begins by depriving the actors of some part of their self-possession or their identity. Frightened and quarrelsome in the wood, the Athenian lovers cannot understand what is happening to them; they remain unaware of the fairies. In the Forest of Arden, Rosalind can meet her lover (unknown to him) 'in a holiday humour', and the Duke with his 'merry men' can live 'like the old Robin Hood of England' – which means, in effect, that they can act out a popular May-game – and can 'fleet the time carelessly, as they did in the golden world'; but they gain this release from high rank because they have been forced into exile. The lords in *Love's Labour's Lost* can only resolve to woo in disguise after some sacrifice of self-respect; they need 'some salve for perjury', and Berowne finds it in his argument,

> Let us once lose our oaths to find ourselves,
> Or else we lose ourselves to keep our oaths.
> It is religion to be thus forsworn...

[1] Barber, *Shakespeare's Festive Comedy*, pp. 6ff; (*cf* Donaldson, *The World Upside-Down*).

This paradox of losing in order to find goes deep into Shakespeare's comedies. It is an essential thread in their composition as festive celebrations.

It comes out in several ways. Sometimes the characters sketch out a festive scenario without realising it, as in the battle between Carnival and Lent in *Love's Labour's Lost* (which is re-enacted in varying forms in the conflicts between Falstaff and the magistrates in *2 Henry IV*,[1] between Sir Toby and Malvolio, and between Lucio's set and Angelo in *Measure for Measure*). Again, even where the 'pastime' is deliberate, Shakespeare tends to keep its planners ignorant of some part of their situation. From their angle, it is necessary that Malvolio should be unsuspecting; likewise Sir Andrew during the mock duel, Falstaff (in the Windsor Forest episode in *The Merry Wives*), and Beatrice and Benedick, during the 'sport' of tricking them into marriage. But this means that Sir Andrew is both participator and victim in practical jokes, while Sir Toby, too, is made to look foolish when he bumps into Sebastian. Similarly, the Windsor Forest plot by the Pages and their friends gives Anne Page the cover she needs for her elopement; and in *Much Ado* Don Pedro and Claudio prepare their 'sport' unaware that Don John is planning a similar trick, in malice, against themselves. This device of providing two layers, as it were, of unsuspectingness makes, of course, for laughter or irony; it was a common (though, again, not a universal) device in comedy.[2] It implies that, for Shakespeare, some loss of self-control or deficiency of awareness is an unavoidable incident in 'pastime', just as it is necessary for some of the participants to hide or lose their identity under a masquerade (and just as it has been argued, in a different context, that the pleasure of giddiness, or letting oneself go, and the pleasure of dressing up comprise two of the fundamental impulses towards the playing of games).[3]

The same paradox reappears in the general outlines of the role that Shakespeare assigns to his clowns. The Fool was a nearly indispensable presence at renaissance revels, a type-personage with a many-sided social, theatrical and literary tradition behind him; he was apart from ordinary men, irresponsible, but adept at uttering home truths which others would be afraid or too proud to acknowledge.[4] Shakespeare follows this tradition. As a rule, his clowns stand aside

[1] *Cf* Barber, *Shakespeare's Festive Comedy*, ch. 8.
[2] *Cf* Evans, *Shakespeare's Comedies*.   [3] Caillois, *Les Jeux*.
[4] See Swain, *Fools and Folly*; Welsford, *The Fool*.

from the intrigue of the play, unlike the crafty servants in Plautus and Jonson; or else, if they affect the plot, they stumble into it blindly, like Bottom and Dogberry, though nevertheless with happy results – 'what your wisdoms could not discover, these shallow fools have brought to light'. They may be simpletons or jesters, or a mixture of both, so that it becomes difficult to distinguish their unconscious humour from their wry wit; but in general, they stand for instinctive human nature as contrasted with culture, for the naïve man or the physical man as against the man of sentiment; whenever they appear, they turn affectation to ridicule. In this respect they are allied to Shakespeare's wits, like Berowne and Benedick, so long as the latter behave as satirists. But the fools in Shakespeare are not exposed to the same temptations as the wits, being excluded from high sentiment or observing it from the outside; they are more humble or more cynical, but in either case more consistent. From Costard to Pompey in *Measure for Measure*, they speak for the flesh, against the pretensions of the spirit. And, beyond this, the two jesters Touchstone and Feste have a sharp eye for human vanities and a kind of professional glee in the trite wisdom of conforming with nature: 'And so, from hour to hour, we ripe and ripe, | And then, from hour to hour, we rot and rot'; or, 'thus the whirligig of time brings in his revenges'. Because of this adherence, or submission, to nature, they can be free to enjoy fantasy (as well as satire) without personal involvement. And such comparative impersonality, which is common to Shakespeare's clowns, is another manifestation of the festive spirit. They appear in a comedy as if by right, not because the plot needs them; more directly than the other characters, they convey a sense of holiday release as part of a natural cycle in life.

On the other hand, no one character in Shakespeare's comedies introduces the festive movement in the play alone or controls it throughout. It is a social spirit, arising in part from the interplay within a group of characters and in part fortuitously from circumstance. It imposes a change of attitude on the leading characters impersonally, from the outside, causing them to lose one identity and acquire another like a *rite de passage*.

But Shakespeare is neither a recorder of fêtes and folklore nor a satirist like Jonson. The festive strains in his comedies always subserve or support the theme of love as initiation to marriage. This is the central, unifying theme that runs through all his comedies and romances. The lovers' feelings inform the lyrico-dramatic poetry in his comic plays and the lovers' bewilderments and discoveries mark the decisive turns of the plot. But Shakespeare makes no use in his purely comic plays of a love-intrigue outside marriage, such as he could have found in Roman or Italian drama, just as he shows little interest – taking his writing as a whole – in the comic possibilities of a plot dealing with a long-married couple, a favoured subject in medieval farce. He was probably fonder of bawdy jokes than other Elizabethans (or perhaps his jokes have received more attention from scholars); but love in his comedies always leads towards marriage, marriage in accordance with the Elizabethan ideal of a free choice of suitable partners and mutual love and trust (subject to the husband's authority). This is the ideal Shakespeare upholds in his sonnets, and similarly in *The Shrew* and *The Merry Wives*, despite their light-hearted tone and their kinship with farce.

His comedies, then, are essentially celebrations of marriage, of the approach to marriage, which he presents in a social as well as a personal aspect. Not content with a single love story, he usually contrives to bring several couples together for common rejoicing in the final scene. And the cohesion of the family, as expressed through the dramatic motif of the separation and then reunion of parents and children, was clearly a second theme of emotional importance to Shakespeare; he introduces this motif in his first (or first surviving) comedy, *The Comedy of Errors*, combining it with the material he was borrowing for his main plot, and he brings it to the forefront again nearly twenty years later, in his last tragi-comedies or romances. Again, the marriage plot in his comedies is often entangled in social or moral considerations affecting society at large, but in such a way that by the end of the comedy marriage appears as the resolution of the broader tensions, as the type or focus of harmony in society as a whole. Shakespeare likes to bring together a crowd of characters from various social ranks for a grand ensemble scene at the end of the play; and, in disregard of classical theory about the social composition of comedy, he usually brings in the head of the state, the ruler or prince, as approving spectator, active agent or final arbiter in this general reunion. A prince figures in one or another of these capacities in the final scene in no less than thirteen of his sixteen comedies and romances.

Partly for this very reason, they cannot be regarded exclusively as festive performances, however; they have too much in them of other moods, besides the mood of holiday. In the eyes of Dr Johnson,

Shakespeare, unlike other playwrights, was an author 'who caught his ideas from the living world, and exhibited only what he saw before him'; and in his *Preface*[1] he goes on to defend the dramatist for breaking through conventional distinctions and mixing tragic and comic scenes together on his stage – thereby

exhibiting the real state of sublunary nature, which partakes of good and evil, joy and sorrow, mingled with endless variety of proportion and innumerable modes of combination; and expressing the course of the world, in which the loss of one is the gain of another; in which, at the same time, the reveller is hasting to his wine, and the mourner burying his friend; in which the malignity of one is sometimes defeated by the frolick of another; and many mischiefs and many benefits are done and hindered without design.

In spite of some rhetorical over-emphasis in Dr Johnson's apology, it would be hard to deny that even in his comedies Shakespeare gives an impression of the varied 'course of the world' to an exceptional degree, and that, if there are many serious moments in them which are transformed by the approach of the festive spirit, there are many other elements which the idea of festivity will not take in at all. This is clearly the case with his late tragi-comedies, even though festive and pageant-like scenes are still important there. Among the plays of his middle years, an interest in character and morality competes with, and threatens or overshadows, the festive mood in *The Merchant of Venice*, *Much Ado*, *All's Well* and *Measure for Measure*. (For this reason, and because of some distinctive common features in their manner of composition, I shall group these four plays together for discussion under the heading of 'problem' comedies, although Professor Barber includes the first two in his group of 'festive' plays, and the term 'problem' plays is usually reserved for the other two.) And, to go back farther, it was, as Barber notes,[2] only with the writing of *Love's Labour's Lost* and *A Midsummer Night's Dream*, probably the fourth and fifth of his comedies in chronological order, that Shakespeare began to concentrate on constructive ideas drawn from festival. In these two plays, indeed, festival motifs form the basis of the plot. But his three earliest comedies (*Errors*, the *Two Gentlemen of Verona* and *The Shrew*) are drawn primarily from other types of literary or dramatic source; and so, of course, are the comedies following the *Dream*, although festival motifs affect their stage construction strongly at least down to *Twelfth Night*, about the mid-point of Shakespeare's

---

[1] *Johnson on Shakespeare*, pp. 13, 15.   [2] Barber, *Shakespeare's Festive Comedy*, p. 11.

career. It seems clear, then, that analysis of Shakespeare's comedies in terms of festive performance will only meet a part of the problem raised by asking how far, or in what way, they are representations of life. There are other conventions, especially conventions of plot, which seem to intervene, as it were, between the festive elements and the plays considered directly as reflections of character in action. Nevertheless, the difficulty of describing Shakespeare's comedies in general terms is due to their variety or miscellaneity, to the way one element of dramatic interest seems to flow into and qualify the others in the total effect. This variety within the bounds of a single play results in part from his position in the history of the stage, at a meeting-place of medieval, classical and renaissance traditions, and in part from his exceptional powers of assimilation. A study of these traditions with respect to their influence on Shakespeare and of the way he utilised and combined them is the main purpose of this book.

CHARACTER AND PLOT

To return first to the question of real people in unreal situations: Coleridge evidently felt this difficulty, and was not content to dismiss it, as Johnson had done, by saying Shakespeare had faults; instead, he emphasised the independence of character interest in the plays. One of his notes on Shakespeare's general virtues as a dramatist (apparently, for his Bristol lectures of 1813) begins:[1]

Independence of the interest on the plot. The plot interests us on account of the characters, not vice versa; it is the canvas only.

And elsewhere, Coleridge repeats that it was enough for Shakespeare if the story he chose was well known and had 'suitableness to his purpose', as with the story of Lear: 'it is the man himself that Shakespeare for the first time makes us acquainted with'.

This argument seems true enough, in the sense that Shakespeare usually puts more into his characters than the plot, considered in bare outline, seems to require, and that we remember the characters more vividly than the intricate turns through which the plot is often, in practice, worked out. But it is false, both in the general, Aristotelian, sense that without a plot of some kind there would be no play for us, and hence no characters, and in its application to Shakespeare, especially in his comedies. For one thing, when Shakespeare takes

---

[1] Coleridge, *Shakespearean Criticism*, vol. I, p. 199; *cf* pp. 53, 117.

over a previous story for the comedy, as he usually does, he always makes it more intricate than before. And, secondly, Shakespeare seldom or never makes the action of his comedy turn entirely on the interplay between the minds or feelings of the leading characters (as Coleridge implies). Only the two farces, *The Shrew* and *The Merry Wives of Windsor*, could be said to come very near this condition, and they are untypical of Shakespeare's general bent. In general, something other than character intervenes. If the initial entanglement in the play springs from the disposition of the characters – which is not always the case – the resolution always calls for something extraordinary. Sometimes, the resolution is brought about, or mainly brought about, by the skill of a single character – Portia, Helena, the Viennese Duke, Prospero; but they all rely on devious and astonishing methods. And even they depend at some point on the help of chance, which is a regular leading agent alongside the characters in the other plays. In all Shakespeare's comedies, the outcome depends in large part on one or both – usually, both – of two factors which lie outside character development: coincidence and mistakes of identity, generally due to disguise. From one point of view, such events are broadly credible, in Johnson's sense that in real life, 'many mischiefs and many benefits are done and hindered without design'; but at the same time, we come back (to quote Johnson again) to situations that 'want credibility', 'though well enough contrived to divert on the stage'. As between the wonderful and the probable for an ending to his comedies, Shakespeare evidently preferred the wonderful. If he could not find sufficiently extraordinary circumstances in the story he was working from, he took care to invent them.

Yet this bias appears to contradict Shakespeare's profound interest in humanity, and to contradict the prevailing impression carried away from his plays by two critics as distinguished, and as different from each other, as were Johnson and Coleridge. In his *Preface*, Johnson singles out Shakespeare's people from those of other dramatists because they 'act and speak by the influence of those general passions and principles by which all minds are agitated, and the whole system of life is continued in motion'; and it is just after this that he draws attention to 'the progress of his fable, and the tenour of his dialogue' as the marks of Shakespeare's 'real power'.[1] The link between these two observations, the point of departure, is the dramatist's sure sense of motivation, of people's typical impulses towards expression and

---

[1] *Johnson on Shakespeare*, p. 12.

action. Similarly with Coleridge: one of his favourite themes of praise for Shakespeare was his '*keeping at all times the high road of life*. With him' (says Coleridge) 'there were no innocent adulteries;... with him we had no benevolent braziers or sentimental ratcatchers.'[1] And, like Johnson, Coleridge finds this centrality of vision to be the clue to the sense of movement, of continuity of interest, he finds in the plays. First in order of his general notes for the Bristol lectures of 1813 comes the capacity to arouse and satisfy 'expectation':[2]

Expectation in preference to surprise. 'God said, let there be *light*, and there was *light*', – not there *was* light. As the feeling with which we startle at a shooting star, compared with that of watching the sunrise at the pre-established moment, such and so low is surprise compared with expectation.

In spite of its personal, romantic colouring, this note surely brings out most effectively the difference between what we experience as truly 'dramatic' in a play and what we feel to be merely 'theatrical'. And probably Coleridge would not have noticed that he was making the distinction easier in Shakespeare's case by minimising the force of plot in his note about plot and character, which follows on the same page. For he would not have admitted that there was any divergence between the wonderful and the natural.

It may be worth while to dwell further on Coleridge's note about expectation. What we expect from the sequence of events on a stage is drawn partly from our general experience of life and partly from our specialised experience in the theatre. We are ready for two kinds of sequence. We do not assume that they will be identical, merely that they will remain in accord; only when they clash do we feel a reaction of strain or a disagreeable shock of surprise.

Anticipation can be more readily canalised in watching a play than in reading a novel because of the time factor in performance and because the stage focuses the attention of a whole assembly of spectators together. So the grip of convention can be strong. No doubt, in comedy much of its strength comes from wish fulfilment, as Northrop Frye has argued. But to hold, as Frye appears to do, that Shakespeare's romantic comedies are composed of nothing more nor less than wish fulfilment[3] is surely to reduce them all to a flat level of sentimentality; plays which were transparently wish fulfilment might please many, but not long. Something else is needed, within the

---

[1] Coleridge, *Shakespearean Criticism*, vol. II, pp. 216–19; *cf* vol. I, p. 53; vol. II, p. 29.
[2] *Ibid.*, vol. I, p. 199.   [3] Frye, *A Natural Perspective*, pp. 123ff.

sphere of convention itself, if only to make the convention portable; a self-respecting dramatist, charged with improbabilities in his plot, would not be likely to reply simply, 'this is how men wish it to be' – 'this is what the public wants' – but at the least, as Aristotle suggests, 'this is how men say it is'; even for convention, he needs as substratum of belief. And Shakespeare's comic and romantic improbabilities do imply a belief, a general attitude towards the world. They imply that, if men can fashion their own unhappiness, they cannot make their happiness unaided, but depend for that on society, and on something beyond human society as well, on Nature or Fortune or Providence. Shakespeare seems neither to blame the social system as he knows it for the misfortunes shown in his comedies nor to suggest that social arrangements as such are self-enclosed and self-sufficient; his world is always subject to wind and weather. For this reason, if for no other, character cannot be fully independent of plot in his comedies. The tendency to think of character in isolation from plot, which amounted almost to a critical doctrine in the course of the nineteenth century, could only flourish in a different stage of civilisation, wherein personal security was normally taken for granted and men were supposed to govern their own prosperity, corporately if not individually.

The way Shakespeare conveys the effects of Fortune in his comedies expresses a traditional scale of values, or attitude towards the world, while at the same time it communicates a sense of the theatre, which is also traditional, though Shakespeare has made it thoroughly his own. In the comedies, Fortune moves in a cycle. And while in one aspect this cycle has a conventional moral significance as a symbol of human insecurity, depriving the characters for a time of their hope or prosperity, in another aspect it is no more than an extension of the circular movement of festivity, whereby some of the characters lose their social identity for a holiday interval of time, only to acquire a fresh identity in result; it would even be generally nearer the mark to say that in the comedies it is the wheel of Fortune that appears to set the 'whirligig' of festivity in motion. This impression still has a kind of moral force, in that it suggests that any personal possession of a social good is no more than relative and temporary, while at the same time the underlying natural course of things remains stable; on the other hand, the convention is shot through with artifice. Since by virtue of Fortune the dress and rank of some of the characters is changeable, it seems as if it is Fortune that makes the play a play.

Broadly speaking, then, the cycle of Fortune in the comedies both answers an intelligible common expectation about the presence of a natural rhythm affecting human affairs, and confirms our intimate knowledge that we are watching a performance. The artifice testifies to a reality within the spectacle. Shakespeare conveys such a relationship between moral truth and artifice in his comedies with varying emphasis and varying success; but it seems to represent one of his most constant aims.

'Let us sit and mock the good housewife Fortune from her wheel', Celia proposes to Rosalind; and soon their 'sport' looks like earnest. In more than half of Shakespeare's comedies, some of the characters are torn from their secure-seeming places in a court or city and take flight to the woods or the wild country, or find themselves in some 'rough and unhospitable' city abroad. They run away from harsh or tyrannical power in *Two Gentlemen of Verona*, *A Midsummer Night's Dream*, *As You Like It* and *Cymbeline*. Or, as in *The Comedy of Errors*, *Twelfth Night*, *Pericles*, *The Winter's Tale* and *The Tempest*, they lose their homes in a sea voyage; in all these plays, Shakespeare connects a storm (and, in *Cymbeline*, a sea voyage) with the violent separation of members of the same family, in the earlier plays owing to accident, in the later to injustice or treachery.[1] All these flights and exiles represent a break in the social order. But flight leads to recovery. Unforeseen meetings in the woodland heal the perfidies of the court, and in the storm plays one sea voyage restores what another has taken away. The wanderers or fugitives return better off than they set out; and in some plays their unintended arrival benefits other characters as well. The wheel completes a circle, beyond any character's control. And chance plays a similar or less conspicuous role of redress in the other comedies too.

All this was patently a convention. 'Authors make tempest and shipwreck at will', observes a rationalising French critic of the generation after Shakespeare;[2] but the same critic concedes that 'the sea is the most fitting scene for great changes, and that some have called it the theatre of inconstancy'. And, with a double-edged caution, he remarks that those writers of romances who 'make so free with the winds do not know that the prophet has told us that God keeps them in his treasury, and that philosophy, with all her clairvoyance,

---

[1] *Cf* Knight, *Shakespearean Tempest*.
[2] de Scudéry, preface to *Ibrahim* (1641), in Allan H. Gilbert (ed.), *Literary Criticism*, pp. 582–3.

has not discovered their hiding place'. For his part, Shakespeare steers between the solemnity and the banality of convention in stories depending on the 'inconstancy' of Fortune by giving his characters a sense of wonder, by making them feel and express the strangeness of their vicissitudes. Their sense of wonder resounds through his comedies, from Antipholus of Syracuse in *The Comedy of Errors* –

> I to the world am like a drop of water
> That in the ocean seeks another drop,
> Who, falling there to find his fellow forth,
> Unseen, inquisitive, confounds himself.
> So I, to find a mother and a brother,
> In quest of them, unhappy, lose myself,

– to Gonzalo in *The Tempest*,

> O, rejoice
> Beyond a common joy, and set it down
> With gold on lasting pillars: in one voyage
> Did Claribel her husband find at Tunis;
> And Ferdinand, her brother, found a wife
> Where he himself was lost; Prospero his dukedom
> In a poor isle; and all of us ourselves
> Where no man was his own.

Shakespeare's actors seem all the more like real characters because they respond to what is improbable, exceptional or extraordinary in their circumstances.

Moreover, the sensation of losing in order to find, as expressed by Antipholus and Gonzalo, indicates the psychological track to be followed by Shakespeare's leading characters in general, whether at Belmont or Bohemia or the Forest of Arden. The sensation may be provoked by the 'inconstancy' of Fortune, but the total experience is no mere gift of luck; as Gonzalo implies, it becomes a phase in their knowledge of themselves and their place in the world. The self-perception of the sea-changed voyagers in *The Comedy of Errors* and *The Tempest* is close, for example, to that of Berowne and his friends, when the latter are on the point of donning their masquerade:

> Let us once lose our oaths to find ourselves,
> Or else we lose ourselves to find our oaths.

The only significant difference here is that the lords of Navarre have initially 'lost themselves' by trying to work against the course of

Nature, while the sense of loss apparent to Antipholus or Gonzalo is due to a stroke of Fortune.

This difference is not fundamental in the general scheme of Shakespeare's comedies, however. Not only does Fortune follow a cycle, like Nature; but, just as Berowne tries to redeem one kind of psychological loss or loss of identity by another, which is disguise, so it appears that Fortune in the comedies cannot complete her cycle without the use of disguise, either. Adversity leads to disguise, as when the heroines, in a crisis, take to masculine dress, or else it leads to mistakes of identity; and, conversely, a mistake of identity invariably precedes the resolution of the comedy, as if it were a necessary preliminary. And where Fortune (coincidence) does not appear to be a direct agent in producing the happy ending of a comedy, its place is taken by conscious deception or trickery involving some form of disguise as a necessary means, as in Shakespeare's 'problem' comedies, his farces and the sub-plots of his romantic plays. In effect, then, misfortune produces disguise and disguise the return of prosperity.

As consequences of Fortune, depicted on perceptibly conventional lines, the improbable circumstances in Shakespeare's comic plots are certainly external to what seems most keenly perceived and most lifelike in each of his separate characters. But a subjection to something which is outside their separate and conscious wills is part of the essential experience they are to live through in the play, the experience of losing in order to find, of relinquishing something of their previous or habitual selves before achieving a social or a psychological recovery. Fortune in Shakespeare's comedies belongs to the human condition.

At the same time, Fortune so considered overlaps with the idea of a theatrical performance. 'Nature to her bias drew in that', says Sebastian, commenting on the series of chances and mistakes that has led to his marriage with Olivia. And earlier, among the first of the mistakes in *Twelfth Night*, Olivia has touched, with unconscious irony, on an evident if ambiguous truth about Viola: 'Are you a comedian?' 'No, . . .' replies the other actor, 'and yet, by the very fangs of malice I swear, I am not that I play.'

Links such as this between disguised identity or play-acting and coincidences which contribute to the cyclical movement of Fortune form a working convention in Shakespeare's comedies which he treats as an important structural principle. He uses the convention to draw **together** the various themes and strands of his plots, to represent an aspect of life outside the theatre, and at the same time to emphasise the immediate reality of the play as a stage performance.

This convention linking disguise and Fortune came ultimately from classical comedy. But in the Elizabethan theatre it seems to have been Shakespeare, more than anyone else, who reintroduced it to the stage. His use of the convention illustrates not merely his tendency to think in terms of the stage but his startling ability to combine elements taken from a variety of sources – an ability which pre-supposes a selection of materials more critical and deliberate than he used to be credited with, as well as a poet's eye for resemblances and unpredictable associations of ideas. For historically the main dis-tinguishable elements combined in almost any of his comedies lead back to widely separated traditions of the stage. In broad terms, the romantic elements in his plots spring from the Middle Ages, while his sense of comic irony stems from the Roman playwrights and his feeling for comedy as festivity expresses the culture of the renaissance. It was a decisive mark of his genius as a playwright that he could bring into unison this diversity of traditions.

In the chapters which follow I try to describe these several traditions as they affected Shakespeare, particularly in the selection and arrange-ment of his plots. Chapter 2 outlines the romantic conventions that were popular in Elizabethan plays just before Shakespeare began writing, conventions that can be traced back in dramatic form as far as Chaucer's time (though the evidence with regard to England is little more than fragmentary) and, in narrative form, much farther still. In Chapters 3 and 4 I discuss the underlying conventions about disguise and Fortune derived from classical comedy (which requires some consideration of the Old Comedy of Aristophanes, who did not influence Shakespeare directly, as well as of the New Comedy of Plautus and Terence, who did); and in Chapter 5 I attempt to describe the revival and modernisation of New Comedy in Italy about the beginning of the sixteenth century and the influence of this renais-sance form of comedy on Shakespeare.

The order of these chapters, taking medieval traditions before classical, may seem illogical at first sight, but I believe it follows the sequence of Shakespeare's formation as a playwright, since his art must have been shaped by medieval traditions first, and only secondly by classical and renaissance conventions. Quite possibly he read some texts of Plautus or Terence at school before he saw any play acted on a stage. But the living theatre he must have known when he became an actor himself was still medieval in many essentials, while performances of classical comedies or of imitations of classical comedy were still rare in England and were mostly confined to academic audiences when he began writing about 1590. It is true, and deserves emphasis, that Shakespeare was probably the first English dramatist, certainly one of the first, to adapt classical and renaissance comedy for the public playhouses in England, and also true (as far as we can tell) that he applied the principles of classical comedy much more thoroughly than any English writer before him. He has received much less than his due as a practical innovator in this respect, largely because Ben Jonson and the critics who followed him were classicists of a more theoretical cast. Nevertheless, I believe that the classical or renaissance strain in Shakespeare's comic writing, vital as it is, can best be appreciated against the background of the romantic stage traditions surviving from the Middle Ages, which he drew upon at the beginning of his career and again, with a renewal of critical interest, at the end.

The last chapter of this book refers to aspects of Shakespeare's comedies that were not derived from previous stage traditions but illustrate his mind and craft as an Elizabethan professional dramatist, working in a situation that was historically new.

2

MEDIEVAL STAGE ROMANCES

Si fait bon oÿr exemplaire
Et bonnes vertus raconter,
Dont on puet par raison monter
En l'estat de perfection.

L'Estoire de Griseldis

It hath been sung at festivals,
On ember-eves and holy-ales;
And lords and ladies in their lives
Have read it for restoratives.
The purchase is to make men glorious;
Et bonum quo antiquius, eo melius.

Gower, in *Pericles*

Several of Shakespeare's comedies depict 'rebels to Love', somewhat like Chaucer's Troilus. Valentine, Berowne and his companions, and Benedick are such rebels at first among Shakespeare's men, Kate and Beatrice and Olivia among his women; while Adriana and Titania resemble them in their rebelliousness as wives. In all seven of the plays where these characters appear, there is a moment of deception for the rebel answering to his own self-deception, and at least a touch of farce in the process by which he is converted. On the other side, Shakespeare's plots depicting constant love are based upon romance. Constancy is first tried and then rewarded by Fortune.

Some of these plots deal with a daughter's flight from an angry father to the woods, where by the aid of chance she is both united with her lover and reconciled with her father. Such is the story of Silvia at the end of *Two Gentlemen of Verona*, where Shakespeare uses this motif for the first time, and where the intervention of the Outlaws redresses the lovers' 'crooked fortune' (IV.i.22); and such again is the story of Hermia, where in effect the fairies take the place of the Outlaws. There is a later echo of this motif in *Cymbeline*, in so far as Imogen's wanderings are partly caused by her father's displeasure at her marriage; and, more distantly, in the story of Perdita's exposure and subsequent adventures in *The Winter's Tale*. A similar thread in the plot of *Two Gentlemen* is the adventure of the disguised Julia in the wood; and both of these motifs are combined in the adventures of Celia and Rosalind in *As You Like It*. Shakespeare borrowed the plot concerning Julia and the plot of *As You Like It* from contemporary stories, by Montemayor and by Lodge; and the spirit of his early heroines in defying their fathers for the sake of the men they intend to marry may owe something to the plays and novels of Robert Greene.[1] No specific narrative source is known for the plots concerning Silvia and Hermia. But the general pattern of all these plots of woodland adventure is much older than the Renaissance.

Shakespeare links the motif of a daughter's wanderings with two others of a similar kind. One consists of the rejection, unhappiness and final vindication of a falsely accused wife – Imogen or Hermione.[2] The other exhibits the vicissitudes of a father as a man tried by Fate, first losing his wife and child in a storm at sea and then, after many years, finding his family again in the course of another voyage.[3] This is the story of Egeon, which Shakespeare provided as a framing plot for *The Comedy of Errors*, and again of *Pericles*; although these two plays were written some sixteen years apart (*c.* 1592 and *c.* 1608), Shakespeare drew both plots in the main from the same narrative source, Gower's version of the old tale of Apollonius of Tyre. And the same, or a closely related, motif appears in the story of Prospero's long exile (for which no specific source has been identified); with all his magical powers, Prospero depends for his restoration, like Egeon and Pericles, on the favours of the sea –

> By accident most strange, bountiful Fortune,
> Now my dear lady, hath mine enemies
> Brought to this shore;

– and, just as Egeon and Pericles are saved from physical or moral danger by their children, so Prospero in his perilous voyage owes his moral survival to Miranda – 'a cherubin | Thou wast that did preserve me!' – and through Miranda makes his peace with Alonso. In an inverted form, this same motif figures also in *Cymbeline* and *The Winter's Tale*, since Bellarius steals the two young princes

---

[1] See Pruvost, *Greene*; Sanders, 'The Comedy of Greene and Shakespeare'.
[2] See Schlauch, *Constance*; Thompson, *Motif-Index*, Motifs K2110.1, K2112.
[3] See Wells, *Manual of Writings in Middle English*, pp. 112–24; Hibbard (Mrs Loomis), *Mediaeval Romance*, pp. 3–11.

(with whose aid he ultimately saves the king from invasion) when he is wrongfully banished by Cymbeline, while in *The Winter's Tale* Camillo and Antigonus are similarly made the scapegoats for Leontes.

These motifs, then, appear singly in Shakespeare's early writing, and intertwined together in his last plays. How powerful the emotional overtones of the motifs concerning father and daughter could be for him is shown by his treatment of the old story of King Lear. But in the early comedies and the late tragi-comedies they take a form that can be described as exemplary romance. A family is divided; one of its members, cut off from civilised security and exposed to hazard, suffers with constancy and devotion; at last he or she is redeemed by an unexpected turn of Fortune, and the life of the family begins afresh. In this way Fortune, seemingly hostile and capricious, acts at the end in concert with the latent powers of Nature and obeys a hidden Providence. A rationalisation on these lines had long been available to writers, from Boethius (of whose *Consolation of Philosophy* it has been said that 'no other book, except the Bible, was so much translated in the Middle Ages').[1] There was no need to make this familiar rationalisation explicit to give Shakespeare's plots their shape, however. In broad outline, they follow the course of many romances of the Middle Ages, romances grounded on folk-tales.

Moreover, Shakespeare was following a tradition of the stage here, as well as romances transmitted in writing (and probably orally, too). It seems very likely that in choosing romantic plots and reshaping them for his early comedies, he was responding to some of the plays he had seen from his boyhood on, which may have awakened his own desire to work in the theatre. The evidence for such a statement must be no better than indirect, and must include a quantum of pure conjecture, if only because so little is known for certain about the acting companies he could have seen and learned from in his youth; nevertheless, the cumulative arguments in its favour are strong. The repertoire of the stage, from Chaucer's time onwards, had included miracles, or saints' plays, and secular romances and farces, besides moralities, quasi-dramatic forms such as pageants and folk-plays, and the mysteries, or biblical cycles, organised by the larger towns, which constituted the dominant dramatic form in England down to the Reformation and survived in many places until 1570; much of this dramatic material was common to western Europe as a whole.

---

[1] Highet, *Classical Tradition*, p. 571; see Patch, *Tradition of Boethius*.

Historians of the French stage have drawn attention to the continuity between the romantic tragi-comedies that began to appear about Shakespeare's time and the romanticised saints' plays of the later Middle Ages.[1] And J. M. Manly and other scholars have advanced a similar view about England, holding that the miracle plays (though scantily represented in surviving texts) must have contributed decisively to the emergence of the romantic drama in the sixteenth century.[2] Now there was already a large admixture of pre-Christian romance in those saints' legends and miracles of the Virgin that were frequently dramatised; and, in addition, a few entirely secular romances have survived in France and the Netherlands from the later fourteenth century (a period of expansion and change in the records of religious drama as well), testifying to the existence, at least by that time, of an independent tradition of secular stage romances – of which the texts have had the less chance of survival because they would be thought less worthy of recording than religious plays.[3] Probably, therefore, Manly's argument should be amended to refer simply to a broad line of romances, secular as well as religious, joining medieval drama to that of the age of the Renaissance. On the other hand, the majority of new English plays surviving from the first three quarters of the sixteeenth century are not romances but moral allegories; so that some scholars have been led to consider the few texts with undoubtedly romantic plots that remain from the time of Shakespeare's youth as hybrids, or late off-shoots from the prevailing stock of moralities.[4] But they are essentially romances, showing evidence of a continuing tradition, and their morality-play features are merely borrowed.

EARLY ELIZABETHAN ROMANCES

The first twenty years of Shakespeare's life, when professional actors were increasingly busy in the provinces and succeeded (from 1576 on) in establishing themselves in permanent theatres in London,

---

[1] Lancaster, *French Tragi-Comedy*, pp. 1–15; *cf* Baskervill, 'Early Romantic Plays', pp. 502–12; Lebègue, 'Traditions dramatico-religieuses en France'.

[2] Manly, 'The Miracle Play in Mediaeval England', *cf* Baskervill, 'Early Romantic Plays in England', pp. 478ff; Doran, *Endeavors of Art*, pp. 102–4.

[3] Hunningher, *The Origin of the Theater*, p. 82; *cf* R. M. Wilson, *The Lost Literature of Medieval England*, pp. 239–40.

[4] See Spivack, *Shakespeare and the Allegory of Evil*, pp. 251–303; Bevington, *From 'Mankind' to Marlowe*, pp. 190–8; Russell, 'Romantic Narrative Plays'.

witnessed a steady increase in the demand for new plays.[1] This was a period of revivals of Latin drama at Oxford and Cambridge; in English drama, it opened with imitations or adaptations of neoclassical plays by Gascoigne and others for audiences at the Inns of Court, and led on to the courtly mythological fantasies of Peele and Lyly, who were very shortly to be followed by Marlowe, Kyd, Greene and then Shakespeare himself as writers for the public theatres. In one form or another, twenty-nine new English plays have survived from the years 1565–84, and nearly a hundred more are known from the record of their titles.[2] Of the twenty-nine surviving plays, five are neoclassical in form and derivation and five others show classical influence in their subject-matter; these were all played before humanist-trained audiences at court or the legal Inns. Thirteen others are predominantly moral interludes, and only three predominantly romances. On the other hand, the number of moralities now available in print gives a misleading impression of their place in the actors' repertoire. Reforming zeal and perhaps literary ambition on their authors' part must have helped to bring many of these moralities into print; eight of them were 'offered for acting' – that is, advertised on the title-page as suitable for performance by small travelling companies – and were not, therefore, directly commissioned by the actors. (An exact contemporary of Shakespeare, R. Willis, was to remember vividly in his old age the edifying moral of a lost play of this kind, *The Cradle of Security*, which he had seen at Gloucester about 1570, as a small boy standing between his father's legs, 'as he sat upon one of the benches, where we saw and heard very well').[3] But while the number of plays 'offered for acting' shows the growing demand of the period, the actors were just as likely to seek out well-tried romantic themes, less commendable to a printer, in their efforts to please popular audiences – and even the audience at court. And the picture changes when the titles of lost plays, which are usually indicative, are taken into account as well as those that have survived in print. Seven plays of the period were evidently biblical plays or miracles; a score or so were comedies, or cannot be classified; the remainder appear to fall into three groups, with some thirty titles in each: moral interludes, plays showing some classical influence, and miscellaneous romances. Moreover, while some of the second group were evidently

---

[1] Salingar, Harrison and Cochrane, 'Les Comédiens...en Angleterre'.
[2] See Harbage and Schoenbaum, *Annals of English Drama*.
[3] R. Willis, *Mount Tabor* (1639), in J. D. Wilson (ed.), *Life in Shakespeare's England*, p. 34.

taken from history (*Catiline's Conspiracies* by Stephen Gosson, for instance, or *Caesar and Pompey*), more than half spring from apologue, mythology or legend, like Edwardes' *Damon and Pithias* (1565), Peele's *Arraignment of Paris* (1581) or Lyly's *Campaspe* (*c.* 1584); while several other titles, like *Theagenes and Chariclea* or *Cupid and Psyche* reveal the influence of the recently translated hellenistic romances. Among the miscellaneous titles that strongly suggest romantic plays, a few spring from renaissance *novelle* (such as *Titus and Gisippus* – the second English play on this theme of noble friendship – and *Ariodante and Genevora,* evidently borrowed from *Orlando Furioso* and hence allied by plot to Shakespeare's *Much Ado*); eight or more clearly belong to the vogue for romances of knighthood, which lasted through the sixteenth century, like Edwardes' *Palamon and Arcite* or the anonymous plays, *Paris and Vienne* or *Herpetulus the Blue Knight and Perobia* or *The Red Knight* or *The Solitary Knight.*[1] Nearly all the titles of lost plays in this period come from the records of performances at court, which may give undue prominence to mythological subjects in my classification; but there is clear evidence that courtly and popular tastes overlapped, and on the whole the actors must have given the same plays at court as they gave before public audiences in London and the provinces.

Three surviving anonymous pieces represent this phase in the tradition of romance: *The History of Sir Clyomon, Knight of the Golden Shield...and Clamydes the White Knight* (*c.* 1570); *Common Conditions* (1576); and *The Rare Triumphs of Love and Fortune* (1582). The first two were meant for unexacting audiences, but *Clyomon* was revived, and printed in 1599, and *Common Conditions* was offered for acting: ('Six may play this Comedy'). The third was acted at court, but is hardly different in substance. All three contain plot motifs that Shakespeare was to use afterwards: besides knights and clowns, they feature wandering damsels faithful through distress, banished fathers, magical charms, disguises and recognitions. All three maintain the promise held out in the Prologue of *Clyomon* – 'Wherein the froward chances oft, of Fortune you shall see'.

The story of *Clyomon*, says the Prologue, is taken from 'the leaves of worthy writers' works'; it is presented as an example of chivalry.[2] The two knights are rivals who challenge each other, miss their tryst,

---

[1] See F. P. Wilson, *English Drama 1485–1585*, pp. 111–25; Prouty, *Sources of 'Much Ado'*, pp. 13, 31.

[2] *Clyomon and Clamydes*, ed. Greg.

meet in opposition again and are reconciled by no less an umpire than Alexander the Great. Meanwhile Clamydes wins the hand of the Princess of Denmark by slaying a monster (a feat described, but not acted), and Clyomon, who is the princess's brother, earns his marriage to Neronis, the daughter of the King of the Strange Marshes. In this, as in most Tudor plays, several parts could be doubled; however, ten actors are required for the grand reunion in the last scene.

Much of the action deals with Neronis, who first appears and succours Clyomon about a third of the way through the play, when he is declaiming against Fortune's spite, having been set ashore feeling seasick. Later, to escape from a tyrannical marriage, she runs away dressed as a page, serves a shepherd named Corin, finds a hearse which, as she wrongly imagines, holds her lover's corpse, is reassured by Providence (a speaking part), then meets Clyomon again and serves him, each disguised from the other until the end. Her attraction for the village lasses when in male disguise is related by the shepherd, in monologue, in his broad Mummerset:

> But an you did zee how Jone Jenkin, and Gilian Giffrey loves my boy Jack,
> Why it is marvelation to see, Jone did so paste Gillian's back,
> That by God's bones I laught till cha be pist my zelfe, when cha zaw it,
> All the maids in town valls out for my boy.

This, with Corin's name, sounds like a crude anticipation of *As You Like It*; while Neronis's later adventures look forward to those of Imogen in disguise, or of Euphrasia in Beaumont and Fletcher's *Philaster*.

A big part is given to the comic servant, Subtle Shift, who changes masters and deceives each in turn for no good reason except that such is his nature:

> Well, such shifting knaves as I am, the ambodexter must play,
> And for commodity serve every man, whatsoever the world say.

Shift is the Vice and, like the Vices in the moralities, he uses an alias (Knowledge) to help his deceptions. But, though he plays the fool, like the allegorical Vices, he is not, like them, the agent of temptation; and, though he causes confusion, and delays the knights' achievement of honour, Fortune affects them as well and the story, such as it is, could have gone forward just the same without him.[1] The slight colouring of comic allegory due to Shift is almost irrelevant to the plot.

[1] *Cf* Russell, 'Romantic Narrative Plays'.

The dramatist turns abruptly from one set of adventures to another in the narrative style of the prose romances, and gets his characters to retail bits of the story as required, without motivation. There is no sense of a situation developing between the characters as the play advances, but no sequence of temptation, fall and repentance, as in the moral interludes, either. New speakers announce themselves when they come on, in the manner common to most kinds of medieval drama; Alexander tells the audience who he is, and so does the evil enchanter, Brian Sans Foy, who adds that he is a notorious caitiff.

The story traverses various shores and countries, from Denmark to 'Swavia', but no scenery is needed; merely a neutral acting space, on which the actors can tell the spectators where they are. Similarly, in *Common Conditions*, where the actors travel from Arabia to Phrygia, with an excursion to quell an ogre on the Isle of Marofus, there is no need for scenery or for solid properties, except perhaps a practicable tree which can represent a 'wood' and on which the servant–Vice can execute one of his japes.[1] But although no buildings are strictly necessary, particular places are localised on the stage. Early in the latter play, the Vice, Conditions, urges his mistress, the heroine:

> …lady! it is not best for us in Arabia longer to tarry,
> Seeing that fortune in every respect against us still doth vary.
> For, seeing we are so nigh the sea, that we may pass, in one day,
> Clean over the sea to Phrygia, I would not wish we stay;
> Whereas [= *where*] now your good father sir Galiarbus is,
> And of your brother, I warrant you, we there shall not miss.

After their exit, and a monologue, evidently in the same stage area, from the brother, whom they have just lost in the wood, *Here entereth Galiarbus out of Phrygia*; and when this speaker has retired from his part of the stage, after explaining where and how unfortunate he is, *Here enters* a new character, *Lamphedon*, also *out of Phrygia*. By the time Lamphedon has declared his name, place and pedigree (he is the Duke's son, as he reminds himself), and has described his falling in love with an unknown beauty seen in the (Phrygian) forest, *Here enter Conditions, standing privily* nearby, and it is obvious that he and Clarisia have crossed the sea, and what is the identity of the mysterious beauty. Such care for naming localities on the stage is foreign to the style of the morality plays, though needful in a complicated romance.

Complicated this one is. Five different strands can be distinguished

---

[1] *Common Conditions*, ed. Tucker Brooke.

in the plot: (*a*) a banished father, separated from his son and daughter; (*b*) a daughter, separated from her brother as well, who marries, but is then divided from her husband at sea; (*c*) the son, rejecting advances from a second heroine, the daughter of a grotesque physician; (*d*) the daughter, sheltered by her father, each unknown to the other, pursued in love by her brother, also ignorant of their identities and unrecognised by both of them; and (*e*) the husband who, after separate adventures, rejoins his wife secretly but is betrayed by a servant and incurs the wrath of the guardian-father, who condemns the lovers to death, in the form of a dram provided by the weird physician. This farrago suggests the influence of some hellenistic romance; by a coincidence – although no direct borrowing seems likely, and no source is known for either play, – the same five strands are found together in the Italian romantic comedy of forty years earlier, *L'Amor costante*, by the humanist, Alessandro Piccolomini.[1] The Italian gives the play a realistic, or at least a topical, setting, and, after a detailed expository prologue, works out the stage action in a single supposed day; by opening the plot with the brother's amatory siege of his unrecognised sister (*d*) and then developing the other motifs concurrently, down to the angry guardian-father's sentence on the lovers, the playwright can bring back the brother to attempt a rescue of his beloved in Act IV and thereby stage a general confrontation with recognitions in Act V; the dram, of course, is harmless (as it presumably was in the English play too, though part of the text is missing). 'Alas', the father can exclaim at the climax of the Italian play (v.iv), when successive recognition scenes have revealed who his victims are, but have not yet disclosed that they are really unhurt, 'what an inhuman fate has made me find my daughter again and kill her in one and the same day!...What Fortune can do, messer Consalvo! to give so much good and so much harm in a moment!' The English dramatist, on the other hand, has no such calculated, interlocking surprises. He plods forward, transferring attention from one character to another in separated scenes, but otherwise following the episodes in chronological order – motifs (*a*) and (*b*) alternately, then (*c*) and (*d*), then (*e*). He sees his play as a narrative, like the author of *Clyomon*.

The Vice uses an alias, and betrays his various masters in turn,

---

[1] Piccolomini, *L'Amor costante* (1536; pub. Venice, 1540). See Brooke (ed.), *Common Conditions*, pp. xiii–xiv, and 'On the Source of *Common Conditions*'; Spivack, *Shakespeare and the Allegory of Evil*, pp. 291–9.

like Subtle Shift. He stands for something else besides moral obliquity; as he tells the audience,

> for my own advantage believe me you may.
> As near as I can I'll use a mediocrity by the way.
> And *Mediocrity* is my name though Conditions they me call,
> Near kin to Dame Fortune to raise and to let fall.   (line 164)

He thus expresses a comment on the plot, as well as taking part in it. But his impersonal aspect is at odds with his moral quality, and in any case he is a trickster rather than a tempter, lacking any moral hold on his victims. He pushes the plot along, but it could easily dispense with him. His role is superfluous; it appears to be borrowed from the morality plays, as an afterthought, to raise laughter and provide a coating of allegory.

In *The Rare Triumphs of Love and Fortune* an arrogant prince interferes in the love of his sister, Fidelia, for Hermione, who by origin is no better than a foundling, their father's ward.[1] Driven from court, Hermione meets Fidelia near the cave of an old hermit, Bomelio, who has told the audience that he is in fact a worthy general, banished long since thanks to perfidy, or, as he says, to 'fickle Fortune's froward check and her continual spite'. Bomelio hails the heroine as a 'nymph or lady fair, | Or else the goddess of the grove', and shelters Hermione, acknowledging him as his own son; meanwhile the lovers have been betrayed to the prince by the court parasite (who replaces the usual Vice), but Bomelio, knowing the wicked prince, has struck him dumb by enchantment. In Act IV, visiting the court 'like a counterfeit Physician' (and speaking garbled English, French and Italian, like the doctor in *Common Conditions*), Bomelio almost unites the lovers by stealing Fidelia away, under the pretence that the cure for her brother's dumbness must be to extract a drop of her blood; but while he is at court, Hermione crosses his father's plans by finding his magic books, which he regards as an understandable insurance against Fortune, but which he destroys as 'vile' and 'blasphemous', adjuring the 'gentlemen' in the audience to 'abhor this study, for it will confound you all'. Bomelio is thrown into a frenzy, and the resolution must be delayed until the gods can intervene.

This is not difficult, for the whole plot has been unfolded as a test case in a *débat* between Venus and Fortune, stirred up by a Fury. At each turn of the action, one or the other of the rival goddesses exults,

---

[1] *The Rare Triumphs of Love and Fortune*, in Dodsley's *Old Plays* (ed. Hazlitt) VI.

to the accompaniment of music and gunshots; until Mercury, sent by Jupiter, arrives to reconcile them, revive Bomelio, and persuade the goddesses to *show themselves* in joint benevolence, sort out the mortals' tangles and, through Fortune's lips, offer a prayer for the Queen. The role of the Olympians (who take up the whole first act with contention and pageantry) could have been suggested by Peele's *Arraignment of Paris*, another courtly mythological show dedicated to Elizabeth; and it could have helped to suggest other supervisory roles, such as those of Revenge and the Ghost in *The Spanish Tragedy* (*c.* 1587) or of Bohan and King Oberon in Greene's *James IV* (1590); in other words, the *Rare Triumphs* has begun to move towards a sophisticated conception of the play-within-the-play.[1] But, again, the allegorical framework is extraneous to the plot, which consists of an exemplary romance showing constancy under distress and incorporates an element of folk-tale.

In his situation, Bomelio resembles Belarius in *Cymbeline*, while the boorish prince resembles Cloten; and Shakespeare uses Fidele as Imogen's disguise name. It has been claimed, therefore (notably by the New Arden editor, J. M. Nosworthy), that, for those parts of *Cymbeline*, 'Shakespeare's obligation, such as it was, was to *Love and Fortune* and to no other literary production of which we have knowledge'; and even, taking other identifiable sources into consideration, that this play should 'be regarded as Shakespeare's primary source or impulse'.[2] As further evidence, there is Shakespeare's use of the name, Hermione, in *The Winter's Tale*, and the broad resemblance between Prospero's comportment as a magician and the magic of Bomelio.[3] The parallels between *Cymbeline* and *Love and Fortune* are certainly close, as far as they go; but as there is little to distinguish the earlier play from other romances (such as *Clyomon*, where also there is some anticipation of Imogen's adventures), it seems more likely that Shakespeare would have recalled the general style of a whole group of similar old plays than that he would have singled out this one in particular. And *Love and Fortune* by itself would not have suggested linking the Belarius sub-plot with the wager plot in *Cymbeline*, or both with the pseudo-historical invasion. Since it must be presumed that there were a number of essentially similar romances among the lost plays Shakespeare could have known in his early years, it may be

[1] Righter, *Shakespeare and the Idea of the Play*, p. 71.
[2] Nosworthy (ed.), *Cymbeline*, pp. xxv–xxvii; *cf* Muir, *Shakespeare's Sources*, vol. I, pp. 232–3.
[3] Kermode (ed.), *The Tempest*, p. lix; *cf* Muir, *Shakespeare's Sources*, vol. I, p. 260.

useful to turn back to medieval drama in order to gain a fuller view of the tradition Shakespeare was drawing on.

MEDIEVAL STAGE HEROINES

The three surviving early Elizabethan romance plays indicate the popularity of the motif of a heroine enduring insecurity and danger for the sake of her love, and of the motif of a banished father restored at last to his family and to fortune. As it happens, they do not illustrate the motifs of the father wandering in search of his family, or of the wife wrongfully accused, like Imogen or Hermione – or Chaucer's Constance. But stories of long-enduring heroines in general, and of calumniated queens in particular, were very popular, both in literary romances and on the stage, through the later Middle Ages. Their vogue was international.[1] On one side, they attached themselves to the perennial literary debate for and against the honour of womankind; on the other side, they embodied time-honoured folk-tales bearing out the theme of the hidden watchfulness of Providence.

Among the handful of entirely secular stage romances surviving from Chaucer's time – the earliest of their kind – no less than three present variations on the theme of the long-suffering heroine. The Dutch (or Flemish) play *Esmoreit* deals with a Sicilian queen, falsely accused and imprisoned, but rescued at length by her son, who had been carried off as an infant to Damascus. Another Dutch play, *Lancelot of Denmark* (possibly by the same author), shows a virtuous plebeian heroine who is persecuted by her lover's queenly mother. Both of these heroines are aided by fervent prayer.[2] The oldest secular stage romance in French, a little later in date, is *L'Estoire de Griseldis* (1395), founded on Petrarch's version of Boccaccio's story. The playwright enlarges his narrative source with a number of scenes where knights, ladies, shepherds and shepherdesses sing the heroine's praises as an ideal wife and marquise; and when at last the Marquis comes to 'recognise her as his true spouse', the writer makes him dilate at length on her matrimonial virtue:[3]

> O Griseldis assez souffist
> Ta vraye foy et loyauté.

---

[1] *Cf*, p. 29, n. 2, above.

[2] *An Ingenious Play of Esmoreit*, trans. Ayres; *A Beautiful Play of Lancelot of Denmark*, trans. Geyl. See Weevers, *Poetry of the Netherlands*, pp. 48–54.

[3] *L'Estoire de Griseldis en rimes et par personnages* (1395; pub. Paris, *c.* 1550), ed. Roques, lines 2453ff; *cf* introduction, pp. vii–ix, xx.

La constance et l'umilité
Et l'amour qu'a moi as eüe
Ay pour esprouver coigneüe,
Et ta parfaitte obedïence
Ay trouvé par experïence;
Et croy que soubz le ciel n'ait homme
Qui, par tant d'experimens comme
Je t'ay ferme et constant trouvee,
Ait en autre femme esprouvee
La bonne amour de marïage,

and so on for another twenty lines; for the sub-title of the play
promises to show forth 'Le miroir des dames mariees'. Heroines like
this represent an ideal of sentiment, a fixed idea; and on the reverse
of the 'mirror' it would have been fitting to engrave the images of
the Wife of Bath or of some of the bullying and faithless spouses who
figure so prominently in medieval farce. Besides this French example,
C. R. Baskervill has noted seven other plays on Griselda in France,
Germany, Italy and the Netherlands between the mid-fifteenth and
the mid-sixteenth century, including one by the popular Nuremberg
dramatist, Hans Sachs (1494–1576); and there were English plays in
her commendation by the schoolmaster, Ralph Radcliffe (who was
evidently fond of elevating subjects) *c.* 1546, by John Phillip (in a
moral allegory 'offered for acting', *c.* 1559), and by Dekker and
Chettle (1600).[1]

Tales of persecuted wives appear to have formed the most popular
group of all. In her study of *Mediaeval Romance in England*, Laura
Hibbard (Mrs Loomis) examines thirty-nine non-cyclical verse
stories, which she classifies as 'romances of trial and faith', 'romances
of legendary English heroes' and 'romances of love and adventure'.[2]
Fifteen of these romances found expression on west European stages
between the fourteenth and the seventeenth century; and among
these, six gave prominence to the motif of a wife falsely accused. One
such, for example, was the story of *Eglamour and Degrebelle*, acted at
St Albans in 1444, one of the earliest recorded non-religious plays in
England. This could well have been the subject that Sidney chose for
ridicule in his account of the popular drama about 1580; it was
certainly enacted in Germany in the next century.[3] A similar story,

1 Baskervill, 'Early Romantic Plays', pp. 487–8; *cf* Saintyves, *Les Contes de Perrault*,
pp. 537–57; Schmidt (ed.), *Le Théâtre populaire européen*, pp. 381ff.
2 See p. 29, n. 3, above.
3 Baskervill, 'An Elizabethan Eglamour Play'; Hibbard, *Mediaeval Romance*, p. 275.

of the False Seneschal's denunciation of Charlemagne's queen (in the Middle English metrical version, the story of *Sir Triamour*), was also dramatised by Hans Sachs, and by other playwrights much later.[1]

In *Valentine and Orson*, one of the romances widely known during the first century of printing, a falsely accused queen is rescued at length by her lost twin sons.[2] This was popular in folk-plays, especially because of the association between Orson, the 'salvage man', and Carnival customs (as in Bruegel's *Carnival and Lent*).[3] There were London plays on the subject in 1595 and 1598; and Baskervill mentions it among medieval survivals in Breton folk-plays down to the nineteenth century.[4]

Besides *Eglamour* and *Triamour*, four of the Middle English romances about distressed queens that Mrs Loomis analyses appeared on the stage in religious as well as secular guise. The major collection of miracle plays, the *Miracles de Notre Dame par Personnages* belonging to a *puy* or literary guild in Paris (*c.* 1345–80), contains forty pieces on varied themes, legendary, heroic and realistic. While all the plays depict an intervention by the Virgin, nineteen of the subjects can be described as bourgeois or, more frequently, chivalric or romantic, rather than hagiological or ecclesiastic.[5] No less than seven of the romantic miracles portray persecuted queens; and nearly all the medieval groups of tales centred on this theme are said to be represented among them[6] (including the four Middle English romances). These romantic miracles – or sanctified romances – had a wide diffusion on the stage.

The acted stories all follow the same pattern, with, of course, many variations of detail as well as cross-borrowings; as Margaret Schlauch has shown, the essential narrative elements in them must be very much older than their early medieval literary sources. The heroine may be accused of giving birth to monsters, or of infanticide, or adultery. Her accuser may be her mother-in-law, or the king her husband's brother or deputy, or a repulsed lover. In any event,

---

[1] *Ibid.*, p. 284.　　[2] *Cf* Schlauch, *Antecedents of the English Novel*, pp. 56ff.
[3] Grossmann (ed.), *Bruegel: the Paintings*, Plate 6; Klein (ed.), *Graphic Worlds of Bruegel*, plate 25; *cf* Baskervill, 'Early Romantic Plays', pp. 495–6; Bernheimer, *Wild Men in the Middle Ages*.
[4] Baskervill, 'Early Romantic Plays,' p. 510.
[5] Paris and Robert (eds.), *Miracles de Nostre Dame*; Petit de Julleville, *Les Mystères*, vol. I, pp. 115–79; vol. II, pp. 226–335; Frank, *Medieval French Drama*, pp. 114–24.
[6] Micha, 'La Femme injustement accusée dans les Miracles de Notre-Dame'.

the king at once condemns his wife to death on hearsay, without trial or inquiry; or at best, as with Chaucer's Constance, his lenient instructions are falsified by his mother. The heroine is exposed, or takes to flight, in a wild forest or in a boat. Sometimes one such ordeal is not enough and, like Constance, she must go through a similar palaver again; as an Angel-prologue jauntily forecasts in the Italian miracle of *Santa Uliva*,

> Vedrete questa donna singulare
> Come due volte fu gettata in mare.

(You shall see how on two occasions this remarkable lady was thrown into the sea.)

But neither the terror of the forest nor the terror of the waves can overcome a chaste heroine who is truly worth her salt. Like Griselda, she accepts a humble, outcast status in patience. And if she sticks it out, as she always does, she can be sure of being protected by the Virgin, of finding her honour vindicated, often with the help of her son, and of being rewarded in the end by the effusive return of her husband's (or of one of her husbands') affections. In order to indicate the prevalence of this theme, and touch on some of the related narrative and dramatic conventions, it will be simplest to give references as far as possible in the form of a list (which cannot pretend to completeness); I shall group the references around the five most popular subjects among the relevant *Miracles de Notre Dame*:[1]

(i) *La Fille du Roi de Hongrie* has the most sensational adventures. Her widowed father, urged to find a new queen, will only marry a woman like his former wife; on his nobles' advice, and with the approval of an all-too-compliant Pope, he chooses his daughter, Jouye, who cuts off her hand to avoid the match. Her father orders her to be burnt, but she is set adrift instead, and floats to Scotland – where the king marries her. While her husband is at a tournament at Senlis, she gives birth (on the stage). Her mother-in-law writes that she has given birth to a monster and falsifies the king's reply, so that Jouye is again cast adrift, this time with her son. She floats to Rome, where she enters a Senator's service, where her husband, penitent, finds her while on a pilgrimage, recognising her thanks to her son's ring, and where she is reconciled with her father as well; her lost hand is

[1] Salingar, 'Time and Art in Shakespeare's Romances'.

miraculously recovered there from the inside of a sturgeon.[1] This is close to the story of Chaucer's Constance, except that Chaucer has eliminated the initial motif of incest and has emphasised the themes of conversion of pagans (in Northumbria) and of war against the Saracens; more than twenty other variants of the story have been noted in European literature from the thirteenth to the fifteenth century, including the Middle English romance, *Emare*.[2] In the fifteenth century there was a Latin play on the subject, and an Italian prose tale, subsequently dramatised.[3] A more famous Italian version was the *sacra rappresentazione* of *Santa Uliva*, also belonging to the fifteenth century but first printed as late as 1568 and running into several editions over the next hundred years; (in this play, the Virgin restores the heroine's mutilated hands in person, without comment or fuss).[4] The Florentine playwright Giovanni Maria Cecchi (1518–84), who turned to the remodelling of *sacre rappresentazioni* after beginning his career as a writer of neoclassical comedies, took one of his subjects (*Romanesca*) from *Santa Uliva*.[5]

This story contains a cluster of motifs from folklore. (*a*) The incestuous father can be traced back from fairy tales to mythology; in some fairy tales and some romances – as in the thirteenth-century *Manekine*, the source of *La Fille du Roi de Hongrie* – the father has promised his dying queen only to remarry if his new wife exactly resembles herself.[6] (*b*) The motif known as 'the Maiden without Hands' also comes from folk-tales.[7] (*c*) The scene of the heroine's delivery on the stage can be paralleled from several miracles and other medieval plays, such as *Griseldis* (who is shown in manuscript drawings, once in childbed and again 'obviously pregnant')[8] and the Towneley Nativity play. (*d*) The motif linking an ill-fated birth to

[1] Paris and Robert (eds.), *Miracles de Nostre Dame*, no. XXIX; see Petit de Julleville, *Les Mystères*, vol. II, pp. 300–3.
[2] Schlauch, *Constance*, pp. 62–78, 132–4; Hibbard, *Mediaeval Romance*, pp. 23–33.
[3] *Ibid.*, pp. 27–8.
[4] *Santa Uliva*, ed. d'Ancona, *Sacre Rappresentazioni*, vol. III. See d'Ancona, *Origini*, vol. I, pp. 436–7; vol. II, pp. 58–60; Herrick, *Italian Comedy*, pp. 2, 8.
[5] D'Ancona, *Origini*, vol. II, pp. 156–7.
[6] Schlauch, *Constance*, pp. 39–47, 70–4, 120; *cf* Cox, *Cinderella*, pp. xxxii–xxxiii.
[7] Aarne and Thompson, *Types of the Folktale*, Type 706.
[8] Roques (ed.), *Griseldis*, lines 1260ff, 1490ff, and plates XII, XIV. *Cf* England (ed.), *Towneley Plays*, no. X, line 156; York *Nativity*, in Adams (ed.), *Chief Pre-Shakespearean Dramas*; d'Ancona (ed.), *Sacre Rappresentazioni*, vol. III, pp. 281, 378, and *Origini*, vol. I, pp. 450–4; Petit de Julleville, *Les Mystères*, vol. I, p. 167; vol. II, pp. 236, 301, 306, 326; Lebègue, 'Quelques Survivances de la mise en scène médiévale', p. 220.

exposure at sea must be one of the oldest in the history of the theatre; ('O what a thoroughly wanton sex we are', Lysistrata exclaims, when her allies in obduracy show signs of wavering, 'No wonder tragedies are made about us; for we are nothing but "Poseidon and a little boat" ').[1] And already in the Athenian plays that offended Lysistrata, the infant's exposure, whether at sea or on a mountainside, led on to (*e*) the motif of his subsequent acknowledgement by his father, thanks to a ring or some similar token, as with the prince of Scotland in *La Fille du Roi de Hongrie*.[2]

Another Parisian miracle obviously derived from the latter play is *La Fille du Roi Habillée en Chevalier*. Here Ysabel, born on the stage and later in flight from a dutifully incestuous father, adopts male disguise and, after a forest adventure, crosses to Constantinople by sea with the help of the Angel Gabriel, who chats in Latin with their shipmaster. At Constantinople, Ysabel champions the Emperor in battle against the Turks and marries him after piously transvestite complications, including her nominal marriage to his daughter.[3] The earliest examples of the romance motif (*f*) of a fugitive heroine in male disguise have been traced to Indian drama, but it may owe its origin to a ritual charm to ward off evil spirits[4] (in the Parisian miracle of *Théodore, la Femme Moine*, the heroine, a virtuous wife who has been seduced while her husband is away at war, cuts off her hair and becomes a monk, adopting man's dress, she says, so as to trick the Devil – 'je le pense trichier, | Puisque comme homme suis vestue').[5]

(ii) In *Le Roi Thierry et Osanne sa Femme* a wicked mother-in-law accuses Osanne of a monstrous birth. Osanne is first imprisoned, then cast adrift, floating to Jerusalem, where she serves an innkeeper. Her real children (triplets) have been rescued by a charcoal-burner, and after twelve years the king finds them while hunting, and discovers who they are; after a victory over the Saracens he meets Osanne again while on pilgrimage.[6] This story is related to romances like the

---

[1] Aristophanes, *Lysistrata*, line 137.

[2] See d'Ancona, *Origini*, vol. II, pp. 58–60; Murray, 'Ritual Elements in New Comedy'.

[3] Paris and Robert (eds.), *Miracles de Nostre Dame*, no. XXXVII. See Petit de Julleville, *Les Mystères*, vol. II, p. 326.

[4] Freeburg, *Disguise Plots*, pp. 39–44; Thompson, *Motif-Index*, Motif K1837; Halliday, *Greek Questions*, p. 216.

[5] Paris and Robert (eds.), *Miracles de Nostre Dame*, no. XVIII. See Petit de Julleville, *Les Mystères*, vol. II, pp. 267–72.

[6] Paris and Robert, *Miracles de Nostre Dame*, no. XXXII. See Petit de Julleville, *Les Mystères*, vol. II, pp. 306–10.

Middle English *Octavian* and *Valentine and Orson* and *The Knight of the Swan*.[1] It reappears in another fifteenth-century Italian miracle, *Stella*,[2] and in another play (1555) by Hans Sachs;[3] while Fletcher remembers the wicked mother-in-law in *Thierry and Theodoret* (c. 1617).

Another betrayed queen in the Parisian collection of miracles is *Berthe, Femme du Roi Pepin*, whose betrayal involves the motif (g) of the substituted bride.[4] (Berthe is an innocent; but the same device is used by the heroine of another miracle, *La Femme du Roi de Portugal*, in order to conceal her adultery. Middleton must have known some version of the latter play, for he follows the same incidents closely in the sub-plot of Diaphanta in *The Changeling*).[5]

(iii) The *Empereris de Rome* is denounced by a lustful brother-in-law, is later rescued from the sea, and is presented by the Virgin with a herb of miraculous healing powers, which she ultimately uses to extort a confession from her false accuser before healing him of leprosy. This is the only play in this French group where the Virgin's intervention makes a tangible difference.[6] Again, the story belongs to a group based on folk-tale; it was well known in England,[7] and it seems almost certain – from the evidence of roof-bosses in Norwich Cathedral – that it was known in the fifteenth century in the form of a play.[8] It also provided another Italian miracle in the same century (*Santa Guglielma*) and, in the sixteenth century, another play by Cecchi, and another by Hans Sachs.[9]

The other two French miracles about accused wives represent a later phase in the history of the theme; they are related to romances of chivalry:

(iv) *Oton* or *Ostes, Roi d'Espagne* is based on another type of folk-tale, the wager on a woman's chastity (in some variants of the story, it is

---

1 Schlauch, *Constance*, pp. 80–94; *cf* p. 41, n. 2, above.
2 *Stella*, ed. d'Ancona, *Sacre Rappresentazioni*, vol. III.
3 Hibbard, *Mediaeval Romance*, p. 267.
4 Paris and Robert (eds.), *Miracles de Nostre Dame*, no. XXXI. See Petit de Julleville, *Les Mystères*, vol. I, pp. 143–9; vol. II, pp. 305–6; *cf* Paris, 'Le Cycle de la *Gageure*', pp. 483–6.
5 Paris and Robert (eds.), *Miracles de Nostre Dame*, no. IV. See Petit de Julleville, *Les Mystères*, vol. I, pp. 136–9; vol. II, pp. 235–6; Baskervill, 'Early Romantic Plays', p. 488.
6 *Miracles de Nostre Dame*, no. XXVII; see Petit de Julleville, *Les Mystères*, vol. II, pp. 293–6.
7 Schlauch, *Constance*, pp. 106–13; Aarne and Thompson, *Types of the Folktale*, Type 712: 'Crescentia'.
8 Anderson, *Drama and Imagery*, pp. 188–92.
9 *Santa Guglielma*, ed. d'Ancona, *Sacre Rappresentazioni*, vol. III. See d'Ancona, *Origini*, vol. II, pp. 156–7; Hibbard, *Mediaeval Romance*, p. 13.

a sister's honour that is at stake).[1] Oton wages his kingdom on his wife's good name, and he fights her accuser at the end of the play. Another and much more famous version of the story of a wager on a wife's honour, Boccaccio's story about Zinevra of Genoa (*Decameron* II.9), was one of Shakespeare's sources for *Cymbeline*; in several forms, the story also appeared in a Spanish play (Lope de Rueda's *Eufemia*, *c*. 1550) and in three German plays, one of them by Sachs (*Ginevra*, 1548) and another by Jakob Ayrer (*c*. 1600).[2]

(v) In *La Marquise de la Gaudine*, as in *Oton*, the accuser is a repulsed lover (the husband's uncle) and there is a trial by combat; the marquise is championed by a knight who owes her a deep obligation of courtesy.[3] A German variant of the romance was dramatised, again by Sachs, in 1552;[4] almost at the same moment, in 1554, Bandello published another form of the story, calling the heroine the Duchess of Savoy. Bandello's *novella* was translated in France and subsequently dramatised (by Jean Behourt, in *La Polyxene, Tragicomedie*, 1597);[5] it was well known to the Elizabethans. In 1576, for example, George Pettie makes the heroine in one of his stories ask herself rhetorically – 'And for the Duchess of Savoy, what hurt sustained she by that false accusation? Did it not make her glory and virtue show more splendently to the whole world?'[6]

What were essentially the same stories about persecuted queens retained their appeal for popular audiences, then, nearly everywhere in western Europe for at least 200 years, from the time of the Parisian *puy* to the time of Hans Sachs. And in France itself they remained popular in the provinces, especially, it seems, on the fringes of the French-speaking area, long after Paris had turned decisively towards classicism. In his survey of the repertoire of Brittany and of the Basque country, as it existed down to the end of the last century, Baskervill notes that 'themes of the Constance and Eustace type – of calumniated women cast away and wrecked at sea, of separated families, etc. –

1 *Oton, Roi d'Espagne*, ed. Paris and Robert, *Miracles de Nostre Dame*, vol. IV, no. XXVIII; also ed. Monmerqué and Michel, in *Théâtre Français au Moyen-Age*. See Petit de Julleville, *Les Mystères*, vol. II, pp. 297–300; Paris, 'Le Cycle de la Gageure'; Aarne and Thompson, *Types of the Folktale*, Type 882: 'The Wager on the Wife's Chastity'.

2 Baskervill, 'Early Romantic Plays', pp. 488–9.

3 Paris and Robert (eds.), *Miracles de Nostre Dame*, no. XII; Petit de Julleville, *Les Mystère*, vol. I, pp. 132, 140–3; vol. II, pp. 252–3.

4 Hibbard, *Mediaeval Romance*, p. 37.

5 Lancaster, *French Tragi-Comedy*, pp. 65–9.

6 George Pettie, *A Petite Pallace* (1576), ed. Gollancz, vol. I, p. 35; *cf* vol. II, pp. 12, 107. See Pruvost, *Bandello*, pp. 16–21, 30, 75n.

...are possibly the most popular themes among the Basque and Breton plays both in miracles and in purer romantic form'.[1]

There can be no doubt that Baskervill is right in adding that much the same continuity with medieval taste held good for Elizabethan England. For example, four romances of 'the Constance and Eustace type' (*Sir Eglamour* and *Sir Triamour*, already mentioned, and two others to be mentioned later, *Sir Isumbras* and the prose *Frederyke of Jennen*) appear, together with several Tudor moral interludes (described as 'auncient playz'), in the list of books said to belong to Captain Cox, the mason with 'great oversight...in matters of storie' who led the Coventry men in the presentation of their traditional Hocktide play before Elizabeth at Kenilworth in 1575; and although the intention of Laneham, the actor in Leicester's company who furnishes the list, was probably satiric, the list is none the less significant of popular taste.[2] Some of the other romances attributed to Captain Cox's library (such as *The Squire of Low Degree* or *The Knight of Courtesy*) recall the titles of lost plays actually given by Leicester's men and other companies about this time, while others again (including *Huon of Bordeaux* and *The Four Sons of Aymon*) were dramatised for the public theatres by the end of the reign. Although there are gaps, therefore, in the records of the English theatre, evidence as to the popular taste in romantic subjects for which much of the drama catered is virtually continuous from about Chaucer's time to Shakespeare's.

Two of the fourteenth-century plays on the theme of the wronged wife are of special interest to the student of Shakespeare because they contain analogues to *The Winter's Tale* and *Cymbeline*: the Dutch romance, *Esmoreit*, and the French miracle, *Oton*. They provide a basis for reasoned speculation about the popular romantic drama Shakespeare could have seen in his youth.

Eighteen or twenty years pass in the Dutch play between the imprisonment of the Queen of Sicily on a false charge of infanticide – 'For twenty years she knew no smile', says the Prologue – and her joyful release on the reappearance of her lost son, Esmoreit. The Queen is 'the King's daughter of Hungary'. The charge against her is brought, and her infant is stolen and then sold, by her husband's

[1] Baskervill, 'Early Romantic Plays', p. 508.

[2] Furnivall (ed.), *Laneham's Letter*, pp. xvff, 26–32; cf Wright, |*Middle-Class Culture*, pp. 24, 375ff; Bradbrook, *Rise of the Common Player*, ch. 6; and the present chapter, pp. 40–1.

ambitious nephew, Robert; the infant is purchased by Master Platus, the astrologer of the King of Damascus, who is sent to Sicily expressly for the transaction in order to avert a portent he has read in the stars. At Damascus Esmoreit is brought up as a Moslem, or pagan, ignorant of his origin, by the King's daughter, Damiette. These events, leading up to the Queen's imprisonment, occupy the first half of the little play. Then, with a jump across time, Esmoreit is 'eighteen' or more, and Damiette is in love with him; in order to remove the bar of her supposed sisterhood, she tells him that he is a foundling – which is all she knows – and encourages him to go in search of his true parents, wearing the 'swaddling-band' he was found with entwined round his forehead as a helpful sign. Esmoreit crosses the stage from Damascus to Sicily, and through the prison window his mother recognises him and identifies her own stitching on the swaddling-band almost at once –

> I set your father's arms thereon,
> As well is seen, in quarters three,
> And the fourth be the arms of Hungary.

Release of the Queen, paternal acknowledgement with conversion for Esmoreit; then Damiette and Platus follow him, dressed as pilgrims, the one to be welcomed in marriage by Esmoreit, the other to denounce Robert, who is hanged.

The time-scale of *Esmoreit* is typical of exemplary romances. It is often essential to the story to imagine a lapse of many years, either to impress on the audience the idea of a life-long saintliness, patience or endurance, or else to give time for a foundling child to grow up and redeem his unhappy parent from misfortune. For much the same reason, the idea of widely separated places is often essential to the play; the naïve topography of *Esmoreit* is also characteristic. Possibly the plot was influenced by some Byzantine (ultimately, hellenistic) romance, such as seems to be present behind some parts of the *Decameron*. But in any case, the place-names in the story are typical. Persecuted queens on the medieval stage are associated with piety (as in *Esmoreit*), with miraculous healing, pilgrimages or conversions, and the setting of their exemplary privations often belongs to the geography of the Crusades.[1] On the other hand, the staging of *Esmoreit* could be very simple indeed – almost as simple as the Flemish folk-plays of *Valentine and Orson*, as illustrated by Bruegel 200 years later.[2]

---

[1] *Esmoreit*, trans. Ayres, introduction. See Schlauch, *Constance*, pp. 9–11, 53–9, 117–19.
[2] See p. 41, n. 3 above.

There is a general likeness between *Esmoreit* and Robert Greene's novel or novelette, *Pandosto, The Triumph of Time* (1588), which was Shakespeare's main direct source for *The Winter's Tale*. Admittedly, it is almost impossible that either Shakespeare or Greene could have heard of *Esmoreit* itself; and if, as seems much more likely, Greene knew some variant form of the old play, he changed it considerably. But the differences between *Pandosto* and *Esmoreit* are consistent with his general policy as a writer, and not at all inconsistent with the assumption that he knew *Esmoreit* indirectly. Greene (1558–92) was a needy, prolific furnisher of plays and stories, who regularly catered for popular taste, in spite of his very evident pride in his graduate status and his up-to-date literary culture.

Greene departs from medieval stories of unhappy queens by making Pandosto himself accuse his wife ('the Emperor's daughter of Russia') of adultery with his friend because of a groundless but 'flaming jealousy', and by making the queen die in prison, even after her innocence has been declared by oracle.[1] It seems that the husband was a very rare accuser, late in coming forward as the originator of his wife's misfortunes in the evolution of these tales of persecuted heroines.[2] But his emergence as the villain was in line with the desire of sixteenth-century authors to rationalise the archetypal story and treat it as an exemplum of vice and virtue in marriage; and Greene follows the same course in his tragi-comedy, *James IV*, based either on the story of Arrenopia in Giraldi's *Hecatommithi* (1565) or on Giraldi's play about the same subject[3] (the transformation of older romance in the style of *La Fille du Roi Habillée en Chevalier* – in group (i), above – is obvious in Giraldi). By making the queen die in *Pandosto*, Greene follows this moralistic purpose; her repentant husband erects an epitaph to her memory.

Secondly, instead of starting his tale from Sicily, Greene shifts it to Sicily and back from Bohemia; and instead of giving the unhappy queen a newborn son to lose, he gives her a daughter. In Sicily, Greene can appropriately introduce fashionably pastoral scenes, reminiscent of Longus and Sidney; but it seems likely that the motif of the foundling princess as shepherdess was suggested to Greene by an episode in the widely read chivalric romance of *Amadis* (which could have provided him with the name of his heroine's dead

---

[1] Greene, *Pandosto*, in *The Winter's Tale*, ed. Pafford, App. iv. See Pruvost, *Greene*, pp. 285–308.
[2] Schlauch, *Constance*, pp. 46, 60.   [3] Herrick, *Tragicomedy*, pp. 82–6, 232–7.

brother, Garinter, just as it may in turn have provided Shakespeare with the name of her lover, Florizel).[1] The elements of renaissance pastoral in Greene's story are prominent but not essential.

Finally, by making his foundling princess, Fawnia, attract the love of Dorastus, the son of her father's former friend, the king of Sicily, and by making the lovers elope, to be driven by storm to Bohemia, Greene gives his story a neatly circular shape – *The Triumph of Time* – and introduces a new tone of moral sentiment. As René Pruvost points out in his study of Greene, the mid-sixteenth century was attracted by stories in which two young lovers, like Romeo and Juliet, ultimately cause a reconciliation between hostile families or countries; but in *Pandosto*, 'for the first time apparently in English literature, love between the children is made use of by Fortune to wipe out the consequences of errors and crimes that the fathers had been guilty of or had suffered from in the previous generation'.[2] The pastoral adventure in *Pandosto* serves to throw into relief the domestic senti-ment (which is much more insistent than in *Esmoreit*). No doubt Greene's innovation appealed to Shakespeare and his contemporaries. On the other hand, the idea of using a love affair in a romance to bring about the reconciliation of friends who have quarrelled is not very far removed from the idea of using it to bring about the conversion of Saracens.

Pandosto was extremely popular; it was the first English novel to be translated into French, and provided two tragicomedies in France by 1631.[3] At the same time, this wide and instant success suggests that it had a familiar ring as well as an air of novelty. (It is worth noting that Mahelot's drawing of his setting for the second *Pandoste* at the Hôtel de Bourgogne reveals a similar mixture of old and new in theatrical design. On the spectator's left, a painted sea and beyond it the Temple of Delphi; facing the spectator, the façade of the Palace of Epirus; to his right, a prison: the visual effect has the frontal perspective of Italian renaissance theatres, but the combination of far-separated localities on the same stage allows the narrative freedom of medieval *décor simultané*.)[4]

Evidently Shakespeare not only recognised the traditional flavour in Greene's romance but in some respects set out to emphasise it. He keeps Hermione alive to the end, having made her a queen of Sicily, even though this means transposing her daughter's pastoral

---

[1] Pruvost, *Greene*, pp. 299–301.   [2] *Ibid*. p. 290.   [3] *Ibid*. pp. 286–7.
[4] Nicoll, *Development of the Theatre*, p. 117.

scene to the unlikely coast of Bohemia. In this respect, *The Winter's Tale* harks back to *Esmoreit*. These changes from *Pandosto* could, of course, have been prompted by any of a dozen causes; but other details in Shakespeare look like a deliberate recall of 'an old tale' – or an old play. One is Hermione's appearance on the stage in advanced pregnancy in the first act;[1] this would have been common form in medieval drama (cf. (i) (c) above), but is almost unknown in surviving plays by Shakespeare's contemporaries. (Dekker keeps the signs of the heroine's pregnancies off the stage in *Patient Grissil*, for example, where they might have been expected.) Possibly the only exceptions to this tacit rule of prudery or delicacy among Elizabethan playwrights are the scene of the birth of the first Prince of Wales in Peele's *Edward I*, some twenty years earlier than *The Winter's Tale*, and the Shakespearean third act of *Pericles*, shortly before *The Winter's Tale* in date, where *enter Thaisa with child, with Lychorida, a nurse*. And *Pericles* is avowedly an imitation of medieval romance, with Gower as 'Chorus' or presenter.

Moreover, Shakespeare recalls the old motif of incest from folktales and the medieval drama. Greene repeats it too, but clumsily veiled: Pandosto tries to seduce Fawnia when he meets her, then kills himself out of shame when he discovers who she is.[2] But Shakespeare restores it with fine appropriateness. Before Perdita reaches Leontes's court in Act V, the nobles have been urging him to remarry, but Paulina has made him promise not to take another wife unless she can find him one 'As like Hermione as is her picture' (v.i.74); and when Perdita appears with Florizel, Leontes is so patently attracted by her that Paulina has to remind him sharply of Hermione – whereupon he replies, 'I thought of her | Even in these looks I made' (v.i.227). This encounter, preparing emotionally for the final episode of recognition, is described in the next scene as 'so like an old tale that the verity of it is in strong suspicion' (v.ii.28). And the rest of Perdita's story is received in the Sicilian court 'like an old tale still' (v.ii.59). Shakespeare evokes the mental world of plays like *Esmoreit* although he detaches himself from it. His use of Time as Chorus (to which it will be necessary to return in a later chapter of this study) conveys the same line of thought. In his rehandling of

---

[1] Coghill, 'Six Points of Stage-craft in *The Winter's Tale*', *Shakespeare Survey 11* (1958), 33.

[2] Greene, *Pandosto*, in Pafford (ed.), *The Winter's Tale*, pp. 218–25. *Cf* p. 43, n. 6, above.

Greene's story he seems deliberately to allude to old romances and old plays.

Oton is prefaced by a sermon, like other *Miracles de Notre Dame*.[1] It is a much longer play than *Esmoreit* – more than 2,000 lines, falling into what may be described as forty scenes, acted continuously. Though the staging follows the same principle as *Esmoreit*, it is more elaborate; it requires a 'heaven' and four other 'places' – Rome, Burgos, Granada and somewhere in Barbary (which could be indicated simply by a crescent sign). Moreover, Burgos consists of several buildings or subordinate parts, indicating a monastery, a building for the city 'parlement', the queen's apartment, and a fortified castle, which must be strong enough not merely to hold defenders above who can parley with invaders below, as in Shakespeare's scenes of sieges, but to enable a realistic battle scene to be staged: '*Ici se fait la bataille*' (line 385), and the defenders pitch down missiles (mangonels, line 388), while the attackers force their way in after setting fire to one of the gates (line 394). But in spite of this local realism, there is the same naïve treatment of distance as in *Esmoreit*. Messengers and others – there are more than twenty speaking parts in all – hurry from Rome to Burgos or back, in view of the audience, in the space of a few lines, sometimes capping the first line of a rhyming couplet, which concludes a scene in one 'place', with the second line, beginning a fresh scene in another 'place'; or a character may cross half Europe in the course of a single speech, as when Berengier leaves Burgos for Rome ('Mais a Romme m'en iray tout droit', line 925), and by the next line has arrived 'straight' at his destination ('L'emperiére voy la endroit | Ou se siet, et Ostes lez lui'). Telling the story is the dominant consideration; and the speakers take care to remind the audience where they are. These are exactly the same conventions that we find much later in Elizabethan plays like *Common Conditions*, though small travelling companies could not afford equally solid scenery.

The tone of *Oton* is feudal. The Emperor Lotaire invades the kingdom of Burgos ('Spain') so as to create a fief for his nephew Oton (or Ostes) and give him the King's Daughter as wife; the King, Alfons, has fled to his brother at Granada, leaving his Daughter in charge of the Citizens. The Daughter accepts marriage by conquest submissively, in two lines (486–7). She even cherishes the 'sign' which

---

[1] See p. 46, n. 1, above.

Oton gives her, as a private token between them, before he hurries away, immediately after the marriage contract, to follow his liege lord back to Rome. (This 'sign' is an odd choice – one of Oton's toe-bones; the important thing for the playwright is that it should be secret, and portable.)

At Rome, Berengier, who, it seems, has been too prudent to risk himself in battle, sneers at Oton for leaving his wife behind. Oton retorts for the honour of women –

> Par foy, Berengier, c'est mau dit
> Dire des dames villenie   (line 658)

– but he accepts the other's challenge, wagering lands for lands, that Berengier will produce proof of his wife's infidelity after a single meeting with her. Crossing to Burgos, Berengier opens fire by telling the Daughter that Oton cares no more for her 'than a cherry stalk', that he has forgotten her for a 'wench' in Rome, and that he, Berengier, has brought the news as her zealous adorer (line 753):

> Ma dame, je le vous diray:
> De fait me sui cy adressié.
> De Romme vien ou j'ay laissié
> Vostre seigneur, qui ne vous prise
> Pas la queue d'une serise;
> D'une garce s'est acointié
> Qu'il a en si grant amistié
> Qu'il ne scet d'elle departir.
> Ce m'a fait de Rome partir
> Pour le vous annuncier et dire,
> Car grant deuil en ay et grant ire;
> Et pour ce qu'ainsi a mespris,
> L'amour de vous m'a si espris
> Que nuit ne jour ne puis durer,
> Tant me fait griefs maulx endurer
> Pour vous, ma dame.

The Daughter is not to be taken in; she knows Berengier and his 'lineage' too well – ('Certes vous ne vostre lignage | Ne sariez dire un seul bien, non, | Fors mauvaistié et traison') – and she sweeps away from him in scorn. Berengier has to bribe her Lady-in-waiting to produce the 'sign' he needs as evidence. When he shows it before the Emperor in Rome, Oton is profoundly afflicted ('adolez', line, 946) in his feelings as a magnate –

> E! Diex, com je sui adolez!
> Je voy bien j'ay perdu ma terre.
> Le cuer d'ire ou ventre me serre.
> Ha! tresfaulse et deloyal femme,
> Conment m'as tu fait tel diffame?

– and he at once determines to put his wife to death.

Forewarned by a hurrying Citizen, the Daughter prays in the monastery to Mary for help. And from Heaven, God sends Our Lady to comfort her, accompanied by angels singing in descent and on departure (lines 1068–140). The advice the Daughter is given, to follow her father to Granada in the disguise of a squire, hardly requires a divine counsellor (in the prose romance on which the play may have been founded, *Le roi Flore et la belle Jehanne*, the heroine forms a similar plan of her own accord).[1] But (unlike Jehanne) the Daughter is still a virgin; and, more important, this scene of a heavenly descent with music forms the central moment of all the Parisian miracles. (In the corresponding passage in *L'Empereris de Romme*, lines 1208–92, Our Lady tells the Empress while she is sleeping, abandoned on a rock, that she is to take away the plants beneath her head because they have the power of curing leprosy.)

In the remaining scenes of *Oton*, the Daughter presents herself to her uncle and her father, unknown, under the name of Denis (line 1275; her true name, Denise, is not mentioned until later, line 1325): she enters her uncle's service as a squire, skilled in battle as well as in carving and cupbearing, and impresses him by the way she can lay a table (lines 1245–92). When the rumour of her death reaches Granada, her uncle and father decide to attack the Emperor in revenge, calling on Moorish allies to help them, and sending the Daughter in advance as their standard-bearer and herald. Meanwhile Oton, in despair, has renounced God and joined the Saracens (lines 1293–310); but, finding no use in their 'servile' and 'trivial' faith, he repents, and prays God to forgive him for his desertion. In a second musical scene of descent from Heaven (lines 1531–97), God orders him back to Rome to confess his sin and ask pardon for his 'grant deffault' in wishing to kill his wife. The Daughter and her knights meet Oton and capture him on their way to Rome; he submits – 'c'est raison'

---

[1] *Le Roi Flore*, ed. Monmerqué and Michel, in *Théâtre Français au Moyen-Age*, p. 421. See Petit de Julleville, *Les Mystères*, vol. I, p. 127.

(line 1703) – only asking not to be imprisoned. Arrived at Rome, the Daughter challenges Berengier before the Emperor on her 'sister's' behalf, but Oton makes sure that he takes on the combat and, naturally, wins, after prayer. Berengier confesses. As her father and uncle also arrive at Rome, the Daughter reveals herself – 'Tenez, regardez ma poitrine' (line 1996) – and makes peace all round, Oton recovering Spain and the Emperor recompensing Alfons with another kingdom which has happened to come his way.

Crude as it is, the play has a certain consistency; the loyalty of a wife is exactly balanced against the faith of a crusader and feudal loyalty. At one time, scholars like Dowden and Gaston Paris were inclined to believe that Shakespeare was indebted to some lost play intermediate between *Oton* and *Cymbeline*; for instance, among the many versions of the wager story examined by Paris, these are the only two in which the villain approaches the wife with the pretence that her husband is unfaithful to her[1] – in each case, at Rome. This opinion seems to have dropped out of sight. J. M. Nosworthy ignores it, confining his attention to Boccaccio's story, which Shakespeare certainly used; to an English variant of Boccaccio (one of Captain Cox's books), the short story of *Frederyke of Jennen* (Genoa), first published in 1518;[2] and to Shakespeare's historical borrowings from Holinshed and others – besides giving importance, as we have seen, to the possible influence of *The Rare Triumphs of Love and Fortune*. But the older opinion has a great deal to recommend. Gaston Paris held that the folk versions of the wager story, recorded subsequently, date back to the sixteenth century; and the booklet, *Westward for Smelts*, contains another form of the tale which must have been current in England in Shakespeare's time, although it was printed too late (1620) to be eligible for consideration as a direct source.[3]

The problem of the narrative origins of *Cymbeline* is elusive because of the way Shakespeare weaves together four plots or sub-plots, those of Imogen, the Queen and Cloten, Belarius and the princes, and the war with Rome. Only for the first is there a definitely known narrative source – Boccaccio's tale, which we can be sure that Shakespeare read, since he repeats specific details from it, both here and

---

[1] Paris, 'Le Cycle de la *Gageure*', pp. 513–15; see Nosworthy (ed.), *Cymbeline*, pp. xxix–xxxiii.

[2] Nosworthy (ed.), *Cymbeline*, pp. xxii–xxv and 198ff (text of *Frederyke of Jennen*); *cf* Wright, *Middle-Class Culture*, p. 473; above, p. 47.

[3] Paris, 'Le Cycle de la *Gageure*', pp. 513–15, 549.

in *The Winter's Tale* (his knowledge of *Frederyke of Jennen* in addition, though probable, does not affect the main lines of his plot).[1] And even for the wager story Boccaccio's narrative is an insufficient source, since Shakespeare departs radically from Boccaccio's ending, where the heroine engineers her own vindication. *Love and Fortune* is a possible source for the Belarius story, but only for part of it, since Shakespeare's sub-plot turns on the reappearance of the princes to save their father from his enemies, as well as on the man their father has wronged. He sets the theft of the princes back 'some twenty years', introducing it with a broad hint of remote improbability (1.i.65):

> Howsoe'er 'tis strange,
> Or that the negligence may well be laugh'd at,
> Yet is it true, sir.

At the same time, the motif of the long-endured injustice inflicted on Belarius is quite distinct from the Imogen motif, though complementary to it in mood. But if Shakespeare chose the wager story from his knowledge of 'an old tale' or an old play (and not, in the first place, from his reading of Boccaccio), then Belarius's story would seem a natural pendant, as part of the same narrative or stage tradition, if not part of the same particular work. The tradition of romances about persecuted queens would also account readily for the presence of the wicked step-mother in Shakespeare's play.

Neither Boccaccio nor *Love and Fortune* give any basis for the story of the invasion, which Shakespeare uses as his dramatic pretext for bringing his main characters together again. Nor could the reading in British history which Shakespeare uses in this play have provided any continuous narrative of an invasion, or any reference to an Imogen in Cymbeline's reign. For the invasion, Shakespeare mixes fragments of history or pseudo-history without compunction from different reigns; and the only information from Holinshed's vague chapter about Cymbeline relevant to Shakespeare's play is that this king '(as some write) was brought up at Rome, and there made knight by Augustus Caesar' and that he sent the youth of Britain to Rome, 'whereby they might learn both to behave themselves like civil men, and to attain to the knowledge of feats of war'. In addition, Shakespeare may have noticed Holinshed's statement about Cymbeline, that 'Little other mention is made of his doings, except that

---

[1] See p. 55 n. 2, above, and Muir, *Shakespeare's Sources*, vol. I, pp. 236–7.

during his reign, the Saviour of the World our Lord Jesus Christ...
was born of a virgin.'[1] Holinshed's chapter, with its open door to
romantic invention, would surely have seemed significant to Shakespeare only if he was already looking, with the wager story in mind,
for some connection of a legendary sort between Britain and Rome.
It would seem the more natural to bring Cymbeline and an Imogen
together on the stage if the latter already belonged in Shakespeare's
mind to a miracle play or something like one; or if he already knew an
old play combining a wager story with romanticised history or
legend.

If Shakespeare did indeed know an old play derived from *Oton* or
resembling it in outline, that is precisely what he would have found.
The idea of knighthood is essential to the miracle play; Oton does
not exist as a lover, he is purely a feudal warrior. And if the miracle
play contains no hint of any contrast in 'civility' between Romans
and barbarians, it is deeply coloured, like its congeners, with the
thought of faith (or renegation), connected with the image of Rome.
Not only does Shakespeare echo the passage in *Oton* where the would-
be seducer approaches the wife with a lie about her husband; where
he changes the wager story as he found it in the *Decameron* and
Frederyke, removing the mercantile setting and altering the wife's
adventures, he brings it much nearer to the old romance. In both
plays, the heroine, in male disguise, serves her own kinsmen, unrecognised, at table, in a manner befitting a chivalric squire (like
Chaucer's Squire, 'curteis..., lowely, and servysable', who 'carf
biforn his fader at the table'). In both plays, she accompanies an
army, and helps to make the peace. And in both plays, the husband,
having condemned his wife, joins the national enemy (the Saracens,
in *Oton*), repents, with the aid of a divine vision, returns to his own
people, is taken prisoner for a time, and fights his wife's accuser man
to man. However varied in detail, these incidents are embedded in
the theme of war as it is treated in each play and to the equivalence
thus set up between the husband's honour and his wife's. While it is
hardly likely that Shakespeare would have looked out for such episodes
because of a reading of Boccaccio, it is easy to believe that if he knew
the wager plot already in some such setting of romance he would
have turned to Boccaccio in order to strengthen some of its details.

[1] Holinshed, *Chronicles* (ed. 1587), pp. 32–3. See Brockbank, 'History and Histrionics
in Cymbeline', *Shakespeare Survey 11* (1958); Salingar, 'Shakespeare's Romances',
pp. 24–5; Harold F. Brooks, in *Cymbeline*, ed. Nosworthy, pp. 212–16; Muir,
Shakespeare's Sources, vol. I, pp. 233–5.

A slight pointer in this direction is the digression in *Frederyke of Jennen* where the disguised heroine defends a kingdom.[1] But more substantial, though still indirect, evidence for the existence of an English play or romance intermediate between *Oton* and *Cymbeline* comes from the booklet, *Westward for Smelts*.[2] Several gossips there are exchanging stories for and against the honour of women; the wager story is told by a Fishwife. Her version is like *Frederyke* in that the main characters are merchants and the husband sends a servant to kill his wife; but the setting is London, during the Wars of the Roses. When the husband receives seeming proof of his wife's adultery his first thought is to commit suicide, but he then decides to have his wife killed 'and himself utterly to forsake his house and lands, and follow the fortunes of king Henry' (*sig*. C1*v*). The wife, wandering in male disguise and nearly starving because of the war, is found near York by King Edward IV, 'being come out of France', and is taken into his service (C3*r*). She discovers her accuser with her crucifix (the stolen 'sign') in his possession while she is nursing the wounded after the battle of Barnet; and she asks the king to send for her husband – 'whom she heard was one of the prisoners that was taken at the battle of Barnet' (C3*v*) – and to judge between them. All these details imply that the writer of *Westward for Smelts* (who calls himself Kind Kit) knew a version of the story which was roughly contemporary with *Frederyke of Jennen* but independent of it, and which (like *Frederyke*) tried to give an air of truth to its contents by dating them in recent history – in other words, a version near the heyday of the miracle plays and not very different from *Oton* in shape. The casual way the meeting between wife and husband after the battle is introduced by Kind Kit is one of the indications that the writer was working from memory of an old story, not with a text in front of him. And one of the listeners in his dialogue hints as much when she comments on the heroine of the tale she has just heard,

I like her as a garment out of fashion; she shewed well in that innocent time, when women had not the wit to know their own liberty: but if she lived now, she would show as vild [*wretched*] as a pair of Yorkshire sleeves in a Goldsmith's shop.   (*sig*. C4*v*)

If a popular compiler of 1620 could have thought of this as a tale remembered 'out of fashion', Shakespeare could have thought so too.

---

[1] Nosworthy (ed.), *Cymbeline*, p. 206.
[2] 'Kind Kit', *Westward for Smelts* (1620): copy in Trinity College, Cambridge.

As with *Pericles* and *The Winter's Tale*, the general scheme of his plot could have been taken from the tradition of exemplary romance.

The passage in *Cymbeline* (v.iv) where Posthumus, asleep in prison, has a vision of Jupiter could have been suggested by Plautus's *Amphitryon*, the noted classical example of *tragicomoedia*, from which Shakespeare had borrowed previously, in *The Comedy of Errors*. In Plautus, Jupiter tells the audience (III.i) that he will save Alcmena from her husband's unjust accusation, as he, the god, would be guilty if he allowed the innocent to suffer; and accordingly Jupiter is described at the climax of the play (v.i) as appearing in thunder, while Amphitryon lies in a faint. The vision scene in *Cymbeline* has been cited by Nosworthy as evidence of Shakespeare's debt to *Love and Fortune*, but the parallel is not very close because in the latter play Jupiter does not show himself to the mortals at all, but sends Mercury to tell Venus and Fortune to show themselves instead. Nevertheless, the archaic verse in Shakespeare's vision scene recalls the style of plays before 1590, as Nosworthy points out;[1] and it strengthens the possibility that, in additon to *Amphitryon*, Shakespeare was remembering plays in the manner of the miracles, with heavenly visions like those of Oton or the Empress of Rome, which that of Posthumus also resembles closely.

Before returning to this possibility directly, however, it will be convenient to discuss the strain of exemplary romance in the earliest of Shakespeare's comedies, *The Comedy of Errors* (*c.* 1592).

EGEON AND APOLLONIUS

The *Comedy of Errors* is usually and, in the main, rightly described as a farce – 'the only specimen of *poetical* farce in our language', according to Coleridge. Yet a spectator inattentive to the title and unaware of the play's reputation would receive a very different impression from the opening scene, an impression not of farce at all but of solemnity. A ruler comes on with attendants, to hear and sentence an elderly merchant who is held captive. And the first lines – the merchant, Egeon, speaking – have a tone of stage heroics, the rhythm and almost the ring of *Tamburlaine*:

> Proceed, Solinus, to procure my fall,
> And by the doom of death end woes and all.

[1] Nosworthy (ed.), *Cymbeline*, pp. xxxvi–xxxvii.

This was the set tone of a tragic play in the early 1590s (as for instance in the first speech of *1 Henry VI* –

> Hung be the heavens with black, yield day to night!);

and the allusions to strife and calamity that follow would not be out of place in a tragedy: on Egeon's side, to the shipwreck which parted him from his wife and one of his sons –

> So that, in this unjust divorce of us,
> Fortune had left to both of us alike
> What to delight in, what to sorrow for; –

on the Duke's side, to the trade war which is made to sound like a civil war:

> the mortal and intestine jars
> 'Twixt thy seditious countrymen and us.

True, Egeon tempers his bitterness with a resigned self-esteem –

> Yet this may comfort; when your words are done,
> My woes end likewise with the setting sun;

and –

> A heavier task could not have been impos'd
> Than I to speak my griefs unspeakable;
> Yet, that the world may witness that my end
> Was wrought by nature, not by vile offence,
> I'll utter what my sorrow gives me leave.

And he speaks his griefs in a deliberate, high style of epic narration[1] – which yet stops short of the braggardism of Marlowe – while Solinus listens with a stern compassion ('For we may pity, though not pardon thee'), and even with a kind of choric awe:

> Hapless Egeon, whom the fates have mark'd
> To bear the extremity of dire mishap!

But by the end of the scene, where

> Hopeless and helpless doth Egeon wend
> But to procrastinate his lifeless end,

Shakespeare has presented him effectively enough as a man who has touched the height and depth of happiness and misery and who, in his own mind, has finished with life.

---

[1] Foakes (ed.), *Comedy of Errors*, notes to I.i.28 and 67.

The experienced playgoer at an early performance would not have been misled, however. He could hardly have anticipated the fast and funny movement of the rest of the play, but he could have recognised in the opening scene the distinctive notes of romance rather than tragedy; in the speakers' inclination towards pathos rather than aggressiveness, for example, and in Egeon's reference to Fortune, which had left him something 'to delight in' as well as something 'to sorrow for'. Such a playgoer might have remembered the first entry of another *senex*, Galiarbus, in *Common Conditions*, and his wordy descant on a similar theme:

Who can but smile and laugh to see the state of fortune, she?...
Ha goddess! thou, whose countenance strange doth ebb and flow each day;
Sometimes thou dost restore to wealth, and sometime to decay.
As proof is plainly seen by me: though banished wight I was,
Thou hast restored to wealth again, far better in each case...
Yet though thy turning wheel and variable change
Hast me restored to wealth again, in foreign countries strange – ...
But ha, Galiarbus! in this thy joy what sorrows doth abound?
What sudden griefs attacked thy mind? what care thy heart doth wound?
What good can all this living do to thee in foreign land?
And seeing children twain remain as yet in tyrant's hand?...

Or the playgoer might have remembered the first entry of old Bomelio, *'like an Hermit'* beside his cave, in *The Rare Triumphs of Love and Fortune*:

He that in his distress despaireth of relief,
Let him begin to tell his tale, to rip up all his grief,
And if that wretched man can more than I recite
Of fickle Fortune's froward check and her continual spite,
Of her inconstant change, of her discourtesy,
I will be partner to that man to live in misery...
...list, lordings, now my tragedy begins...
Go walk the path of plaint, go wander, wretched, now
In uncouth ways, blind corners fit for such a wretch as thou...

In spite of the new dramatist's superior artfulness in preparing for the old man's narrative, the elevated tone of his blank verse, still relatively novel when the play was first acted, and his incomparably greater ability to humanise his speakers, the playgoer would have had a strong inkling of what to expect. He could have recognised the literary conventions behind Egeon's narrative, akin both to the plaints against Fortune in works like *The Mirror for Magistrates* and to interpolated life-stories in romance; and from Egeon's pointed references to his lost wife and sons, he could have felt sure, again, that it was romance and not tragedy he was watching.

Indeed, without searching his memory for specific parallels, a moderately literate or experienced playgoer listening to Egeon's story could have responded to the echoes in it from the best-known of exemplary romances, *Apollonius of Tyre*.[1] Gower's version of the story, in *Confessio Amantis* VIII, had been printed in 1493 by Caxton, and again in 1532 and 1554; and Shakespeare was evidently drawing upon it here, as again much later in *Pericles*. Like Egeon, Apollonius is apparently a victim of Fortune, manifested through tempests:

> Fortune that evere be muable
> And mai no while stonde stable:...
> His cours he nam with Seil updrawe,
> Wher as fortune doth the lawe,...
> The which upon the See sche ferketh.
> The wynd aros, the weder derketh,
> It blew and made such tempeste,...
> The mast tobrak, the Sail torof,
> The Schip upon the wawes drof,
> Till that thei sihe a londes cooste...   (lines 585ff)

At Pentapolis, where this storm wrecks Apollonius, he is to marry the princess – only to lose her, in childbirth, in another tempest. Nevertheless, Gower observes, reassuringly,

> Lo, thus fortune his hap hath lad;
> In sondri wise he was travailed,
> Bot hou so evere he be assailed,
> His latere ende schal be good.   (line 1320)

The turning-point for Apollonius (which I shall emphasise in the next quotation) is delayed, however, until some fourteen years later, when he is falsely told at Tarsus that the daughter he had left in charge there is dead:

> He curseth and seith al the worste
> Unto fortune, as to the blinde,
> Which can no seker weie finde:
> For sche him neweth evere among,
> And medleth sorwe with his song.

[1] See Foakes (ed.), *Comedy of Errors*, p. xxxi; Smyth, *Shakespeare's Pericles*.

> But sithe it mai no betre be,
> *He thonketh god* and forth goth he
> Seilande toward Tyr ayein.   (line 1584)

With divine aid (line 1710) he finds his daughter, again on shipboard; and

> For this day forth fortune hath sworn
> To sette him upward on the whiel.   (line 1736)

Moreover, she is as good as her word. Instructed in a dream by 'The hihe god, which wolde him kepe' (1789), Apollonius changes course at sea and makes for Ephesus – where he is to rediscover his wife; and thereupon,

> The wynd, which was tofore strange,
> Upon the point began to change,
> And torneth thider as it scholde...   (line 1807)

Egeon's listeners in the theatre, learning that he too was a victim of 'the always-wind-obeying deep', that he too, in quest of his family, had arrived at Ephesus, and that he too, though hardly 'thanking God', was at least resigned to his fate, would have strong motives to expect that he likewise in the end would be 'set upward on the wheel'.

Except that it focuses interest on the father instead of the children, the story of Apollonius resembles in outline those hellenistic romances of separation, adventure and reunion, like Heliodorus's *Theagenes and Chariclea*, which met with a literary revival in the sixteenth century. *Apollonius* springs from the same phase in the history of popular fiction; it seems to have originated as a Latin romance of the third century A.D., the century of Heliodorus.[1] And other romances of similar origin, giving a Christian turn to hellenistic fiction, remained current down to Shakespeare's time. One such was the story known as the Pseudo-Clementine *Recognitions*, written in its Latin form in the fourth century, but 'derived from a pre-Christian Greek romance' on the lines of *Apollonius*;[2] this was inserted into a saint's legend. Another was the legend of St Eustace, or Placidas, which belongs in its core to the same tradition, and has been traced back to origins of the eighth century or earlier in the Byzantine world.[3] In all three of these

---

[1] Perry, *Ancient Romances*, pp. 294ff, 350.
[2] *Ibid.*, pp. 285–93; Trenkner, *Greek Novella*, pp. 101–2.
[3] Monteverdi, 'La Leggenda di S. Eustachio', pp. 169–226; Trenkner, *Greek Novella*, pp. 103ff; Hibbard, *Mediaeval Romance*, p. 6.

romances, a father, fallen from high estate, loses his wife and children (his daughter in *Apollonius*, his twin sons in the other two) and finds them again in extraordinary circumstances, after many years of wandering about the Mediterranean. In all three, the unhappy wife (in *Apollonius*, the daughter as well) preserves her chastity against assault. In this respect, they resemble both Chariclea and her counterparts in earlier hellenistic romances, and the afflicted queens in later miracle plays. But, not content with showing virtue defending itself as in Heliodorus, the writers of these Christianised romances state or imply that the buffetings of Fortune are really the hidden trials of Providence. This theme is made explicit in the *Recognitions*, where Clement, the future saint, travelling with St Peter from Rome towards Antioch, meets an old man, in fact Clement's long-lost father, who denies the existence of Providence and attributes his own sufferings (in Caxton's translation of the story) to 'that which fortune hath destined'; but it is the old man's autobiography, recounted in order to support his denial, that leads to his recognition and hence to his conversion.[1] Gower makes the same theme almost equally explicit in his version of *Apollonius*; and similarly the afflictions in the legend of St Eustace show borrowings from the Book of Job. The same spirit governs the romances of persecuted queens in the miracle plays; as Oton exclaims when he is reconciled with Denise in the Parisian miracle (line 2010),

> Ha! biau sire Diex, tost ou tart
> Rens tu des biens faits les merites,
> Et de punir les maux t'aquittes...

The exemplary romances of both kinds, concerning sorely-tried parents and much-enduring wives, were connected in spirit as in plot.

The stories of St Clement and St Eustace were incorporated in *The Golden Legend*, where Shakespeare could have read them; and the latter was an enduring subject for the stage. In the fifteenth century, for example, it was acted in a Florentine miracle play (which was to be printed in many editions) and in two French versions;[2] it was still a chosen subject for Jesuit college plays in France in the early seventeenth century,[3] and in Brittany it was acted at the end of the sixteenth

---

[1] Caxton, *The Golden Legend* (ed. Ellis), vol. VI, p. 260. See Perry, *Ancient Romances*, p. 290; Monteverdi, 'La Leggenda di S. Eustachio', p. 199.

[2] Monteverdi, 'I Testi della leggenda di S. Eustachio', pp. 445ff, 481ff.

[3] Stegmann, 'Le rôle des Jésuites dans la dramaturgie française', p. 446.

century, while (as I have noted from Baskervill) themes like that of the Eustace legend and themes like that of Constance were still popular in the province 300 years later.[1] In England, several metrical romances of the late Middle Ages, such as *Sir Isumbras* and *Sir Eglamour*, contained variants of the same legend;[2] a play of *Placidas* or *St Eustace* was acted at Braintree in 1534; and in 1581, Barnabe Riche opened the collection of tales he called his *Farewell to Military Profession* with his own rehandling of the legend, the story of Sappho, Duke of Mantona.

As stories involving the extraordinary reunion of twin brothers, both the Clement and the Eustace legend are related to Plautus's *Menaechmi*, which Shakespeare certainly quarried from extensively in *The Comedy of Errors* (though the father has dropped out of the action of the Roman play, being relegated to the Prologue, where his loss of one boy on a business voyage and his death from sorrow are described); and it seems likely that Shakespeare remembered both legends when constructing his own play.[3] The way Egeon's family has been separated – the rock splitting their mast after the shipwreck, the two ships each rescuing one of the parents and one of the children, but unable to join, and then the grown son leaving his father to find his brother (1.i.76–132) – recalls the father's tantalising, successive losses in the Placidas story; while Shakespeare's dénouement – the prepared execution transformed into a scene of rejoicing – could have been suggested to him by the similar ending devised by Barnabe Riche. And the dénouement in *The Comedy of Errors* also borrows from the Clement legend (as well as from *Apollonius*, which Shakespeare is following to the extent of locating his play at Ephesus and making the mother an 'Abbess' there). In the Clement legend, Peter's enemy, Simon Magus ('Simon the enchanter'), wishing to escape from execution as a magician, casts his own appearance on Clement's father – in Caxton's translation, 'he imprinted his similitude and likeness in this old man Faustinian, in such wise that of every man he was supposed to be Simon Magus'; with the result that, although the sons recognise their father's 'voice', they would run away from him but for St Peter's intervention. Egeon meets with a similar

---

[1] Lebègue, 'Traditions dramatico-religieuses en France', p. 248; *cf* p. 47, n. 1, above.

[2] Hibbard, *Mediaeval Romance*, pp. 88–120, 274–8; *cf* Wells, *Manual of Writings in Middle English*, pp. 112–24; Harbage and Schoenbaum, *Annals of English Drama*; Barnabe Riche, *His Farewell to Military Profession* (1581).

[3] Trenkner, *Greek Novella*, pp. 105–8.

incomprehension from Antipholus of Ephesus, just before the other twin comes back on the stage:

> EGEON Why look you strange on me? You know me well.
> ANTIPHOLUS OF EPHESUS
> I never saw you in my life before.
> EGEON O! grief hath chang'd me since you saw me last;
>   And careful hours with time's deformed hand
>   Have written strange defeatures in my face.
>   But tell me yet, dost thou not know my voice?...
>
> Not know my voice! O time's extremity,
> Hast thou so cracked and splitted my poor tongue
> In seven short years that here my only son
> Knows not my feeble key of untun'd cares?   (v.i.295, 306)

There is nothing like this in the Apollonius story; but transformation by strange means, the proximity of an enchanter or 'conjurer' (for so Pinch is described in the same scene, v.i.242), the quasi-biblical setting and the danger of an execution are details all common here to the play and the saint's legend.[1] Here, then, where Shakespeare is bringing to a climax the tale of Egeon as a man tried by fate or Providence over a period of many years, it is clear that he is not following one narrative source alone but fusing scattered incidents together from a broad tradition of exemplary romance.

It is customary for scholars to reconstruct Shakespeare's procedure in writing *The Comedy of Errors* by saying that he took Plautus's *Menaechmi* for his primary source, enlarging it with other material including the sub-plot of the reunion of the parents, borrowed mainly from *Apollonius*.[2] And, clearly, Plautus furnished the basis for the bulk of Shakespeare's play. But it is far from obvious that an Elizabethan dramatist setting out to imitate Plautus would naturally think of adding a sub-plot in an elevated tone of romance; among the many renaissance copiers of *The Menaechmi*, Shakespeare seems to have been the only one to attempt such an opening gambit. All things considered, it seems more plausible to suppose that Shakespeare set out with something like the Eustace or Clement legend in mind, and then (as I have suggested with his employment of Boccaccio's tale in

---

[1] Caxton, *Golden Legend* (ed. Ellis), vol. VI, pp. 261–2. See Salingar, 'Shakespeare's Romances', pp. 17–8.

[2] See Baldwin, *Five-Act Structure*, chs. 28–9; Muir, *Shakespeare's Sources*, vol. I, pp. 18–20; Bullough, *Sources*, vol. I, pp. 3–11; Foakes (ed.), *Comedy of Errors*, pp. xxxi–xxxii.

Cymbeline) decided that he could strengthen his plot of a family re-union by means of extensive borrowing from Plautus; or else that from the outset, both forms of the story of family reunion, the romantic and the farcical, were present to his mind together. This conjecture is consistent with his lasting interests, as shown by his choice of plots. It is also more in keeping than the usual account of Shakespeare's approach to the sources of *The Comedy of Errors* with the position this play occupies in the history and development of the Elizabethan drama.

SURVIVALS OF MEDIEVAL STAGING

Although so few dramatic romances – as distinguishable from moral interludes – have survived from the first half of Elizabeth's reign, the evidence of recorded titles goes to show, as I have argued, that roughly a third, perhaps more, of the actors' repertoire must have consisted of plays of this type. Scattered evidence as to the staging of popular Tudor plays down to the beginning of Shakespeare's career points the same way, confirming the view of scholars like Manly and Baskervill that a tradition of romantic plays, religious and secular, continued unbroken from the fourteenth and fifteenth centuries.

References which hint at romantic plots are, of course, directly significant here. But such hints are doubly significant when they allude to methods of staging and construction on the lines of plays like *Esmoreit* and *Oton*. Biblical plays could be acted in processional manner, on moveable pageants, as they often were in England, because the dramatist's object was not to unfold a narrative but to commemorate and exhibit the meaning of sacred events. On the other hand, the more a dramatist's subject consisted of circumstantial episodes of wandering or adventure, recounted for their cumulative effect, the more it required to be acted in a fixed area, with *décor simultané*; in other words, with the possibility for the actors to move quickly, in sight of the audience, to and fro between 'Sicily' and 'Damascus' or 'Rome' and 'Burgos' or whatever such removed localities the story called for. Hence evidence of *décor simultané* in England, though not nearly so well attested as in France, suggests the presence of a common tradition of romantic drama, such as one might expect to find also from the independent showing of literary history. Again, the same kind of subject required extreme freedom in the dramatic representation of the passage of time, so as not merely to describe but to show, in successive visible episodes, half a lifetime or more of exploits or sufferings. And where indications of this sort come together with references to scenes of heavenly apparitions in English plays, there is a strong presumption in favour of the influence of the miracles, as distinct from the better-known English tradition of biblical drama.

The only dramatised life-story remaining from among the many recorded examples of saints' plays in England is the East Midlands play from the Digby MS, *Mary Magdalene* (*c.* 1480–1520).[1] It runs to 2,100 lines, in 51 continuous scenes requiring *décor simultané*. After biblical or apocryphal scenes, partly in allegorical form, of Mary's sins and repentance and the resurrection, the play turns to episodes from *The Golden Legend*: Jesus sends Mary from Judea to Marcyll (Marseilles) to convert the pagan king (she crosses in scene 34: '*Here xall* [shall] *entyre a shyp with a mery song*... *Here goth the shep owt of the place*'); Mary converts him with the help of miracles, destroying his Temple of Mahomet with fire out of a cloud (scene 36) and blessing his wife with pregnancy; the King and Queen set out for Jerusalem, but the Queen has to be left for dead with her newborn child on a rocky island (scene 41); on his return from pilgrimage, however, the King finds wife and child miraculously alive (scene 44); Mary leaves the pious monarchs, and '*goth*... *in-to the wyldyrnesse*', where she has been living in her cell 'this xxx wynter', as she says (scene 49, line 2055), before her death. While in the wilderness, she converses only with angels, and is sustained by divine grace (scene 48):

Here xall to [two] *angylles desend In-to wyldyrnesse; and other to xall bryng an oble* [consecrated wafer], *opynly aperyng a-loft In the clowddes; the to be-nethyn xall bryng mari, and she xall receyve the bred, and than go a-yen In-to wyldyrnesse*... *Her xall she be halsyd* [welcomed] *with angelles with reverent song.*

This scene, with Jesus above, is exactly similar to the scenes of heavenly apparitions and musical descents in the French *miracles*; all the composite parts of medieval romantic drama are present in the play.

That this was not a unique or rare example of such a scene on an English stage is shown by a reference from the next generation. In

[1] *Mary Magdalene*, ed. Furnivall, *The Digby Mysteries*. See Craig, *English Religious Drama*, pp. 310–34; Hoeniger (ed.), *Pericles*, pp. lxxxviiiff; *cf* Cohen, 'Marie-Madeleine dans le Théâtre du Moyen-Age'.

1540 John Palsgrave published the text of a Dutch neoLatin play, *Acolastus*, with a translation and notes intended for school use. When the Prodigal Son in the play wishes for a *deus ex machina* to help him in his misery, Palsgrave paraphrases him with a wish for 'god him self, or some good saint appearing to me forth of a cloud'; and he explains the Latin 'adage' by means of a lengthy note, comparing ancient with modern practice;[1]

What this adage meaneth is declared by Suidas, for such as in old time were players of tragedies, when they had brought the audience to have pity upon some great adversity or cruelty, which was towards to be done unto some innocent person, and that they had brought such persons into the hatred of the multitude, as...should put any such cruelty in execution,...then to quiet the minds of the auditory, and to bring them suddenly to a rest and peace again, there should some god suddenly appear from some high place, near unto the Theatre [the stage], by whose commandment and divine authority all parties should at once be put to silence.

At this point, a marginal comment indicates, 'The like manner used now at our days in stage plays', and Palsgrave's note continues,

Of which the like thing is used to be showed now-a-days in stage plays, when God or some saint is made to appear forth of a cloud, and succoureth the parties which seemed to be towards some great danger, through the Soudan's [Sultan's] cruelty.

From the way he speaks of danger and the Sultan, it is evident that Palsgrave is thinking of a romantic miracle, of chivalric adventure.

That highly unoriginal piece, *Sir Clyomon and Sir Clamydes*, shows that the same convention was in force some thirty years later, well after the Reformation. When Clyomon has killed the King of Norway, he buries him in a hearse fetched by the shepherd and goes off in search of Neronis, leaving his sword and golden shield with 'verses writ' beside the hearse as 'a true report' of his deed; whereupon Neronis, finding the hearse and shield and imagining her lover dead, prepares to kill herself too with his sword. '*Sing here*', instructs the stage direction towards the end of her monologue (line 1546); but a moment later, '*Descend Providence*' – who announces that he has been sent 'from seat of mighty Jove' expressly 'to let [prevent] this wilful fact [crime]', and, showing her the sheet of 'verses', tells her to 'Read that, if case thou canst it read, and see if he be slain'; which done, he obeys the next instruction, to '*Ascend*'.

---

1 John Palsgrave, *Acolastus* (ed. Carver), pp. 171–2.

Since it seems probable that Shakespeare knew this scene or some other very like it and remembered it with amusement, it is worth quoting Neronis's speech at some length:[1]

> Ah woeful sight, what is, alas, with these mine eyes beheld,
> That to my loving Knight belong'd, I view the Golden Shield:
> Ah heavens, this Hearse doth signify my Knight is slain,
> Ah death no longer do delay, but rid the lives of twain:
> Heart, hand, and every sense prepare unto the Hearse draw nigh:
> And thereupon submit yourselves, disdain not for to die
> With him that was your mistress' joy, her life and death like case,
> And well I know in seeking me, he did his end embrace.
> That cruel wretch that Norway King, this cursed deed hath done,
> But now to cut that ling'ring thread, that Lachis [*sic*] long hath spun,
> The sword of this my loving knight, behold I here do take,
> Of this my woeful corpse alas, a final end to make:
> Yet ere I strike that deadly strokes that shall my life deprave, [*sic*]
> Ye muses aid me to the Gods, for mercy first to crave.

> *Sing here.*

> Well now you heavens receive my ghost, my corpse I leave behind,
> To be inclos'd with his in earth, by those that shall it find.

So Thisby, or Francis Flute, finds the misleading sign of the death of Pyramus and prepares to slay herself, also with her lover's sword and – except for the improvement of internal rhymes – in similar fourteeners:

Asleep, my love? What, dead, my dove? O Pyramus, arise,
Speak, speak. Quite dumb? Dead, dead? A tomb must cover thy sweet eyes.
These lily lips, this cherry nose, those yellow cowslip cheeks,
Are gone, are gone; lovers, make moan; his eyes were green as leeks.
O Sisters Three, come, come to me, with hands as pale as milk;
Lay them in gore, since you have shore with shears his thread of silk.
Tongue, not a word. Come, trusty sword; come, blade, my breast imbrue.
And farewell, friends; thus Thisby ends; adieu, adieu, adieu.

Either Shakespeare remembered this passage from *Clyomon* in some detail or, as seems even more probable if his parody was to take full effect, he and his audience had heard a number of passages in the same strain.

---

1 *Clyomon and Clamydes*, ed. Greg, lines 1532ff; Russell, 'Romantic Narrative Plays', p. 108.

But criticism preceded parody. The absurd Providence episode in
Clyomon suggests that the stage conventions common to secular
romances and saints' plays lingered on in the former although the
Reformation had brought the latter to an end. But when after 1576
the building of playhouses on the edge of London made the acting
profession seem a social menace which the City authorities strove to
repress,[1] the situation changed, and romantic plays of the school of
Clyomon and *Common Conditions* came in for special attack. Since the
outcry against the theatres was led by preachers, it is hardly surprising that comedies and romances should be singled out, rather than
moral interludes; at the same time, the dispute incidentally furnishes
more evidence about the dramatic form, as well as the popularity, of
many plays which can never have found their way into print. For the
attack was conducted on literary or cultural as well as religious and
administrative lines. And it was precisely the remnants of medieval
tradition in the romances that provoked criticism, both from an
outright opponent – or convert to opposition – of the drama like
Stephen Gosson, and from those who, like George Whetstone and
Sir Philip Sidney, hoped to disarm opposition by introducing reform.

In 1578 Whetstone published his play, *Promos and Cassandra*,
dedicating it to 'his worshipful friend, and Kinsman, William
Fleetwood Esquire, Recorder of London'[2] – a very influential
personage, prominent in the campaign against the stage.[3] Whetstone
evidently wished to show in his play that a semi-realistic fiction
(based on a modern *novella*, by Giraldi) could work even more
effectively towards 'the confusion of Vice, and the cherishing of
Virtue' than the old-fashioned edifying moral allegories;[4] and he
clears the ground in his dedicatory Epistle by reproving the abuses of
contemporary dramatists everywhere – Italian and French playwrights for licentiousness, the Germans for competing with preachers
and thus bringing religion into disrespect, and the English for both
social and artistic indecorum. His literary standard is taken from
Horace[5] and he puts it forward as a corrective to the typically
medieval customs of the popular theatres (the italics are mine):

---

[1] See Chambers, *Elizabethan Stage*, vol. I, chs. 8–9; Bradbrook, *Rise of the Common
Player*, chs. 2–3; Salingar *et al.*, 'Les Comédiens en Angleterre', pp. 547–8.

[2] Bullough, *Sources*, vol. II, pp. 442–4.

[3] Chambers, *Elizabethan Stage*, vol. I, pp. 265, 285; vol. IV, pp. 219, 277.

[4] *Cf* p. 32, n. 3, above; Wright, 'Social Aspects of Some Belated Moralities'.

[5] See Horace, *Ars Poetica*, lines 89–118; *cf* Edwardes, *Damon and Pithias* (ed. Adams,
Pre-Shakespearean Dramas), prologue, lines 14–26.

The Englishman in this quality, is most vain, indiscreet, and out of order: he first grounds his work on impossibilities: then in three hours *runs he through the world*: marries, *gets Children, makes Children men,* men to conquer kingdoms, murder Monsters, and *bringeth Gods from Heaven,* and fetcheth Devils from Hell. And (that which is worst) their ground is not so unperfect, as their working indiscreet: not weighing, so the people laugh, though they laugh them (for their follies) to scorn: Many times (to make mirth) they make a Clown companion with a King: in their grave Counsels, they allow the advice of fools: yea they use one order of speech for all persons: a gross Indecorum, for a Crow will ill counterfeit the Nightingale's sweet voice: even so, affected speech doth misbecome a Clown. For to work a Comedy kindly [naturally], grave old men should instruct: young men should show the imperfections of youth: Strumpets should be lascivious: Boys unhappy: and Clowns should speak disorderly: intermingling all these actions, in such sort, as the grave matter, may instruct: and the pleasant, delight.

Whetstone is not a thoroughgoing neoclassicist, in spite of his precepts from Horace. Nevertheless, he objects, in the name of decorum, to the intrusion of the comic Vice into romantic or semi-historic plays (like *Common Conditions* or Preston's *Cambyses*), and also objects to the fabric of romance as such. Except for the getting and growing up of children, all his strictures can be matched against extant plays from the period. And his evidence shows that Shakespeare need not have depended on *Clyomon* alone (or on *Love and Fortune,* which appeared a few years later than Whetstone's Epistle) for recollections of romantic plays which 'bring Gods from Heaven' as in the Jupiter scene in *Cymbeline*.[1]

In the third of Stephen Gosson's pamphlets against the stage, *Plays Confuted,* in 1582, this ex-playwright takes up the same theme, more fiercely. Gosson gives a general account of the current repertoire, including borrowings from renaissance and classical sources, and from recent translations, as well as from romances:[2]

I may boldly say it because I have seen it, that *The Palace of Pleasure, The Golden Ass, The Ethiopian History, Amadis of France,* the Round Table, bawdy Comedies in Latin, French, Italian, and Spanish, have been thoroughly ransacked to furnish the Play houses in London.

But, while this passage may reflect an increasing demand for new subjects about 1580, Gosson reserves his particular scorn for the older romances:

[1] *Cf* F. P. Wilson, *English Drama 1485–1585,* pp. 141, 160.
[2] Gosson, *Plays Confuted,* ed. Chambers, *Elizabethan Stage,* vol. IV, pp. 215–16.

Comedies so tickle our senses with a pleasanter vein, that they make us lovers of laughter, and pleasure, without any mean, both foes to temperance. What schooling is this? Sometime you shall see nothing but the adventures of an amorous knight, passing from country to country for the love of his lady, encountering many a terrible monster made of brown paper, and at his return, is so wonderfully changed, that he cannot be known but by some posy in his tablet, or by a broken ring, or a handkercher, or a piece of a cockle shell. What learn you by that? When the soul of your plays is either mere trifles, or Italian bawdry, or wooing of gentlewomen, what are we taught?

One thing we may learn from this list of particulars is that in Gosson's view, as in Whetstone's, a piece like *Clyomon* would be representative; also, that romances connected with pilgrimage were still to be seen. Again, Gosson draws attention to the typical plot-motif of long-drawn-out separation, followed by a recognition.

When Sidney answered Gosson's first pamphlet against the drama, without naming the pamphleteer, his reply took the form of an extensive and philosophical *Apology for Poetry* (written *c.* 1583, but not printed until 1595). It was the first comprehensive essay on literature in English, ranging far beyond Gosson's parochial censures. But in his account of a typical popular play of the moment, Sidney merely substantiates Gosson and Whetstone again, with rather more precision and more picturesque detail (again, my italics):[1]

you shall have Asia of the one side, and Africk of the other, and so many other under-kingdoms, that the Player, when he cometh in, must ever begin with telling where he is, or else the tale will not be conceived. Now ye shall have three Ladies walk to gather flowers, and then we must believe the stage to be a Garden. By and by, we hear news of shipwreck in the same place, and then we are to blame if we accept it not for a Rock. Upon the back of that, comes out a hideous Monster, with fire and smoke, and then the miserable beholders are bound to take it for a Cave. While in the meantime two Armies fly in, represented with four swords and bucklers, and then what hard heart will not receive it for a pitched field? Now, of *time* they are much more liberal, for *ordinary* it is that two young Princes fall in love. After many traverses, she is got with child, *delivered* of a fair boy; he is *lost, groweth a man,* and is ready to get another chld; and all this in two hours' space: which how absurd it is even sense may imagine, and Art hath taught, and all ancient examples justified, and at this day, the ordinary Players in Italy will not err in.

[1] Sidney, *Apology for Poetry*, ed. Smith, in *Elizabethan Critical Essays*, vol. I, p. 197.

Sidney is much more concerned with renaissance theory and the unities than Whetstone or Gosson, but he has evidently been watching the same sort of play. And the plays he has seen have evidently been constructed on medieval principles, except that the actors appear to have been poorer in resources than the producers of *Oton* or of *Mary Magdalene*. And although no examples have survived from the 1580s of plays where a child is born and grows up in the course of the action, the details of the plots that Sidney calls 'ordinary' could have come from *Esmoreit* or the French *miracles*; or, again, from *Cymbeline* or *The Winter's Tale*. If indeed, as seems reasonably certain, Shakespeare saw more than one 'old tale' dramatised on these lines, it must have been just about the time that Sidney was writing.

Finally, Robert Greene gives a similar sarcastic account of the popular repertoire in his semi-autobiographical booklet, the *Groat's-worth of Wit*, where the splendidly dressed strolling player who takes the poor scholar, Roberto, into his service, boasts of his own unaided accomplishments:[1]

Nay then, said the player. I mislike your judgement: why, I am as famous for Delphrigus, and the king of Fairies, as ever was any of my time. The twelve labours of Hercules have I terribly thundered on the stage, and played three scenes of the devil on the highway to heaven...Nay more (quoth the player) I can serve to make a pretty speech, for I was a country Author, passing at a moral, for it was I that penned the Moral of man's wit, the Dialogue of Dives, and for seven years' space was absolute interpreter of the puppets.

'But now', he adds, 'my Almanac is out of date'; this mixture of romances, *diableries*, moral interludes and mythological pageants, eked out by puppet-plays, is no longer sufficient to please the public; and he hires Roberto to improve on it. This meeting with the player must represent the time shortly before 1587, the time when Greene and the other university wits began writing for the public theatres. The few years between that time and 1592, when the *Groat's-worth of Wit* was written, were the decisive years for the formation of Elizabethan poetic drama, including Shakespeare's first beginnings as a dramatist. It is in the same pamphlet, where Greene warns his fellow-scholars, Marlowe, Nashe and Peele, against bohemianism and exploitation by the players, that he utters his famous gibe against their rival actor-poet, the 'upstart Crow, beautified with our feathers', who

---

[1] See Chambers, *Elizabethan Stage*, vol. III, p. 324; vol. IV, p. 241; Greene, *Groat's-worth of Wit*, ed. Saintsbury, in *Elizabethan and Jacobean Pamphlets*.

'supposes he is as well able to bombast out a blank verse as the best of you' and 'is in his own conceit the only Shake-scene in a country'.

When *The Comedy of Errors* was first performed, then, plays in the medieval tradition that Sidney and Whetstone had ridiculed belonged, at furthest, to the very recent past. Theirs were the

> jigging veins of rhyming mother wits,
> And such conceits as clownage keeps in pay,

that Marlowe dismisses in the Prologue to *Tamburlaine*. Yet Marlowe himself wrote a modern miracle-play in *Faustus*, while Greene was content to refurbish the themes of romance. As for Shakespeare, if he was aware of Sidney's arguments when he began his career, they never fully persuaded him. Not only did he draw on the popular tradition that must have been familiar to him from childhood for the framing plot of Egeon in *The Comedy of Errors*, but he returned to it again and again, as a practised playwright, most obviously in his last romances, from *Pericles* onwards. Plots involving prolonged trials by Fortune and the division and reintegration of a family must have attracted the dramatist emotionally, as well as appealing to his public. The medieval tradition was Shakespeare's starting-point; its hold was too deep to be shaken off.

On the other hand, *The Comedy of Errors*, with its patent borrowings from Plautus, represents a direct challenge to Elizabethan classical taste. It showed that the 'upstart Crow' had not only picked up some of the lessons of classical art, but was prepared to apply them more thoroughly than anyone else. And here, too, the early play was much more than a passing experiment in Shakespeare's work. If medieval romance illuminates Shakespeare's point of departure as a dramatist, his borrowings from classical comedy show the direction in which his mind was moving.

3

'ERRORS' AND DECEIT IN CLASSICAL COMEDY

Comedy aims at representing men as worse...than in actual life.
Aristotle, Poetics

C'est une étrange entreprise que celle de faire rire les honnêtes gens.
La Critique de l'Ecole des Femmes

In spite of Shakespeare's attachment to medieval stage traditions, the classical revival affected his comedies decisively. No doubt he was not unduly attentive to the imitative rules of 'art' instilled by scholars and schoolmasters; but this is far from saying that he met them with indifference. Art, as the humanists expounded it, largely with Terence and Plautus in mind, stood for an approach to dramatic structure which was foreign to the medieval theatre and in that sense new: not the staging of impressive moments in a loose chronological sequence, 'the natural order' as it could be called, but 'the artificial order' of a continuous plot unfolding causal connexions between its incidents as it advances. And this involves a continuous interaction between character and situation and a constant awareness of each of the characters as a separate and consistent personage, whose speeches may forward the general action, but may also invite contrast with the rest of what the audience knows or believes about it – in other words, a constant inclination towards dramatic irony. A modern playwright can take for granted that his audience will notice a logical progression in his plot and will be ready to receive an actor's speeches ironically; indeed, he is almost obliged to start from these assumptions for the sake of dramatic perspective. But they are not the natural, invariable concomitants of every tradition of play-acting, any more than visual perspective is an invariable factor in painting. They were the discovery, or invention, of the Athenian dramatists, handed on to their Roman imitators and thence to the Renaissance. Shakespeare absorbed the lessons of classical drama very thoroughly, not only in those comedies (perhaps a third of his output) which probably or certainly show some direct use of Roman models, but in the spirit and construction of his

76

comic writing as a whole. He was not, of course, a classicist on principle, like Ben Jonson. But then the vital difference between them was not one of more scholarship or less, as Jonson implied in the superb epitaph which moulded his rival's fame for generations, but one of flexibility of mind, attitude and temperament. Jonson associated classical comedy with correction and satire, following a sixteenth-century tradition, while Shakespeare, also, however, following tradition, associated it with romance.[1] The opposition we habitually set up between the terms 'romantic' and 'classical' should not lead us to underestimate his deliberate adaptation of classical methods and motifs.

The standard classical method of dramatising a story was to concentrate on the climax, leaving the remoter antecedent events, if not already known to the audience as parts of a myth, to be narrated separately in a prologue or disclosed in the course of the action. Horace gives a general formula for this when he says in his *Ars Poetica*[2] that a good poet does not 'begin...the war of Troy from the twin eggs' (from which Helen was born), but, like Homer,

he hastens to the issue, and hurries his hearer into the story's midst, as if already known, and what he fears he cannot make attractive with his touch he abandons; and so skilfully does he invent, so closely does he blend facts and fiction, that the middle is not discordant with the beginning, nor the end with the middle.

Similarly, a dramatic poet should distinguish, he adds, between what is to be narrated and what shown. Terence, whom Horace praises elsewhere for his 'art', had carried the device of retrospective exposition a step further by keeping his audience in the dark or in doubt about essential information (such as the heroine's true origins in *The Andrian*), disclosing it in the recognition scene at the end with an effect of timely surprise.[3]

The first renaissance commentator on the *Ars Poetica*, Cristofero Landino, drew attention (in 1482) to Horace's principle of 'order' in literature: 'The artificial order is when, contrary to the usual reckoning of time, we very often begin at the end and then return to earlier events'.[4] During the intensive discussion of Aristotle's *Poetics* which raged in Italy from the 1540s to the 1570s and established the

---

[1] See Coghill, 'Shakespearian Comedy'; Doran, *Endeavors of Art*, ch. 7.
[2] Horace, *Ars Poetica*, lines 146–52; cf 179–82; *Epistles* II, i, 59.
[3] See Frank, *Literature in the Roman Republic*, ch. 4.
[4] See Herrick, *Comic Theory*, p. 99.

canons of neoclassical theory, including the so-called rules of the three unities in drama, this concept of 'artificial order' was absorbed, in effect, into the rule of unity of time, mainly on the assumption, borrowed (or distorted) from Aristotle, that, since a play is an imitation of an action, the performance must seem lifelike in duration as in other ways.[1] But the revival of Terence and Plautus on Italian stages at the end of the fifteenth century and the renewed study of Horace as a critical authority made the general shape of classical plots familiar, at least in Italy, even before the rediscovery of the *Poetics*; and throughout the sixteenth century Horace continued to be cited as a guide to ancient drama on much the same footing as Aristotle.[2] This was particularly so in England. When Sidney expounds the unities of place and time, it is Horace, not Aristotle, he refers to for authority:[3]

many things may be told which cannot be shewed, if they [playwrights] know the difference betwixt reporting and representing...If they will represent an history, they must not (as Horace saith) begin *Ab ovo*, but they must come to the principal point of that one action which they will represent.

Similarly, Jonson, who translated the *Ars Poetica*, cites Horace, but not Aristotle, in the critical preface he published with *Sejanus* (1605).

In Italy, comedies on the Roman pattern, beginning in mid-course (often, however, with an explanatory prologue) and ending in 'rediscoveries', became so common and so stereotyped that in 1551 the Florentine playwright, Grazzini, protested; when the spectators learn from a prologue, he says, 'that in the capture of a certain City, or the sack of a certain Castle, some little boys or girls went astray or were lost', then they feel sure they know the plot beforehand and would be willing to go away.[4] In England, however, the first handful of imitations of Plautus and Terence, from *Ralph Roister Doister* and *Gammer Gurton's Needle* in the 1550s to Lyly's *Mother Bombie* (*c.* 1589), were farces of trickery, not recognition plays; and the first comedy in English turning on 'rediscoveries' was Gascoigne's translation from Ariosto, *Supposes*, acted at Gray's Inn in 1566, with

1 Scaliger, *Poetics* (1561), trans. Padelford, pp. 60–1. See Spingarn, *Literary Criticism in the Renaissance*, pp. 91–2.
2 Herrick, *Comic Theory*; Weinberg, *Literary Criticism in the Italian Renaissance*, chs. 3–6; Smith (ed.), *Elizabethan Critical Essays*, vol. I, pp. lxxivff; Allan H. Gilbert (ed.), *Literary Criticism*, pp. 274, 534, 575.
3 Sidney, *Apology for Poetry*, ed. Smith, *Elizabethan Critical Essays*, vol. I, p. 198.
4 Salingar, 'Shakespeare's Romances', p. 8.

an explanatory prologue, and printed in 1573 and again, with marginal notes, in 1575 and 1576. Shakespeare read Gascoigne, probably before writing *The Comedy of Errors* and certainly before *The Taming of the Shrew*.[1] But his own *Comedy of Errors* was the first original play in English which not merely adapted material from Plautus but followed 'the artificial order', beginning at a high point of action, relating antecedent events in the course of the action, and pursuing a unified plot to a climax of 'rediscoveries'.

The main plan of *The Comedy of Errors* is a rehandling of Plautus's *Menaechmi*, with incidental borrowings from his *Amphitryon*. Similarly, in *Twelfth Night*, where Shakespeare may have taken suggestions from several allied sources, his principal model was the anonymous Sienese play, *Gl'Ingannati* (1531), in itself a variant of *Menaechmi*, but (as I shall try to show in detail later) he deliberately turned back to the Roman original as well. These two Shakespearian comedies can be described as recognition plays and so, too, can the four late romances, from *Pericles* to *The Tempest*, in the first and last of which some scholars have noted possible echoes from Plautus's *Rudens*.[2] Certainly, the form of *The Tempest* is unimaginable without classical example; and, like *The Comedy of Errors*, it observes the unity of time.

These two comedies, out of sixteen, are enough to show that Shakespeare could apply the 'rules' when he chose. If he neglected them elsewhere, it was not out of carelessness. In *The Taming of the Shrew*, where he borrows the sub-plot of Lucentio's wooing from Gascoigne's *Supposes* (and takes the names Tranio and Grumio from Plautus's *Mostellaria*), he stretches the time of the sub-plot so as to make it coincide with the main action. But as a rule he works for concentration. He hurries through the plot of *Two Gentlemen of Verona*, drastically foreshortening the borrowed part, Julia's adventures; and although he emphasises in the first lines of *A Midsummer Night's Dream* that four days must elapse before the wedding celebration, the effective action races through a single night. In these two plays he seems to have invented his main plot, though he probably owed some debt still to the criss-cross arrangement of the *Menaechmi*. In other comedies, like *The Merchant of Venice*, *Much Ado* and *As You Like It*, he sharply accelerates the time-scheme of his narrative sources. It is as if Shakespeare was carrying out the precept of that other independent, Lope de Vega, to 'let the action take place

---

[1] Baldwin, *Five-Act Structure*, p. 674; Bullough, *Sources*, vol. I, p. 4.
[2] Simpson, 'Shakespeare's Use of Latin Authors', pp. 17–22.

in the least time possible'. Lope, who similarly borrowed from Italian stories while he kept his distance from Italian theories, said, 'when I have to write a play I lock the rules away with six keys; I remove Terence and Plautus from my study that they may not cry out at me' – because 'in Spain...whatever is written is against art', and play-goers demand an immensely varied action;[1] to which Shakespeare could largely have agreed. Or he could have assented to the apologetic prologue to Act II of Cervantes's biographical or miracle play, *El Rufian dichoso*, where it is said that time has brought changes, and even improvements, since the days of Plautus and Terence, and that no spectator cares if a stage action leaps 'from Germany to Guinea', because 'thought is nimble'.[2] The comparison is appropriate in that the English public, like the Spanish, clung to medieval stage traditions; but also because the Spanish dramatists make explicit a conscious choice in face of the rules which is implicit in Shakespeare.

The Chorus-prologues to *Henry V* plainly show Shakespeare as much aware as Cervantes of the technical problem of encompassing time and space; from the outset, the Chorus invites the audience to supplement the deficiencies of a theatre with their 'imaginary forces':

> For 'tis your thoughts that now must deck our kings,
> Carry them here and there, jumping o'er times,
> Turning th'accomplishment of many years
> Into an hour-glass;

and at each pause in the action he returns to the same theme, with an occasional glance at the objections of literary purists:

> The King is set from London, and the scene
> Is now transported, gentles, to Southampton;
> There is the play-house now, there must you sit,
> And hence to France shall we convey you safe
> And bring you back, charming the narrow seas
> To give you gentle pass; for, if we may,
> We'll not offend one stomach with our play.

> Thus with imagin'd wing our swift scene flies,

---

[1] Lope de Vega, *The New Art of Making Comedies* (1609), trans. Perlzweig, in Allan H. Gilbert (ed.), *Literary Criticism*, pp. 542–5.
[2] Cervantes, *El Rufian dichoso* (trans. Reyer). Cf Rennert, *Spanish Stage*, p. 94; *Don Quixote*, part I, ch. 48; Tirso de Molina, *The Orchards of Toledo* (1624), in Barrett H. Clark (ed.), *Theories of the Drama*, pp. 94–5.

> In motion of no less celerity
> Than that of thought.

and, again:

> Vouchsafe to those that have not read the story
> That I may prompt them; and of such as have,
> I humbly pray them to admit th'excuse
> Of time, of numbers, and due course of things,
> Which cannot in their huge and proper life
> Be here presented.

Even here, of course, where the nature of the subject seems to require a special respect for the written book, Shakespeare ignores Sidney's injunction to English playwrights to represent history in a classical style; the Chorus's deference to 'the story' rather recalls a medieval Presenter – or Gower, in the consciously archaic expositions in *Pericles*.[1] But what counts in *Henry V* is not simply respect for the chronicle as such, but realism or vividness of presentation; Shakespeare is in fact applying one of the maxims Sidney had repeated from Horace, to the effect that a dramatist should discriminate between showing and narrating. And that Shakespeare was quite aware of Sidney's second Horatian maxim as well – to begin *in medias res*, and not *ab ovo* – seems plain from his prologue, some three years later (1601–3), to *Troilus and Cressida*, where again he is dramatising a famous passage of history:

> hither am I come
> A Prologue arm'd, but not in confidence
> Of author's pen or actor's voice, but suited
> In like conditions as our argument,
> To tell you, fair beholders, that our play
> Leaps o'er the vaunt and firstlings of those broils,
> Beginning in the middle; starting thence away
> To what may be digested in a play.

Since the 'argument' here is precisely that of the Trojan war, which Horace had taken as his example, and since the 'Prologue arm'd' recalls the Prologue in armour who had introduced Jonson's *Poetaster* (1601), where Horace was the spokesman and hero, the conclusion seems certain that Shakespeare had the *Ars Poetica* in mind. If he usually disregarded the rules extracted from or attached to Horace by the classicists, it was not the fault of his 'small Latin'.

---

[1] Salingar, 'Shakespeare's Romances', p. 22.

Horace's commonsense observations deal in the first place with epic. Transferred to the theatre, they imply, not necessarily a standard measure of unity, with an approximation, conventional at best, between acting time and the time-span of the play's fictitious events, but a principle of continuous and mounting interest in what is immediately present to the spectator's imagination. In Henry James's phrase, there should be no 'leakage of interest'; the technical problem is not to relieve the spectator from imagining a lapse of time within the scope of the play, but to avoid distracting his attention with dramatically empty time, imaginary gaps without service to the action. Such continuity is presumably part of Shakespeare's meaning in 'what may be digested in a play', and part of his aim in altering the story-teller's chronology for plays like *Much Ado*. At the same time, it appears that, before any other English playwright, he experimented with a method of concentrating dramatic interest adapted from the 'artificial order' of Plautus and Terence. Egeon's narrative at Ephesus in *The Comedy of Errors*, beginning some thirty lines after the opening of the play instead of coming in a separate and preliminary prologue speech like the equivalent narration in the *Menaechmi*, recalls in form the deferred prologue in *Miles Gloriosus* (II.i) where Palaestrio recounts how the heroine of that play (together with her pretended twin) comes also to find herself in Ephesus. Shakespeare's method here is not only more exciting but serves to bind together more diverse strands than in any of the plots of Terence or Plautus; nevertheless, it is basically a classical device. And the same device reappears in his late recognition plays. In *Cymbeline*, where the time-span of the heroine's adventures is sharply contracted (certainly by comparison with Boccaccio's story) but where the plot as a whole is greatly extended in range, Belarius's soliloquy, binding two parts of the total plot together (III.iii.79), is virtually another deferred prologue; so is Prospero's narrative in the second scene of *The Tempest*. Conversely, in *The Winter's Tale*, where a plot in classical form with retrospective exposition would destroy the role of Leontes, and where a felt sense of the passage of time is part of the substance of the play, Shakespeare introduces the figure of Time himself (IV.i) to speak what is virtually an apologetic prologue in Terence's manner,[1] dealing with the critical problems the dramatist is tackling, as well as affording a preface to the second, climactic phase of the action:

[1] *Ibid.* pp. 3–6.

> Impute it not a crime
> To me or my swift passage that I slide
> O'er sixteen years, and leave the growth untried
> Of that wide gap, since it is in my pow'r
> To o'erthrow law, and in one self-born hour
> To plant and o'erwhelm custom. Let me pass
> The same I am, ere ancient'st order was
> Or what is now receiv'd.

This is very close to the argument that Cervantes composed, nearly at the same date, for Comedy to expound in *El Rufián dichoso* (except that Cervantes calls the unities a heritage from the past, whereas Shakespeare, presumably with critics like Jonson in view, alludes to them ambiguously under the 'order' which is 'receiv'd' in the present; but then it would have seemed equally appropriate in England or Spain during the years around 1600 to refer to them as ancient or as modern). And it is only when Time in *The Winter's Tale* has asserted his authority as a power beyond 'law' and 'custom' that he begins to revert to the details of his story:

> Your patience this allowing
> I turn my glass, and give my scene such growing
> As you had slept between.

Time's speech as a whole is a more subtle variant of the Chorus's addresses in *Henry V* and the Prologue to *Troilus*. It illustrates once again that when Shakespeare departs from the unities he does so consciously, with a purpose. But the 'artificial order', the compact arrangement of a classical play, is still his central point of reference.

There is more involved here than the time-scale of the episodes shown on the stage. In classical comedy – Athenian New Comedy and the copies or adaptations by Plautus and Terence – the technique of retrospective exposition, whether in prologue form or by way of the dialogue, is regularly employed to the same end, a scene of recognition; and the motif of recognition appears in all of Shakespeare's comedies, prominently in more than half of them. It is true that recognition scenes were also prominent in medieval stage romances, from *Esmoreit* to *Common Conditions*, since they were based on stories akin to (if not descended from) the stories dramatised by the Greeks. But whereas the medieval playwrights exhibit the long-drawn-out pathos of their leading characters without a hint of irony, Terence and Plautus, by preparing for the recognition as a sudden resolution of a human entanglement, bring out the irony of characters struggling unawares against their imminent good fortune. And the compressed scheme of time and place in the classical theatre serves to focus such ironies of situation. This ironic bias means that, even with recognition plots, Plautus and Terence move towards comedy, not romance as exhibited on the medieval stage. And in this direction Shakespeare follows their lead.

The lesson of classical 'art' for the comic playwright was the pleasure of contrivance. And the other leading motif in Roman comedy, readopted and constantly diversified by Shakespeare and his renaissance predecessors, was deception – the irony of the trickster, as distinct from irony of situation. Historically, the former came first, since the motif of trickery was taken over by Athenian New Comedy from Old Comedy, while the irony of situation, depending on the concept of Fortune's wheel, was borrowed from tragedy. New Comedy (Greek and Roman) occupies a kind of middle ground between romance and farce, combining elements of both. Donatus the grammarian (fourth century A.D.), whose commentary on Terence, published in the fifteenth century, served as a guide to renaissance scholars and teachers, tends to assimilate New Comedy plots to Aristotle's schematic analysis of tragedy, emphasising 'errors', or mistakes of identity; for example, in his note on *The Andrian*, where Davus sceptically repeats the heroine's incomplete story about her Athenian birth (I.iii; 220ff), Donatus comments: 'He narrates part of the argument [of the play] and does not believe that what he says has been done, that there might remain a place for error [*ut supersit locus errori*]...Now the whole argument in summary is narrated to the people [the audience], but in order that there might remain something toward error, belief is taken away [*sed ut restet aliquid ad errorem, abrogatur fides*].' Donatus might have added that scepticism is in keeping here with the speaker's character, but he is interested in mistakes of identity as constitutive elements in the plot.[1] Similarly, Diomedes and Evanthius (whose notes on comedy were printed together with Donatus in renaissance editions) treat comic plots as complications of 'error': Diomedes describes New Comedy as 'plots about agreeable mistakes' [*gratis erroribus*]; and Evanthius, in a passage much elaborated in the sixteenth century, divides comic plots into three parts (following the Prologue) – the Protasis, or beginning of the action, the Epitasis, or complication, and the

---

[1] Baldwin, *Five-Act Structure*, p. 36.

Discovery or *catastrophe* (in the sense of sudden change). The Epitasis he describes as 'the growth and progress of the confusions and as I might say of the knot of the whole misunderstanding' [*totius...nodus erroris*], while the Catastrophe is 'the turning round of things to happy issues, made clear to all by a full knowledge of the actions'.[1] The emphasis of these late-classical grammarians, then, falls on the recognition plot, where New Comedy approaches tragi-comedy or romance; but the notion of 'agreeable mistakes' leading on to a clarification does not exclude, what is obvious enough, the large part taken by the tricks of the cunning slave in Plautus and Terence. As George Duckworth observes, both playwrights base their plots on a dual 'conception of error'; 'innocent mistakes, guileful deceptions – these, either separately or in combination, produce the errors and misapprehensions to be found in all [their] plays'.[2]

Many renaissance theorists followed Donatus by analysing comic plots in terms of mistakes of identity leading through complications to a recognition; his method was transferred from Terence to Plautus, and in 1576 an influential edition of Plautus (by Lambinus) appeared, annotating the 'errors' in the *Menaechmi* along these lines. (T. W. Baldwin thinks that Shakespeare knew this edition, as well as one of the earlier sixteenth-century editions of the play, which he would have studied at school.)[3] And meanwhile Castiglione and other Italian writers had been trying to work out a general theory of the ridiculous applicable to comedy, drawing on Aristotle and Cicero and on examples from Boccaccio as well as Plautus and Terence, in order to explain the sources and mechanism of laughter. Their approach is rationalising and analytic; they bring out the sense of detachment and intellectual superiority connected with ridicule, and they emphasise the effects of irony, ambiguity and surprise, and of the perception of contrast between the latent and the surface meaning of a speech or gesture, or of contrast between anticipation and outcome in a repartee or a series of events. In his *Poetica*, published in 1563 but evidently written much earlier, Trissino distinguishes between 'moral' and 'ridiculous' comedies, and between the sources of laughter in deformities of the mind and deformities of the body. As to mental deformities, 'in jokes we laugh at the ignorance, imprudence, and credulity of someone else, and especially when we see them in

---

[1] Coghill, 'Shakespearian Comedy', pp. 2–3; Herrick, *Comic Theory*, pp. 57ff.
[2] Duckworth, *Roman Comedy*, pp. 141–2.
[3] Baldwin, *Five-Act Structure*, pp. 667, 691–4.

persons who are thought substantial and of good intelligence, for in such as these many times opinion and hope are deceived'; and in general, Trissino finds the most potent source of laughter in 'that which deceives expectation' – as in the *Menaechmi* and his own play, the *Simillimi*, adapted from it.[1] This analysis finds a common ground between an audience's reaction to 'errors' in the plot of a comedy and their amusement at an act of folly or a deliberate jest.

Castelvetro carries this theory further in the exhaustive dissection of causes of laughter in his *Poetics* (1571), where the mainspring of comedy is found in deceptions [*inganni*]. There are four main causes of laughter according to Castelvetro: sympathy (with children, for example, or people we love); deceptions; deformities of mind or body; and obscenity. It is a sign of original sin, he says, that we laugh at deceptions, since we pride ourselves on our superiority to the folly in others; nevertheless, he examines the sub-species of such occasions of laughter in detail:[2]

Now the deceptions that are material for laughter can be divided in four ways. The first is of the deceptions that come about through ignorance of those things which are in ordinary use and in the common understanding of men, as through drunkenness or sleep or delirium. The next class contains the deceptions that come about through ignorance of the arts and the sciences and of the powers of the body or of the mind, when someone, before he has correctly estimated his capacity, boasts of something he cannot do.

In these two classes, it is self-deception that is uppermost. In the next, it is not quite clear whether it is the dupe or the spectator who is 'deceived', but in either case the laughter follows from the reversal of an expectation, as in Trissino:

The third class contains those deceptions that result from an unexpected movement of things in another direction [*per traviamento delle cose in altra parte*] or through the turning of the point of a jest against the person who is the author of it.

Evidently, then, renaissance critics took a conscious pleasure in the deft juggling with misunderstandings exercised in plays like the *Menaechmi*. But only in his last category does Castelvetro touch on mistakes of identity as a source of laughter:

[1] Giangiorgio Trissino, *Poetica*: see Allan H. Gilbert (ed.), *Literary Criticism*, pp. 212, 224–32.
[2] Lodovico Castelvetro, *Poetica d'Aristotele vulgarrizata e sposta* (Basel, 1576), p. 93; trans. Allan H. Gilbert, *Literary Criticism*, p. 313; see Weinberg, *Literary Criticism in the Italian Renaissance*, pp. 502–11.

The last class contains those deceptions that proceed from tricks or from chance [*per insidie altrui, o dal caso*];

and even here, it is noticeable that he combines under a single heading the 'innocent mistakes' and the 'guileful deceptions' that Professor Duckworth distinguishes in Plautus and Terence. Moreover, although Castelvetro is nominally discussing drama – his work is 'Aristotle's Poetics translated and explained' – he takes his examples of comic situations from the *Decameron*. In other words, he has subsumed the notion of comic 'error' found in Donatus under a more inclusive view of humour, framed in a rationalist psychology, which depends either on trickery or, more generally, on a tension between two minds – the man deceived and his deceiver or else the spectator. It is partly a moral or educational view, since it singles out self-deception, but it is mainly an aesthetic view, a declaration of taste. It corresponds with the bias of Italian learned comedy in the sixteenth century, from Ariosto onwards; and it was quickly followed by other Italian critics.[1] When that self-conscious artist, Guarini, defends the new genre of tragi-comedy introduced by his *Pastor Fido*, in a pamphlet of 1601, he takes it for granted that the constitutive factor in comedy is 'deceit'; the 'order' of a comic plot, he says, is more 'artificial' than tragedy, which takes shape from 'passion or accident or fortune or the nature of the [historical] event itself' [*dalla costituzione del fatto stesso*]:[2]

But in the comic [order], artifice, guile, falsehood, deceit [*lo 'nganno*], adroitness, mischievous tricks are the expedients of the intrigue; which is a manner as remote as possible from tragical dignity.

Here the two favoured themes of renaissance theory – when it deals with technique, and not the moral function of comedy – stand out in parallel: the artifice of the playwright and the 'deceptions' of his characters.

Shakespeare could have met this Italian interpretation of New Comedy in Gascoigne's *Supposes*, translated from Ariosto's *Suppositi*. As if to compensate for the relative novelty of the form of his play in England, even to a sophisticated audience, Gascoigne as translator supplies a Prologue in which he jokes about the meaning of his English title:

---

1 See *ibid.* pp. 539, 587, 934 (quoting Bonciani [1574], Antonio Riccoboni [1579] and Celso Giraldi [1583]).
2 Giambattista Guarini, *Il Pastor Fido e il compendio della poesia tragicomica* (ed. Brognoligo), p. 280.

the very name whereof may peradventure drive into every of your heads a sundry suppose, to suppose the meaning of our supposes...But understand, this our Suppose is nothing else but a mistaking or imagination of one thing for another. For you shall see the master supposed for the servant, the servant for the master: the freeman for a slave, and the bondslave for a freeman: the stranger for a well-known friend, and the familiar for a stranger. But what? I suppose that even already you suppose me very fond, that have so simply disclosed unto you the subtleties of these our Supposes: where otherwise indeed I suppose you should have heard almost the last of our Supposes, before you could have supposed any of them aright.

And in his marginal notes Gascoigne draws attention to the various 'supposes' that motivate Ariosto's plot – avowedly extracted from Plautus and Terence – much as Donatus had pointed out the 'errors' governing the action in Terence. These errors in the *Supposes* are partly 'innocent mistakes' due to coincidence, but are mainly due to the 'shifts' and 'deceits' of the comic servant, the 'feigned Erostrato'. And Gascoigne's prologue picks out, not Fortune's share in the plot, but, in the Italian manner, the subjective experience of 'a mistaking or imagination' for the characters and the pleasure of puzzles or 'subtleties' anticipated for the audience.

Shakespeare's *Comedy of Errors* marks the beginning of his own synthesis of the elements of classical comedy, as interpreted by the Renaissance. In choosing the *Menaechmi* as his principal model, he was taking what was probably the best-known of all classical plays in the sixteenth century, by way of stage revivals and imitations.[1] And, like *Supposes*, his title is a pointer to renaissance classicism. But in order to show more fully the bearings of the idea of 'error' for playwrights during the Renaissance, and its crucial place in their view of comedy, it will be necessary to discuss their classical models at some length in the remainder of this and in the following chapter, beginning with Aristophanes, at the point of origin of comedy as a form of art.

THE TRICKSTER IN CLASSICAL COMEDY

Unless they are downright opponents of the theatre, renaissance critics, in spite of their unvarying preoccupation with the moral effect of literature, never seem to take notice of the ethics of comic deceivers.

[1] Salingar, 'Shakespeare's Romances', p. 15n.

Moralists though they are, they assume, almost without question, that, within certain limits or on certain licensed occasions (such as Carnival), double dealing and practical jokes are permissible and even admirable. This assumption, or something like it, goes far back into the origins of literary comedy; without it, most European comedy as we know it would disappear.

The leading characters in Aristophanes have a great deal in common with the trickster-heroes and sacred buffoons of a number of primitive societies and the enigmatic Fools of the Middle Ages.[1] Grotesquely masked and padded, and often accompanied on the stage by choruses in non-human guise – horses, clouds, wasps, birds, frogs – the heroes of Old Comedy, certainly in Aristophanes, express through one part of their complex make-up the animal, the instinctive or the childish in man; in Aristotle's terms, they represent men as 'lower' or 'worse' than they really are, being 'ludicrous' precisely because they exhibit 'defect or ugliness' without pain. They are greedy, lustful and cheerfully unscrupulous, incalculable, refractory and blind to common-sense. Yet, on another level (not mentioned by Aristotle), they are shrewd, resourceful, far-sighted, patriotic and capable of superhuman achievements. They resemble in this respect other Greek heroes of guile and inventiveness: Odysseus; the Titan, Prometheus, one of the creators of mankind, who cheated Zeus of the meat in his burnt-offering, and furnished mankind with fire; or Hermes, patron of merchants and thieves and herald of the gods, who even from his cradle could steal the cattle of Apollo and invent the lyre.[2]

With minor variations, each of the eleven surviving plays of Aristophanes (*c.* 448–*c.* 380 B.C.) consists of the exposition of a scheme invented by the hero (or heroine); his success against opponents in a battle of words and slapstick; and – usually after the parabasis, or direct address to the audience by the chorus, the actors having temporarily left the stage – scenes of the hero's triumph and cele-bration. Most of the schemes have a plainly self-interested motive – to escape from the discomforts of the Peloponnesian war, from debts, from lawsuits, from want, from political bullying. But, except perhaps in the *Thesmophoriazusae* (or 'Ladies' Day', as Dudley Fitts has translated

[1] Chambers, *Medieval Stage*, vol. I, bk II; Nicoll, *Masks*; Welsford, *The Fool*; *cf* Radin, *Primitive Religion* and *The World of Primitive Man*.
[2] See Kerényi, 'The Trickster in Relation to Greek Mythology', in Radin, *The Trickster*, pp. 173–91; Whitman, *Aristophanes*, pp. 18–58.

it), where Euripides, as an alleged misogynist, has to invent a pack of stratagems to avoid being mobbed by the Athenian women, the public import of the scheme becomes even more prominent as each play advances – to revive the peace and prosperity of the city, to purge it of false policies, wrong-headed philosophy or bad poetry. And the schemers are not infantile sub-men or mysterious visitants, like primitive tricksters and buffoons, or subjugated outsiders, like medieval Fools, or even mythological rogue-heroes as a rule, but in status typical, often elderly, Athenian citizens. Dicaeopolis in the *Acharnians* and Trygaeus in *Peace* are elderly farmers from Attica, and so is Strepsiades in the *Clouds*, though he has married and settled in the city. The Sausage-seller in the *Knights* comes from the riff-raff of the market, on his own admission a 'rascal', hardly a 'man' at all,[1] but he shares the honours of the play with the master of the household, old Demos (the People). Lysistrata and Praxagora, who equal the comic initiative of their male counterparts, are by origin model wives in typical bourgeois families. And in the *Frogs*, not for the first time in Old Comedy, the principal schemer is Dionysus, the representative of the theatre, the god in whose honour the great civic festivals which included the dramatic competitions were maintained.[2] Whether their sex allows them to vote or not, all these schemers behave as full members of Athenian democracy after Pericles, confident in their right to political opinions and initiative.

Nevertheless, they are aggressive twisters, with ways as devious as the Heathen Chinee and yet often as absurd as the Wise Men of Gotham. In the *Acharnians* (425 B.C.) – the first comedy of Aristophanes to survive complete – Dicaeopolis side-steps the sovereign Assembly to make his own peace with Sparta. Pursued by a chorus of bellicose Acharnians, he saves his neck and wins them over with a cock-and-bull version of the origins of the war, after snatching a coal-basket from one of his fiery pursuers as a hostage, to gain time, and wheedling a stage-kit from Euripides in preparation for his speech of defence; his peace secured, he exploits his private, contraband market with other Greek cities to the full, and gleefully scores off the warrior, Lamachus. In the *Knights* (424 B.C.), the Sausage-seller ejects his rival, who represents Cleon, the dominant politician of the

---

[1] *Knights*, lines 178–86; see Whitman, *Aristophanes*, p. 87.

[2] See fragments of Hermippus, *Birth of Athena* (*c* 439 B.C.); Cratinus, *Dionysalexandros* (430 B.C.); Eupolis, *The Colonels* (427 B.C.) and Aristophanes, *The Babylonians* (426 B.C.) in Edmonds (ed.), *Attic Comedy*, vol. I, pp. 33, 307, 401, 589. *Cf* Norwood, *Greek Comedy*, pp. 118ff; Webster, *Greek Art and Literature, 700–530 B.C.*, pp. 60–2.

day, by outdoing him in bawling, abuse, flattery, demagogic swindling, faked oracles and, finally, theft. When Strepsiades in the *Clouds*
(423 B.C.) goes to school with the alleged arch-sophist, Socrates, so as
to learn how to wriggle out of his debts, he abjures the gods and hopes
to earn the name of being 'uppish, glib-tongued, bold, impudent,
shameless', 'a sly fox, a slippery customer, an impostor'. Having
colonised the air and founded Cloudcuckootown on the inspiration
of the moment, Peithetairus in the *Birds* (414 B.C.) coolly proceeds to
blockade the gods and, with advice from Prometheus, to extort the
goddess Sovereignty from Zeus. Even the passionately altruistic
Lysistrata raids the Acropolis, douses the member of the Committee
of Public Safety and bundles him off the scene in grave-clothes,
forges an oracle, and eggs on Myrrhine to torment her sex-starved
husband (411 B.C.). To the hero of the comedy and his friends, his
exploit is 'a dread and mighty deed' or 'a daring and novel device', or
even a manifestation of 'audacity, wisdom, patriotism and prudence';[1]
but their opponents, who stand for the régime or policy legally in
force, decry it as 'shamelessness', 'insolence' (*hubris*), an act of
'unheard-of, unendurable lawlessness'.[2] Not only is the leading
character an outrageous law-breaker, he is often ridiculously hare-
brained or doltish as well. Strepsiades is a dullard in sophistry. Old
Philocleon in the *Wasps* (422 B.C.), a very similar character, is tricked
out of his craze for jury-service by his more rational son, and inducted
into a round of fashionable pleasures, only to disgrace the young man
by his riotous conduct. Old Trygaeus, who is also 'mad' in his way,
with his noble obsession with flying to heaven to bring Peace back
to the Greeks (421 B.C.), chooses, of all conceivable mounts, a dung-
eating beetle; and when, even so, he is more than half-way through
the air, he has a moment when he loses his nerve, and yells to the
stage-machinist to be careful (line 175). Dionysus in the *Frogs*
(405 B.C.) longs to restore the recently-dead Euripides to the theatre.
In many ways, he is a typically smart young Athenian, and he sets
off with his slave, Xanthias, taking an inordinate amount of baggage;
moreover, as a precaution before descending to Hades, he adopts an
incongruous disguise as Heracles (who has been there before). Once
there, he rapidly changes dress with his slave and back again, as he is
alternately threatened and welcomed by the inhabitants below, who
have scores to settle with Heracles, or else intimacies to renew; and

[1] *Acharnians*, 128; *Peace*, 94; *Lysistrata*, 545–7.
[2] *Acharnians*, 289, 491; *Lysistrata*, 399, 425; *Plutus*, 415–21.

he is not admitted to Pluto's court until he has undergone a beating by the porter, to settle which of the travellers is really the slave. Even then, he changes his mind in the end, and comes back to Athens with Aeschylus.

Much of the content of Aristophanic comedy springs, as Cornford showed, from fertility ritual – the insistent jokes about food, sex, excrement and death, the unlimited mockery and personal abuse, the horseplay, the wearing of grotesque masks by actors and chorus. And many recurrent features of his scenarios seem to belong to the same source – the semi-formalised role of the chorus, the *agon* or mock-battle, followed by a triumphal feast and a processional revel (the *komos*), which is accompanied by some form of mock-marriage or a general spree at the end.[1] Together, actors and chorus seem to represent the whole city in festival, as if by delegation; they act to and for their audience, address them directly, and almost draw them into the play. It is in keeping with this cardinal aspect of the plays that the main figure should be of the type of a folklore hero, a shrewd buffoon – especially when the buffoon is also a tough-minded rustic (as in Aristophanes' early plays and his last surviving work, *Plutus*), exasperated by urban changes and the discomforts of war. The opponent the hero overthrows is a warlike power-seeker or else a charlatan with public influence (Cleon, Socrates and Euripides, as they appear in the plays); and, as Cornford pointed out, in nearly every play the hero drives off, beats or jeers at intruders who claim a share in his feast. In several plays the intruders are described as *alazones* – vagabonds and impostors (Cleon in the *Knights*, the soothsayer, Hierocles, in *Peace*, another oracle-monger and Meton, the land-surveyor, in the *Birds*);[2] and similar figures are common in the other plays. Hence some critics, notably Northrop Frye, have found the basic meaning of Old Comedy – indeed, of comedy in general – in an opposition between Impostor types and the hero as *eiron*, the Ironical Man who dissembles his understanding; and the basic movement of comedy, in an advance from false opinion towards knowledge, or truth.[3]

---

[1] See Cornford, *Origin of Attic Comedy* (ed. Gaster); Mazon, 'La Farce dans Aristophane'; Pickard-Cambridge, *Dithyramb*; Dover, 'Greek Comedy'.

[2] *Knights*, 269, 290; *Peace*, 1045, 1069, 1120; *Birds*, 983, 1016: see *alazon* and derivatives in Todd, *Index Aristophaneus*; Cornford, *Origin of Attic Comedy* (ed. Gaster), pp. 115ff.

[3] Frye, *Anatomy of Criticism*, pp. 169–75; cf Cornford, *Origin of Attic Comedy* (ed. Gaster), p. 119; Cooper, *Aristotelian Theory of Comedy*, pp. 117ff, 224–6.

But this theory does not altogether work. For one thing, many intruders at feasts in Aristophanes are not called *alazones*; while some *alazones* are not intruders at feasts. To the first group belong the informers and other minions of the law in three of the plays, angry shopkeepers and creditors, a poet and a would-be parricide; to the second, the ambassadors and public orators in the *Acharnians* and Socrates and his school in the *Clouds*. In addition, the gods are called impostors (*alazones*) in the *Birds*, and Heracles and Aeschylus in the *Frogs*.[1] The verbal inconsistency here hardly matters. But, though soothsayers and informers are assumed to be legalised scoundrels (like Chaucer's Pardoner and Summoner), and some of the others, charlatans, all the comic victims are not obviously impostors; what most of the two groups, the named *alazones* and the rest, have in common is rather that they stand for authority and the law (even Socrates is accepted as a teacher for the time being, and the young man in the *Birds* who wants to get rid of his father has come to Cloudcuckootown on a deceptive promise, believing parricide will be legal there). They are like the policeman who is knocked about by Punch. The treatment they receive brings out an ironic quality in the hero, but also his strain of wilfulness and bland anarchy. Moreover, in the *Knights* (903), the Sausage-seller boasts to Cleon that 'the goddess has ordered me to be more of an *alazon* than you are'; while in the *Clouds* (449), Strepsiades hopes to be accounted *both* impostor and dissembler (*eiron*). This seems to be the only place where Aristophanes uses the latter noun.[2]

The view of Aristophanes' typical hero as an ironist is too narrow. It leaves out of account much of his primitive theatricality on one side, his intellectual acrobatics on the other.

The primary significance of wearing a mask (or masquerade), according to anthropologists, is not simply to hide the wearer's everyday personality but to change and transcend it, by bringing him into direct, magical contact with images of the supranormal powers in nature, in the animal world, in the dead.[3] In this sense, there is a residue of magic in all the performers in Old Comedy. But the special mark of the leading actor is that very often he changes his own garb, or causes others to change visibly, in the course of the play. When the

[1] *Acharnians*, 63, 87, 109, 135, 373; *Clouds*, 102, 1492; *Birds*, 825; *Frogs*, 280, 709.
[2] Whitman, *Aristophanes*, p. 27; (but see *Wasps*, 174; *Birds*, 1211).
[3] See Eliade, 'Masks'; cf Krien-Kummrow, 'Maschera Teatrale'; Jeanmaire, *Dionysos*, ch. 7; Webster, *Greek Art and Literature, 700–530 B.C.*, pp. 65ff; Bédouin, *Les Masques*; Lévi-Strauss, *Anthropologie structurale*, pp. 269–94.

Sausage-seller has won his slanging-match for Demos's favour, he announces that he has transformed his master by cooking him, and the old man re-enters, much more splendid than before. Conversely, Lysistrata dresses the Committee-man like a corpse. Peithetaerus acquires wings. In *The Women in the Assembly* (392 B.C.) the female revolutionaries steal their husbands' clothes. In the *Thesmophoriazusae* (411 B.C.) Euripides persuades his kinsman to dress as a woman (so as to spy on the women in their sex-closed festival and defend the poet's cause) and then, to extricate his champion, assumes four different roles, three from his own plays. In the *Acharnians*, similarly, Dicaeopolis had already borrowed a stage outfit from Euripides, the rags worn by King Telephus when disguised as a beggar. Dionysus goes to the underworld dressed as Heracles, in a lion-skin. Some of these rig-outs, especially the last two, may seem pointless or even futile as contributions to the theme or plot. But they bring out the comic hero's gift and role as a shape-changer – a more positive (and magical) function than that of the ironist, who conceals what he really thinks. By a long tradition, the leader of a troupe of comedians has been the clown, the performer whose mask or make-up is the most glaring, who mimics or changes costume more than the others, who plays at playing and visibly reduplicates the act of acting.

This bias towards playfulness within the field of performance makes one of the main differences, of course, between comedy and tragedy. It is intimately related to some of the distinctive modes of comedic irony (not the irony of a character, but the ironies of the form). However complex in structure or meaning, a tragedy is single-minded, in the sense that all the speakers are intent on thoughts connected with the plot, and the actors may not emerge from behind the characters they represent. No one talks to the audience or acknowledges the stage-machinist. The masks of Greek tragedy contributed to uphold the illusion of a heroic world, remote, even if it suggested parallels with Periclean Athens, and internally self-consistent. The subject of a tragedy was its *mythos* – its legend, or plot. But the usual word for the subject of comedy was *logos* or *hypothesis* – argument, or supposition – or else 'fiction', as opposed to 'history'.[1] The story element in comedy was a free invention. And, by custom, Old Comedy was topical and mythical (or pseudo-mythical) at once. It could, and was expected to, name living people and recent measures, and attack them freely (this extreme freedom of speech, the licence

---

1 Cooper, *Aristotelian Theory of Comedy*, pp. 50–1.

of extended democracy, was the special mark of Old Comedy in the eyes of critics after the fifth century); it caricatured current events and well-known personalities, somewhat like a revue or a cartoon. But it also regularly brought in gods and characters from history or legend, alongside representatives of various professions, fictitious Athenians with significant invented names (Pheidippides, 'Skimp-horse'; Lysistrata, 'Disbander-of-armies'), talking animals and personified abstractions like War and Poverty. And it regularly employed burlesque for the elements of the scenario, weaving current allusions into parodies of epic, tragedy, myth, fable, or religious ritual or state procedure. Because a comedy in Athens was topical and mythical together, neither satire nor burlesque could operate alone. No comedy of Aristophanes is simply a myth or fable turned to ridicule; still less is any of them a consistent reconstruction, even in caricature, of current events. When a real person, a Cleon, Socrates or Euripides, figures prominently in a play, he is a comic type as well as an individual, and it is the type rather than the real man that governs the role, without the slightest pretence at a sequential life-story or even a *roman à clef* (however much subsequent biographers and historians may have extracted from the plays in the form of inferential evidence or echoes of gossip). To intermix ritual and pamphleteering, actuality and fable is precisely the central aim of Old Comedy, because it is a contribution to the annual politico-religious festivals when the past and the ideals of Athens merge with her present, and the life of the whole city is symbolically renewed.

On the other hand, a comedy is not simply a ritual (any more than a tragedy is simply the repetition of a myth); and Aristophanes and the other poets of Old Comedy cannot treat past and present, fable and reality simply as interchangeable equivalents or as moments of the same unquestionable continuum, because the poets are consciously removed from archaic modes of thought. They are writing at a time and place of deep political change – partly under the stress of war – and of incessant public discussion, writing as contemporaries and fellow-citizens of the first generation of critical historians, logicians and sociologists. Hence the dualism of Old Comedy is complicated further; it includes attitudes of belief and unbelief, rationalism and magic, as well as the two planes of contemporaneity and the mythical. And hence the plays of Aristophanes are thoroughly imbued with irony, with the awareness of multiple, but in part conflicting, inter-pretations and possibilities. To borrow Castelvetro's formulas, they are based upon 'deceit'; not merely the delusions or impostures of the characters, but the structural 'deceptions that result from an unexpected movement of things in another direction' – save that Castelvetro is speaking primarily of successive instants on a single narrative plane, whereas in Aristophanes there is also the unexpected copresence of divergent lines of meaning, which may leap out in an incongruous image or pun, or dart through his argument as a whole. It is an irony of values, reaching far beyond the dissembling of a sly buffoon. At the same time, the sly buffoon, the trickster, part common man and part folklore hero, is the indispensable personage to hold such an imaginative complex together, to interpret it, in the theatrical sense of the word.

Aristophanes deliberately plays with historical time; for instance, the choruses of old men who dance in three of his comedies are Marathon veterans, of incredible longevity. Similarly with place: not only can his scene shift from one spot in or near Athens to another, and from earth to Olympus, or Hades, or Cloudcuckootown, but it can shift with a flagrant contradiction of logic, and his acting space can be the imaginary place and the real stage at the same time. When Trygaeus shouts to the machinist who is hoisting him towards the stage roof, he is supposed to be looking down from an immense height on the Piraeus; after he has flown to Olympus, he summons the chorus, who at once join him by some means of locomotion unspecified; and later, while the chorus, like all Greek choruses, remain in front of the audience, and while they are delivering their parabasis to the spectators, he leaves them (on Olympus) and rejoins them (in Athens), explaining to the public that he has come down painfully on foot, and that 'it's a tough business to go straight among the gods'. A similar joke is turned against the audience in the *Birds*, where the chorus, in the parabasis (753ff), invite those of the spectators who wish to follow a natural, unrestrained, lawless existence to join them in Cloudcuckootown, so that the *alazones* who are ridiculed in the second half of the play appear to have hurried on to the stage in response to this summons.[1] Or, again, the main theme of the comedy may indeed consist of what Castelvetro calls 'an unexpected movement of things in another direction', as when the re-education of Strepsiades, in the *Clouds*, and Philocleon, in the *Wasps*, recoils extravagantly on their tutors. The chorus of horse-men in the *Knights*, who might be expected to represent the aristocratic or

---

[1] Whitman, *Aristophanes*, pp. 185–6; Guthrie, *Greek Philosophy*, vol. III, p. 104.

oligarchic party opposed to Cleon, applaud the victory of the Sausage-seller, which, on the political level, implies an even more unbridled demagoguery.[1] Again, when Aristophanes mocks Euripides as a woman-hater in the *Thesmophoriazusae*, he takes the occasion to malign the sex himself without limit.

This kind of ironic 'deceit' (or 'double take') is intimately related to burlesque, or rather, to the dualism of Old Comedy as what might be called topicalised myth. The rejuvenative 'cooking' of Demos by the Sausage-seller, for instance, resembles the witchcraft of Medea; Trygaeus's flight on his beetle is compared to the heroic exploit of Bellerophon on Pegasus, but also to one of Aesop's fables.[2] And this is more than parody. While strict parody is purely reductive, mimicking the original so as to make it seem ridiculous and confining itself within the bounds of mimicry, Aristophanes will turn the similitude round for an unexpected but searching comment on social realities, or treat it freely as a springboard for new fantasies of his own. When Trygaeus's Daughter complains, in mock-tragic tones (*Peace*, 114ff) that he will go 'to the birds, to the crows' (attempt the impossible, kill himself), that he has chosen an incredibly smelly beast for a visit to the gods, and that at least he should take care not to fall and provide a subject for Euripides, the old man points out, on Aesop's authority, that the dung-beetle is the only winged creature to have reached heaven and adds that his steed's unsavoury appetite is a capital merit, since with any other Pegasus he would need 'double rations'. Here the parody plays back into the old man's character as both a canny farmer and a heroic buffoon, obsessed by the ravages of the war; it sparks across the gap between opposing fantasies, on the themes of excrement and of aspiration; and it casts a weird, flickering light on the human situation, on man's complicated nature as a food-requiring and a myth-making animal.

When Peithetaerus ('Comrade-Persuader') thinks of urging the birds to establish Cloudcuckootown, a fantasy of escape from the city (from lawsuits and war-neurosis) turns into a parody of the founding of a new city (a subject close to the minds of the imperialistic Athenians, particularly in 414 B.C., at the critical moment of the Sicilian expedition), a parody of the contemporary sophists, with their emphasis on the contrast between Nature and Law and on

---

[1] See Ehrenberg, *People of Aristophanes*, pp. 47–8; *cf* Walker, 'The Periclean Democracy'; Navarre, *Les Cavaliers*, pp. 100ff.
[2] *Peace*, 129ff. See Lever, *Art of Greek Comedy*, pp. 23, 115, 155; Trenkner, *Greek Novella*, p. 79.

language as the arbiter of opinion (there being no great difference, as the hero points out to his feathery hosts, between *polos*, the heavenly sphere, and *polis*, a city),[1] a parody of cosmologies and creation-myths (in the birds' ensuing claim to sovereignty by ancestral right),[2] and, finally, a parody of the fable of Prometheus. The play is at once a satire on the Athenians, gullible to the pitch of megalomania – 'mankind is always and every way by nature deceitful' (451) – and a celebration of their inventiveness, their 'subtle reasonings' and 'ingenious conceptions' (195, 317). The same impulses are both absurd and splendid; 'deceit' here gives rise to lyricism, as well as burlesque. In a world where 'democracy' can induce the gods to elect an incomprehensible barbarian as one of their delegates (1570), and where the Olympians themselves are no more than 'braggarts' (825), a gift of the gab and cool bluffing may be sufficient to gain Sovereignty (that 'beautiful maiden, who manages God's thunderbolt and everything else, wise counsel, good laws, moderation, the dockyards, vilification [as in comedies], the judges' pay-clerk, their three-obol fees' (1537)); but only a consummate, Promethean trickster can uphold a humane metropolis in the air.[3]

Similarly, only a sublime simpleton could dream of combining all the women of Greece in a sex-strike to end the Peloponnesian War – and get away with it. But Lysistrata's scheme is not merely an 'insolent', yet 'awe-inspiring', trick to stop the war, it is also a searching observation on a cardinal rule of Athenian democracy, the restriction of political rights to men, and at the same time a fantastic application of the magico-religious principle of abstinence as a means to fertility (as in the women's rituals in the Thesmophoria, which Aristophanes parodied in the same year).[4] Again, only a god or a fool could hope to restore the glory of Athens in 405 B.C., when Euripides and Sophocles had recently died, and in military affairs the city was driven to the brink of disaster. Yet Dionysus's adventures in the *Frogs* form a serio-comic *rite de passage*.[5] Heracles, whom he 'imitates'

---

1 *Birds,* 172–84. See Whitman, *Aristophanes,* ch. 5; Guthrie, *Greek Philosophy,* vol. III, chs. 3–4, 8.

2 *Birds,* 684ff. See Harrison, *Themis,* pp. 453–61, 630ff; Kirk and Raven, *Presocratic Philosophers,* pp. 44–8; Guthrie, *Greek Philosophy,* vol. III, pp. 236–42; Whitman, *Aristophanes,* pp. 182–4.

3 Whitman, *Aristophanes,* pp. 182–4; but see also Vandrik, *Prometheus,* pp. 71–5; Ehrenberg, *People of Aristophanes,* pp. 57–60, 253–73.

4 Harrison, *Prolegomena to Greek Religion,* p. 128; Halliday, *Greek Questions,* p. 144.

5 See Whitman, *Aristophanes,* ch. 7; Ehrenberg, *People of Aristophanes,* ch. 10; Harrison, *Themis,* pp. 376–81; Thomson, *Aeschylus and Athens,* ch. 7; Guthrie, *The Greeks*

in dress as in exploit, and whom he therefore consults before his journey to Hades, is both the brawny glutton of farce and, in popular belief, the protector of young men; besides the chorus of frogs – creatures of an intermediate world – the main chorus Dionysus meets consists of his own worshippers, initiates in the Eleusinian mysteries. His haggling with the corpse (who would rather go back to life than carry the god's baggage, after all), his surprise encounters underground, his interchanges of dress with his slave, the ordeal of buffetings he has to undergo at Pluto's gate, his umpiring of the dispute between Euripides and Aeschylus, which becomes a burlesque of poetic contests in his own theatre but culminates in a parodied weighing of souls,[1] and, finally, his mocking change of front towards his recent hero, are all moments of initiation, steps towards a new life, before he returns in torchlight procession with 'him whom his soul desires', Aeschylus, the poet of an earlier and more hopeful generation, who may bring the city 'good thoughts of great blessings' and deliver it from 'distress and the harsh assembly of arms'.

These parodies, then, go beyond parody, and Aristophanes reinstates the serious fantasy contained in myth on a different plane. The peculiar 'deceit' or sleight-of-hand in Aristophanes, his unpredictable transitions between ridicule of myth and identification with it, spring from his partial scepticism, the attitude of mind he shares with the very contemporaries he attacks, like Euripides and the sophists,[2] but more particularly, it seems, from his critical self-awareness as a comic poet. Through his parabases, he complains, or pretends to complain, of his 'fickle-minded', 'novelty-loving' public, who make 'comedy-writing the most arduous task on earth';[3] he boasts to them of his dismissal of stale, vulgar jokes, of his ever-fresh inventiveness, his 'ingenuity' and his daring.[4] Though these self-advertisements may express a genuine pride, they are also part of the ritual of competition, and part of the aura of the dissembling buffoon (in that, for example, he will re-utilise the very gags he has been deriding). Such resounding claims are in keeping with that 'deceit' which Gorgias the sophist said was inseparable from persuasion, the

---

and their Gods, pp. 240, 277–94; Jeanmaire, *Dionysos*, pp. 268–73, 436–8. *Cf* p. 90, n. 2, above.

[1] Homer, *Iliad*, VIII, 69. See Murray, 'Excursus', in Harrison, *Themis*, p. 350; Murray, *Aristophanes*, pp. 118–34; Huizinga, *Homo Ludens*, p. 79.

[2] Murray, *Aristophanes*, p. 108; Ehrenberg, *People of Aristophanes*, pp. 64–5.

[3] *Acharnians*, 632; *Women in the Assembly*, 586–7; *Knights*, 514ff.

[4] *Acharnians*, 629; *Clouds*, 537–48; *Wasps*, 1029; *Peace*, 738–53; *Frogs*, 1370–7. See Ehrenberg, *People of Aristophanes*, pp. 27–36; Lever, *Art of Greek Comedy*, ch. 4.

essence of rhetoric (and hence, in the sophist's view, of drama, or at least, of tragedy).[1] But competitive involvement is the life-blood of criticism. And there is at least potential literary criticism in parody or burlesque, the favourite genre of Old Comedy – often a very effective genre for criticism, as English poetry has shown, from Chaucer or Ben Jonson to Eliot. The *Frogs*, which has been described as 'a remarkable piece of impressionistic criticism',[2] is probably the earliest surviving continuous discussion of literature in Europe; and in Aristophanes, who has literary or theatrical allusions in every play, the critical attitude towards his own task is inseparable from the creative.

In the argument between Philocleon and his son about the sort of anecdotes befitting a well-bred banquet, Bdelycleon brushes aside his father's penchant for grotesque fables (*Wasps*, 1179): 'But, no! No myths, but human affairs, the household things we mostly talk about'. This aptly describes the domain of comedy, both in what Bdelycleon rejects and, more significant for the future, in what he approves.[3] It suggests a difference of generations as well, and touches on a distinction of genres; the comic poet's charge against Euripides is precisely that he has brought down tragedy from the mythical and heroic to the everyday (and the sophistic). 'I taught these [Athenians] to speechify', Euripides is made to boast in the *Frogs* (954), '...to apply subtle rules, to square off lines of verse, to notice, to see, to understand, to love twisting, to employ contrivances, to suspect mischief, to deliberate everything...introducing affairs on the stage, common and familiar, where I could be tested.' Not that the fabulous monsters and 'unaccountable high-riding terms' (929) of Aeschylus escape ridicule, either; but Euripides has lowered the dignity of tragedy. It can be inferred that he is satirised for poaching on comedy's ground as well.

In any case, Euripides, or the 'enlightenment' he stands for, has destroyed critical innocence; distinctions like that between 'myths' and 'household affairs' are inescapable. And for Aristophanes they stand at the centre of comic poetry. The mythical and the familiar, the magical and the rational, the fantastic and the pragmatic, the metaphorical and the literal – Aristophanes repeatedly brings such concepts together, both to play off one against the other and to

[1] Lucas (ed.), *Aristotle: Poetics*, p. xix; Guthrie, *Greek Philosophy*, vol. III, pp. 25, 51, 180.

[2] Lucas (ed.), *Aristotle: Poetics*, p. xvii.

[3] Ehrenberg, *People of Aristophanes*, pp. 53, 289ff; Trenkner, *Greek Novella*, pp. 16–22.

employ both sides of the antithesis in unexpected combinations; and to these should be added the varying contrasts between reality and 'deceit', 'imposture', or acting. In the *Clouds* (225), Socrates, aloft in his Thinkery, explains that he is 'treading the air', because 'he would never investigate heavenly bodies correctly, if he did not suspend his brain and mingle his subtle thoughts with the congruent air'. Otherwise 'the sap of his thought' would be earthy; 'exactly the same thing happens with water-cress'. Here it is not simply the (allegedly impious) 'imposture' of astronomers that receives attention,[1] but a pre-scientific habit of mind. By claiming to 'mingle' his thoughts with a substance 'of the like nature' in order to penetrate and understand it, Socrates is reviving the basic principle of sympathetic magic, that like affects like;[2] and Aristophanes takes the occasion to reduce the principle to absurdity. 'Up-in-the-air imagery' (as Whitman points out) is frequent in Aristophanes, and is 'almost a fixed symbol of vaporous nonsense, intellectual twaddle, delirium, and vertigo' – though 'it also has its own heroic madness, at times'.[3] As in this play, where the chorus of Clouds is given a strong but expressively elusive personality, it may be only a short step from the ridiculous to the sublime. But the essential comic instrument for Aristophanes is his dual treatment of metaphor. When the Informer applies to Peithetaerus for wings (so as to speed up his prosecutions), Peithetaerus proffers good advice (to turn to honest work) instead; and these 'words' are genuine 'wings', he says, because by words 'the mind is raised aloft, and man is exalted' (*Birds*, 1447). He uses picture-thinking very like the (pseudo-)Socrates, although his moral intention for the moment is the opposite. Similarly, in the *Frogs* (1365), when Aeschylus demands to decide his controversy with Euripides by 'testing the weight of our expressions', a huge pair of scales is brought in, whereupon the chorus exclaims in admiration, 'What trouble clever people go to! Another freakish, unprecedented prodigy! Who else would have thought of it?' But the burlesque is turned around when Dionysus decides (1394) in favour of the 'gravity' of Aeschylus – his 'Death' against Euripides's 'Persuasion'.[4]

In a metaphor (as Aristotle says) there is a 'transfer' of properties

---

[1] Bury, 'The Age of Illumination', pp. 382–3; Dodds, *Greeks and the Irrational*, pp. 189ff; Guthrie, *Greek Philosophy*, vol. III, pp. 359ff.

[2] See Dodds, *Greeks and the Irrational*, pp. 194–5; H. and H. A. Frankfort (eds.), *Before Philosophy*, p. 27; Kirk and Raven, *Presocratic Philosophers*, pp. 372–5.

[3] Whitman, *Aristophanes*, pp. 139, 181.

[4] Navarre, *Les Cavaliers*, p. 221; *cf* p. 99, n. 1, above.

from an object in one class to an object in another, often using analogy. This is a description in terms of logic. But there is also an emotional leap, an act of participation or identification, without which there would be no force in metaphors like 'weighty thoughts' or 'winged words'. Empathy is another name for this mental act of participation; but it also seems closely allied to the volitional identification with nature involved in magic and mythopoeic thinking – the projection, as it has been called, of an 'I and Thou' relationship between man and his world[1] – and closely allied to the motive of self-transformation through direct contact with another nature involved in the making and wearing of a primitive mask. A metaphor, in brief, is one meaning impersonating another; an actor is a living metaphor. This, at least, seems to correspond to Aristophanes's view, though he is also aware of the logical gulf bridged by analogy in a metaphor and, equally, of the actor's 'deceit' in assuming a role. *Mimesis* (here, the actor's art and all that goes with it on the stage) is both 'imitation' in the rational, Aristotelian sense, a semblance of voluntary human actions transferred to a special medium, and 'impersonation' with an irrational, quasi-magical overtone of possession through contact with an alien power, somewhat like the state of possession that Plato attributes to the declaimer of poetry in his *Ion*.[2] But it is the second, the irrational aspect, that Aristophanes stresses for comic purposes.

When Dicaeopolis is harried by the chorus of Acharnians (somewhere in the country), he knocks for help, without leaving sight of the chorus, at the house of Euripides (somewhere in Athens) (*Acharnians*, 393). Before pleading his case to his enemies, he wants to borrow the stage rags worn by the tragic poet's King Telephus in disguise as a beggar, as if a stage costume, particularly a stage disguise, constituted a sort of talisman. He hears at first from a servant that Euripides is not at home: 'His mind has gone out gathering versicles, and is not within; but he himself *is* within, with his feet in the air, composing a tragedy.' 'You write with your feet in the air', Dicaeopolis tells him when he sees him, 'when you could just as well keep them on the ground. No wonder your works are halting.' He accuses the poet, then, of the charlatanism, or mock-magic, pinned again on Socrates in the *Clouds*. Nevertheless, he insists on the loan, for he can only save himself, apparently, by acting the part analogous

---

[1] H. and H. A. Frankfort (eds.), *Before Philosophy*, ch. 1; *cf* p. 93, n. 3, above.
[2] See McKeon, 'Literary Criticism and the Concept of Imitation in Antiquity'; Lucas (ed.), *Aristotle: Poetics*, app. 1; Jeanmaire, *Dionysos*, pp. 316–21.

to his own situation from Euripides, and to this end mere words are not sufficient, but he must have the costume as well:

'For today I must make myself a beggar, – To be what I am, yet not appear it.' The spectators will know quite well who I am, but the Chorus must stand by like a set of boobies while I nettle them with my 'little phrases'.

The buffoon here pretends to be a simpleton, in order to mock the stupid rustics on one side and the clever charlatan on the other, to ridicule the idea of make-believe and laugh at the audience for accepting it – and to use it himself. For Dicaeopolis does, in effect, acquire Euripides's sophistic eloquence. When he delivers his oration, he opens (496) with two 'little phrases' from the beggar-king, as preamble to a part-serious, part-burlesque appeal for a 'just' policy, uttered in the name of Comedy. 'Even Comedy can sometimes discern' what is just or right, he says. But there is no pretence of consistency. Quite the reverse; Comedy is avowedly masquerade – in Bernard Shaw's phrase, 'the fine art of disillusion'.

In the *Thesmophoriazusae*, where it is Euripides's turn to need help, he calls on his friend Agathon. When Agathon, after much palaver, shows himself out-of-doors, he is dressed as a woman (95). This garb, he at last explains (146), is needed for his inspiration:

I wear a costume that goes with my thoughts. For if one is a poet, he should have the habits appropriate to the play he must write. For example's sake, if he is writing a women's play, he should participate in their habits in person...If he is writing a men's play, he has the bodily equipment already. What doesn't belong to us in the first place, we must capture by *mimesis*.

Agathon's principles (which are not utterly remote, however, from those of 'method' acting) again imply changing the personality by means of magical contagion; and they tally with some of Plato's reasons for banning *mimesis* from his Republic.[1] But, in this 'women's play', they work: when the transvestite kinsman is trapped, he 'imitates [Euripides's] new *Helen*' to call for rescue; and, though the poet's responding impersonations of three separate roles from his own plays are dismal failures, he gains his end at last in a female disguise. In a like manner, Dionysus's attempt to 'imitate' Heracles in the *Frogs* (109) is first ridiculously futile but in the end significant. Just as the metaphors of 'winging' thoughts and 'weighing' them are first exposed as logical absurdities, with visual aids in costume or stage

---

[1] *Republic* III, 395.

properties, and then taken seriously for their emotional value, so the principle of Dionysiac possession in *mimesis* is both deflated and developed. Even in the unambiguous passage in *Plutus* (291, 306) where the slave 'imitates' the Cyclops and Circe with the chorus in a miniature dance-drama to express their joy, their cathartic relief at escape from the 'madness' of poverty, there is still a strong trace of the idea of Dionysiac possession.[1]

This dual attitude towards *mimesis* governs Aristophanes's comedy in general, in his serious purpose, whether 'advice', as he calls it, or fantasy, as well as in his burlesque. His object is not purely to caricature present-day realities, or to launch into fantasy or a mythical ideal, but to change the mental life of his audience by bringing the two kinds of emotional drive, the two modes of perception, into tension and interplay. Unlike tragedy, his comedy insists on the reality of the present moment, even while practising its own form of 'deceit'. It offers illusion without wish-fulfilment and wish-fulfilment without illusion. The trickster hero is a projection of the 'ingenious' poet.

THE TRICKSTER, CONTINUED

Throughout the period traditionally assigned by Alexandrian scholars to Middle Comedy[2] – from the end of the Peloponnesian War in 404 B.C. until her defeat by Philip of Macedon at Chaeronea in 338 B.C. or, at latest, until 322, the year after Alexander's death, when the Macedonians again crushed her army and her fleet – Athens, though shorn of her empire, still kept her independence. But Menander's first play came out in 321 B.C., in the shadow of a Macedonian garrison; New Comedy was the product of a half-century when Athens was indirectly governed from Macedon and overmastered by struggles between the successor-kingdoms to Alexander. It was still a living form, however, though already in decline, when the first Roman translation of a Greek play was performed in 240, early in the lifetime of Plautus (*c.* 254–184); (very much of our knowledge about Athenian New Comedy is taken, of course, from Roman adaptations). Menander (342–292) was Athenian by birth, but most of the authors of New Comedy were naturalised Athenians, Philemon (*c.* 363–264) coming from Syracuse, and Diphilus (*c.* 355–*c.* 290?) from

---

[1] *Cf* Wasps, 118–23; see Dodds, *Greeks and the Irrational*, pp. 78–9; Jeanmaire, *Dionysos*, pp. 316–21.
[2] Lesky, *Greek Literature*, p. 418; Norwood, *Greek Comedy*, pp. 37–58; Lever, *Art of Greek Comedy*, ch. 7.

Sinope on the Black Sea. Athens was now the intellectual centre of the hellenistic civilisation, Greek in official culture but multi-racial in beliefs and customs, bequeathed by Alexander's vast empire. The resulting cosmopolitanism was no doubt an important factor in diffusing New Comedy through the hellenistic and the Roman world, but this also meant that the intense city-consciousness of Old Comedy had been diluted. The prestige of the old gods had long been fading, with their intimacy and their reassurance. Menander was deeply influenced by Aristotle, whom he could possibly have heard lecture, and whose successor at the Lyceum, Theophrastus, was his master;[1] but the new philosophies emerging after Aristotle's flight from Athens and death in 322 were individualistic and apolitical (in the sense that they were no longer centred on the city). And, within the limits of self-government left to the Athenians, democracy was receding; in spite of a struggle, the poorer citizens were disfranchised and at the same time (in 321) deprived of the state festival fund that had enabled them to attend the theatre without the loss of a day's pay. Although Menander's ultimate audience, in his own time and much later, was much wider than that of Aristophanes, therefore, his immediate, effective public came from less than half the citizen population, from perhaps some 9,000 propertied families, out of about 21,000 citizen families in all.[2]

As major political themes and then mythological extravaganza (still traceable in the surviving fragments of Middle Comedy) disappeared from the theatre, New Comedy concentrated on 'household matters', especially marriage arrangements for the sons of well-to-do families and the sons' love-affairs with courtesans. Personal satisfaction became all-important, though still within the social framework of the city. Money made the chief dividing line between the characters in fourth-century comedy,[3] and obtaining money for a young lover is the typical object of a New Comedy intrigue. Menander's positive code is a gentle humanitarianism (echoed and summed up in Terence's '*Homo sum: humani nihil a me alienum puto*'); a guiding thread in his writing is the idea of reconciliation – between lovers who have quarrelled, between fathers and sons, rich and poor, masters and slaves, even Greeks and barbarians.[4] And this attitude seems characteristic of New

[1] Tierney, 'Aristotle and Menander'; Webster, *Menander*.
[2] Ferguson, *Hellenistic Athens*, chs. 1–2.
[3] Ehrenberg, *People of Aristophanes*, ch. 12; Lever, *Art of Greek Comedy*, pp. 165ff.
[4] Gomme, 'Menander', pp. 291–2; Webster, *Menander*, pp. 21–5.

Comedy at large. There are sympathetic, perhaps indulgent, pictures of the honest poor, and of grumpy old citizens soured by inequality. Heroines in several plays have been abandoned at birth because their parents could not afford to keep them; wealthy men are urged, as a social obligation, to marry poor girls or provide for their dowries. There is a strong feeling that money forms an unjust or unnatural barrier between fellow-citizens, just as it is taken for granted that slaves, however subject to the lash, are human beings, with as much inborn intelligence as their owners. But the comedies lead towards reconciliation, the reaffirmation of citizenship and the re-knitting of family ties, not towards social criticism.

New Comedy, especially Menander, was praised by hellenistic and Roman critics for well-made plots and insight into character-types, for truth to life and good breeding.[1] The gods had left the stage, except for minor deities or abstractions to speak an occasional prologue; choruses had shrunk to bands of revellers appearing at intervals with nothing to say. Costume was contemporary, and the actors' masks and wigs, like the stage settings, took on a stylised naturalism.[2] The fantastic puns and metaphors and incongruous word-lists of Old Comedy were excised, together with lampooning, obscenity and exaggerated stage phalluses. Buffoonery, which Aristotle as well as Plato had disapproved of, was toned down.

Nevertheless, much of the underlying structure of Old Comedy remains. Although money and status are now the fields of contention, instead of state policy and culture, the shaping lines of group cleavage between rich and poor, men and women, fathers and sons, and revellers and intruders, are still evident, as in Aristophanes. A feast, shown or described, is still a symbolically important element in the plot, and the comic butts, though no longer demagogues, informers, soothsayers or sophists, are functionally related still to Old Comedy *alazones*. There is the boastful cook, for example, a heritage from Middle Comedy, and the parasite (when he is treated as a nuisance and not a friend). The types more engaged in New Comedy plots, the money-lenders, slave-dealers (or procurers), grasping courtesans and braggart soldiers, all, in their dramatic functions, represent money as an obstacle to pleasure. In fourth-century Athens (we are told), 'there was, perhaps, no business more capitalistic in its organisation

---

[1] Norwood, *Greek Comedy*, pp. 314–17.
[2] Webster, *Greek Theatre Production*, pp. 26, 73ff, and 'The Comedy of Menander', in Dorey and Dudley (eds.), *Roman Drama*, pp. 8ff.

and international in its scope than the traffic in courtesans';[1] while the soldiers, though still valiant only in show (like Lamachus in the *Acharnians*), are now wealthy mercenaries, rejoicing in the favour of foreign kings, boasting of the fantastic luxuries they have seen in their travels,[2] and, above all, of their prowess in love. Like the slave-dealer and the (unsympathetic) courtesan, the mercenary excites dislike or envy as a successful outsider – an intruder – without roots or loyalties in the city; he is the supreme example of the impostor as the young man's rival in love, which is his effective dramatic role in New Comedy (*Alazon* was the Greek play from which Plautus says he took his *Miles Gloriosus*). The *alazon* remains, then, though his special mark in New Comedy is the false pretence of pleasure in love or the interposition of money-power.

Similarly, the schemer remains, as an almost indispensable motive force in the plot, although his achievement is very often reduced by the large share in the action accorded to chance and his scope diminished further by the disappearance of politics and overtly mythical themes. No longer a wonder-worker or public saviour, he is merely the contriver of success in a private love-affair. Moreover, in keeping with the assumption that buffoonery degrades a gentle-man, the role of trickster is now usually (though not invariably) delegated from citizens to slaves. And the cunning slave is not, as a rule, working on his own behalf (though Plautus's *Persian* and *Stichus* show that there could be exceptions), but as an agent for his young master, usually scheming for the son of the house in opposition to his real master, the father. Being a slave, the trickster is now no more than an instrument. He is set to solve a problem for somebody else. On the other hand, a regular situation in New Comedy – most con-spicuously in those examples that have survived through Plautus – is that the young lover, in a state of helplessness, turns to his servant for advice. The mental initiative is passed to the servant and, quite as much as in Old Comedy, his tricks and contrivances make up the plot. His effrontery and his escape scot-free are quite incredible if con-sidered as pictures of typical domestic life, even in the easy-going régime obtaining in Athens.[3] But nothing illustrates the primacy of

---

[1] Ferguson, *Hellenistic Athens*, p. 71.

[2] See Webster, *Later Greek Comedy*, pp. 6, 64, 116, 173; Finley, *The Ancient Greeks*, p. 89; *cf* Antiphanes, *The Soldier* (394 B.C.), in Edmonds (ed. and trans.), *Attic Comedy*, vol. II, p. 267.

[3] Duckworth, *Roman Comedy*, pp. 288–91; *cf* Gomme, 'Menander', p. 287; Ehrenberg, *People of Aristophanes*, pp. 165–91, 361; Glotz and Cohen, *La Grèce au Ve siècle*,

the trickster's role more forcibly than its persistence in the semi-realistic bourgeois setting of New Comedy, even though the trickster's function is now mostly attributed to slaves.

The slaves in Aristophanes, like Xanthias in the *Frogs* and Cario in *Plutus* (388 B.C.), are greedy, light-fingered, self-confident and sly. Cario has been enslaved (evidently, not in Athens) 'merely for want of a little cash' to pay his debts;[1] he finds it 'a hard thing...to become the slave of a master who is out of his senses', who will not listen to 'the best advice', and whose vexations the slave is compelled, willy-nilly, to share (1–7). Among the surviving fragments of Menander there are several that point to a similar master–slave relationship: 'this troubles me – a slave who thinks more deeply than a servant should', says one line, and another, 'Retain a free man's mind though slave, and slave thou shalt not be.'[2] But the slaves in Aristophanes are grumblingly loyal and obedient, and – except in the *Knights*, where, however, as servants of Demos, they represent two generals – they take no initiative of their own. In New Comedy they have become intriguers. Two anonymous fragments illustrate different sides of their general role.[3] In one, the slave is offering help:

Master, why so deep in thought, all alone, talking to yourself? One might think, you present the picture of a man in sorrow. Refer it to me, take me for fellow-counsellor in your trouble. Don't despise the counsel of a servant – slaves of good character have often proved wiser than their masters. Though fortune may have made the body a slave, the mind still has a free man's character.

The slave from the other comedy is less sententious and more cynical; he is debating with himself how to avoid being implicated in his young master's love-intrigue, and calculating his risks:

It is we – not the hot-headed youth in love – who tremble at the penalty for mistakes.

Knowing he has the lover's father to reckon with, and wanting his freedom, he dismisses one 'policy' as 'too old-fashioned' and another as too obsequious, yet he savours uncertainty like a gamester: 'Pleasure is doubled when it proceeds from a humble and unexpected

pp. 257–67; Kitto, *The Greeks*, pp. 132, 237; Finley, *The Ancient Greeks*, pp. 148–50.
[1] *Plutus*, 147; see Ehrenberg, *People of Aristophanes*, p. 169.
[2] *Menander*, ed. and trans. Allinson, pp. 531, 533.
[3] Page (ed. and trans.), *Select Papyri III*, pp. 317, 319. See Harsh, 'The Intriguing Slave in Greek Comedy'.

source.' Similarly, Davus, in Menander's *Perinthian* (one of Terence's sources for his *Andrian*) contemplates the risk of torture by fire, but, even so, welcomes the prospect of an intrigue:[1]

A slave who is blessed with an easy-going, empty-headed master and cheats him hasn't accomplished any mighty deed in making a yet greater dolt of the one who was a dolt long since.

This is the authentic note of the slave as master-schemer in New Comedy. He prides himself on his intellectual superiority, on the daring, cleverness and originality of his undertaking, as much as any Dicaeopolis or Peithetaerus. And, though the slave sometimes hopes for, or wins, his freedom, this is not his real object in the comedy; as Erich Segal has emphasised, the main delight of the slave-intriguer (at least, in Plautus) is to enjoy the sensation of becoming his master's master for the time being, to play the game of a temporary reversal of roles.[2] Whether it is his own master or the *alazon* he scores off, his aim is the buffoon's pleasure in downing someone who stands for power or authority, like Philocleon's glee in his delusive supremacy as a juryman in the *Wasps* (575): 'Is not this a mighty rule, and a derision of wealth?' The note of self-appreciation in the intriguing slave is supererogatory in the plot as such, but essential to the comedy; in the love-intrigue, it is 'motiveless' (as Coleridge said of Iago's 'malignity'), but it is vital to the slave's quality as trickster.

No doubt Plautus brings out the spirit of buffoonery much more than Terence or, as far as can be seen from the rediscovered play and surviving passages and fragments, Menander; the other two are more consciously refined. Plautus was evidently close to the Italian (or Graeco-Italian) traditions of farce; he delights in word-play and puns, and he changes the even dialogue of Greek New Comedy into a mixture of verse dialogue and polymetrical song, in a spirit of comic opera;[3] in a sense, he comes nearer to Aristophanes than either Menander or Terence. And, as a writer of *palliata* (comedies with Greek costumes and subjects), he may have exaggerated the role of the impudent slave as he found it in order to magnify the indulgence of 'going Greek' for the amusement of his Roman public; it is disputed whether there were many slaves or not in Plautus's Rome, but in any case Donatus records that slaves in the *togata* (Roman-dressed

---

[1] *Menander*, ed. and trans. Allinson, p. 423.
[2] Segal, *Roman Laughter*, p. 113, and ch. 4 *passim*.
[3] See Arnaldi, *Da Plauto a Terenzio*, vol. 1; Beare, *Roman Stage*, chs. 8, 16; Duckworth, *Roman Comedy*, chs. 12–13.

comedies) were kept in their place.[1] But there is no evidence that either Plautus or Terence (c. 185–159 B.C.) introduced any radically new dramatic motifs in their adaptations from the Greek. They altered the details of some social customs and brought in fresh jokes; they rearranged episodes and combined parts of plots from separate originals; and Terence constructed his plays with a novel effect of suspense in view.[2] But it seems extremely probable that such re-shuffling of the elements of the plot was normal practice with their Athenian predecessors as well; neither Plautus nor Terence seems to have invented any new cards.

Moreover, while the crafty slave is the commonest type of trickster in Roman comedy, he is not the only one. In *Curculio* and Terence's *Phormio* the trickster is a helpful parasite; in *Truculentus*, a wily courtesan. In *Amphitryon*, it is Mercury; in *Casina* it is the old matron, Cleustrata, and the 'good-for-nothing young slave', Chalinus, merely carries out her plan. Apart from Aristophanes's *Plutus*, *Amphitryon* is the only nearly complete surviving representative of a type of play still popular in Middle Comedy, the mythological burlesque (especially the travesty of a myth of a divine birth); T. B. L. Webster would attribute the unknown Greek original to a date c. 330 B.C.[3] In *Casina* (from a play by Diphilus, c. 330/20),[4] old Lysidamus, who schemes to seduce his son's girl by means of a faked marriage, harks back to the riotously rejuvenated elders in the *Wasps* and the *Clouds*, like the other fathers who compete with their sons in Plautus's *Bacchides* (from Menander) and his *Mercator* (from Philemon). Neither the heroine nor the son appears on the stage in *Casina* (the latter, says the prologue, because 'Plautus did not wish it'); so that the characters who do appear are divided into two camps, the women against the men, except that Chalinus plays the women's game by deceiving the old would-be deceiver and dressing up as the mock-bride. This farcical scheme recalls the 'women's plays' of Aristophanes, with their quasi-ritualistic sex battles,[5] and particularly the female impersonations in the *Thesmophoriazusae*. The vein of comic trickery is continuous.

---

[1] *Ibid.* p. 69; cf Legrand, *New Greek Comedy*, pp. 104–16; Frank, *Literature in the Roman Republic*, p. 80; Chalmers, 'Plautus and his Audience', pp. 24, 39; Segal, *Roman Laughter*, pp. 36–7.

[2] Gordon Williams, '*Pseudolus*' and 'Roman Marriage Ceremonies'; cf Frank, *Literature in the Roman Republic*, ch. 4; Beare, *Roman Stage*, pp. 88ff, 300ff; Duckworth, *Roman Comedy*, ch. 7; Laidlaw, 'Roman Drama', pp. 246, 254–6; Hanson, 'Scholarship on Plautus since 1950', pp. 106ff.

[3] Webster, *Later Greek Comedy*, pp. 16–19, 85–97.

[4] *Ibid.*, pp. 161ff, 240.   [5] *Cf* Huizinga, *Homo Ludens*, p. 68.

In order to buy out the heroine from the establishment of the slave-dealer and procurer Ballio, on his young master's behalf, the comic slave Pseudolus (who gives his name to another comedy by Plautus) devises a series of confidence tricks and impersonates one of Ballio's servants, thus intercepting the purchase-money for the girl from a wealthy soldier. Here the trickster pretends to be another individual of the same status. But in *Amphitryon* and *Casina* the trickster's disguise crosses the boundaries of status or sex and appears to combine opposing qualities – man and woman, or god and slave. And transpositions of role as extreme as these are typical of Old Comedy. Dicaeopolis, the displaced farmer, becomes lord of the market; and so, in effect, does Chremylus, in *Plutus*. Philocleon tells the dancing-girl he has carried off in his drunken spree that she will be his concubine when his son dies (*Wasps*, 1351), but at present his son watches over him strictly, 'because I am young...and his only father'. The sexes change political roles (and dress) in Aristophanes's 'women's plays'. Trygaeus and Peithetaerus become like birds, and marry goddesses, while the gods come down to the level of *alazones*. Dionysus, intermediary between the living and the dead, is both dandy and hero and (like Mercury) god and slave. Some of these disguises or transformations in Aristophanes (like the loan of stage costume to Dicaeopolis) cannot be explained in terms of plot, or of plot alone; and some can hardly be called disguises at all, since (as Dicaeopolis emphasises) there is no doubt who the trickster is, in spite of the change in his appearance or his attributes. But a metamorphosis is essential to each play.

From a surviving summary (*c.* A.D. 200) and the surviving fragments of a play by Cratinus, the major predecessor of Aristophanes, it appears that such theatrical metamorphoses were specially connected with Dionysus: in the *Dionysalexandros* (430 B.C. – 'Dionysus-as-Alexander', another name for Paris of Troy), Dionysus, disguised as Paris, first contrived the famous contest of the goddesses on Mount Ida, with himself as arbiter, carried off Helen as his prize, and then, taking fright on the arrival of the Greeks, took on the form of a ram – an ineffective disguise, since the real Paris easily detected him, married Helen and sent Dionysus to the Greeks. The ancient commentator observes that 'in the play Pericles is satirised most convincingly by innuendo for having involved Athens in the war'; but it is clear that, as in Aristophanes, much of the sacred myth is preserved beside the political innuendo, since at the beginning of the play as summarised the chorus of Satyrs 'mock and jeer' at Dionysus, but in the end they accompany him to Greece, 'comforting him and declaring that they will not desert him'.[1] The burlesque ridicules the god and then restores his mythical image and function, after a paradoxically appropriate double metamorphosis.

The related examples of the *Frogs* in particular, but also of the travestied ritual in the *Thesmophoriazusae* and of the re-education of the two fathers in the *Wasps* and the *Clouds*, suggest that the underlying pattern of these changes of personality springs from rituals of initiation; and, if so, the central and ambiguous role of the buffoon may be shaped by reminiscences both of the hierophant (or medicine-man) who guides the initiate through a sequence of ordeals and illusions, and of the initiate himself, who thereby gains a new personality and passes from one phase of existence to another. The stage trickster overcomes contradictions and conjoins two (or more) styles of life in one. And the more extreme and farcical a situation in classical comedy, the more likely its connexion with ritual or myth. It is the rational, critical strain in the mind of Aristophanes's age, however, that makes fantastic situations palpable as logical absurdity or paradox and transfers the mystery of shape-changing from ritual to comedy. And the idea of shape-changing, as a self-evident game which yet has latent mythical and Dionysiac associations, remains closely identified with the idea of comedy as such, down to Plautus and Terence. In Plautus, particularly, the trickster is a go-between in several senses. Not only is he an agent in a sexual intrigue, but he causes apparent changes of status in himself or others, often across extremes, as in Old Comedy, and he brings about an ironic meeting and exchange between opposing social attitudes or values.

Mercury's usurpation of the appearance of Amphitryon's slave, Sosia, is plainly a sub-plot added to the principal tragic myth of Jupiter's impersonation of the general, his liaison with Alcmena and his fathering of Hercules. Its effect in Plautus's 'tragicomedy' is partly to double the scenes of human bewilderment, partly to reassure the audience about Alcmena (I.ii), partly to ridicule Sosia's boasting, cowardice and greed, and theatrical slaves at large, and partly to underline the mortal frailties of the gods in myth. In his long prologue, requesting a favourable hearing from the audience and explaining the

---

1 Cratinus, *Dionysalexandros*, ed. and trans. Edmonds, *Attic Comedy*, vol. I, pp. 33ff. See Norwood, *Greek Comedy*, pp. 118–22; Pieters, *Cratinus*, p. 211; Guthrie, *Greeks and their Gods*, ch. 6; Jeanmaire, *Dionysos*, pp. 97ff, 278ff; cf p. 90, n. 2, above.

plot, Mercury speaks for the gods as actors (20ff, 86ff):

My father... well knows the reverence and fear due to Jupiter. Just the same, he has ordered me to appeal to you politely and mildly. For the Jupiter who has ordered me here dreads a fiasco like any of you. Born of a mortal mother and a mortal father, it's hardly surprising if he's apprehensive... Don't wonder why Jupiter should concern himself about actors today. There's nothing surprising in it: Jupiter himself is going to play this comedy.

And Jupiter (presumably the 'father' of the troupe) likewise reminds the spectators that he is not the Amphitryon he appears to be (III.i):

I'm the one who lives in the upper story and is pleased to be Jupiter now and then. But the moment I arrive here, I become Amphitryon and change my costume. This time I've come in your honour, so as not to leave the comedy unfinished; also, to bring help to Alcmena.

Far from being extra-dramatic, as alleged by many critics, with their dogma of stage illusion, such asides and *doubles-entendres* addressed to the audience in the prologue or in the course of the play, like the parabasis in Aristophanes, are of the very stuff of ancient comedy. To say that the gods are actors and the actors are gods is to insinuate a special claim for the art, however modest or equivocal. And the theme of dual personality becomes the main current of the play. Even before he meets Mercury, Sosia, noticing how the night has stopped still (on Jupiter's command), thinks that the stars or the sun must be 'drunk' (I.i; 272, 282). He is easily terrified by his double, and almost convinced (438):

– Who am I, at all events, if I'm not Sosia? I'm asking you, as a question.
– When I don't want to be Sosia, you are Sosia, for sure.

The slave believes he must have been 'changed' or have died without remembering it, or have been deprived of his own 'image' (455–9), as if by magic (*imago* meant a mask, as well as a likeness or an apparition). When Sosia assures his master that he is in two places at once – in the house and on the stage (II.i.561) – Amphitryon believes he is drunk (574) or crazy (580, 585) or bewitched (605); and when Alcmena, in good faith, duplicates the confusion (II.ii), Amphitryon thinks that his wife must be dreaming (726) or raving (696, 728) or possessed (777) or enchanted (830), while Sosia – who has had more direct experience in such matters – advances the suggestion that she has been seized by a Bacchic frenzy (703–4) and that her condition is a false pregnancy, due to her madness (718–19). He so far persuades

Amphitryon that the latter believes Alcmena may be a sorceress, who has made him doubt his own whereabouts (789, 844). By this point the comedy has reached the ground of Euripides's *Alcmena*, and also, as has been pointed out, the territory of his *Bacchae*.[1] Sosia has even infected the heroic theme of the birth of Hercules with the idea of Dionysiac mania. But the play ends, after an earth-shaking miracle (as in the *Bacchae*), with an explanatory assurance to Amphitryon from Jupiter that there is no call to send for exorcists or soothsayers, and an appeal from Amphitryon to the audience to applaud 'for the high Jupiter's sake'. Much as in Cratinus and Aristophanes, mythical travesty returns by a comic detour towards serious myth. The divine and the histrionic interweave until they almost change places.

The concept of mysteries or initiation seems at first far removed from the women's counter-intrigue in *Casina*, whereby the supposed serving-maid is married, ostensibly to another servant of the household, and the real Chalinus, the young slave in disguise, thrashes his pretended husband and his old master. But besides these reversals of role due to a deception and a counter-deception, there is another, in the form of parody. The Greek play evidently contained a mock-ceremony of marriage, which Plautus has embellished and Romanised (IV.iii–iv).[2] In a mock-prothalamion, the older woman leading the pretended bride across the threshold exhorts her to 'begin this journey auspiciously', so as always to be 'uppermost' with her husband, to 'triumph' over him, to 'command', 'despoil' and 'deceive' him, night and day (815–24). Throughout the song, with its liturgical insistence, the idea of a wife's military domination over her husband, the complete reversal of Roman ethics, runs along with the obscene joke the singer has in view. And after the bridal night, the housemaid who is in the secret mocks the ostensible bridegroom (v.i.896) by asking him whether 'Casina' has been sufficiently *morigera* – using the quasi-ceremonial word, 'almost a technical term' (it has been explained), that incapsulated the faithful complyingness and submissiveness expected of a Roman wife.[3] The sex-disguise is extended to become the triumph of a shrew. And this initiation-in-reverse has been identified with the essence of the comedy, first by the prologue, which reminds the audience that 'Plautus' controls the story (65)

[1] Stewart, 'The *Amphitruo* of Plautus and Euripides' *Bacchae*'; Webster, *Later Greek Comedy*, pp. 86–8; Costa, 'The Amphitryo Theme'.

[2] Williams, 'Roman Marriage Ceremonies'; *cf* Ernout (ed. and trans.), *Plaute*, vol. II, p. 209n.

[3] Williams, 'Roman Marriage Ceremonies', pp. 19–21.

and points out, tongue in cheek, that marriage ceremonies between slaves, however strange to Roman eyes, are customary in 'Greece' and elsewhere, where they are celebrated 'with even more pomp' than the weddings of freemen (67–78); and then again by the housemaid, who tells the audience (IV.i; 759–62) that there has never been a 'game' like the trick her mistress is springing on her master, 'not even at the Nemean or Olympic games'. *Facere ludos* meant both 'to celebrate the games' or festival and 'to deceive, to play a trick' on someone;[1] this double meaning is central to the idea of comedy in Plautus.

Towards the end of *Mostellaria* (*The Haunted House*), again, Tranio mocks his master, old Theopropides (v.iii; 1149):

If you are a friend of Diphilus or Philemon, you can tell them how your slave played the fool with you. You'll provide them with first-rate deceptions for comedies.

Tranio has set himself the impossible task of preventing the father, unexpectedly returned to Athens after a business voyage, from discovering the son's debauchery; his *ludificationes* have made the substance of the farce. To keep the father from entering his own home, he has pretended that the house is haunted; to explain away the son's debts, he has pretended that the young man has bought the house next door. He even imposes on their next-door neighbour to second him while he shows Theopropides what an admirable investment the purchase has been; and during the tour of inspection he amuses himself by drawing his master's attention to a non-existent picture of a crow teasing a pair of vultures (III.ii; 832–40). This is an echo from Aristophanes' buffoons. Early in the play (I.ii; 85–156) the young rake has compared himself to a well-built, expensively decorated house where the roof leaks and the beams rot because of the tenant's neglect; but Tranio's lies have emptied a house, bought another and improved it as well. Having helped to debauch his young master (I.i), he saves him from his father's anger; in a sense, he is a real guardian. And he communicates with the dead. It was possibly the motif of superstition in this play that suggested it to Jonson as his working model for *The Alchemist*.

The trickster's connexion with ironic transposition of values comes out again in the *Miles Gloriosus* (one of the most influential of Latin

[1] Ernout (ed. and trans.), *Plaute*, vol. II, p. 205n; *cf* Huizinga, *Homo Ludens*, pp. 35–6.

plays in the Renaissance). The braggart warrior, Pyrgopolynices, has bought out a young Athenian's mistress from her mother, taking the girl with him to Ephesus, and has also by chance acquired the Athenian's slave, Palaestrio; the plot consists of the slave's 'fine fetches and skilful stratagems' against the soldier. The first is a *trompe-l'oeil* – making the heroine appear as both herself and her (fictitious) identical twin. The second is two-sided – wheedling the soldier into sending away the heroine with her lover (who is disguised as a shipmaster) in exchange for a rendezvous with a supposedly adoring and supposedly married woman next door (so that he can then be thrashed as a would-be adulterer). For these tricks Palaestrio and his original master need the willing and 'obedient' connivance of the next-door neighbour, a wealthy and white-haired citizen named Periplectomenus; and a lengthy dialogue (III.i; 615–737) is devoted to explaining why this eldery Ephesian patrician should go so far out of his way for a young Athenian stranger. Periplectomenus is a youthful and amorous '*semisenex*' (649) in the style of Old Comedy, the direct opposite of the bombastic, absurdly gullible mercenary. He is what Bdelycleon in *The Wasps* had wanted his father to become, 'a witty raconteur and an agreeable boon companion' (*vel cauillator facetus uel conuiua commodus*, 642). Unlike Philocleon, he knows better than to drink out of turn or paw a fellow-guest's *protégée* (652); but his 'youthful manners' have something of the clown, just the same, since he can turn himself at will into a stern adviser or a consoler mild as the zephyr, a merry guest, a bounteous host, or even a lascivious dancer (661–8). At the same time, he refuses to marry and raise a family; he means to keep his freedom and be flattered by his expectant kinsmen (678–715). Upon which Palaestrio observes that, if the gods were really just (like good inspectors fixing prices in the market), they would reward such delightful characters with long life, and cut short the lives of rascals (725–35). But these social paradoxes do not prevent the two of them from leading the soldier into a trap, ostensibly to vindicate the cause of matrimony.

The bachelor's enjoyment in keeping his heirs on a string seems like a Roman touch; otherwise, his character and the nature of the story are in keeping with the reputation of Ephesus.[1] He is the quintessential, semi-mythical reveller, as opposed to the *alazon* – and to Roman *gravitas*. Presumably this scheme of things is part of Shakespeare's meaning when he calls Falstaff's ageing light-o'-loves at the

[1] Trenkner, *Greek Novella*, pp. 8, 131, 171.

Boar's Head 'Ephesians,...of the old church' (*2 Henry IV*, II.ii.143). And a recollection of Plautus is almost certainly active at the Garter Inn in *The Merry Wives*, where Falstaff occupies a room 'painted about with the story of the Prodigal' while he spins intrigues that fall out like the braggart soldier's, and where his jovial Host is a self-styled 'Ephesian' (IV.v). Especially in the latter play, the elements of Plautus's reveller and his impostor have been re-combined to form the role of Falstaff.

The glorification and self-commendation of the trickster are carried even further in Plautus than the praise of the schemer's daring and cleverness and the poet's self-praise for originality in Aristophanes. Palaestrio, urged to rally his forces and summon auxiliaries, to intercept the enemy's convoys and preserve his legions' line of supply, tersely accepts the responsibility of command, and admits Periplectomenus to his council of war (II.ii; 218ff); he will mount his 'engines' (or contrivances: *machinas*, 813) against Pyrgopolynices, as soon as he has 'his troops ranged by centuries'; they spring to his orders as their 'general' (IV.iii; 1160). Similarly, Pseudolus in his play will 'engage his enemies' – Ballio the slave-dealer, the soldier and his old master – with 'a double and triple line of ruses and stratagems', 'investing' and 'storming' Ballio's 'stronghold' (*Pseudolus* II.i; 573ff); he will 'lead his legions to battle in rank beneath their standards, since the birds are on the left and the auspices are clear' (II.iv; 761). Tranio, in *The Haunted House*, rates his own 'immortal, single-handed exploits' above the 'vaunted feats' of Alexander and Agathocles (775), even before he has 'disengaged his troops from the blockade' (1048). In a long monologue in the *Bacchides* (IV.ix; 925–77) the contriving slave, Chrysalus, compares himself in detail with Ulysses – a favourite paragon – and elevates himself above the Greek commanders for their reputed glory in subduing Troy, with all their equipment, their fleet and their warriors, after a ten-year siege:

Child's play, beside the assault I'm going to make on my master, without any fleet or any army or any such array of troops.

Such rodomontade and self-comparison with Greek heroes is frequent with Plautus's comic characters and significant of his attitude towards his world;[1] writing in the first age of the Republic's military expansion (and contact with Greek literature), he ridicules the

---

[1] Ernout (ed. and trans.), *Plaute*, vol. V, p. 62n; Arnaldi, *Da Plauto a Terenzio*, vol. I, p. 183; *cf* Grenier, *Le Génie Romain*, p. 171.

pompous language of triumphal announcements for the entertainment of an audience of citizen-campaigners: his vainglorious slave is a counterpart to the vainglorious soldier.[1] But the honorific descriptions bestowed on tricksters are not drawn only from warfare; Palaestrio is a 'senator' and an 'architect', for instance (592, 915). And Plautus makes a great show of the trickster's rising to difficulties and thinking out his plans. Palaestrio asks for 'a little silence', while he 'convokes his thoughts in council' (II.ii; 196); and Periplectomenus, respectfully stepping aside, points out to the audience how he frowns in cogitation, taps his breast 'as if to call out his intelligence', turns, counts with his fingers, slaps his thigh in the strain of thinking, shakes his head and rests his chin on his hand, monumentally, 'just like a comedy slave', while the man of thought obviously goes through the motions. Pseudolus (said to be one if the author's favourite creations) is more explicit about his brain-work. At first (I.iv; 394) he has to admit to himself that he has no plan at all to back up his promises; nevertheless –

just as a poet, tablets in hand, wants to find something that is nowhere on earth, and discovers it after all, giving the likeness of truth to a lie, so I, too, will be a poet.

Alone again at the end of this scene (562), he ventures a guess that the audience still think he is bluffing, but manages to turn their doubts to his own credit by a show of candour:

When an actor appears on the stage, he should really introduce some new device in a new manner. If he cannot, he should give place to someone who can. I want to take myself off for a while inside, while I mentally marshal my snares... You won't be kept waiting long; meanwhile, the flute player will entertain you.

If the trickster in Plautus is no longer a magician, he is at least a conjurer who takes the audience part-way into his secrets, the better to display his skill. His confidential, self-appreciative monologue became common form in the Renaissance; for example, with Corbolo, the servant in Ariosto's *Lena* (1528):

Now I'd need the artful dodges of the servants I've seen invented in comedies to know the fraud and deceit to milk this sum from the old man's purse. But even if I am no Davus or Sosia, and wasn't born in Syria or Thrace

[1] See Hanson, 'The Glorious Military'; Frank, *Literature in the Roman Republic*, pp. 68–69.

haven't I some trickery in this noddle as well? Don't I also know how to plot a device that fortune can weave, who usually favours the bold, they say? But what shall I do, as I don't have a credulous old man to deal with, like the Chremes or Simo Terence or Plautus usually invent? Still, the greater his caution, isn't mine the greater glory if I catch him in a trap? (III.1)

The renaissance schemer tries to surpass the classics in the very act of imitating them; but the impulse in this direction comes from classical comedy, too.

Besides the speeches in *Pseudolus* where the slave appears to discuss his part with the audience, there are other asides and references to comedy in the dialogue, which may either break the illusion (or rather, the thread of the plot) for a moment, or unexpectedly reinforce it. When the young lover, Calidorus, asks Pseudolus to explain a part of his intrigue, the latter replies (II.iii; 720): 'This play is being acted for the spectators' benefit; they know what happened, because they were present; I'll tell you afterwards.' But later, when the slave's confidence tricks on Ballio and on his old master, Simo, have been carried out, but the dupes are as yet unaware of it, a similar allusion works the other way. Simo comes to meet the procurer, asking himself ironically whether his own 'Ulysses' (Pseudolus) has carried off the 'palladium' (the mistress his son had wanted but could not pay for) from the 'Ballionian citadel' (IV.vi; 1063); he hopes to collect a wager from Ballio if the enterprise has failed. And Ballio reassures him gleefully, since he is persuaded that the soldier has bought the girl from him instead. Describing an earlier scene, his meeting with Calidorus and Pseudolus, he brushes off their abuse of him as theatrical commonplace (1080):

– What did he say [asks Simo]? What did he tell you? Tell me, what did he talk about?
– Theatrical nonsense; the insults they always hurl the procurer in comedies, which every child knows: he called me a blight and a scoundrel and a perjurer.

The irony of values here and the irony of situation are clinched by the reference to comedies; as a modern Italian critic, Arnaldi, remarks on this passage, 'it is the usual game, typical of *Pseudolus*, of playing with perspectives, between the stage and living reality, which in this case is going to work out ironically in a striking victory for comedy over life'. The remark, and the passage, suggest Pirandello; but, as Arnaldi also says, Plautus must be doing no more than refining on the motif of 'a comedy about comedy' (*'la commedia della commedia'*) that he found in Menander.[1] Comedy had been a kind of play that dealt with other plays, in the form of burlesque, since the time of Cratinus and Aristophanes; the *Thesmophoriazusae* has inset scenes from Euripides, and the *Frogs* dramatises a dramatic contest. And complicity between actors and audience, round the edge, as it were, of the subject for the time being, recalling the permanence of the festival as against the topicality of the present argument, had been inherent in the dual nature of Old Comedy. The performance belonged to the city's festival, the actors were actors, the stage was the stage.

Echoes of this department of irony, with respect to the theatre itself, are also found in Plautus, and passed from him to the Renaissance. In the prologue to the *Menaechmi*, for instance (there are no such confidential prologues in tragedy, naturally):

This city is Epidamnus, while the present play is being acted. When the play is changed, it will be another town. The members of the company change in the same way: the same one is sometimes a procurer, sometimes a youth, sometimes an old man; poor man, beggar, king, parasite, soothsayer...

In the theatre Plautus knew, the scenery, 'such as it was,...probably remained unchanged from play to play';[2] in Menander's theatre, there were probably three sets, one each for tragedies, comedies and satyr plays,[3] but, even so, the architectural background was still plainly visible while 'the imaginary background changed', as one play succeeded another in the course of each day of the festival.[4] And the same literary or imaginative convention about the scene of comedy held good for the enclosed theatres, temporary or lasting, in Italian renaissance courts, decorated with illusionistic painted scenery. For the first production, at Urbino in 1513, of Bibbiena's comedy, *La Calandria* (based on the *Menaechmi*), the stage (according to a letter of Castiglione) 'represented a very beautiful city, with streets, palaces, churches, and towers', where 'the streets looked as if they were real, and everything was done in relief, and made even more striking through the art of painting and well-conceived perspective'.[5] But Bibbiena's Argument (or second prologue), while stating that the scene is Rome, plays against the illusion:

Don't imagine, though, that they [the actors] could come here so quickly

---

[1] Arnaldi, *Da Plauto a Terenzio*, vol I, pp. 174, 188.
[2] Beare, *Roman Stage*, p. 170.
[3] Webster, *Greek Theatre Production*, pp. 17–28, 109, 166–70.
[4] Beare, *Roman Stage*, p. 266.
[5] Castiglione's letter, in Nagler (ed.), *Source Book*, p. 71.

from Rome by witchcraft; because the city you see here is Rome: which used to be so extensive, so spacious, so great that, in her days of triumph, she could receive many cities and countries and rivers spread out within her; but now has become so little that, as you see, she fits comfortably into this city of yours. So goes the world.

Similarly, Ariosto, in the prologue to his *Negromante*, performed at the ducal palace in Ferrara just after his *Lena*, in the Carnival of 1528, plays with the relationship between the visible and the imaginary scene. Just as Orpheus caused beasts and even trees to follow him, and Apollo's song built the walls of Troy, so, says the actor, 'here today you will find all of Cremona moved hither with its people':

I know that some will say that [the city] is like, perhaps even that it is the same, that was called Ferrara, when *Lena* was acted; but take heed and remember that it is Carnival, when people disguise themselves; and the costumes they wear today were someone else's yesterday, and tomorrow they will give them to someone else again; and tomorrow they will put on another dress, which someone else has today. This, as I've said, is Cremona, the noble city of Lombardy, which presents itself here with the clothes and the mask that Ferrara wore formerly.

This quizzical moralising about the physical properties of the stage[1] clearly goes back, through Plautus, to Aristophanes.

Despite the continuity in the spirit of comedy from Aristophanes to Plautus, however, there were, of course, fundamental changes in the transition to New Comedy, which affected renaissance comedy deeply as well. These changes were mainly connected with the shift of the centre of interest within comedy from the city to the individual. The other large-scale shifts of interest, from politics to money-power and from myth to domestic conditions, tended towards the same results, if they were not at bottom expressions of the same historical process.

The irony of Old Comedy affected the mental image of the whole city-state, its myths, ideals and principles of thought and conduct; it is hardly surprising that Plato gave Aristophanes a place of honour in his *Symposium*, in spite of the latter's caricature of Socrates. In New Comedy, little more than a persistent memory of irony on this scale remains. The people in Old Comedy represent the collective personality of the city; in New Comedy, little more than themselves.

[1] Ariosto, *Commedie*, ed. Catilano; *cf* Radcliffe-Umstead, *Birth of Modern Comedy*, p. 85.

From wonder-worker, paradoxical sage and king of the revels, the comic buffoon has shrunk to an impudent trickster, the abetter of youthful debaucheries, dealing in 'pelting matters' fit for 'Bridewell' (as Ascham was to say) such as theft, fraud and false pretences. This marks one decisive change: the demotion of the comic trickster, the devolution of his still indispensable role from citizen to slave.

Secondly, in New Comedy the personal aspect of sexual life has been almost separated from the social aspect. Sexual themes in Aristophanes combine noisy obscenity with ideas of pleasure and domestic happiness, of the continuity of the city and of natural fertility. His typical heroes are not only buffoons, but full citizens, elderly or apparently ageless, husbands and fathers; or else mature women like Lysistrata and Praxagora who take over the political role of their husbands (it is significant, perhaps that the myth Aristophanes expounds in the *Symposium* deals with a primordial unity of the sexes). Menander's heroes are young lovers or newly-created fathers, with, as yet, no family experience or responsibilities, just as they seem to have no voice in the state. Love for them, whether pleasure or sentiment, has no public resonance, either solemn or obscene. The implicit theme of most of the comedies is their sexual initiation, their entry into manhood. And in this they are regularly opposed to their fathers – another split in the central personality-role of Aristophanes. The opposition between fathers and sons in the *Clouds* and the *Wasps* turns on social philosophy, not sex; in New Comedy it is a conflict between two age-groups whose essential outlook is the same, usually a struggle over money occasioned by love, but sometimes (as in *Casina* and *Mercator*) a direct sexual rivalry. Occasionally, as in Terence's *Self-Tormentor* and his *Brothers* (both from Menander) the father's attitude towards his son is brought forward for discussion; but in general the action is presented entirely from the younger man's point of view. This shift in what may be called the operative age-level of comedy was, of course, to be lasting.

Thirdly, town is separated from country. It is true that this split was apparent by the end of Aristophanes' career; *Plutus* reflects the impoverishment of Attic farmers after the Peloponnesian War, while the contrast there between the Just Man and the Informer symbolises the chicanery and injustice of the town.[1] But the heroes and elders of his early plays were both farmers and town-dwellers (if town-dwellers against their will) and, in any case, full citizens. The old

---

[1] *Cf* Ehrenberg, *People of Aristophanes*, pp. 82–94.

men in the *Wasps*, town-dwellers with a rustic outlook,[1] are 'morose' (*dyskolos*, 106, 1105) from poverty and from envy of young careerists (1059–121); they find compensation in their fees for jury-service – the equivalent of an old age pension[2] – and in the sense of power this brings them, with its 'derision of wealth'; in other words, through the politico-legal institutions of the city. In contrast, Cnemon, the *Bad-tempered Man* (*Dyskolos*) in Menander, who has resented money-grabbing and inequality in much the same way,[3] has reacted by re-treating in dudgeon to his farm; the just society he dreams of is a world of solitaries, like himself. The father in *The Self-Tormentor* punishes himself by hard work on his farm, whereas a return to their farms had been the longing of Dicaeopolis and Trygaeus. Urban and rustic manners are contrasted in plays like Plautus's *Haunted House* and *Truculentus* and Terence's *Brothers*, sometimes with the hint that the latter preserve an old-fashioned probity, but always with the presumption that their interest is no more than marginal.

Instead of farming, the background of New Comedy is trade. War affects the plot of Plautus's *Captives* (from an original by Philemon, *c.* 280 B.C.),[4] and young soldiers (not braggarts) have just returned from service in Menander's *Perikeiromene* (*The Unkindest Cut*) and his *Sicyonian* (*c.* 313); Daemones, in Plautus's *Rudens* (from a play by Diphilus, *c.* 310), is an Athenian driven into exile by legal, or possibly, political oppression.[5] But there is little or no discussion of state policy in the plays. And, by contrast with the occasional influence of war on the action, nearly every plot surviving from New Comedy is affected by a business journey at one point or another. The people of Aristophanes seem to be cooped up in Athens; the people in New Comedy are repeatedly travelling, and come from as far afield as Carthage and Persia. Menaechmus (the traveller) was born at Syracuse; his twin brother was lost during a business trip to Tarentum; when he lands at Epidamnus in Illyria (the modern Durazzo), in search of his brother, he and his slave are already supposed to have visited Spain, Marseilles and the cities on both sides of the Adriatic. Sometimes (as in *The Andrian* and *Phormio*) a business voyage long before the action of the play begins has produced a daughter in a secret liaison; more often, it is the return of the father or of the son he has sent abroad on

---

[1] *Ibid.* p. 85.   [2] Walker, 'The Periclean Democracy', p. 105.
[3] Menander, *Plays and Fragments*, trans. Vellacott, p. 91; (*Il Misantropo* [*Dyskolos*], ed. and trans. Marzullo, lines 718ff).
[4] Webster, *Later Greek Comedy*, pp. 145–7.   [5] *Ibid.* p. 104.

family business that precipitates the immediate action. Sometimes kidnapping by pirates affects the story; conversely, poverty induces parents (as in *Casina*) to abandon an infant daughter they cannot afford to keep. Again, the typical *alazones* – the slave-dealers and mercenaries – are outsiders who owe their place in the story to finance. The scene is still usually Athens, but not always; it may be Epidamnus or Ephesus or near Cyrene, anywhere on the broad inner ring of hellenistic civilisation. But the urban institutions at the basis of the play (partly romanised by Plautus and Terence, to be sure) and the imagined network of travel and sea-trade are always much the same. The results of trading and finance dictate the tricksters' schemes in New Comedy and govern the direction of the plots.

In spite of the impression of movement and adventure, however, and the geographical extension of the stories in the plays composed during the generation after Alexander the Great, New Comedy is still curiously inward-looking. It is still focused on the typical bourgeois family, embedded in familiar urban surroundings, with 'friends and kinsfolk and festivals',[1] clinging to the social privilege of citizenship, and preoccupied with the internal and personal tensions that will affect its survival as a patrilineal group.[2] Marriage is a burden, especially marriage with a woman who, as the wife's father says in the *Menaechmi* (v.ii), is overbearing and presumptuous because of her dowry. The old fathers in the plays resent it, almost unanimously; but that does not prevent them from interfering, with a show of moral authority, in the affairs of their sons- and daughters-in-law (as in Menander's *Arbitration*, *Stichus*, and Terence's *Mother-in-Law*). For their sons, a love-match is all the more precious (as in *The Andrian*) because it implies an alternative to a marriage of convenience. Or else they seek their love outside marriage, with professionals. But in the plays dealing with love and marriage, the issue at stake in the plot is the recognition of an infant's paternity, his right of membership in a citizen family – as it is even in *Amphitryon*, the rule-proving exception of a play which deals with a wife's adultery. (Even in the *Menaechmi*, which is also exceptional because it shows a marriage breaking up, the Epidamnian husband returns to his father's home in Syracuse.) Similarly, in those comedies, like *Pseudolus*, which

---

[1] Terence, *The Mother-in-Law*, IV.ii.591.
[2] See Gomme, 'Menander', p. 264; Legrand, *New Greek Comedy*, pp. 135–8; Post, *From Homer to Menander*, pp. 237, 242; Webster, *Menander*, pp. 59ff. *Cf* Ferguson, *Hellenistic Athens*, pp. 68, 78–85; Tarn, *Hellenistic Civilization*, pp. 100–2.

deal with love outside marriage, the courtesan figures in the plot largely as a cause of opposition over money between father and son; or, by way of variation, the son finds an unexpected ally in his father (in Plautus's *Asinaria*) or in a father-substitute, as with Periplectomenus in *The Braggart Soldier*; or the concealment and subsequent revelation of a child's paternity makes the groundwork of the intrigue, as in *Truculentus*, with its sardonic picture of a courtesan's machinations. A common motif, as in *The Andrian*, again, and *Rudens*, is the discovery that a desired mistress too poor to make an acceptable match, or apparently in servile status as a courtesan, is in fact the daughter of a citizen family. On the other hand, the occasional liberation of a male slave at the end of a play is merely a bonus, not an objective of the plot. In spite of the opening out of the hellenistic world, and the breakdown of the political framework of the city – the very factors making for a new ethic of cosmopolitanism, as in the philosophy of the Stoics – the writers of New Comedy cling to the institution of the family at the heart of the old *polis*.

Indeed, hellenistic scholars traced the origins of New Comedy, not to the period when Athens was overwhelmed by Macedon, but to the period of the loss of her empire and the crisis in her democracy at the end of the Peloponnesian War. According to some, it was Aristophanes who led the way; when financial depression made elaborate choruses too expensive and the eclipse of democracy made personal satire dangerous, it was said that he turned away from politics and, at the end of his career, produced one new play (*Cocalus*, 387 B.C.), which contained 'rape, recognition, and all the other characteristics imitated by Menander'.[1] Others attributed New Comedy plots to the influence of Euripides, who (as Aristophanes had scornfully noted) had first brought love-stories to the forefront in tragedy.[2] According to the Alexandrian biographer of Euripides, Satyrus (*c.* 200 B.C.),

quarrels between husband and wife, father and son, servant and master, or situations involving sudden changes of fortune [*peripeteia*], substitution of children, violations of girls, and recognition by rings and necklaces;...all this is really the mainstay of New Comedy, and it was Euripides who perfected it.

There can be little question that Euripides influenced the writers of New Comedy profoundly, and that one of the main differences

[1] Edmonds (ed. and trans.), *Attic Comedy*, vol. I, pp. 572, 671.
[2] Lesky, *Greek Literature*, pp. 370, 385–7, 655–6.

between them and their predecessors is their using tragedy as a model instead of as a subject for burlesque,[1] though it is also possible that some stories reached Euripides and New Comedy alike by way of folk-tales.[2] What is significant in the development of Athenian comedy, however, is the writers' preference for 'household matters' and tensions affecting the family.

With this development goes a new form of comedic 'deceit', the concealment of a character's identity. This is never a crucial motif in the surviving plays of Aristophanes, except perhaps where he is guying Euripides in the *Thesmophoriazusae*, and even there the lifting of a disguise leads to a quasi-political reconciliation between Euripides and the women of Athens. But New Comedy plots frequently turn, for their complications and solutions, on an 'error' about someone's personal identity, the removal of which will enable the family to reunite and close its ranks once again. The error often concerns the marriageability of the heroine – who may arouse pathos as a seeming orphan (in *Rudens* and *The Self-Tormentor*, for instance), but seldom appears on the stage (which means, in public) if she is a temporary courtesan destined for rehabilitation, and never if she is already known as a citizen's daughter. Sometimes it is an error within the family itself, involving real or apparent dangers of incest between brother and sister (in *Perikeiromene* and *Epidicus*, for example). Or the mistake may arise from the presence of twins – in the *Menaechmi* and *Bacchides* and, in a sense, *Amphitryon* – or feigned twins, like the heroine in *The Braggart Soldier* who appears and reappears in two adjoining houses thanks to a hidden passage through the wall.

The fondness for twins and doubles in New Comedy implies the influence of folklore.[3] But the most general working rule, which seems to have made such stories appear suitable for treatment in New Comedy, is that there should be confusion over someone's identity; not primarily his psychological identity, his inner self, but his birth, his original name and status. To quote the late grammarian, Diomedes, again, New Comedy can be paralleled with tragedy precisely because the latter contains 'a Discovery of former fortune and family' which takes 'an ill turn', whereas in comedy, 'love-affairs and the abduction of maidens' lead to nothing worse than 'agreeable mistakes'.[4] They are equally mistakes about family status, however. They appear to

[1] Dover, 'Greek Comedy', p. 122.   [2] Trenkner, *Greek Novella*, ch. 4.
[3] *Ibid.*; Murray, 'Ritual Elements in New Comedy', pp. 46–50.
[4] See p. 84, above.

express the anxieties and nostalgias of an age when the tight family structure is felt to be vital and yet insecure. Menaechmus's sister-in-law, to whom he is really a foreigner, mistakes him for his twin. In Plautus's *Captives*, Tyndarus, a purchased prisoner-of-war who had been kidnapped in infancy, imagines himself, in his father's house, to be a slave masquerading as a freeman, while his father imagines that he has merely bought a hostage to exchange for his other son. The slave Sosia, in *Amphitryon*, who is driven to doubt whether he is inside the house or out of it, is another extreme example of such confusion about one's identity (again, not with reference to personal feelings, but with reference to social position, to place). But such 'mistakes' can turn out to be 'agreeable' in New Comedy when the son of the house is free to marry the girl he has seduced, the baby's paternity is acknowledged, or the orphan reclaimed.

The trickster figure has several necessary functions in this comedic society. In a sense, he helps to keep the family going precisely by conveying money from one generation to another (as notably in Plautus's *Aulularia* (*The Pot of Gold*)) – typically, from the father's use to the son's; or, better still, by transferring it to the son's use from unsympathetic outsiders. In a deeper sense, he is the son's guide or guardian, by helping him in his love affairs, where his father is most apt to fail him. His tricks involving doubled or feigned *personae* reproduce the 'agreeable mistakes' that evidently cover (and then assuage) a deep-seated feeling of uneasiness about the family as a well-defined, enduring social entity. And by parodying, sometimes mocking, the qualities of authoritative bourgeois and military men, he is at least a safety-valve for wider feelings of social incongruity. Just as the son's impulsive love releases tension within the family, so the cocksure impudence of the trickster, especially the trickster slave, releases tension in society at large. And, just as the young man's love holds a promise of life-renewal, if not salvation, so with the quick wits of the slave. A man who 'retains a free man's mind though slave', a helpful slave who can be wiser than his master, even a mischievous slave who enjoys cheating his master only when the latter is not a fool,[1] stands for qualities making for human survival against the pressures of fortune and social constriction. With his mock-heroic display of 'cleverness', he is almost (one suspects) a refuge for national pride, in a world where that much-vaunted Greek distinction is of no political avail. And, more generally, as the slave who is not a mere human

[1] See p. 108, above.

instrument, the man who keeps his mental initiative and thereby contradicts his servile status, he brings out the ambiguousness but also the hope of the whole imagined society to which he belongs. He personifies the 'deceit' in social values and circumstances. It is true that the trickster's scope is reduced in New Comedy, as well as his dignity, while the idea of Fortune, borrowed from tragedy, comes to govern much of the plot. But the ironies attaching to the trickster's part run through New Comedy as a whole, where it is indebted to Euripides as well as where it stems from Aristophanes in a continuous line of descent.

And the trickster or the ironies that belong to his part reassume their importance, despite a long series of variations in detail, throughout the tradition of imitating or modernising New Comedy that was introduced by the Renaissance. Ariosto's *I Suppositi* (or *The Substitutes*: the original of Gascoigne's *Supposes*); *Gl'Ingannati* (or *The Deceived*); *A Midsummer Night's Dream*; *Volpone, or The Fox*; *A Trick to Catch the Old One*; *Le Menteur, Les Fourberies de Scapin, Le Malade imaginaire*; *The Way of the World*; *She Stoops to Conquer*...titles such as these denote the omnipresent theme of deceit. More than anything else, it is the invitation to the audience to enjoy an exhibition of some form of deceit that distinguishes comedy from romance in the theatre. The influence given to Fortune in many plots of New Comedy (and hence, in many renaissance comedies as well) makes no fundamental difference here. Nevertheless, it is a complicating factor sufficiently important to require separate consideration.

4

FORTUNE IN CLASSICAL COMEDY

I well consider all that ye have sayd,
And find that all things stedfastnes doe hate
And changed be: yet being rightly wayd
They are not changed from their first estate.

Spenser

This is a matter of no small importance to me. I insist on knowing where you deposited the hand-bag that contained that infant.

The Importance of Being Earnest

Errors prompted by unreason, by vanity, by double meanings, by guile – all these types of 'deceit' listed by Castelvetro can be traced back to Old Comedy. But so far in this discussion of the legacy of classical comedy to the Renaissance there has been no occasion, except in passing, to mention Castelvetro's remaining sub-category, of deceptions caused by chance or fortune. In the main, this important motif was introduced by New Comedy, where it marks one of the main departures from the comic scheme of Aristophanes. But its origins go back earlier.

THE WHEEL OF FORTUNE

In its synonyms and associations, down to the present, the idea of 'fortune' touches a wide span of meanings: haphazard, chance, accident, coincidence, luck, wealth, the unpredictable, adversity, the force of circumstance, even fate. The primary scope of meaning of *tyche*, fortune, in Greek has been explained as the way things 'hit' or turn out, where there is no evident reason;[1] and the connotations of the word were neutral or favourable at first. It stood for a vaguely personified minor deity or daemon, a subordinate nature-spirit. Hesiod (?c. 700 B.C.) includes Tyche among the daughters of Ocean, together with river-deities like the Nile, personifications of wealth such as Plutus, and personifications of aspects of good government like Metis (Wisdom); and the slightly later *Hymn to Demeter* similarly

---

[1] See Pack, 'Tyche'; Lattimore, *Poetry of Greek Tragedy*, p. 88.

names Tyche among the nymphs who welcome Persephone in the underworld, the realm of Pluto, imagined as both the home of the dead and the natural source of wealth.[1] Along this line of mythopoeic thinking, *tyche* was almost indistinguishable from *dike*, the natural, the rightful order of things; it was associated with the profit that came from farming or shipping, with the prosperity of a city. The earliest recorded statue of Tyche (fifth- to fourth-century) showed her with the attributes of a fertility-daemon, carrying a horn of plenty and holding the infant Plutus (Wealth) in her arms.[2] Or *tyche* could mean the 'luck' that (as if by birthright) would never completely forsake a man of noble descent;[3] thus Pindar hails Fortune (472 B.C.) as the 'daughter of Zeus', the 'lady of salvation', who has favoured a political exile in the Olympian games.[4] Most of the references to *tyche* in Aristophanes carry a similarly benign, faintly divinised significance.

In the later fifth and the fourth centuries, however, the Greek conception of Fortune passed through an evolution which implies an intellectual advance, a relapse and a contradiction. Writers began to emphasise the adverse side of *tyche*, contrasting it with human reason and foresight; this indicates the pressure of rationalism, a movement from mythological thinking towards abstraction and systematic analysis,[5] though it may also contain a trace of belief in the natural cussedness of things. On the other side, Fortune was divinised again, no longer, however, encompassed within the old mythology as a daughter of Ocean or of Zeus, but as the unpredictable aspect of a generalised divine power, whether friendly or hurtful; or, finally, as an independent goddess, lacking a mythical ancestry or life-story and a place in the traditional Greek city cults, yet, in popular belief, immensely powerful, more coercive than the Olympians. This semi-mythical, semi-allegorical goddess of hellenistic Greece and of republican and imperial Rome lived on as Dame Fortune in the poetry of the Middle Ages and the sixteenth century.[6] Her well-known

---

[1] Hesiod, *Theogony*, 336–70; *cf Hymn to Demeter*, 405–33. See Lesky, *Greek Literature*, p. 85; Hild, 'Fortuna', p. 1265.

[2] Hinks, *Myth and Allegory in Ancient Art*, pp. 76–83; *cf* Hild, 'Fortuna', p. 1266; Harrison, *Themis*, pp. 241, 282–5, 525–8.

[3] Dodds, *Greeks and the Irrational*, pp. 42, 58.

[4] Pindar, *Olympian* XII (trans. Lattimore). See Pack, 'Tyche'; W. C. Greene, *Moira*, pp. 34, 39, 72.   [5] See Hild, 'Fortuna', p. 1265.

[6] Hild, 'Fortuna', pp. 1266ff; Stock, 'Fortune (Greek)', pp. 94–5; Murray, *Greek Religion*, pp. 131ff; *cf* Coleman-Norton, 'Fortune in Roman Drama', pp. 61–71; Patch, *The Goddess Fortuna*; Chew, 'Time and Fortune'; Mason, *Shakespeare's Tragedies*, pp. 4–19.

attributes, such as the horn of plenty, the rudder and the wheel or sphere, were sufficient to identify her in an emblematic image but not enough to endow her with a humanised personality; she was blind or capricious, unaccountable, unlocatable, the obverse of human intentions and efforts. And yet, by a striking contradiction of thought, one at least of her principal emblems, the wheel, suggests the exact opposite of caprice or unpredictability; it is the very image of regularity. As Cornford observes, 'the wheel of Fortune...does not symbolise chance or accident, but the very reverse'.[1] The persistent association of Fortune with a wheel (or sphere) looks at first like an instinctive effort to rationalise the factor of chance in life and to reconcile it with natural justice, the natural course of things, *dike*; it corresponds to the effort of philosophers, from Plato onwards, to reduce the concept of Fortune to the status of an imperfectly understood expression of the divine reason, providence.[2] But the image of Fortune's wheel also springs from a much older complex of ideas, which were fundamental to drama and which Greek drama helped to perpetuate.

The opposing sides in later conceptions of Fortune can be illustrated by comparing passages from the two great fifth-century historians. For Herodotus (died *c.* 425) the notion of the wheel is important. He makes Croesus, for example, warn Cyrus the Persian that, as a ruler, he should always remember that 'there is a wheel of human affairs whose movement suffers not the same men always to be fortunate' (I.207); ironically, Croesus, who claims that his own fall from fabulous wealth into captivity has made him 'keen-sighted', gives Cyrus advice that leads him to disaster. This 'wheel' gives the outline of Herodotus's main narrative, the conquests and defeat of the Persian empire; kings and plutocrats cannot escape from it, because 'the gods are jealous' of extreme human prosperity (I.32; III.40). And elsewhere, Herodotus mentions 'divine chance' (III.139; IV.8); his view of fortune is basically religious.[3]

In contrast, Thucydides (*c.* 460–*c.* 400 B.C.) expresses, or records, an entirely pragmatic view; in his account of the Athenian debates leading to the Peloponnesian War (in 432–431), he quotes Pericles as telling the assembly that 'sometimes the course of things is as arbitrary as the plans of men; indeed this is why we usually blame

[1] Cornford, *From Religion to Philosophy*, p. 175 and ch. 6, *passim*.
[2] W. C. Greene, *Moira*, ch. 9; *cf*. Cioffari, *Fortune and Fate*, pp. 34ff.
[3] W. C. Greene, *Moira*, pp. 84–8; *cf* Robinson, 'The Wheel of Fortune', p. 208.

chance for whatever does not happen as we expected' (1.140).[1] The only ground common to the two historians in these passages is that each is thinking of the course of political events somewhat like a dramatist, in the light of the main actors' deliberations.

Fortune was depicted by the Romans as standing on a globe and, in the Middle Ages, after Boethius, as turning a wheel.[2] But (as Herodotus shows) the elements of the icon were Greek before they were adopted by the Romans.[3] It comes nearer to the primary meaning of the image to say, not that Fortune stands on a wheel (instability) or that she turns a wheel (volition), but that Fortune *is* the wheel; or rather, in this metaphor, which has never, it seems, expressed a single, unitary idea, but always a state of mental tension, the element of the wheel, that which revolves, is primary, and the personification of Fortune, that which happens to men, is secondary. The wheel image as such stands for the rotation of the stars and the seasons and also recalls one of the crucial technical devices in the archaic civilisations of India and the Near East; in magical and metaphysical thinking, it is a symbol of perfection.[4] Among early Greek philosophers, for example, Parmenides (mid-sixth century) maintained that reality, the One, was 'bounded on every side, like the bulk of a well-rounded sphere'.[5] Parmenides was denying that motion, change, diversity, becoming, inhere in reality at all; but those who took the contrary view also resorted to the concept of rotation or the image of a spherical body in order to convey their theory of the universe. This comes out, for instance, in the earlier saying of Anaximander of Miletus (early sixth century), that all existing things come into being and pass away 'according to necessity; for they pay penalty and retribution to each other for their injustice according to the assessment of Time'; here the notion of a cosmos governed by law, like a well-ordered society, coalesces with the notion of a process in time, through change to a reversion to the original state of composition.[6] As against this, Heraclitus (sixth century) held that conflict within the universe is just and necessary; but the cosmos is nevertheless a unity, and the way of understanding it is like a circle: 'the way up and down

---

[1] W. C. Greene, *Moira*, pp. 268–71.
[2] Hild, 'Fortuna', p. 1277; Patch, *The Goddess Fortuna*, pp. 147–77.
[3] Robinson, 'The Wheel of Fortune'; Harrison, *Themis*, pp. 525–30.
[4] Lenoble, *Histoire de l'idée de Nature*, p. 67; cf Childe, *Man Makes Himself*, pp. 43–6.
[5] Kirk and Raven, *Presocratic Philosophers*, pp. 276, 284; cf Bréhier, *Histoire de la Philosophie*, vol. I, p. 63; Guthrie, *Greek Philosophy*, vol. II, pp. 42–9.
[6] Kirk and Raven, *Presocratic Philosophers*, pp. 117–22; cf Bréhier, *Histoire de la Philosophie*, vol. I, p. 47.

is one and the same'.[1] Empedocles (fifth century), the critic of Parmenides, held a mystical vision of the cosmic cycle, not unlike Anaximander; the universe passed from the rule of love to the rule of strife and back again, so that although 'things never cease from continual shifting,...in so far as they never cease from continual interchange of places, thus far are they ever changeless in the cycle.'[2]

The image of rotation, of spherical movement, was almost compulsive for Greek thinkers when they tried to speculate about the destiny of the soul or to describe the ultimate nature of the universe, the relationship between appearances and reality, change and the unchanging; from the Pythagoreans to the Stoics, 'Greek cosmology was always dominated by the image of a period or great year at the end of which things return to their point of departure and recommence a new cycle *ad infinitum*.'[3] The basic notion, of the circular movement of time, was a familiar one. The word *eniautos* (a year, or any complete space of time) implied a return to the starting-point;[4] and the comic poet, Hermippus, represented Time (?c. 440) as a 'round' figure, with 'all things spinning in a circle' inside him, bringing them forth as 'he goes round the earth in a circuit'.[5] Similarly, Aristotle quotes the saying (of medical provenance) that, like the heavens, 'human life is a circle'.[6]

Obviously, the later popular image of the *wheel* of Fortune comes much closer to this conception of a natural, cosmic cycle than to the rational analysis of *chance* (as mere accident or contingency) touched on by Thucydides and worked out later by Aristotle.[7] But the logical contradiction implicit in the image of Fortune's wheel (the contradiction between regularity and fortuitousness) also corresponds to something in the older images of the cosmic cycle. It is noticeable that in Herodotus the 'wheel' is kept turning by divine 'jealousy' and that in several of the early philosophers the cycle is maintained

[1] Kirk and Raven, *Presocratic Philosophers*, pp. 189–91, 195; *cf* Guthrie, *Greek Philosophy*, vol. I, p. 352.

[2] Kirk and Raven, *Presocratic Philosophers*, pp. 326ff; Guthrie, *Greek Philosophy*, vol. II, p. 168.

[3] Bréhier, *Histoire de la Philosophie*, vol. I, pp. 309ff (*cf* pp. 59, 63, 68, 138ff, 214ff, 452ff); Kirk and Raven, *Presocratic Philosophers*, pp. 202, 222, 352; Guthrie, *Greek Philosophy*, vol. I, p. 352; vol. II, p. 47; Trouillard, 'Le néoplatonisme', p. 903.

[4] Harrison, *Themis*, p. 182.

[5] Hermippus, *Birth of Athena*, frag. 4, ed. and trans. Edmonds, *Attic Comedy*, vol. I, p. 287.

[6] Guthrie, *Greek Philosophy*, vol. I, p. 352.

[7] *Cf* Greene, *Moira*, ch. 10; Cioffari, *Fortune and Fate*, ch. 2.

by some form of tension or 'strife'. The circular movement of time is not imagined as impersonal, uniform, automatic; some quasi-human effort intervenes. This idea of the cycle requiring tension is allied to mythopoeic thinking; and it comes out again as one of the shaping ideas in comedy.

A belief in the need for human effort to be exerted periodically in order to renew the cycle of nature would seem to explain the basic function of seasonal mimetic rituals in the archaic civilisations of the Near East, and hence the ultimate origin of dramatic festivals. In Mesopotamia and similarly in Egypt (write the Frankforts), 'the business of everyday life was interrupted several times in the course of each month when the moon completed one of its phases or other natural events called for appropriate action on the part of the community'. At the New Year in both civilisations there were mock battles miming the primordial battles of the gods; for centuries in Babylon – the source of Greek astronomy and possibly of much in Greek cosmogony as well – the king at each New Year 'took on the identity of Marduk' and 're-enacted the victory which Marduk had won over the powers of chaos in the first New Year's Day, when the world was created. At the annual festival the Epic of Creation was recited.'[1] These solemnities socialised nature, projected an image of legal order on to the cosmos, but they were not supposed to replace the need for everyday human labour, but to complete it. Similar rituals were performed in the ancient world at each significant point of transition in the public existence of the community, such as the enthronement of a king, or the founding of a new temple or city; and ritual was likewise called for at each turning-point in the existence of an individual – birth, puberty, marriage, death. This need for rituals (the Frankforts continue) springs from what has been called a 'dramatic conception of nature', in which there is a constant struggle of opposing powers, and in which time is not imagined abstractly but is 'experienced in the periodicity and rhythm' in life, wherein 'the transition from one phase to another is a crisis' calling for united human effort to overcome it.[2]

Moreover, there were mythical ' "regions" of time', 'withdrawn from direct experience' but 'normative' for religious thought: the future Kingdom of God for the Jews, the past time of creation for the

[1] H. and H. A. Frankfort, *Before Philosophy*, pp. 16, 34, 215, 238; *cf* Kirk and Raven, *Presocratic Philosophers*, pp. 9, 34, 39, 71, 80, 102.
[2] *Before Philosophy*, pp. 22, 32–6; *cf* Hocart, *The Life-giving Myth*.

Babylonians and the Egyptians. It was essential for the Babylonians to revive the moment of creation at the New Year; while 'no pharaoh could hope to achieve more than the establishment of the conditions "as they were in the time of Rē, in the beginning" '.[1] According to Mircea Eliade, this complex of beliefs and rituals expresses a desire, universal in pre-industrial societies, to escape from historic time and re-enter the timeless, mythical world of their origins;[2] this interpretation may be too sweeping, but is nevertheless suggestive for an understanding of the myth of the eternal return in Greek philosophy and of the way mythical and historical time overlap in Old Comedy. Within the Near Eastern rituals themselves, Theodor Gaster distinguishes two recurrent pairs of motifs – rites of mortification (such as fasting) at the crisis of the time-cycle and purging of the evils of the old, dying season; and rites of invigoration and jubilation (such as ritual marriage and feasting) to initiate the new season. Like Murray and Cornford before him, Gaster finds in this seasonal pattern of mimetic rites the underlying pattern of drama.[3]

The renewal of the cycle of social time is a fundamental theme in Greek comedy. Hardly anything remains to show the nature of Old Comedy after its official inauguration at Athens (a half-century later than tragedy) as part of the spring festival of the City Dionysia in 486 B.C., until a decade or so before its inclusion (*c.* 442) in the winter festival of the Lenaea as well. But from the more numerous fragments surviving from Aristophanes' contemporaries and immediate predecessors, as well as from his own extant plays, it seems clear that in the second half of the fifth century (the age of Pericles and his successors) there were regularly two sides to Old Comedy: 'invectives' against present-day opinions and policies and individuals (especially, it was said at the time, against 'the wealthy, the well-born or the influential'),[4] and 'advice' to the city, which was bound up with an imagined recall of legendary or historical heroes or of a mythical régime from the past. The combination of ridicule and revival was probably more important to the scheme of comedy than any specific

---

[1] *Before Philosophy*, pp. 35, 215; but see also p. 240.

[2] Eliade, *Myth of the Eternal Return*; (but see also Radin, *World of Primitive Man*, ch. 1; Kirk, *Myth*, pp. 254–7).

[3] Gaster, *Thespis*, pp. 26, 83; Webster, 'Greek Tragedy', in Platnauer (ed.), *Fifty Years of Classical Scholarship*, pp. 80–3; *cf* p. 92, n. 1, above.

[4] Pseudo-Xenophon, *Constitution of the Athenians* (trans. Frisch) II.18; *cf* Platonius, *On the Classification of Comedies*, in Edmonds (ed. and trans.), *Attic Comedy*, vol. I, p. 313. See Robert J. Bonner, *Athenian Democracy*, p. 123.

programme or line of political attack (for instance, in 411, Eupolis, who had satirised Pericles like the other comic poets during the statesman's lifetime, 'brought [him] back to life' with other historic lawgivers so as to correct the misgovernment of the day).[1] It is hardly credible that the Athenian democratic majority, who were not defeatists, would have tolerated plays attacking their leading politicians and declared policies throughout the tense years of the Peloponnesian War (431–404), still less sponsored such plays officially and awarded prizes to them, if the motif of revival did not hold a strong emotional appeal for them.

In all of Aristophanes' extant plays, the 'argument' or 'hypothesis' is the restoration of a natural order for the city by means of fantastic schemes involving the trickster-hero. In three of them (the *Acharnians*, *Peace* and *Lysistrata*) the political object is the ending of the war. The *Knights* and the *Wasps* attack Pericles' first successor as leading politician, Cleon. The *Clouds* and then the *Thesmophoriazusae* and the *Frogs* mock intellectual innovations in the persons of Socrates and then Euripides. The *Birds* and the two late plays, the *Women in the Assembly* and *Plutus*, present fantastic utopias, in the form of the restoration of a mythical golden age. In nearly all of them, the object of the hero's 'daring and novel device' is to cure the evils of the present by returning to the past; or else, as in the *Clouds* and the *Wasps*, 'nature' recoils against new-fangled ideas, or, at least, as in the *Thesmophoriazusae*, peace is restored between the buffoon and the women as a consequence of his 'innumerable devices'. The immediate purpose of Dicaeopolis in making his private treaty with Sparta in the *Acharnians* is to return to the pre-war pleasures of his farm and celebrate the rural Dionysia once more. And, just as Dicaeopolis (the natural *dike* of the city) speaks in the name of comedy and wishes to return to the festive condition of comedy, so Trygaeus (Vine-reaper, whose name also suggests a nickname for comedy, *trygodia*) restores Theoria (Festivals) to the Council when he brings back Peace to Athens and marries the second companion of Peace, Opora (Fruits-of-summer). The object of Trygaeus's fantastic raid on Olympus for Peace has been to enjoy again 'the olden way of life the goddess used to dispense to us' (571–81); and while the comedy ends amid jubilation, following his feast, he prays for 'wealth for the Greeks' (not the Athenians alone), an abundant harvest 'for all alike' in barley, wine,

---

[1] Eupolis, *The Demes*: see Page (ed. and trans.), *Select Papyri III*, pp. 202ff; Edmonds (ed. and trans.), *Attic Comedy*, vol. I, pp. 337ff, 399, 978ff.

figs and children, and the recovery of 'all the good things we have lost since the beginning' (1316–32). Comedy in these two plays seeks its own perpetuation, not as a satiric art-form, but as a symbol of the periodic renewal of society. And in nearly all the comedies, the result, if not the first intention, of the central 'device' is either the rejuvenation of a principal actor or of the Marathon veterans in the chorus who embody the ancient spirit of Athens, or else the recreation of a mythical condition of peace, justice and effortless plenty 'for all alike', much as in Trygaeus's prayer. The Chorus of Farmers who support Trygaeus dance for joy as if they had 'sloughed off old age' (*Peace*, 336) and old Philocleon in the *Wasps* becomes 'young' again. In the *Knights*, the Sausage-seller, 'inventor of marvellous schemes', crowns his success with the magical rejuvenation of Demos, so that when Demos returns to the stage newly dressed, he is already 'dwelling in the violet-crowned Athens of old,...as he was formerly, when he sat at table with Aristides and Miltiades' (1321–5). The past supervenes here on the present. And similarly, in the *Frogs*, that other wonder-worker, Dionysus himself, brings back the old hero-poet, Aeschylus, from the past. (This propitious return of the dead, in a torchlight procession with Dionysus, seems to be related, through folklore, to Carnival masquerades).[1]

Besides bringing joy through the vine and prosperity through the wine trade, Dionysus, as Euripides shows in the *Bacchae*, was also a magician who aroused ecstasy in his worshippers and caused the land to flow with milk and honey. The paradisiac side of his cult overlapped with earlier beliefs or tales about the bliss of the golden age.[2] According to the oldest poetic statement of the myth, in Hesiod (*Works and Days*, 109–26), the men of 'the golden race' lived a blameless, untroubled existence, 'like gods', never feeling the weight of 'miserable age' and enjoying perpetual feasting, 'for the grain-giving earth bore fruit for them abundantly and ungrudgingly of its own accord'.[3] (Hesiod's personification of harvest-bloom and feasting, Thalia, was later to be appropriated as the muse of Comedy.)[4]

---

[1] See Jeanmaire, *Dionysos*, pp. 47, 268–73; Lawson, *Greek Folklore*, pp. 190–255; Welsford, *Court Masque*, pp. 7, 17, 35, 92–7, and *The Fool*, p. 291.
[2] See Campbell Bonner, 'Dionysiac Magic and the Greek Land of Cockaigne'; Euripides, *The Bacchae*, ed. Dodds; Jeanmaire, *Dionysos*, ch. 1; Guthrie, *Greeks and their Gods*, ch. 6; Gaster, *Thespis*, pp. 442ff.
[3] See Solmsen, *Hesiod and Aeschylus*, pp. 83ff; Baldry, 'Who Invented the Golden Age?'
[4] Jeanmaire, *Dionysos*, pp. 29–30; see Plato, *Laws*, 653D; Robert J. Bonner, *Athenian Democracy*, pp. 136ff.

Although Hesiod is not consistent, he describes the golden race here as the first breed of men to be created by the gods; they lived 'in the time of Cronus', the father and predecessor of Zeus. When they had passed away, they became benevolent earth-daemons, watchful guardians over the living and 'givers of wealth'; while Zeus, having deposed Cronus, allowed him to rule over the race of heroes in the ever-fertile Isles of the Blest, 'at the ends of the earth' (*Works and Days*, 121–6, 166–73). The myth of the metal races (or ages) follows Hesiod's reference to the entry of labour and sickness into human life with the curse of Pandora's box, and it is meant to illustrate the progressive degeneration of mankind through injustice and greed.

There is no return of the cycle here (as there is in Virgil, however). But according to one version of the legend, Zeus later released Cronus from his bonds; and Hesiod says that even now, in the age of iron, the city where justice prevails is blessed with peace, feasting and earth-given abundance – as in the age of Cronus.[1] By the time of Pericles, if not earlier, the dream of labour-free abundance, mythically remote in time or place, could be identified with the ideal of equality and the hopes and ambitions of the poor: for example, Plutarch, in his life of Pericles' rival, Cimon, in the course of a passage where he quotes from a play by Cratinus – the *Archilochoi*, 449 B.C. – to exemplify Cimon's popularity, goes on to say that by his open-handed hospitality Cimon 'seemed to restore to the world that community of goods which is fabled to have existed in the reign of Cronus'.[2] The festivals of Cronus (which later antiquity assimilated to the Roman Saturnalia) were holidays of social release, the exchange of gifts, and mimic equality between rich and poor, masters and slaves.[3] The life of the golden race is the polar opposite of a society that knows hardship and inequality. Old Comedy alludes to it frequently; often satirically, perhaps, but usually in company with the dominant motif of renewal.[4]

It seems clear, for example, that the earliest play which certainly alluded to the golden race, the *Plutuses* (436 B.C.) by Cratinus, included an attack on the *nouveaux-riches* associates of Pericles, the new 'Zeus', and depicted some kind of *coup d'état* by the Wealth-gods, companions

[1] Hesiod, *Works and Days*, 225–37. See Solmsen, *Hesiod and Aeschylus*, pp. 86ff, 107ff; Lovejoy and Boas, *Primitivism in Antiquity*, pp. 24ff; Ryberg, 'Vergil's Golden Age'.
[2] Plutarch, *Cimon* 10; see Thomson, *Aeschylus and Athens*, p. 234.
[3] Lucian, *Saturnalian Letters* 19–20; Athenaeus, *Deipnosophists* XIV, 639–40. See Frazer, *The Golden Bough, Pt VI: The Scapegoat*, ch. 8; Lovejoy and Boas, *Primitivism in Antiquity*, pp. 67ff; Baldry, 'Who Invented the Golden Age?'
[4] Norwood, *Greek Comedy*, p. 139; Lever, *Art of Greek Comedy*, pp. 74ff; Lovejoy and Boas, *Primitivism in Antiquity*, pp. 38–41.

of Cronus, who have broken free and returned to Athens.[1] Aeschylus had brought the conflict between the Olympians and the older gods into tragedy; an imagined return of the older dispensation is a sign of the mythical time-cycle at work in comedy. In the *Animals*, by Crates, near in date to the *Plutuses*, there was apparently 'a contest between two Popular Leaders promising (in the form of a return to the Golden Age?) a servantless millennium', whereas 'the Chorus consisted of Animals, who (in the coming new conditions) refuse to be eaten'; while one speaker promises a primitive Land of Cockaigne, the other tries to outbid him with an automatic hot-water supply, in a spirit of advanced technology. Here it looks as if the myth was used primarily for satire.[2] Cratinus's *Cheirons* (*c.* 435) revived Solon with a chorus of wise centaurs to contrast the idyllic simplicity of the past with the régime of Pericles, the 'tyrant', 'son of Faction and Cronus'.[3] A Land of Cockaigne appears once more in the *Amphictyons* (*c.* 431) by Teleclides, where a speaker, presumably Cronus, dilates on 'the life which [he] gave to mankind', when, 'of their own accord', 'every stream flowed with wine, barley cakes fought with wheat cakes' to be eaten, and 'fish came into the house, frying themselves and lying down ready on the tables'; no doubt the poet here was ridiculing the food-fantasies of ordinary Athenians, but (as the title suggests) he may at the same time have been putting forward an argument for peace.[4]

Other comedies also parodied the dream of a Land of Cockaigne (for instance, in a description of a rocky island where weeds and rushes grew abundantly 'of their own accord'), or used it to satirise the inordinate hopes of the war party in Athens (much as Aristophanes ridicules them in the *Acharnians*);[5] in *The Golden Race* (423), Eupolis attacked Cleon, and brought in a chorus of Cyclopes, whose way of life corresponded to the simplicity and fertility of the reign of Cronus.[6] Many variations were therefore possible on the themes Aristophanes introduced into his utopian comedies, but two features

[1] Edmonds (ed. and trans.), *Attic Comedy*, vol. I, pp. 73ff; Pieters, *Cratinus*, pp. 206, 208; Ehrenberg, *People of Aristophanes*, pp. 64n, 239, 320.

[2] Edmonds (ed. and trans.), *Attic Comedy*, vol. I, pp. 159ff.

[3] *Ibid.*, pp. 105ff; *cf* Plutarch, *Pericles* 3; Ehrenberg, *People of Aristophanes*, p. 340.

[4] Edmonds (ed. and trans.), *Attic Comedy*, vol. I, pp. 183ff. See Lovejoy and Boas, *Primitivism in Antiquity*, p. 40; Ehrenberg, *People of Aristophanes*, pp. 130–1, 320–1.

[5] Cratinus, *The Seriphians* (*c.* 426 B.C.), Pherecrates, *The Persians* (? 425 B.C.), in Edmonds (ed. and trans.), *Attic Comedy*, vol. I, pp. 97ff, 253ff; *cf Acharnians*, 61–125.

[6] Edmonds (ed. and trans.), *Attic Comedy*, vol. I, pp. 411ff; see Ehrenberg, *People of Aristophanes*, pp. 239, 349; Kirk, *Myth*, pp. 162ff.

seem to be constant in the fragments from his contemporaries – a social ideal, treated with conscious exaggeration, ambiguously or ironically, and a return to Athens of characters or social conditions from the remote mythical past.

Peace is related to the comic myth of the golden age, with Trygaeus's defiance of the gods for the sake of benefits 'for all alike', as they were at 'the beginning', and his marriage to a goddess. And where Aristophanes introduces the myth directly, he follows the same pattern of outwardly conservative revolution. When the flight of Peithetaerus and Euelpides from Athens in the *Birds* turns, first, into a proposal to found a new Athens-in-the-air, Cloudcuckootown (124, 172), and then – before the city is even founded – into a proposal immediately to 'demand the rule back from Zeus' (554), the claim propounded, and adopted by the birds, rests on a parody of Hesiod (and of other cosmogonies), on the fiction that birds are a race 'of older and remoter origin than Cronus and the Titans and Earth', closely descended from primeval Chaos through Eros, born 'in the revolving seasons' (469, 693ff).[1] Recalling their services to mankind (on which Hesiod had had much to say), the birds promise 'health and wealth' to their human allies, 'life, peace, youth, laughter, choric dances, festivals...', an excess of 'riches for all', to the second and third generation (729ff), and, in addition, freedom from the restraints of law (755ff). It is fitting that the birds should be assisted also by another fugitive, Prometheus, the rebel from the race of Titans whom Zeus in his day had overthrown, and that Prometheus should suggest their supreme demand, that Zeus be forced not merely to 'restore the sceptre to the birds' but to let Peithetaerus marry Sovereignty as well (1536). The *Birds* is a fantasy of a cosmic cycle.

Similarly, in the *Women in the Assembly* (392 B.C.), a double revolution – first government by women and then a quasi-Platonic system of communism in wives and property (with 'plenty for everyone') – is preceded by the ironic argument that, as the city has had enough of dissension and innovation, it is time for the women to rule, since they are more conservative than the men (214ff).[2] And in *Plutus* (388 B.C.), the poverty-crazed farmer, Chremylus, persuades the Wealth-god to visit the temple of Asclepius and be cured of his blindness by the holy snakes there, with the result that the golden

[1] Navarre, *Les Cavaliers*, p. 187.
[2] Ehrenberg, *People of Aristophanes*, pp. 67, 127, 204; Cloché, *Démocratie athénienne*, pp. 210, 233, 238, 285; Thomson, *Aeschylus and Athens*, p. 366.

age is restored for Chremylus and the Attic farmers; Plutus now consorts with the 'god-fearing and righteous' instead of the un-deserving, 'a heap of blessings has burst into our house, without our committing any injustice' (804), and at the same time (somewhat as in the *Birds*), not merely does the Priest of Zeus the Preserver hurry to Chremylus to beg for food and lodging, because no one troubles to offer sacrifices any longer, but he learns that Zeus the Preserver has forestalled him there 'of his own accord' (1190).

Here again, Aristophanes incorporates ancient beliefs in a revolu-tionary utopia. Before the farmer takes Wealth into his house, he has to beat down the objections of an old hag, Poverty, whom he finally drives away (419–609). Poverty objects that without her – without the pressure of need (but not beggary) – there would be no handi-crafts, no husbandry, not even any provision of slaves; the decent life Chremylus longs for would simply collapse. To this Chremylus can give no answer, except his nostalgia for social justice.[1] At one level, therefore, the play exposes the contradictions in the popular myth of a golden age. But at another level, it re-enacts it; the expulsion of Poverty is almost a ritual expulsion of hunger.[2] And Asclepius, the semi-divine wonder-worker with his holy snakes, though a newcomer to rationalistic Athens during the comic poet's lifetime, had an immemorial cult behind him. He had been introduced to the city in 420 B.C. (where he was housed with Sophocles until a temple could be built for him), as a result of the terrible plague of ten years earlier brought on by the war; his faith-healing has been described as 'a religion of emergencies', a manifestation of the psychology of a time of crisis.[3]

Like other Old Comedies, these plays depicting the return of a golden age follow the rhythm of purgation and invigoration common to ancient seasonal rituals; and, like the ancient rituals, their *logos* or rationale assumes the need for human exertion at a critical juncture to renew the natural cycle of time. Thanks to some 'inventor of marvellous schemes', the mythical world rejoins the world of every day. On the other hand, there is no sacred king ruling in Athens to maintain or restore the world as it was 'in the beginning', and no royal founder is as much as considered in the comedies; they pay

---

[1] Ehrenberg, *People of Aristophanes*, pp. 69ff, 238ff; Cloché, *Démocratie athénienne*, p. 233.

[2] *Plutus*, 610–12; cf Frazer, *Golden Bough* (abridged edn.), p. 578.

[3] Dodds, *Greeks and the Irrational*, pp. 110–16, 128, 193, 203; Willetts, *Blind Wealth and Aristophanes*.

virtually no attention to Theseus, for instance. Old Comedy was created by and for a new type of society, conscious of a revolutionary break with tradition in its recent historical past, 'addicted to innovation',[1] committed to a trading empire and the championship of democracy, proud of its freedom of speech and the right of the sovereign people to govern themselves through their Assembly. Hence the social order is recreated in Old Comedy by means of political revolutions, not battles with monsters, and the 'inventor' of the life-renewing 'scheme' is usually a private citizen, never a deity (except for the popular god, Dionysus), and never a legendary hero.

And the gods themselves are insecure or impermanent. Both the competitive terms of the dramatic festivals and the intellectual temper of the enlightenment during Aristophanes' time favoured a treatment of myth which was inventive, not repetitive, and critical, not ritualistic. Herodotus (who was interested in comparative religion) wrote that Homer and Hesiod had been the first of the Greeks 'to compose Theogonies, and give the gods their epithets, to allot them their several offices and occupations, and describe their forms', and in his 'opinion' these myth-makers had lived only 400 years previously (an over-estimate).[2] And the sophist Protagoras was prepared to carry the relativism implicit in such a statement much further, maintaining that the social world is essentially man-made, not god-given, and that 'Man is the measure of all things, of the things that are that they are, and of the things that are not that they are not.'[3] Whether exactly in the sense that Protagoras intended or not, the burlesque of myth in Old Comedy involved treating 'Man' as 'the measure'; the poets shifted the myths to the human plane and exploited their improbabilities. Or they brought out contradictions between one myth and another; in the utopian comedies, for instance, the idea of technical progress associated with Prometheus conflicts with the theme of a return to the reign of Cronus, implying regression to the state of a primitive food-gathering society, for which 'the grain-giving earth bore fruit...ungrudgingly of its own accord'.[4]

---

1 Thucydides, I. 70. See Glotz and Cohen, *La Grèce au Ve siècle*, chs. 4–7; Robert J. Bonner, *Athenian Democracy*; Ehrenberg, *People of Aristophanes*, ch. 13; Cloché, *Démocratie athénienne*, ch. 9; Finley, *The Ancient Greeks*, pp. 70–82.

2 Herodotus, II. 53; *cf* Murray, *Greek Religion*, p. 44.

3 Guthrie, *Greek Philosophy*, vol. III, pp. 63ff, 181ff, 234, 262ff; Whitman, *Aristophanes*, ch. 5.

4 See Lovejoy and Boas, *Primitivism in Antiquity*; Havelock, *The Liberal Temper in Greek Politics*.

And in the *Birds*, Aristophanes presents an even more radical criticism of myth; the birds' herald-like boast of primordial ancestry, which Peithetaerus has put into their heads, not only burlesques Hesiod and other more recent cosmogonists, but ridicules the whole principle of employing myth to assert a claim to political rule or territory or to justify a system of law or custom. The play explodes its own version of the cosmic cycle into fantasy, and what remains is the lure of words and the elasticity of human inventiveness – 'mankind is always and every way by nature deceitful'.

Man invents deceits or illusions for himself, therefore. Nevertheless, this is not a purely rationalising, reductive line of criticism. Peithetaerus's imperial myth-making is a tribute to human potentialities; conversely, the patent absurdities in the 'beautiful and noble, all-purpose plan' of a Chremylus or a Trygaeus serve to emphasise the drive of human need and desire behind their fantasies. The tension between caricature and myth-making, between 'invectives' and 'advice' at the heart of Old Comedy, is a tension between the sense of actuality and a vision of the desirable; it is not myth that magically reinforces practical life, as in ancient rituals, but the power of the imagination. The trickster replaces the sacred king. The particular ambitions and conventions of Old Comedy disappeared with Periclean Athens. But it left behind, as guide-lines for New Comedy, the assumption of men's hopes and desires striving to identify themselves with the cycle of nature, and the master-concept of the 'deceit' entailed in such striving. From New Comedy, these guide-lines have been extended to shape the art of comedy in the Renaissance and later.

There is a 'wheel', then, in Old Comedy, but it is not the wheel of chance; there is no place for mere contingency in this world of as-if. Nothing that happens in the plays is unpredictable, in Thucydides' sense, because probability has been eliminated; and either there are no 'jealous' gods to turn the wheel, as in Herodotus, or else their jealousy is inoperative. Most of Aristophanes' references to *tyche* stand closer to Herodotus's 'divine chance', in the propitious sense. The Sausage-seller comes on the stage in the *Knights*, for example, like the genie of Aladdin's lamp, at a moment of 'good fortune' (151), just when Demos's slaves, who need a champion, have drunk a libation to the Good Daemon; in *Peace*, after a similar appeal by Trygaeus to 'the propitious moment', the moment of the Good Daemon (292–300), the Chorus of Farmers hail him as their 'absolute commander, chosen for us by good fortune' (359–60). 'How all things go right,' they exclaim as they celebrate their successful return with Peace, 'when a god and Fortune wish it!...For now a divine spirit is visibly bearing us to prosperity' (939–46). Fortune can 'quickly turn around and present its evil side', but only against the sacrilegious, so that it is still 'divine chance'; in the scheme of the plays, it is prosperous.[1] It carries no hint of caprice or adversity towards mankind in general; it expresses a vote of confidence in the gods of the Athenian *polis*.

Similarly, it carries no real hint of chance as contingency or coincidence, opposed to probability. When Trygaeus speaks of 'the propitious moment', for example, he means that now is the time to rescue Peace from her cave, because the attention of the giant, War, has been distracted; but in this fairy-tale plot where space can be twisted at will, his time-sense is of no consequence, and his words only have a genuine meaning in the real world, outside the play. The *absence* of probability (and hence of meaningful chance) is essential to the fiction, which arouses a tension between hope and the sense of actuality in the immediate present.

In *Plutus*, on the other hand, there is a different sense of *tyche*, which now stands for a depressing contrast between economic conditions and human rights. Cario says a slave may 'chance' to give good advice which his master ignores (3), and he has been enslaved merely for lack of money (147); Wealth speaks of the misers and spendthrifts into whose houses, in his blindness, he used to stumble 'by chance' (237, 242); and to Chremylus, life as it is seems a 'madness' or the work of 'an evil spirit', where men of good 'character' or 'manners' always suffer (32ff, 245, 500ff). This tone is significant for the fourth century; a writer of Middle Comedy says, for instance, that slaves have no permanent city or status, but shift about as Fortune decides.[2] The desacralisation of Fortune in *Plutus*, while greater influence on real life is attributed to it, the emphasis on an irrational distribution of wealth, the withdrawal of interest from politics (in the old sense) to 'manners', and the subdued tone of the play are all signs of the passing of Old Comedy. In spite of this, however, Fortune plays no part in arranging the events on the stage (not even, it seems, the meeting between Chremylus and Plutus); and Chremylus creates

---

[1] *Thesmophoriazusae*, 721–5; cf *Clouds*, 804–12; *Wasps*, 869, 1450; *Birds*, 544, 675, 1721–7; *Women in the Assembly*, 131, 172, 504. Cf p. 131, n. 3, above.

[2] Anaxandrides, *Anchises* (? 352 B.C.), in Edmonds (ed. and trans.), *Attic Comedy*, vol. II, p. 47; cf Lever, *Art of Greek Comedy*, p. 165.

his utopia, diminished though it is, very much like his predecessors in Aristophanes. The wheel of prosperity turns, but not by the agency of a hidden power, Fortune. And the relationship between the events in the play and an image of real life remains, as before, an ambiguous one, part allegorical and part fantastic.

In classical tragedy, by contrast, the relationship between life and drama is more straightforward. Although the play presents an image of the heroic age, not contemporary Greece, it contains within itself a model of the life it talks about. In Aristotle's formula, it is 'an imitation of an action'. And the action is subject to the conditions of real actions, deliberation, forethought and ignorance about the outcome. But since the story comes from a well-known myth as a rule, the spectators know more about the future than the characters; hence the type of dramatic irony, turning on men's ignorance about their situation and their fate, which tragedy handed on to New Comedy.

Sophocles, who knew Herodotus, held a similar conception of fortune: 'like a wheel, fortune turns in a circle'.[1] Like the philosophers, he compares human life to a natural cycle, governed by time, to the waxing and waning of the moon, the alternation of the seasons, the course of the stars. By the will of Zeus, the chorus tell Deianeira in the *Women of Trachis* (129–31), 'sorrow and joy come round to all in turn, as if in the circling path of the Bear'.[2] In *Oedipus Rex* (?c. 425 B.C.), when Jocasta learns that Oedipus's supposed father has died a natural death, she ridicules her husband's fear of the oracle: 'what should a mortal have to fear, dominated by fortune, never foreseeing clearly?' (977). But when the Messenger goes on to reveal that in fact Oedipus had been a foundling, she guesses the truth and rushes away in horror. This partial revelation brings fresh confidence to Oedipus, however; he attributes Jocasta's revulsion to 'a woman's pride' and contempt for him as a bastard. But, he proclaims,

I hold myself the son of beneficent Fortune, and will not be dishonoured. She is the mother who bore me; and my kinsmen, the months, have marked me as lowly and great in turn. Such being my origin, nothing can change it; why should I give up finding out my birth?

(1080–5)

[1] Robinson, 'The Wheel of Fortune', p. 208; Greene, *Moira*, ch. 6.
[2] Musurillo, 'Fortune's Wheel: the Symbolism of Sophocles' *Women of Trachis*'.

Oedipus the self-made king is right in acknowledging his luck, and Oedipus the prince exposed at birth is right in thinking that chance has brought him round to his point of departure. Only, he is wrong to imagine that he will welcome the result. He is right in thinking of time as a cycle. The essential for Oedipus, however, is to know, to find out, and it is here that the cycle of Fortune is treacherous. It both reveals and masks the true rhythm of things, as determined by the gods.[1] The tragic irony of his speech depends in part on the foreknowledge in the minds of the audience. But it also depends on the way Sophocles introduces the implied metaphor of Fortune's wheel, so as to suggest that human affairs – those that matter to the individual – are neither predictable (in which case there would be no point in talking in this way of Fortune) nor entirely random (in which case there would be no point in the image of the wheel), but follow a course which is unknowable in detail but in its ultimate form regular and certain, conforming to the order of nature. *Oedipus Rex* is the type of those plays which led Diomedes the grammarian to define tragedy as 'a Discovery of former fortune and family taking an ill turn'. But even without thinking about the last phase in the story, an audience here can see that Oedipus is both right and wrong.

Although Euripides has more explicit speculation, and more varied opinions, about Fortune than Sophocles – for instance, in a fragment from one of his plays a speaker wonders whether 'Fortune or some divine powers sway the life of man?'[2] – the way he uses the concept for dramatic irony is closely similar. In *The Trojan Women* (415 B.C.) he makes the despairing Hecuba say that no one can rely on Fortune's crazy moods (1203–6), when the spectators already know that the gods have sworn to wreck the victorious and vindictive Greeks on their homebound voyage. In those plays which can be described as romantic tragi-comedies – like *Ion*, *Helen* and *Iphigenia in Tauris* (414 B.C.) – Euripides exploits the irony of Fortune for the sake of a neat but exciting theatrical manoeuvre. In one day at the temple of Apollo at Delphi, the temple-foundling, Ion, both finds a foster-father in Xuthus (who has married the Athenian princess, Creusa, and who acknowledges the youth in error as his own illegitimate son), and discovers who his real parents are – Apollo and Creusa, whom the god had raped and who had exposed her infant secretly at birth. Unaware at first of each other's identity, Creusa and her son come

[1] *Cf* Ehrenberg, *Sophocles and Pericles*, pp. 69–73; Diano, 'Edipo Figlio della Tyche'.
[2] W. C. Greene, *Moira*, p. 217; *cf* ch. 7, *passim*, and pp. 408ff.

near to murdering each other, Ion's vengeance being only prevented by the Priestess of the temple, who had brought him up and who produces his birth-tokens at the critical moment:

O Fortune, [he exclaims] incessantly changing the lot of men and making them miserable and happy by turns, how near I have come to killing my own mother and to sufferings undeserved! Can it be that all this could happen in one bright circuit of the sun? (1512-15)

Athena appears, and makes out that her brother Apollo had contrived all for the best; but – quite apart from the vexed question whether Euripides wrote this passage with his tongue in his cheek[1] – the main dramatic emphasis falls on men's ignorance of their lot. The 'circuit of the sun' in Ion's speech is both a reference to his divine (but delinquent) father, whose identity is still ironically hidden from the speaker, and another image of Fortune's wheel.

Similarly, in *Iphigenia in Tauris*, Orestes, the Greek prince fallen into the hands of barbarians, says that his true name should be 'Misfortune' (500), but Pylades reminds him (721) that 'the excess of our adversities often brings about sudden changes of fortune'; and these words preface the scene of recognition between Orestes and his sister in which they plan to escape together.

It was no doubt plays like these that Satyrus had in mind when he said that Euripides 'perfected' plots containing quarrels within a family, rape or abduction, 'sudden changes of fortune' and recognitions by means of tokens, and that these became the 'mainstay' of New Comedy. Taking this statement as substantially correct (though it may exaggerate Euripides' contribution), it can be said that Euripides' influence reached much further still in this direction, and shaped romantic fiction and drama down to the Renaissance. His direct influence on renaissance tragi-comedy may have been slight, but his indirect influence was enormous. Euripides and New Comedy together provided the principal literary models for the plots of the prose romances of the late hellenistic age, like Heliodorus's *Ethiopian History*, and these in turn were pillaged by fiction-writers like Sidney and Greene and (as Gosson noted) by playwrights when they were rediscovered in the sixteenth century.[2] And the hellenistic romances

---

[1] Kitto, *Greek Tragedy*, ch. 11; Lesky, *Greek Literature*, pp. 389–90; Conacher, 'The Paradox of Euripides' *Ion*'.

[2] See chapter 2, pp. 63, 72, above; *cf* Lesky, *Greek Literature*, pp. 858–9, 866; Wolff, *Greek Romances*.

prepared the ground, as it were, for their own reception in the Renaissance through the influence they exerted on near-contemporary pious tales with a Christian colouring like *Apollonius of Tyre*, which were well known throughout the Middle Ages. I have called the latter exemplary romances, because they exhibit models of patience and long-suffering rewarded by providence.[1] By contrast, the pagan plays and stories, which can be called Euripidean romances, emphasise the irony of fortune. They depend on complications and surprise, whereas exemplary romances are concerned with the trials of virtue. But the distinction of tone or outlook between hellenistic romances and pious tales like *Apollonius* is not very sharp.

Another channel of influence for Euripidean romance, though it was not the author's intention, was Aristotle's theory of tragedy. But when Aristotle delivered the lectures that form his *Poetics* (?c. 330 B.C.), Euripides was the most popular of the classical dramatists in Athens and the main interest in tragedy apparently lay with complications of plot.[2] Not only does the working out of the plot take primacy among the factors Aristotle examines in a tragedy, but the idea of the wheel of Fortune is crucial to his analysis of the complex plot, the type he most approves. It is true that he would like to see accidental or haphazard events reduced to a minimum in drama; everything in a tragedy, he insists, should happen 'in accordance with necessity and probability', and any extraordinary or irrational details forming part of the *donnée* of the story should be kept in the background. However, the function of the pivotal episodes of *peripeteia* and recognition, the hallmarks of a complex plot, is to bring about a change of fortunes in a striking way; and Aristotle draws no fundamental distinction between *Oedipus Rex*, which ends in horror, and *Iphigenia in Tauris*, where death is averted, because the conclusion in both plays has been produced by the same mechanism. Since a *peripeteia* is not simply an episode showing a sudden change in the situation, or one which works out *differently* from the agent's intention, but 'a change' which is *contrary* to the actor's intention and 'by which the action veers round to its opposite' (*Poetics* XI; Butcher's translation), it represents the wheel-like motion of events with redoubled force. And since the 'recognition' Aristotle is concerned with is primarily a recognition

---

1 Salingar, 'Time and Art in Shakespeare's Romances'.
2 Webster, *Fourth Century Athens*, pp. 62–9.

of persons ('a change from ignorance [*agnoia*] to knowledge, producing love or hate between the persons destined by the poet for good or bad fortune' (XI)), coincidence is a necessary precondition for the ideal plot: that is, two kinsmen must meet, in potential hostility, one of them at least being unknown to the other. This, in turn, requires that some exceptional circumstance shall have separated them earlier on; in other words, the high point of a complex plot in Aristotle's analysis is the point where the wheel has completed its turn, and an Oedipus, an Ion or an Orestes establishes his true identity: he finds his parents or rejoins his family.

As Aristotle admits, such conjunctions of circumstance are so rare that, from all the sources of mythology, 'a few families only...furnish the subjects of tragedy' (XIV). Hence it was 'not art', he adds, 'but happy chance' that drew the writers of tragedy towards 'those houses whose history contains moving incidents like these'.

Plot, *mythos*, is more vital than character in Aristotle's theory of tragedy precisely because it contains situations which,- whether engineered by the gods or not, arise outside of human intention or control and provide 'moving incidents like these', bearing forcibly on men's ignorance of their true place in the world (which is first of all their place in their family). As the theory passed into academic tradition, it was simplified into a formula: according to Theophrastus, tragedy was 'an action involving a reversal in the fortunes of heroic chracters';[1] and 'changes of fortune' remained at the centre of definitions of drama down to Dryden's time. The early Renaissance found the formula in the grammarians of the fourth century A.D., even before the *Poetics* was made available; and medieval readers like Chaucer knew it from Boethius. 'What other thing doth the outcry of tragedies lament', asks Boethius, 'but that fortune, having no respect, overturneth happy states?' It was in the shape of a narrative about Fortune's wheel that the notion of tragedy was passed on to the Middle Ages, long after any knowledge of the classical theatre had disappeared.[2]

New Comedy it was that came to be defined as 'an imitation of life', like tragedy, differing only from tragedy in that its characters were citizens, not heroes, and its incidents led to a happy outcome, by way

[1] Atkins, *Literary Criticism in Antiquity*, vol. I, p. 159.
[2] Boethius, *Consolation of Philosophy* II, prose ii (trans. 'I.T.', 1609). See Farnham, *Medieval Heritage of Elizabethan Tragedy*.

of 'agreeable mistakes' without 'serious dangers'.[1] And whereas Old Comedy had been grounded on the assumption of the self-determination of Athens (an assumption without which its 'advice' would have been meaningless), for New Comedy that basis had gone. The city festivals remained (at least, for the wealthy), but there could be no serious pretence that the gods they celebrated stood for the collective personality of the city any longer, or its will to make its own decisions. The city was almost helpless, and the private wealth it still contained was a source of division, not strength. There could be no public fantasy of a recall of the golden age; the life to be imitated was contemporary, life in the age of iron.

Belief in the cyclic movement of human destiny had not been challenged, but in what must have been a reflex of hope and despair, control of the wheel was now committed more firmly than ever before to the personification of uncertainty, Fortune; Fortune, says Tarn, 'was a thoroughly hellenistic conception...She was not blind chance, but some order of affairs which men could not comprehend. But all could see her.'[2] Her increased prestige was directly connected with the Macedonian conquests; towards 290 B.C., Menander's former patron, the oligarch, Demetrius of Phalerum, wrote a treatise on Fortune, in which he asked whether anyone, fifty years earlier, could have dreamt that the Macedonians would overwhelm Persia:

Fortune, who makes no covenant with us mortals but surprises us by innovations contrary to our calculations and shows her power by the unexpected, now seems to me to show all men, by putting the Macedonians to live among Persian riches, that they too have only been lent these benefits, until she has a new plan for them.

This recalls the wheel Herodotus spoke of, except that Fortune governs it now, not the 'jealousy' of the gods; and there is no contact with Fortune through worship – she 'makes no covenant'. As for the Olympians, when Demetrius I of Macedon entered the city in triumph in 290, the Athenians hailed him as a 'god', considering that 'other gods are either far away or have no ears or do not exist or do not attend to us at all'.[3] The central concern of the philosophies of the day, the older Cynic school and the newer Epicureans and Stoics, was

---

1 *Cf* Coghill, 'Shakespearian Comedy'; Atkins, *Literary Criticism in Antiquity*, vol. I, p. 159.
2 Tarn, *Hellenistic Civilization*, pp. 340–51; Angus, 'Athens', pp. 224–30.
3 Webster, *Fourth Century Athens*, pp. 110, 116; *cf* Murray, *Greek Religion*, ch. 4; Dodds, *Greeks and the Irrational*, p. 242.

with man as an individual – not his loyalties or decisions as a citizen – and with affording him a moral insurance against Fortune, or against a superstitious belief in Fortune.[1] In the acclamations to Demetrius I of Macedon there was already a sign of the oriental king-worship that was to obliterate the moral basis of Old Comedy completely and pass control over the ordinary citizen's life to a human power far above him. Men could believe that each individual had his own Fortune (his *daemon* or *genius*). But by the second century B.C. the hellenistic world was beginning to accept Babylonian astrology, and the idea of Fortune began to merge with the sterner notion of Fate. This was acceptable to Stoic philosophers, hostile as they were to a belief in mere chance.[2]

It was no longer, then, an 'inventor of marvellous schemes' who apparently caused the wheel to turn in New Comedy (though the trickster figure still had an essential role there, as we have partly seen), but usually the hidden power of Fortune, operating through human ignorance, as in Aristotelian theory and Euripidean romance. The experience of Menander's characters has been likened to a religious (as well as a social or sexual) initiation;[3] as the wheel turns, they pass from ignorance to knowledge; they must lose in order to gain. But this initiation is not due to their own impulse – as it had been with Dionysus in the *Frogs*, who found what he had not expected but had at least set out with a quest, – it is guided for them from above. After the first scene in *Perikeiromene*, Menander gives an explanatory prologue to Agnoia (Ignorance, as in the *Poetics*), as if she were a presiding goddess from Euripides:[4]

all this blaze [of the lovers' quarrel] was kindled for the sake of what is coming. It has made Polemon fall into a rage. That was my doing; he's not that kind of person naturally. And it is the first step towards bringing the rest of the story to light, so that the twins may find their friends at last...; for a god may overrule the evil that is done and turn it to good.

There is still a faint trace here of the old ideas of demonic possession and 'divine chance'; but Ignorance here is chiefly deputising for Fortune, turning harm into good over Polemon's head.

In another play by Menander, Fortune herself speaks the prologue

1 Bevan, 'Hellenistic Popular Philosophy'; Festugière, *Epicurus*.
2 Tarn, *Hellenistic Civilization*, pp. 340–51.
3 Post, *From Homer to Menander*, p. 220.
4 *Perikeiromene*, trans. Post, in Oates and O'Neill (eds.), *The Complete Greek Drama*, vol. II, p. 1177.

– 'I am the mistress, arbiter and disposer of these events.' Like Ignorance, Fortune is contradistinguished from natural disposition or character, but she shows herself beneficent none the less; the moral opponents from Aristophanes' *Plutus* are still there, but their relationship has changed. In other passages from Menander, Fortune is variously described as a pilot 'ever holding the tiller', as a false name men give to their own mistakes, as a force competing with a man's nature, as a favourer of the just. But the underlying view which shapes the benevolent irony of Menander's plots seems to be expressed by the speaker who says, 'I have been reviling Fortune unjustly', since, far from being 'blind', Fortune has been leading the way: 'I suffered terribly, but by my sufferings I was working out these present blessings, for I had never gained this had I not then suffered.'[1] Outside the scope of the plays, Fortune meant, among other things, empire over against city, money over against personality; it meant disfranchisement and a foreign garrison. Within the plays, it tends to mean psychological insecurity, but also, in compensation, the pull of the family, as the most natural social group. The wheel of the plots comes round to a recognition scene; by attaching her to the wheel, the playwrights correct Fortune's arbitrariness.

New Comedy plots in general follow the same lines as Menander. In Plautus's *Menaechmi*, for instance (from an unidentified Greek source, probably earlier than Menander – ?*c.* 340),[2] the brother landing at Epidamnus is warned by his slave against stopping there, because the very name of the city shows it to be a place of bad luck, whence no stranger escapes '*sine damno*' from its drunkards, informers, swindlers and courtesans (II.i; 255–64); but precisely – in the logic of the play – because he listens to the 'wheedling courtesan' who mistakes his identity, and gets himself entangled in the resulting confusions, he is enabled to find his twin. The tone here is farcical; but in *The Captives* (probably from Philemon, *c.* 280/70),[3] where Plautus draws attention to his seriousness, the action takes a similar course, and Tyndarus, like Menaechmus's slave – or like Orestes at Tauris – misconstrues the intentions of Fortune. 'Human fortune moulds and reduces us as she wishes', he exclaims, having taken his master's place in captivity: 'Me, who was free, she has made a slave; from the heights, she has thrown me down to the depths' (II.ii; 304).

[1] Page (ed. and trans.), *Select Papyri III*, p. 251; Allinson (ed.), *Menander*, pp. 399, 445, 491, 503, 505.
[2] Webster, *Later Greek Comedy*, pp. 67–74.   [3] *Ibid.*, p. 146.

Again, in Plautus's *Rudens* (*The Fisherman's Rope*: from Diphilus, ?*c.* 310/300), the heroine is shipwrecked near Cyrene. She had been kidnapped as a child and sold to a procurer; she complains of the gods' injustice towards her piety (I.iii; 185–219) – but the storm has wrecked her beside the cottage where her father lives in exile. (The connexion of the story with the sea, here as in the *Menaechmi*, recalls another traditional image of Fortune.) The prologue in *Rudens* has been spoken by the star-god, Arcturus, who explains that he has raised the storm, in obedience to Jupiter; for 'the supreme commander of gods and men' has appointed the stars as guardian spirits, to watch men's faith and actions, to punish the fraudulent and reward the deserving. In this way, the romance expresses a religious conception of providence, which Diphilus may have taken from Plato.[1] But this makes no difference to the working out of the plot and the juxtaposition of Fortune and Ignorance; when the father, Daemones, recounts a dream, which is clearly meant to be prophetic and lucky, he begins by exclaiming how strangely the gods delude us ('*Miris modis di ludos faciunt hominibus,* | *Mirisque exemplis somnia in somnis danunt*': III.i; 593). The sententiousness here and in Tyndarus's lines from *The Captives* bespeaks the influence of Euripides (whose *Alcmena* – where Zeus or Jupiter emerged with a similar protective role – is named directly in the description of the storm in *Rudens*).[2] But such 'agreeable mistakes' were typical of New Comedy (since it had 'palliated all the bitterness of [Old] Comedy') according to the late classical grammarians.[3]

That the representation of Fortune in New Comedy should be borrowed from philosophy or from popular beliefs was only to be expected. But it also seems very probable that the theatre, with its immense prestige in Greek culture, served to crystallise the artistic and literary image of Fortune for many centuries. Plato (and others) had said that the gods had created mankind as their plaything, or had arranged human life like a stage-play – a form of aphorism with a long subsequent history[4] (similarly, Daemones in *Rudens* implies that the gods *play* with men by means of dreams – '*di ludos faciunt hominibus*'). But moralists writing under the influence of New Comedy

---

[1] See Fraenkel, 'The Stars in the Prologue of the *Rudens*'; Hanson, 'Plautus as a Source Book for Roman Religion', pp. 70, 91–5; Webster, *Later Greek Comedy*, p. 154.
[2] *Rudens*, I.i; 86.   [3] *Cf* p. 84, above.
[4] Curtius, *European Literature*, p. 138; Jacquot, ' "Le Théâtre du Monde" de Shakespeare à Calderón', pp. 348ff.

or Euripidean romance often linked this general theatrical image specifically with the idea of Fortune. For example, in the third century B.C., the popular preacher, Teles, expounding the Cynic doctrine of moral self-sufficiency, showed how the conventions of the drama could be adapted for a moral sermon:

Fortune is like a playwright, who designs a number of parts – the shipwrecked man, the poor man, the exile, the king, the beggar. What the good man has to do is to play well any part with which Fortune may invest him.

Here a distinction is drawn between external, unstable prosperity or status and the moral self.[1] The hellenistic prose romances which were widely read in the first centuries A.D. repeatedly equate Fortune with a theatrical show, or a spectacular, theatrical episode with the manipulations of Fortune, as they recount their heroes' vicissitudes.[2] Again, Lucian, the rhetorician and satirical moralist (second century A.D.), compares mankind, rich and poor, to a tragic actor sent hobbling on to the stage by his manager, Fortune, with one foot buskined and the other bare.[3] But the most important statement of this theme comes from the Roman patrician and Christian moralist, Boethius, who in this as in other departments of learning summarised a great deal of classical thought and preserved it for the Middle Ages.[4]

When Boethius wrote his *Consolation of Philosophy* (A.D. 523–4) in his prison at Pavia, he had been thrown arbitrarily from a position of high power under the Gothic King Theodoric, and was threatened with death. The visionary figure of Philosophy comes to his cell to argue with him, so as to persuade him to understand his plight correctly. She teaches him wisdom, in a traditional literary style, without bringing in revelation; her arguments are borrowed from the Platonists and Aristotle; but when she deals with the crucial problem of Fortune, they are taken from, or associated with, the theatre. What right, Philosophy asks, has Boethius to blame Fortune? Fortune has always behaved dissemblingly (like a play-actor: '*sic*

---

1 See Bevan, 'Hellenistic Popular Philosophy', p. 91; *cf* Bréhier, *Histoire de la Philosophie*, vol. I, p. 367.
2 See Petronius, *Satyricon* (first century A.D.), 80; Chariton, *Chaereas and Callirhoe* (second century) IV.4; V.8; Heliodorus, *Ethiopian History* (*Theagenes and Chariclea*) (third century) V.6; VII.8; VII.6; X.39; Achilles Tatius, *Leucippe and Clitophon* (second to third century) I.3; III.15–21; V.11; VI.3; VII.5. *Cf* Wolff, *Greek Romances*, pp. 176–89; Calderini, *Le Avventure di Cherea e Calliroe*, pp. 159–69; Perry, *Ancient Romances*; Lesky, *Greek Literature*, pp. 857ff.
3 Lucian, *Saturnalian Letters* 19.
4 See Patch, *The Goddess Fortuna* and *The Tradition of Boethius*; Highet, *The Classical Tradition*, pp. 41–6, 571.

illa ludit..."*hunc continuum ludum ludimus*" "). And this capriciousness or untrustworthiness of Fortune is in the very nature of things:

If thou settest up thy sails to the wind, thou shalt be carried not whither thy will desirest, but whither the gale driveth...Endeavourest thou to stay the force of the turning wheel? But thou foolishest man that ever was, if it beginneth to stay, it ceaseth to be fortune.

These time-honoured images of the sailing wind and the wheel already begin to illustrate Philosophy's main thesis, that Fortune belongs to the cosmic order; and the wheel, the cycle, *is* Fortune, for Boethius (later in the dialogue, he introduces the image of Fortune *turning* her wheel, an image which was to be repeated many times in the Middle Ages, but it is evident from the argument as a whole that this is no more for him than a figure of speech). Using a rhetorical, semi-theatrical device, Philosophy now assumes the part of Fortune towards the author, and puts to him the case that Fortune would make for herself. 'When Nature produced thee out of thy mother's womb', she makes Fortune remind Boethius, she – Fortune – provided him with education, wealth and honours; but these things were hers, to revoke as to concede:

Must I only be forbidden to use my right? It is lawful for the heaven to bring forth fair days, and to hide them again in darksome nights. It is lawful for the year sometime to compass the face of the earth with flowers and fruits, and sometime to cover it with clouds and cold. The sea hath right sometime to fawn with calms, and sometime to frown with storms and waves. And shall the insatiable desire of men tie me to constancy, so contrary to my custom? This is my force, this is the sport [*ludum*] which I continually use. I turn about my wheel with speed, and take a pleasure to turn things upside down...What other thing doth the outcry of tragedies lament, but that fortune, having no respect, overturneth happy states?

(II, prose i–prose ii)

'Happy states' (princes) are like Oedipus, the moment before his fall; like Oedipus, Boethius has been guilty of *hubris*; and, like Oedipus, he is reconducted by Fortune to his mother's womb. Fortune is not outraging Nature, however; she has her own *dike*, her natural right, which is part of the justice and course of the cosmos. Most of Fortune's argument would have been familiar to Sophocles, a thousand years earlier, except perhaps for the emphasis on her caprice – and this is coloured by the theatre. By the end of this passage, the association with tragedies in the writer's mind is made explicit.

As soon, however, as Fortune (or Philosophy speaking in her name) has reminded Boethius of tragedies, she asks him, 'What if this mutability of mine be a just cause for thee to hope for better?' And now the mood of the dialogue begins to come nearer to Euripidean romance. The ancient metaphor of the cosmic wheel still governs the writer's imagination, but it comes to be used again as an expression for the ultimate order in the universe, for providence itself. When towards the end of their dialogue (IV, prose iv) Philosophy turns to the first cause of things, she uses a figure of concentric spheres, or wheels within wheels. Providence, she explains, is the divine reason, the unmoved mover at the centre of the cosmos, from which radiate outer and lesser powers, including Fate, which is really the natural order perceptible to man. Like the relation of 'a circle to the centre', such, she tells Boethius, is 'the course of moveable Fate to the stable simplicity of Providence'. She combines this geometrical or astronomical image with imagery drawn from nature, as in the earlier speech of Fortune:

That course [of Fate] moveth the heaven and stars, tempereth the elements one with another, and transformeth them by mutual changing. The same reneweth all rising and dying things by like proceeding of fruits and seeds. This comprehendeth also the actions and fortunes of men by an unloosable connexion of causes, which since it proceeds from the principles of unmovable Providence, the causes also must needs be immutable.

The revolutions of Fortune, then, are nothing else but an outer ring to 'the course of moveable Fate', and, like Fate, Fortune in turn is subject, in the last resort, to 'the stable simplicity of Providence'. The wheel expunges Fortune's malice. Her play-acting is mere appearance, but to be appearance is her reality.

Boethius's dialogue appealed strongly to readers for centuries. It was translated by Alfred, by Chaucer, by Elizabeth I; its essential arguments reappear in Spenser's *Mutability Cantos*. And it affects renaissance drama and Elizabethan drama in particular at several levels. But while Boethius's conception of Fortune's wheel reaches back to early Greek philosophy and, beyond that, to ancient myth and ritual, it is guided by images borrowed from the theatre. In applying his teachings to theatrical purposes again, renaissance dramatists, therefore, if in part unconsciously, were repaying a debt. And, within the tradition of comedy at least, the theatrical associations of the conception of Fortune carry with them the persistent irony or paradox, that Fortune's play-acting is at once a deception and an expression of truth.

FORTUNE AS TRICKSTER

Fortune is a deceiver; external goods are not only transient but unreal by comparison with man's true nature. Such is the burden of moralists, from the age of Teles the Cynic to Boethius. The equivalent in New Comedy is the theme that adversity also is delusive. Happiness is temporary and precarious. 'Everything human is completely mad', says a speaker in a fragment from the Middle Comedy writer, Alexis (?360 B.C.):[1]

We, the living, have the chance of a leave of absence, as if we had been released from death and darkness to go to a carnival [a festival: *panegyris*], into amusements and into this light upon which we look. He who laughs the most and drinks and plays with Aphrodite during his leaves of absence, and also dines, he enjoys his holiday the most before he goes home.

'Men's life is like a game of dice', says Micio, in Terence's *Brothers* (739: after Menander, ★*c.* 300 B.C.);[2] 'if the throw you most want doesn't turn up, you must correct what chance gives by means of skill.' But if happiness is provisional, so is misfortune. The trickiness of chance reveals man's true nature, his true place in the world, which is indistinguishable from his need for society and his position as a link in the continuity of the family.

Conversely, the trickster in New Comedy is nearly always lucky. True, he depends on Fortune also for his complete success as a rule. The intriguing slave, who inherits in an underhand fashion the mental initiative or inventiveness that the citizen-protagonists in comedy have lost, usually requires the help of coincidence; either he counterfeits a coincidence to make his deception plausible or else he is luckier than he knows. His function is to set the wheel of Fortune spinning. But on the other hand, the wheel never completes its turn in New Comedy without the help of a deceiver, whether an impudent slave or a free citizen who keeps something of the buffoon or trickster in him. The deceptiveness of Fortune is thus illustrated on yet another

[1] Lever, *Art of Greek Comedy*, p. 168; *cf* Edmonds (ed. and trans.), *Attic Comedy*, vol. II, p. 479.
[2] ★ marks the probable or conjectured dates of the Greek originals behind the comedies of Plautus and Terence, as given by T. B. L. Webster in *Menander and Later Greek Comedy*.

plane. But in spite of the apparent distance in the world of New Comedy between men and the power that disposes their happiness, in spite of the disappearance of those magical transformations of the social world that had been usual in Old Comedy, trickery remains in intimate collaboration with the cycle of Nature. The two are still inseparable.

In many comedies, the 'agreeable mistakes' result from a concealed identity or a duplicated identity (twinship) within the family of the play. In effect, the concealment or doubling of identities in these plots reproduces the duality of the actor and his mask on the plane of a more or less life-like fiction; while the recognition scene, the public disclosure of the disguising, shows that chance has been working, concealed, to renew the family cycle. And in some plays from New Comedy the collaboration of tricks and chance has a religious colouring, as a means of rewarding virtue or as a sign of providence. These tendencies point back towards the ancient hinterland of comedy, where masquerade and the life-cycle were interdependent, in that the purpose of assuming a ritual disguise was life-enhancement, and the task of reanimating Nature for society involved ritual disguising and *mimesis*. With all its domesticity and surface realism, therefore, New Comedy still follows the outlines of myth.[1] But it also shows its descent from the critical art, as distinct from the ritual survivals, in Old Comedy through its emphasis on deception, irony and moral ambiguity. The function of disguising has been abstracted from natural magic, to become an attribute of mind or character and of social behaviour. Just the same, fortunate dissembling, 'agreeable mistakes', remain at the centre of comedy still, whether it leans towards farce, as with Plautus, or comedy of manners, as with Terence.

Several plays are recorded from Middle Comedy with titles like *The Twins* or *The Namesakes*; others dealt with legends of a birth from a divine father. Plautus's *Amphitryon* (?*c.* 330) evidently represents both of these types; here the deceptive duplications of identity in Amphitryon's household, before the birth of Hercules and his human twin, are caused by the gods, in a manner reminiscent of the period of the *Frogs* and Euripides' *Bacchae*.[2] In other comedies by Plautus, from Greek originals mostly earlier than Menander (*The Persian*,

---

1 Murray, 'Ritual Elements in New Comedy'.
2 See p. 114, n. 1, above; also Edmonds (ed. and trans.), *Attic Comedy*, vol. II, pp. 659ff; Norwood, *Greek Comedy*, p. 51; Webster, *Later Greek Comedy*, pp. 68, 71–4, 83ff.

*c. 330; Casina, *c. 330/20; The Haunted House, *c. 320/10), there are
disguises or impostures on a purely human plane; trickery provides
sufficient comic material here, with very little help from coincidence.
The obscure agency of Fortune causes the separation, the confusion
and then the reuniting of the twin brothers in the *Menaechmi*
(?*c. 340); but this play – the favourite of the Renaissance – illustrates
how in New Comedy Fortune's wheel cannot complete its turn without the help of trickery.

One boy, according to the Prologue, had been lost and stolen at
Tarentum, when 'it so happened' that the games were being held
('*Tarenti ludei forte erant*', 29) – a typical concurrence of chance and
festivity at the starting-point of the mistakes in the story. Each step
in the plot thereafter involves a kind of interchange between equivalents which are also opposites; between money values and family
values, status and pleasure, liberty and duress, and, of course,
between the married resident twin who has been lost to his family
and his travelling bachelor brother who still belongs to it. The
Epidamnian citizen who had abducted Menaechmus I had adopted
the boy as his heir, says the Prologue, having 'no children of his own
except his wealth' (59), and had married him to a well-dowered (and
therefore domineering) wife; meanwhile the father's family at
Syracuse had given the lost boy's name to the remaining twin (37–
48). At bottom, therefore, the plot arises from the search by
Menaechmus II for his namesake, his other self. But that is not quite
how it is worked out. The play opens at Epidamnus with a monologue by the parasite, Peniculus, who, having great hopes from
Menaechmus I, dilates on the paradox that it is stupid to try to confine
a man's will by 'fetters' when a well-heaped table is the real means to
'chain' and enslave him (I.i); whereupon his patron is shown caught in
the same paradox. Breaking from home to spend the day with his
mistress, the courtesan Erotium, Menaechmus I is 'kept back and
called back and questioned' by his 'customs-officer' of a wife ('*me
retinas, reuocas, rogitas*': I.ii; 114, 117); having arranged a banquet with
Erotium and Peniculus, he is 'retained and detained' ('*ita med attinuit,
ita detinuit*': IV.ii; 589) beyond his appointed time by one of his
vociferous clients in the Forum,[1] while his brother has unsuspectingly
taken his place; and he is again restrained, with force and humiliation,
by his father-in-law's slaves (v.viii), this time in lieu of his brother,
who is supposed to be mad. But his own roguery has caused this

---

[1] See Segal, *Roman Laughter*, pp. 51, 189.

confusion; in the mock-military terms habitual with Plautus's tricksters,[1] he boasts in his first scene of the mantle he has stolen from his wife to give to his mistress (I.ii; 131):

This is the right, the elegant way to double-cross a sharp watchman! A beautiful, honourable, delightful exploit, a workmanlike job! I've carried this off from my plague at my own risk, to give it to my destruction [*Meo malo a mala abstuli, hoc ad damnum deferetur*]. I've diverted this plunder from the enemy to the benefit of our allies.

Nor is his twin any less of a rogue. Warned by his faithful slave, Messenio, against the same kind of 'destruction' prevalent at Epidamnus (II.i; 264, 267), he is at first guarded and scornful when Erotium's Cook (II.ii) and then Erotium herself claim to remind him of his dinner-appointment; but he warms to the chance of a free meal (II.iii; 418) and finally shakes off Messenio when Erotium asks him to take the stolen mantle to an embroiderer's to be refashioned; 'the plunder's mine; the manoeuvre has begun', he tells Messenio, echoing his brother (435). And when he comes away from his banquet *à deux* (having told Peniculus to be off, for a madman: 517), he is carrying the stolen mantle and a bracelet similarly acquired as well, and determines to abscond while the going is good (III.iii; 551):

Why, all the gods are helping me, enriching me, loving me! But why am I hanging about, when I'm given the time and opportunity to slip away from these haunts of procuring? Quick, Menaechmus, forward march!

Menaechmus I is berated by his Wife (who has been informed by the disappointed parasite) for stealing her mantle, and has the door shut in his face by Erotium for returning to her without it (IV.ii–iii); but in the next scene (v.i) the Wife catches Menaechmus II with the offending garment and blocks his escape. This 'plunder' becomes a mock recognition token; it is almost a talisman (like the stage rags in the *Acharnians*), the symbol of the apparent bad luck of Epidamnus, the 'destruction', whether through sex or marriage, that seems to threaten each of the brothers there in turn. But their trickery saves them. When the Wife and her father declare that Menaechmus II (who, of course, denies all knowledge of them) must be mad, he decides accordingly that his best move is to feign madness, and he burlesques a tragic frenzy, with echoes from Euripides, so as to frighten them away (v.ii; 832ff).[2] Once again, deception rebounds from

---

[1] Hanson, 'The Glorious Military'.

[2] Webster, *Later Greek Comedy*, p. 69; *cf* Arnaldi, *Da Plauto a Terenzio*, vol. I, p. 38.

brother to brother; Menaechmus I is now trapped by his father-in-law's slaves (in company with an *alazon*, the quack doctor). But he is rescued, in mistake, by Messenio; and when the slave then proposes to fetch the traveller's money from their inn so as to leave Epidamnus, bargaining for his freedom in exchange for his timely intervention, Menaechmus I, puzzled as he is (he thinks he is living in a dream), blandly encourages him, with the private intention of keeping this unexpected windfall for his pains (v.viii; 1044). This last turn of rascality precipitates the recognition scene between the slave and the two brothers; after which Menaechmus I decides to leave his disagreeable wife, put up his property, wife included, for auction, and go back to Syracuse.

The whole farce depends on convention, rather than character. Although the Greek author was evidently writing before Aristotle had lectured on the *Poetics*, he has adopted the scheme of a complex plot by making Peniculus and the Wife intervene with results contrary to their intentions; he has worked on the principle that a recognition may not be allowed to take place on the stage until the situation has been well and truly reversed. There is no reason, except the convention of stage ignorance borrowed from tragedy, why Menaechmus II should not guess why strangers in Epidamnus hail him by name; and there is no apparent reason, except the comic convention of trickery, why Menaechmus I, who is evidently a rich man, should provide a gift for his mistress by stealing from his wife. Fortune turns by way of theft, mistakes and dissimulation; deception is the answer to bad luck. Bewildering double identities have something apparently supernatural behind them, almost as in *Amphitryon*; and each of the brothers regains his true self by means of a masquerade.

The theft by Menaechmus I corresponds to his early abduction by his foster-father, who was fittingly drowned (says the Prologue) by a swollen river. A similar complex of ideas, interweaving Fortune, poetic justice and trickery, reappears in *Rudens*, which Plautus acknowledges as an adaptation from Diphilus (*c. 310/300?).[1] The setting here is unusual, more like a satyr-play than the street scene normal in comedy;[2] it represents a rocky coast in Africa, near Cyrene, with the storm-battered cottage of Daemones, the Athenian exile, a poor temple dedicated to Venus, and an altar. A slave-dealing procurer named Labrax has broken faith with a young Athenian in Cyrene by setting

[1] *Cf* above, p. 153.
[2] Beare, *Roman Stage*, p. 170; Webster, *Greek Theatre Production*, pp. 26–8.

sail with the two girls in his possession (the young man's beloved, Palaestra, and Ampelisca, her maid), hoping to make more money out of them in Sicily; but Labrax and his companion in villainy and the two girls have been wrecked and scattered here by a storm. Since the altar has been the place dishonestly appointed by Labrax for a meeting with the Athenian, it is possible for the latter and his slave, Trachalio, to find Palaestra and Ampelisca before Labrax can snatch them back from the temple, where they have taken sanctuary with the priestess. And the characteristic perjury of the slave-dealer recoils further still; when he breaks into the temple, Trachalio shouts for help, and Daemones rescues the girls, taking them into his protection (III.iv), and later (IV.iv) discovering in Palaestra his own long-lost daughter, whom Labrax had purchased illegally (since she had trinkets giving evidence of her freeborn parentage). Here the wheel of Fortune goes further than in the *Menaechmi*, or any other Roman comedy; it virtually reproduces as well as recompensing the past: Labrax meets Palaestra's lover at the appointed place, against his will, and in effect he tries to kidnap her a second time from her father. Although Daemones has never seen the procurer before, he exclaims that he has met 'many a man like that – it's because of that sort that I'm living in poverty', when the lover, in his search, asks about 'a grey-headed, frizzle-haired scoundrel, a fawning perjurer' (I.ii; 125); and this interchange, and Daemones' subsequent rescue of the girls, in response to Trachalio's cry for help in the name of the law (621), recall the Prologue's first description of him (33–8) as a virtuous Athenian, driven into exile and poverty as a consequence of his generosity in helping others. The wheel has come full circle – 'is there anyone more fortunate than me?' he asks (1191) – when it turns out that the young Athenian, to whom he at once agrees to marry his rediscovered daughter, is well-born and a kinsman (1198).

All this follows from the prologue, where the star-god Arcturus explains that the storm has been his doing, in keeping with his charge from Jupiter to punish faith-breakers and watch over the good. It is romance, with strong overtones from Euripides – in the subject-matter of Athenians or Greeks reunited when far from home (as in *Ion*) or when stranded on a distant, barbarian coast (as in *Helen* and *Iphigenia in Tauris*); in the passages about the storm (where Euripides is directly mentioned: I.i; 86); in the heroine's despair when she is shipwrecked (I.iii); and in the succour of a noble-minded priestess (I.v); as in each of the three rescue plays by Euripides. And the dramatist connects Daemones strongly with the ideas of Athenian solidarity and sense of law. When he responds to Trachalio's appeal for law to be upheld against sacrilege (because Labrax has broken into the temple), he becomes an arbiter as between Trachalio and Labrax (III.iv; 714ff), with a warm interest in the disputed girls once he hears that they are Athenians (738–9). His recognition scene comes about through a second arbitration (IV.iv), because his fisherman-slave, Gripus, has found the travelling-bag containing Labrax's money and the casket with Palaestra's trinkets in the sea, Trachalio has observed Gripus and claimed the casket for Palaestra, and both have referred their dispute to Daemones. He is an arbiter yet again in the final scene, when Labrax claims his bag from Gripus and Gripus claims a huge reward; and there is even a fourth arbitration in the play, reported off-stage at Cyrene (III.vi, V.i), where the lover has haled the perjurer to court. The recognition plot, therefore, is subordinated to the theme of justice, to the reassertion of the general values of Athens as a civilised city. Here again, in the motif of re-cognition through arbitration, the comedy harks back to Euripides, possibly by way of Menander's *Arbitration* (?c. 300), where an ill-tempered grandfather brings his grandson's true position to light unawares by agreeing to umpire a dispute between two slaves; at a decisive moment later in this play, the grandfather is pointedly told that the gods have allotted 'character' to each of us as his guardian or commander.[1]

But just here, in the reinstatement of Athenian values, *Rudens* also recalls Aristophanes, especially, perhaps, the *Birds*. One marked thread in the play is the theme of poverty – the poverty of Gripus and of the chorus of fishermen who come in chiefly to deplore the results of the storm (II.i), the poverty of the Priestess and her temple, the poverty of Daemones in his battered cottage.[2] A contrary theme is the idea of expectation or hope – there are twenty occasions where *spes* comes into the dialogue, from the lover's search (92) to Palaestra's monologue after the shipwreck and her meeting with Ampelisca (204, 209, 222, 231, 247), onwards to the recognition scene (1145, 1161, 1175) and the final scene (1414), where Daemones dashes Gripus's hopes of a profit. And the junction between these two ideas lies in the comic motif of quick wits or trickery, as opposed to

---

[1] Allinson (ed.), *Menander: The Arbitrants*, line 881. See Webster, *Menander*, p. 21; *Later Greek Comedy*, pp. 168–9; Post, *From Homer to Menander*, chs. 6–8.

[2] See Arnaldi, *Da Plauto a Terenzio*, vol. I, pp. 222–5.

extravagant delusions or imposture. The first phase of the action has resulted from the attempt of Labrax, the *alazon*, to cheat Palaestra's lover by sailing away 'with the fond expectation' (as his half-drowned accomplice puts it) 'of gobbling up the whole island of Sicily' (II.vi; 543); and the second phase begins with the introduction of poor Gripus, whose rope gives the play its title, who has just fished up Labrax's travelling-bag (his only catch for the day) and who launches at once into a euphoric chant of anticipation, as he imagines himself not merely free by use of its contents but a rich man, a 'Croesus', a famous traveller and the founder of a city named after himself, 'the monument of my glory and deeds' (IV.ii).[1] These imperial day-dreams sound like an echo from Aristophanes.

In the same vein, Trachalio behaves like a trickster when he springs on Gripus (for the sake of Palaestra's casket) and corners him with arguments about property-rights, so that Gripus calls him a 'philo-sopher' or sophist (IV.iii; 986) and complains sarcastically that he doesn't understand hair-splitting 'city laws' (1024). And Daemones, the just man, is something of a trickster himself. At first, he is merely given touches of the ironic buffoon; when, for instance, he tells his slave, Sceparnio, to stop wasting time watching storm-tossed maidens if he means to earn his supper (181); when he congratulates himself on finding two attractive clients by sheltering them (893); or when he ridicules his wife's effusions over their daughter (1204). But in the last arbitration, when the gods have already repaid his mainly dis-interested dealings, he acquires a bonus for himself by sagacious opportunism. Again, property-rights are in question. After the dispute over Palaestra's casket. Gripus has criticised his master for holding the other contents of the travelling-bag ('a gift from the gods') in trust, instead of keeping them for himself, Daemones has replied that honesty is the best policy (with the nuance that he values the pleasure of a game more than the profit), Gripus has retorted that such fine sentiments are applauded in a comedy, but none of the spectators apply them in practice; and Daemones, as he goes off to prepare a sacrifice to the gods, has let it be seen that he has spoken from wariness rather than high principle. In any case, there has been a difference between his unguarded generosity at Athens, as described in the prologue, and the 'prudence, skill and astuteness' he professes now (IV.vii). And these are the qualities that come to the fore when he arbitrates between Gripus and Labrax over the travelling-bag,

---

[1] *Ibid.*, pp. 232–4.

for which the latter has offered the slave a huge reward, with his usual glibness and bad faith. Half the disputed sum Daemones adjudges to Labrax, in exchange for liberating Ampelisca (so that she can marry Trachalio, who has also been set free); the other half he allots to the plaintiff, keeping it himself, however (by 'fraud', according to Gripus), as the price of the slave's freedom. In effect, he shows Gripus what really happens in comedies. The circumstances of Daemones' exile from Athens have recalled Peithetaerus's flight from the unjust city, and now his astute judgment resembles Peithetaerus's reception of the would-be intruders to Cloudcuckootown. In spite of the strongly romantic tone of the play, it leads up to trickery in order to complete the restoration of desirable social relationships.

In *Rudens*, as in the *Menaechmi*, the trickster completes the work of Fortune's wheel without premeditation. But in several plays due to Menander or his influence, the trickster collaborates intentionally with Fortune, or Fortune comes in to cap his efforts. In working out plots in these lines, it looks as if Menander gradually devised a new pattern for comedy.

Probably the earliest of his known plays was *The Bad-Tempered Man* (316 B.C.). Here the god Pan, who speaks the prologue, presides over the action; the lover's success is due partly to disguise (when he works as a farm-labourer, on the advice of a slave), but mainly to coincidence (the coming of the revellers; the accidents at the well). The effects of inventiveness and the effects of chance are merely linked together by contiguity. Similarly, in Plautus's *Pot of Gold* (from Menander, *c. 310), the results due to Fortune – or rather, to the Household God, who speaks the prologue and who watches over the hidden treasure near the temple of Faith on behalf of Euclio's family – and the results due to the lover's knavish servant simply follow one another (except that they have a point of contact in the neurotic behaviour of old Euclio when he has found the treasure). But Menander's *Double Deceiver* (*c. 310) – Plautus's *Bacchides* – has a different approach: the first deception by Chrysalus founders because of a chance mistake of identities (when his young master confuses one twin sister with the other), whereupon Chrysalus deliberately stages a tableau of misleading identities for his second deception (the blackmail story), enlisting the captain, who arrives by chance at the moment, as well. Here the trickster deliberately and successfully reproduces the deceptions due to chance. And in comedies of later origin the same device is repeated. In *Pseudolus* (?*309) –

possibly from Menander[1] – Plautus makes the intriguing slave descant at length on the way a chance arrival has perfected his plans (II.iii; 667ff) (this is said to be the earliest reference in Roman literature to Fortune as a goddess):[2]

Immortal gods! this man has saved me by his coming. The supply he brings leads me back from wandering off the right way. Opportunity herself couldn't come to me more opportunely than this letter he so opportunely brings. It's a horn of plenty to me, where I can find all I want: my ruses are here, all my needed deceptions and impostures, the money, the girl-friend my young master's in love with. Now I can really brag and let myself go! I had my plan of action ready prepared...But really, you can say this – the goddess Fortune can prevail over the plans of a hundred clever men. And this is true, too: when Fortune's on your side, you excel and everyone says how wise you are...Fools that we are, when we seek so vainly and so greedily for something to be given to us, as if we could know our own interests! We leave certainty, to pursue uncertainty...But that's enough philosophising.

And from this pre-Juvenalian reflection, the Roman intriguer returns to the business of the play – which means turning an improvised lie to advantage and deceiving three other characters at once. Again, in *The Braggart Soldier* (from Diphilus, *c. 300), Palaestrio, favoured by chance, begins his operations with an artistic imitation of coincidence, in the manner of Chrysalus. And there is another variant on this theme in Menander's *Arbitration*: the slave-girl Habrotonon acts a part in order to find out the truth (as if in a detective story). Chance provides her with clues, but the rest is the work of her own 'persuasion' and 'pretence' – or 'malice and roguery', as her admiring fellow-conspirator calls it.

In these plays, the trickster juggles knowingly with coincidence. In others, he is luckier than he realises. In Plautus's *Carthaginian* (from Menander, *c. 300), the slave-intriguer invites a Carthaginian stranger to pose as the heroine's father – whereupon it is discovered that that is who the stranger is (since the Carthaginian is exceptionally god-fearing and the occasion is a festival of Venus, coincidence here looks like 'divine chance').[3] Similarly, in *Curculio*, *The Threepenny Day*, *Epidicus* and Terence's *Phormio* (from several Greek authors, *c. 310–270), a trickster's ruse leads to the unexpected discovery of a lost

---

[1] Webster, *Later Greek Comedy*, p. 190; see Gordon Williams, '*Pseudolus*'.
[2] Coleman-Norton, 'Fortune in Roman Drama', p. 70; but see Hanson, 'Plautus as a Source Book for Roman Religion', p. 81.
[3] *Ibid.*, p. 92.

sister or daughter (or a family fortune), either by pure coincidence in theatrical timing or by cause and effect. The trickster works in the dark, but his trickery is needed to bring the truth to light. This convention is worked out most thoroughly in Plautus's *Captives* (★280/70), where Tyndarus and his master from Elis have been purchased by Tyndarus's father in Aetolia as prisoners of war. When Tyndarus undertakes to impersonate his master in order to help him to escape, he has no idea that this trick will lead to his own reinstatement in his family. Since he is really a freeborn citizen, he does not behave like a trickster except for the impersonation. But, like the Menaechmi brothers, he discovers his own identity by acting a part.

In the plays that attracted Terence there are further variations. In *The Andrian*, *The Eunuch* and *The Self-Tormentor* – all three from Menander, ★*c*. 304–298 – the slaves overreach themselves by their cunning; in *The Brothers* (also from Menander, ★*c*. 300) the impudent slave has only a minor part; and in *The Mother-in-law* (from Menander's follower, Apollodorus, ?★ *c*. 270) the hero sends his knowing servant on a fool's errand in order to keep him out of the way. Self-deception is the governing factor in most of these comedies, rather than downright trickery; Terence is interested in the way people with plausible or respectable motives deviate from an Aristotelian mean in their conduct. Dissembling belongs firstly to the ordinary give-and-take of a civilised domestic life for his citizen characters, and only secondly to the fabrications of his slaves. On the other hand, the desire in his people to live amicably together is stronger than their impulse to quarrel, so that coincidence has as it were a natural purchase to grip on. But in his social world of inverted trickery, Fortune, though benevolent, still operates through deceit.

'Report' and 'dissimulation' are the two key concepts in *The Andrian*. Chremes has approached Simo to arrange a match between his daughter and Simo's son, Pamphilus, because he has heard reports (*fama*, 99) that the young man has a steady character. Then he has broken off the match because he has heard that Pamphilus is living with a foreign girl, an orphan from Andros, whom he treats as if she were a legal wife (144). Simo has denied this, although he has found out that it is true; nevertheless, he means to pretend to his son that the match with Chremes' daughter is still agreed – partly in order to test his son's obedience, and partly, he says, so as to forestall the wiles of his slave, 'that rascal Davus' (1.i). Davus, on his side, sees through his old master's plan and advises Pamphilus to pretend to obey his father's pretended commands (II.ii–iii). Hence the main intrigue consists of a bluffing match between master and slave, in which, just as the slave had guessed that the master's preparations for a wedding were only feigned, so the master assumes that the labour pains of his son's mistress are really an imposture devised by the slave (III.i). But Davus's astuteness leads to awkward results when Pamphilus's mistress, Glycerium, and his friend, Charinus, both misinterpret reports that Pamphilus has promised to marry into Chremes's family; and again when the slave is forced by the too-thorough success of his first deception to practise a second, inducing Chremes to withdraw his consent to the marriage once more by means of a cleverly improvised tableau with the newly-born baby (IV.i–iv). Davus is only saved from his master's anger, and the situation is only resolved, by the timely arrival of Crito, a newcomer from Andros (IV.v), who, like a god from the machine (as Donatus points out in his notes on the play), brings with him the disclosure that Glycerium is, in fact, a lost daughter of Chremes (V.iv). In a sense, therefore, this is one of the comedies where Fortune simply caps a schemer's blind invention; had Crito landed in Athens either earlier or later, it is easy to suppose that the whole tangle would have worked out differently. But as it is, the misunderstandings have lasted just long enough for the leading characters to measure the distortions of gossip and hasty judgments and test each other's true intentions. And Terence (or Menander) camouflages the intrusion of accident by working it into the psychological texture of the play, the excessive mistrust typified by Simo and Davus. Thus Davus, in his first monologue, refers to talk between the lovers to the effect that Glycerium is Athenian by birth, only to dismiss it from his mind as a childish invention (I.iii; 220–4); and similarly, although Crito has a good legal reason for intervening when he does, he is afraid of being thought a blackmailer for his pains (815). Like other characters who transpose convention in this lightly sophisticated play where fiction parades as reality and reality is masked as fiction, he suggests a traditional role, that of the *alazon*, in reverse. Through Donatus's notes, drawing attention to the chain of 'errors', *The Andrian* had a deep influence on Renaissance theory of comedy,[1] although Terence was less frequently acted and imitated than Plautus.

The alliance between Fortune and the trickster, based on the

---

[1] *Cf* p. 84, above.

capacity for self-deception in the serious characters, is more conspicuous still in *The Self-Tormentor*, where again there are two fathers
(Menedemus and another Chremes) and two young lovers in perplexities. Chremes's slave, Syrus, has the impudence to introduce
the mistress of Menedemus's son into Chremes's household under a
false identity and then to switch households with a variant of this
unforeseeably lucky imposture for the benefit of his own young
master's liaison:

this is the plan I give the palm to; this is where I'm really superbly exalted,
that I have the resource and the artful capacity to deceive both [the fathers]
by telling the truth.   (IV.iii; 709)

But this trickster's boast is no more than an extension of the central
moral subject of the play, the difficulty of candour, sincerity. Earlier,
for instance, Syrus has given an intimate sketch – in the style of the
Characters of Theophrastus – of the heroine weaving at her loom. He
had burst into her house with another slave, he says there, so as to
catch her unawares and thus seize 'an opportunity of judging the
course of her daily life, which reveals a person's character [*ingenium*]
better than anything else' (II.iii; 275–95). And this speech follows
the same train of thought as that of Chremes previously, when he had
been explaining to his self-tormenting neighbour (Menedemus) that
lack of candour had been the cause of his troubles with his son: 'You
really didn't know him well enough, nor he you. And why? It's
when people don't live frankly together' (I.i; 153). But Chremes is
not exactly sincere himself, and he will even recommend deceit in
his officious eagerness to set his neighbour right (I.ii–II.i; III.i; IV.v).
When, therefore, the trickster boasts that on the strength of his
cunning he will deceive the two fathers by telling the truth, he has
the logic of the moral situation behind him.

The Mother-in-law is a striking play, unusual among its kind. As
Donatus says in his preface, 'in the whole comedy, things are kept
moving so as to bring in innovations, yet without revolting from
custom. For instance, it introduces a kindly mother-in-law, a bashful
daughter-in-law, a husband extremely gentle with his wife and also
devoted to his mother, an honourable courtesan.'[1] Pamphilus has
returned to Athens, in a mood closer (as Donatus observes) to tragedy
than comedy, cursing his lot and the inconstancy of Fortune (III.i,
iii). He has found his parents and his wife's parents at sixes and sevens

---

[1] See Donatus's notes in *Terentii . . . Comoediae*, ed. Stallbaum.

because his wife, Philumena, has inexplicably left his mother's house during his absence and gone back to her own mother. Pamphilus arrives in time to learn the secret; she has given birth to a baby which both have reason to believe is not his. He had married her against his will, had then come to love her, and now finds himself in a dilemma; he can neither bring himself to take her back nor to explain his reason to the two families. The play consists, then, of a series of concealments and recriminations, in which the men blame the women (the two mothers and Pamphilus's former mistress, the courtesan, Bacchis) in a manner recalling older sex-war comedies like *Lysistrata*, while most of the characters brush past the truth without seeing it. Parmeno the slave tries to soothe Pamphilus, for instance, by pointing out that the angriest quarrels often spring from the slightest causes; women in particular, he adds, are like children in this respect (III.i). Pamphilus's father, Laches, first blames his wife for causing him 'undeserved vexations' (II.i), then accuses first Pamphilus and then Philumena's father, Phidippus, of showing obstinate resentment, resolving, in the next breath, to discharge his feelings on his wife again (III.v); then reproaches his son once more for expecting perfection of other people or else 'trumping up false grounds for discord' (IV.iv); then admits that he had accused the women, including the attractive Bacchis, mistakenly, and finally declares (still on mistaken evidence) that there has been nothing in the whole squabble to merit a divorce (v.ii); and Laches throughout has been the character who has goaded the others into action. When, as a last resort, Bacchis is sent for to help, she produces the evidence, surprising to all those in the secret of the birth, that one night, shortly before his wedding, Pamphilus, who was then still her lover, had come to her, drunk, and, after 'pretending' to ignore her 'suspicious' questions, had confessed that he had just raped an unknown girl – who, of course, was Philumena (v.iii). As in other New Comedies, then, the wheel comes round full circle. And, although *The Mother-in-law* is the most consistent and penetrating Roman comedy of manners, the wheel spins as usual (as Donatus again notes) through a series of 'errors'. Nearly all of Castelvetro's categories of deceit, from drunkenness to chance, are present here together. Had Pamphilus been capable of remembering his crime distinctly, there would have been no dilemma; but if the others had not blindly and obstinately interfered, there would have been no solution. Like the Menaechmi and other heroes in New Comedy, Pamphilus restores the continuity of his family as a result of confusions, concealments and false assumptions affecting the identity, the moral if not the legal identity, of the principal characters in the play; his road to his true self passes through social disguise. And Pamphilus feels the human need for concealment, the tension between private and social life, until the end: 'I don't want this to be like comedies', he says in the last scene, 'where everyone discovers everything'. 'As if', Donatus subjoins in his notes, 'this were not a comedy, but real life' – a remark which the neoclassical dogmatists on stage illusion might have done well to take note of.

One of the chief 'technical novelties' of Ibsen and his successors, according to Shaw, was to get rid of 'the old stage tricks' dealing with 'unreal people and improbable circumstances' and to substitute 'a forensic technique of recrimination, disillusion and penetration through ideals to the truth'. Novelty in the arts is relative. On one side of the argument, Ibsen himself is not altogether free from 'old stage tricks' involving a cycle of coincidences. On the other side, priority for devising a technique of penetration through false conventions to the truth, at least in serious domestic drama, should rather go to Menander and Apollodorus, or else to Terence, who added his own polish to their methods, and made them accessible to the playwrights of modern Europe. From *The Mother-in-law* it is not a very long step, in subject-matter or construction, to *Pillars of Society* or *Mrs Warren's Profession*. In comedy of manners, the Way of the World has always been deceit; and the lie that becomes a truth has been a staple of post-Renaissance comedy from the time of Corneille to Pirandello or Synge. Already by Shakespeare's day, dramatists had rediscovered the ironic possibilities in the motif of false impressions giving place to moral recognition, in comedies as unlike each other as *The Honest Whore*, *Volpone* and *Measure for Measure*. And in the Renaissance, as in classical comedy, the episodes of delusion that carry the plot forward are not intended as a straightforward picture of life, but rather as a duplication of the primary function of comedy – a seasonal celebration by masked performers.

There was much in classical comedy that the Elizabethans could not accept. Their attitude towards trickery, for instance, is morally cautious, if not ambiguous – it is funny when applied to moral deviants, but otherwise reprehensible. Shakespeare accepts it, in farcical terms, as a weapon defending marriage in the battle of the sexes, or, in serious terms, as a means of restoring the moral order:

'Craft against vice I must apply', says the Duke in *Measure for Measure*. But, although the renaissance stage abounded in servant buffoons – Harlequin, Hanswurst, the Vice, the *gracioso* and others – who were plainly related in several ways to the impudent slaves of New Comedy, in Shakespeare at least the relationship is not one of direct descent; his clowns are commentators, not intriguers. In the main plots of his romantic comedies, the initiative in disguise or witty improvisation has passed to his heroines, at the same time as the typical motive for intrigue has become the securing of love, not the finding of monetary means to enjoy it. By comparison with Plautus or Terence, Shakespeare's comic scene is at some removes from the everyday bourgeois world, thanks to the influence of medieval romance; just as his comic intrigue is less of a vestigial ritual, and more of a game, because of the self-consciousness clinging to renaissance imitations of antiquity and thanks to the influence of renaissance courtly culture. Yet the process of acting within the comedy and the function of disguise in renewing the cycle of nature are as much vital to Shakespeare as to any other inheritor of the classical tradition. Whereas in Jonson, for example, the typical movement in a comedy is an advance towards moral truth by way of the unmasking of impostors, in Shakespeare it is an advance towards self-discovery by way of disguise and illusion.

Shakespeare's great innovation was to treat comedy lyrically as an emotional and imaginative experience, an inward metamorphosis. But his conception of a comic plot as a cycle of changing relationships is still essentially classical. As between Terence and Plautus, he almost certainly owed less to Terence's comedy of manners, and more to the comic-opera methods of Plautus. But, directly and indirectly, he borrowed heavily from both. He probably took hints from Terence (especially *The Andrian*) in the eavesdropping scenes in *Love's Labour's Lost* and the scenes of gossip and eavesdropping and true or misleading report which are added to Don John's intrigue in *Much Ado About Nothing* (no direct narrative source has been found for these passages in either play). His debt to Plautus is more certain and more extensive, beginning with his use of the *Menaechmi* and *Amphitryon* in *The Comedy of Errors*. He probably re-employed the device of rebounding confusions and transpositions of identity from these two plays, especially the *Menaechmi*, in two other early comedies, in episodes for which (again) there is no identified source – the crisscross of intrigues and errors affecting the two pairs of lovers in *Two*

Gentlemen and in *A Midsummer Night's Dream*. There is an echo from *The Haunted House* in *The Taming of the Shrew*, besides the indirect borrowing from Roman comedy by way of Ariosto and Gascoigne's *Supposes*; Shylock's pathetico-ridiculous outcry about his daughter and his ducats recalls Euclio in *The Pot of Gold*; and the intrigues against Falstaff in *The Merry Wives* are evidently indebted to the plot of *The Braggart Soldier*, while Anne Page's elopement recalls *Casina*. At the end of the first phase of his romantic comedies, in *Twelfth Night*, which becomes a 'comedy about comedy' and a kind of summing-up of his previous work, Shakespeare not merely draws his main plot from one of the most famous of Italian variants on the *Menaechmi* but supplements it by a direct (and evidently conscious) return to the Roman source; and while the main plot, with its latent allusion to Plautus, associates disguise with the benevolent deceptions of Fortune, the sub-plot deals, also in classical manner, with revelling and trickery.

Similarly, the central preoccupation in Shakespeare's late tragi-comedies is also the central theme of Euripidean romance, the cycle of Fortune affecting a family. At first, in *Pericles*, *Cymbeline* and *The Winter's Tale*, Shakespeare tackles the problem of dramatising a lengthy passage of time in his characters' lives by returning to the techniques, as well as the narrative material, of late-medieval stage romance, though even here he is still thinking of classical recognition plays and Horace's principle of selective narration. But in *The Tempest* he adopts the classical unities of time and place once more, there is a retrospective narration, and in addition the cycle of Fortune is completed by re-enacting on the island something very like the crimes committed against Prospero in Milan. Again, scholars have found no direct source for Shakespeare's plot. But for this play, with its incidental fantasies of empire and its dominant motif of the just man in exile requited by Providence through a storm, it seems very likely that Shakespeare took strong hints, if not his shaping ideas, from Plautus's *Rudens*. Even the poetic motif of life as a dream, or life as a stage-play, stems from the mental world of New Comedy. In so far as Fortune governs, or appears to govern, men's affairs, their rank and prosperity are deceptive; they are disguised from themselves as well as others. To this extent, an art that is based upon disguise presents a faithful image of reality, on condition that, as in classical comedy, it makes disguise and deception evident. At the same time, a plot in circular form, reuniting lovers or restoring children to their parents, provides an image of the course of Nature, hidden behind the apparent interference of Fortune.

The classical delineation of Fortune in dramatic plots, the role of the trickster in conditioning the presentation of Fortune, and the tradition of drama as an adjunct to seasonal celebrations provided fundamental guide-lines in comedy for Shakespeare as for other dramatists in the Renaissance. He owed to the classical tradition not merely occasional episodes or situations but his underlying conception of comedy as a form of theatrical art using logically connected plots to arouse and satisfy expectation and at the same time addressing itself to the spectators' sense of irony. Medieval romance provided him with stories, but the medieval stage tradition, as it survived to the time when he began his career, could not have given him the distinctively theatrical mode of presentation, the impulse to carry forward a plot by means of deceptive appearances and ironic reversals, that he drew from Plautus and Terence. In this connection, however, it is not easy to disentangle Shakespeare's direct debt to the Roman playwrights from his debt to their renaissance imitators.

5

SHAKESPEARE AND ITALIAN COMEDY

It's true that neither vulgar prose nor rhyme
Can be compared with ancient prose or verse,
And eloquence has fallen from its prime;
   But seeing wits are not indeed diverse
From those the heavenly Artist used of old,
What's done by them today need not be worse.

Ariosto

I travail with another objection, signior, which I fear will be enforced against
the author...That the argument of his comedy might have been of some
other nature, as of a duke to be in love with a countess, and that countess
to be in love with the duke's son, and the son to love the lady's waiting-maid;
some such cross wooing, with a clown to their servingman, better than to be
thus near, and familiarly allied to the time.

Jonson

Athenian Old Comedy had been a political celebration, Roman comedy
a festive entertainment. The achievement of the Italians in the early
sixteenth century was to reintroduce the methods as well as the
spirit of Roman comedy to modern Europe, though in reviving them
they inevitably changed them, making of comedy more of an intellectual game and setting the dramatist to range as best he could
between open-minded observation and technical virtuosity. But by
modifying as well as retrieving an art-form from the past, Ariosto's
generation prepared the way for both Molière and Shakespeare.[1]

The renaissance of New Comedy in Italy spread across a century.
It was heralded by the recovery of twelve new texts of Plautus in
1429 and of Donatus's commentary on Terence in 1433 – so that
scholars could now read nearly twice as many Roman comedies as
before and had a better means of appreciating their structure. There
were scholastic productions of Latin drama in Rome, by Pomponio
Leto, just before 1470, and in 1488 a Florentine seminary performed

---

[1] For a list of editions and translations of Italian plays, see Bibliography.

the *Menaechmi* amid some public excitement;[1] meanwhile the revival of the ancient dramatists on the stage began in earnest with the production of the *Menaechmi* in Italian at the ducal court of Ferrara in 1486. Over the next fifty years there were frequent performances, usually in translation, of the classical dramatists – more often Plautus than Terence, and much more of the comic playwrights than Seneca, hardly anything of the Greeks – in the principal Italian cities, especially in Florence and Venice and the courts of Rome, Ferrara and Mantua;[2] so that in the course of the last third of the fifteenth century a cultivated public became familiar with the old dramatic texts.

In the first third of the sixteenth century came the second phase of the renaissance, the creation, for the same public, of a new form of Italian drama, the *commedia erudita* or 'learned comedy', imitating Plautus and Terence; this phase began effectively, again at Ferrara, with the production of Ariosto's *Cassaria* and his *Suppositi* in the carnival seasons of 1508 and 1509. The production of such plays was not simply a humanistic experiment, still less a scholastic exercise, but an expression of Renaissance Carnival, part of a grandiose entertainment; magnificently staged, the plays exhibited modern characters in the setting of a contemporary Italian city; and the dramatists' unconcealed and even assiduous borrowing of situations and mechanisms of the plot from classical comedy was itself at first an affirmation of contemporary thought and feeling. Writers demonstrated their modernity by imitation of the classical past.

But what was really a third phase in this renaissance of classical drama opened about 1540, when, in the changing atmosphere that accompanied the Counter-Reformation, Italian men-of-letters began to expound the newly available text of the *Poetics* in order to frame rules for literature in accordance with Aristotle (though in the theory of comedy the more familiar rhetorical precepts of Donatus, Cicero and Horace carried as much weight as Aristotle's formulations).[3] Even when the theorists also wrote plays themselves, their purpose was not to analyse or describe the procedures of comedy, but rather to fit them into a rational moral system that was neither contemporary nor

---

1 See Borlenghi (ed.), *Commedie*, vol. I, p. 15; Rossi, *Quattrocento*, pp. 523–31.
2 See D'Ancona, *Origini*; articles on Ferrara, Florence, Mantua, Rome, Venice in D'Amico (ed.), *Enciclopedia dello Spettacolo*.
3 See Toffanin, *Cinquecento*, part 2, book VIII; *cf* Herrick, *Comic Theory*; Allan H. Gilbert (ed.), *Literary Criticism*; Spingarn, *Renaissance*; Weinberg, *Italian Renaissance*.

ancient but preordained and everlasting. And a fourth phase in the renaissance began almost at the same time, with the appearance in Italy of companies of full-time professional actors, 'vulgarly called Comedians', who are first recorded at Padua in the carnival of 1545. The aim of these specialists in what is now known as *commedia dell'arte* – professional comedy – was to display their virtuosity in miming and declamation by identifying themselves with fixed and well recognised stage roles, whether lovers or comic 'masks'. Their skill was to 'improvise' on a given scenario or 'subject'; although they sometimes gave literary comedies and occasionally tragedies, they formed their own repertory out of elements from learned comedy, reduced to schematic outline so that they could be combined and recombined at will.[1] Hence the actors produced a second kind of stereotype, though far removed in spirit from that of the theorists; (meanwhile literary playwrights in Italy, partly in reaction against the 'comedians', tried to give regular comedy a loftier sentimental tone or turned instead to pastoral). This dual process of rationalisation, academic and professional, had already begun when Italian comedy reached France and then England in the middle decades of the century; so that when Sidney, for example, wanted to trounce the slipshod practice of the English stage about 1580, he could confidently appeal to an abstract but definitive-looking standard of 'Art', which 'at this day, the ordinary Players in Italy will not err in'.

For critics like Sidney, the Italian canons of drama meant essentially a return to the ancients and hence to the abiding principles of Reason and Nature – as in Vasari's view of the rebirth of painting since Giotto. But although the Italians copied the plot structures of Plautus and Terence, and observed the unities of time and place even before these were erected into rules, they did not of course follow the ancients in everything: for instance, they invariably portrayed modern settings and circumstances; they employed Italian, though the exact form of the language was subject to keen debate; and, with some exceptions, and amid much critical controversy, they wrote their comedies in prose. The lavish sets for Italian stages were new in design, however much they owed to antiquarian research and enthusiasm, and the festivities of which the dramatic shows formed part belonged to a modern (or late-medieval) civilisation. It was the demands of these festivals and of the expanding lay culture which they

---

[1] See Nicoll, *Masks*, pp. 300ff; Apollonio, *Storia*, vol. II, pp. 250–3; Croce, *Poesia popolare*, pp. 503–14.

represented that called the comedies into being and gave a meaning to their deliberate evocation of the past.

Moreover, the Italian and the European stages of Ariosto's lifetime (1473–1533) presented a wide variety of dramatic forms, in Latin and the vernacular languages – not only the surviving liturgical plays and the huge civic biblical and saints' plays, then at the height of their organisation in Florence as well as England and France, but many forms of folk-play and, within the sphere of literature, dramatised romances and *novelle*, mythological pageants, moral allegories, and farces and *sotties* (satiric revues). The plays of John Heywood, Vicente, Gringore, Hans Sachs and, in Italy, Ruzzante show that this medieval tradition of miscellaneous, unregulated secular drama was far from declining, but was flourishing and developing among Ariosto's contemporaries. And the vigour and artistic potential of *sotties* and farces are indicated by no less a classical scholar than Erasmus, in his letter from Antwerp in 1515 to his friend and critic, Martin Dorp, when he defends his own outspokenness in *The Praise of Folly* by appealing to the licence granted by 'even the ignorant crowd' to the 'popular comedies' in which so 'many taunts are freely thrown out...against monarchs, priests, monks, wives, husbands – against anyone in fact'.[1] Ribald and often realistic though it was, Italian learned comedy did not aspire to the same freedom of speech; it absorbed much but it rejected much from other kinds of contemporary drama, just as it adapted some things but ignored others from the example of the classics. The forms it took, the conventions it transmitted to the rest of Europe, represented not a theoretical conclusion, but a cultural choice.

For a century before Ariosto, Italian scholars (and some Germans studying in Italian universities) had written comedies in Latin – still the spoken language of the universities – dealing with contemporary life, usually student life.[2] The authors were humanists; in this as in many other branches of literature it seems to have been Petrarch who led the way, although his comedies have disappeared. Among those who followed his precedent in the fifteenth century were the many-talented Leon Battista Alberti, Tito Livio dei Frulovisi or 'Titus Livius' (who had five of his Latin comedies acted at Venice in

---

[1] Erasmus, *Letter to Dorp* XIV (in *Praise of Folly*, trans. Radice, p. 222); see Swain, *Fools and Folly*, pp. 135–7; Mason, *Humanism*, pp. 90–1.
[2] See Sanesi, *Commedia*, vol. I, pp. 61–133; Apollonio, *Storia*, vol. I, pp. 251–4; Herrick, *Italian Comedy*, pp. 15–25; Radcliff–Umstead, *Birth of Modern Comedy*, pp. 23–58.

the 1430s before he left for England, where he wrote the first *Life* of Henry V for his patron, Humphrey, Duke of Gloucester)[1] and Aeneas Sylvius Piccolomini, the future Pope Pius II. In one sense, the learned comedy of the sixteenth century merely transposed this tradition into Italian. Ariosto, the court poet and official, Bibbiena, the Medicean adviser and future cardinal, Machiavelli, the diplomat–historian, and other writers of learned comedy were also humanists, from the same sections of society. The plots of humanist (Latin) comedies often recall *novelle*[2] and learned comedy similarly owes more to Boccaccio than to Plautus in spirit and, of course, language. But, unlike their successors, the humanist authors do not modernise Roman comic plots or adopt the unities of time and place and the five-act division, at least until the turn of the century,[3] when the stage revivals of Plautus and Terence have already begun. The innovation of 'learned' comedy was not simply the use of Italian but the combination of Italian material with externally classical form. The new form expressed, or proclaimed, a sense of affinity between modern Italy and the ancient world. One factor behind it was the increasing grasp of antiquity in the visual arts, as shown for instance by the archaeological realism of Mantegna's paintings and, in architecture, by the renewed study of Vitruvius (which led in turn to the frontal perspective and illusionistic scenery of modern European theatres). The visual arts affected the revival of Roman comedy by way of the wealth of the rulers of north Italian cities and their use of spectacle as an instrument for policy or prestige. And, under the shock of the foreign invasions that overclouded the first productions of learned comedy, the Italians, nationalists in culture if not in politics, were even more determined to assert their special identity with ancient Rome.

The creators of learned comedy were very conscious of their position in cultural history. As humanists, they adapted the convention of the Roman comic prologue, sometimes to prepare the audience for a very complicated intrigue, but also to defend their practice with theory or deliver an amusing lecture. Ariosto, for example, explains precisely what he is going to do in his first play, *La Cassaria* ('the play of the *cassa*', or chest; the title is one of several meant to recall Plautine

[1] *Ibid.* pp. 36–40; Bullough, *Sources*, vol. IV, pp. 159, 349.
[2] See Apollonio, *Storia*, vol. I, pp. 251–2; Radcliff–Umstead, *Birth of Modern Comedy*, pp. 27–45.
[3] Sanesi, *Commedia*, vol. I, pp. 118ff; Radcliff–Umstead, *Birth of Modern Comedy*, pp. 47–57.

titles like *Aulularia* and *Mostellaria*).[1] As soon as I have said 'a new comedy...never yet acted in Latin or in Greek' (says the Prologue, in effect), I can see that most of you disapprove:

such an undertaking does not seem to [the majority] amenable to modern wits, and only what the ancients have said do [they] think perfect.

But in themselves, wits (*ingegni*) have not changed; a good Italian can be spoken without a 'barbarous' mixture of Latin, and a story can be made enjoyable with 'jests'. And he goes on to announce the title, to give the name of the city depicted on the stage, and to explain that a servant, who comes on right away, will make known the 'argument'.

Ariosto wrote his first plays in prose; and a justification of prose – departing from classical precedent – is the main theme of the prologue which Castiglione wrote on behalf of the next notable contributor to learned comedy, his friend Bibbiena, when Bibbiena's *Calandria* was given at the ducal palace of Urbino for the carnival of 1513. The play is full of verbal echoes from the *Decameron*, which provides the title-part as well;[2] Castiglione's prologue points the same way:

Today you will be the spectators of a new comedy intitled *Calandria*: in prose, not in verse; modern, not ancient; vernacular, not Latin...That it is not ancient should not displease you,...because modern and new things always please and delight more than...the old...It is not in Latin: because ...the author wanted it...to be understood by everyone and to give everyone pleasure. Besides which, the language which God and Nature have given us should not be less esteemed among us or held in less favour than Latin, Greek and Hebrew: to which ours would be in no way inferior if we would only exalt it, observe it and polish it with the same diligent care that the Greeks and the rest applied to theirs.

As for the author's obvious 'theft' from Plautus, the prologue dismisses it with a joke; the play is introduced as a contribution to Italian prose.

A similar, even more pointed, concern for Italian – specifically, Florentine – speech comes out in the *Dialogue on Language* which Machiavelli composed a year or two later, shortly before his own comedy, *Mandragola* (1518):[3] the correct defence of one's language is a

---

[1] Ariosto, *Opere minori*, ed. Segre, p. 241.
[2] Edns of *La Calandria* in Borlenghi, *Commedie*, vol. I, Borsellino, *Commedie*, vol. II.
[3] Machiavelli, *Literary Works*, pp. 173–90. See Toffanin, *Cinquecento*, p. 116; Hall,

patriotic duty, and comedy, in particular, cannot be written with humour and 'a certain urbanity' unless 'native words and expressions are used'. Much as they differed in other respects, Machiavelli would have agreed with Castiglione in this, that a modern comedy should be 'natural' and Italian, even when it recalled the classics – as it should. In his prologue to *Clizia* (1525), which is closely modelled on Plautus's *Casina*, Machiavelli makes play with his theory that history repeats itself; he outlines the case of a certain old 'gentleman', 'once upon a time, in Athens'. . . but,

> What would you say to this same case having occurred again a few years ago in Florence? As our author wanted to represent one of them, he has chosen the Florentine, thinking that you would enjoy it more than the other. For Athens has been destroyed. . . [and] its citizens spoke Greek, a language you don't understand.

This urbane joking rests on the pretence that Plautus (who is not named this time) had been recounting an anecdote about a real person (as Boccaccio often did); but there is a second, latent irony when it turns out that *Clizia* contains a potentially much more serious domestic turmoil than its original. Machiavelli uses literary borrowing to subserve a playfully ironic treatment of actuality, realistic character-study and 'natural' Florentine speech. An even more insistent defender of the actual, the spontaneous and the natural in comedy was Angelo Beolco, known by his stage name as Ruzzante (*c.* 1500–42).[1] For Ruzzante, the 'natural' meant Paduan peasant dialect (which was compatible with Venetian patriotism, however); nearly all his characters are peasants, and his first comedies are based on folk-play motifs, introducing humanistic literature by way of parody. On the other hand, by the end of his short career as an actor–dramatist (spanning the 1520s) Ruzzante too had conceded to literary fashion to the extent of modernising two plays of Plautus in dialect.

The fashion stemmed from the courts, which launched learned comedy and indirectly governed its conventions. At Florence, the Medici had used a display of classical culture to impress diplomatic visitors; and Machiavelli says of Lorenzo (who governed alone, 'in the greatest prosperity', from 1480 to 1492) that he used tournaments and shows and 'triumphs in the antique manner' to keep Florence 'in a

'The Italian *Questione della Lingua*'; Grayson, 'Lorenzo, Machiavelli and the Italian Language'; *cf* Ridolfi, *Machiavelli*, pp. 170ff.

[1] See Zorzi (ed.), *Ruzante*, introduction.

state of continuous festivity', in which 'his aim was to keep his city in abundance, the people united, and the nobility in honour'.[1] At Ferrara, the dukes professed an educational purpose: the prologue written for a revival of Terence's *Phormio* in 1509 said it was the policy of Alfonso d'Este – Ariosto's patron – to sponsor Roman plays in translation so that everyone, learned and unlearned alike, 'could acquire the examples of antiquity from them';[2] but Alfonso's father, Duke Ercole, had initiated the policy with an eye to dynastic prestige. He supervised every side of the productions himself, while his daughter Isabella described those she saw in minute detail in order that her husband's productions at Mantua should not be outdone. For Alfonso's wedding during the carnival of 1502, she writes that their father had constructed a theatre in his palace capable of holding 5,000 spectators ('but the seats will be given first to foreigners and then, if there is room, to Ferrarese gentlemen'); he showed her a display of no less than 110 costumes, in readiness for the five Roman comedies that were to be given during the festivities, 'so that I should know that they were made specially, and that those for one play would not have to serve for the others'.[3] For Isabella, as for other letter-writers of the time, what counted most in such theatrical occasions were their public and spectacular aspects. They noted the 'vast expense' of the wedding shows at Ferrara. They were vividly impressed by decorations and scenery – the view of Epidamnus showing the town with ships in the harbour at the first Ferrarese production of the *Menaechmi* in 1486, for example; or the resplendent theatrical decoration at the Mantuan court in 1501, the roof blazing with 'hundreds of lights like shining stars', the scene presenting 'an ancient and eternal temple of rare beauty', in 'admirable perspective', and the sides of the stage 'adorned with six paintings of the Triumphs of Caesar by the famous Mantegna'; or, again at Ferrara, the 'view in perspective of a town with houses, churches, belfries and gardens, such that one could never tire of looking at it'. This was in 1508, at the *première* of Ariosto's *Cassaria*, a historic moment for the drama; but, for Isabella d'Este's correspondent, Bernardino Prosperi, the court painter's scenery was the 'best' thing in all the carnival shows

---

1 Machiavelli, *Istorie fiorentine* VII.36 [1532], in *Opere*, ed. Bonfantini, p. 977. See Welsford, *Court Masque*, pp. 98–102; Bowra, 'Songs of Dance and Carnival'; Borlenghi (ed.), *Commedie*, vol. I, pp. 10ff.

2 Sanesi, *Commedia*, vol. I, p. 174; Apollonio, *Storia*, vol. I, pp. 270ff; vol. II, pp. 1–37.

3 Apollonio, *Storia*, vol. I, pp. 273–4; Gage, *Life in Italy*, p. 130.

and festivities, 'because of the different things that are there, all most cleverly designed and excuted'. 'I suppose', he adds, 'that this will not be destroyed, but that they will preserve it to use on other occasions.'[1] Even Castiglione, relating the success (in which he had a literary share) of the first night of *Calandria* at Urbino, devotes most of his enthusiasm to the scenery – another 'beautiful city' (Rome) in 'well-conceived perspective', including an octagonal temple surrounded by statues in imitation marble and a triumphal arch surmounted by a warrior on horseback – and to the Latin slogans (Caesarism and 'popular sports') illuminated from the roof of the theatre and projecting above the stage.[2] After the decoration of the theatre, contemporary observers paid attention as much to the *intermezzi* – the dances between the acts – and their mythological significance or allegorical message as to the contents of the play.

No doubt they had good reason. Not simply because of the glories of contemporary art, but because the performance of a learned comedy was merely one incident within the festivities for Carnival, or to celebrate a royal entry, a royal wedding or a royal birth.[3] Throughout the sixteenth century in Italy, the comedy usually followed a pageant (or 'triumph') and a tournament or mock-battle; it was a form of entertainment devised for the princes, as they took over civic and popular festivities and turned them into celebrations for the court, or, at most, into court shows which the populace could witness.[4] The prince's architects and designers transformed the main streets of the city with pageants, but the pageants culminated in the palace and it was there that the learned comedy was produced. Until Palladio's Olympic Theatre was opened for an aristocratic academy at Vicenza in 1584, there were no permanent playhouses in Italy; a theatre, however magnificent, was a temporary structure within a great house or a palace. It reflected the patron's taste and splendour, even his superiority to his own possessions; when, for instance, Leone di Somi, stage designer and theatrical manager for the Duke of Mantua in the 1560s, describes how his patron had built a theatre in his palace courtyard for the tournaments in celebration of his wedding

---

[1] Lily B. Campbell, *Scenes and Machines*, pp. 45–9; Nicoll, *Development of the Theatre*, pp. 85–8.

[2] Campbell, *Scenes and Machines*, pp. 49–52; Gage, *Life in Italy*, p. 131; *cf* Nagler, *Source Book*, p. 71.

[3] Leone di Somi, *Dialogues* (1565?), trans. Nicoll, in *Development of the Theatre*, app. B, p. 260. *Cf* Apollonio, *Storia*, vol. II, p. 35; Toschi, *Origini*, p. 723.

[4] D'Ancona, *Origini*, vol. II, p. 162–72; Apollonio, *Storia*, vol. II, pp. 6–27.

and then allowed the structure to be dismantled, the writer adds: 'all the greater was Duke Guglielmo's magnanimity in spending so many thousands of ducats on that marvellous set and then destroying it when it had served its immediate purpose'.[1] In Athens, each year's comedies had been ephemeral but the theatre was a lasting, solid demonstration of the city's wealth and its will to a collective life. In renaissance Italy, the theatre itself was a temporary creation of the prince.

Evidently the scenery dominated the plays. In the first place, the patrons' and their designers' taste for impressive urban settings – almost experiments in town-planning – confirmed without question the classical convention that the actors in a comedy should only meet each other in an open place or the street (so that it seemed odd and 'awkward' to Leone di Somi to witness scenes in theatres in Spain acted as if within a room, a room 'lacking, as it must, a fourth wall').[2] Secondly, since it was technically very difficult during most of the sixteenth century to change the architectual setting on the stage in the course of the action, it was the scene-designer, not Aristotle or Terence, who came to dictate the critical 'law' of unity of place.[3] And thirdly, though the setting could be called illusionistic, and it often represented the very city in which the play was performed, it was not required to be faithful or realistic or functional. The temple and the triumphal arch in Genga's townscape for the stage at Urbino, for instance, were quite unnecessary for the action of *Calandria* and must have conjured up a mood of idealised grandeur quite at variance with the comedy's ribald tone. But it would have seemed far from incongruous in the artistry of the festival as a whole. As André Chastel points out, the visual effect of such a festival was to deck out the real city with architectural fantasy and to give fantasy an illusory appearance of reality; and the architectural setting for the carnival play at Urbino was 'une ville imaginaire, condensant tous les aspects de la ville "transfigurée" de la fête'.[4]

This cultural environment conditioned the literary conventions of learned comedy indirectly as well. There was no difficulty in reconciling Plautus with Boccaccio and with the spirit of Italian carnivals, with their mockery and sense of erotic release, practical jokes and

[1] Leone di Somi, *Dialogues*, trans. Nicoll, *Development of the Theatre*, p. 258.
[2] *Ibid.* p. 260.
[3] See Neri, *La Tragedia*, p. 170; Toffanin, 'Il Teatro del Rinascimento', pp. 94–5; *cf* Spingarn, *Renaissance*, pp. 97–9; Nagler, *Theatre Festivals of the Medici*, p. 41.
[4] Chastel, 'Le Lieu de la Fête', p. 421.

masquerade. And there was no difficulty in preserving the old convention that in a comedy all the characters were citizens or their servants, with no one of higher rank. But a convention which had meant one thing in Periclean Athens meant another in the hierarchic society of the Renaissance. Apart from the writings of a rebel like Ruzzante, it meant excluding peasants from the stage, except as figures of fun. It also meant that no princes or courtiers could be represented in a comedy, either. Decorum was not only a matter of psychological and artistic consistency but of social convention and distinctions of rank. Theorists maintained, for example, that the crucial distinction between tragedy and comedy was not 'the happy ending or the sad' but 'the quality of the persons introduced' and their situations.[1] More commonly, they explained that when Aristotle said the characters in comedy were of 'a lower type', he meant, of lower rank; or else that the architectonic end of comedy, the purpose it should serve, was to make ordinary citizens contented with their government.[2] (Scaliger was more realistic when he recalled that the free speech of Old Comedy had died out with Athenian democracy, and so was Castelvetro, when he added that the style of New Comedy was acceptable to monarchs and aristocrats 'because it does not rebuke any of their operations,...or stir up the common people'.)[3] In any case, whatever was said in addition about drama as a mirror of life, the convention meant that comedy depicted characters below the social rank of the principal spectators. Citizen life could still be portrayed outwardly much as Boccaccio had portrayed it, but with a different tone, a tone of amused superiority, to which the formation of the authors themselves, as humanists, must also have contributed. It is significant that Castiglione and Trissino and Castelvetro stress a feeling of superiority among the causes that provoke laughter.[4]

Another cause of laughter, it was noted, was surprise. And with a search for surprise went a search for variety and a sense of wonder which had some connexion with classical practice and theory but

[1] Leone di Somi, *Dialogues*, trans. Nicoll, *Development of the Theatre*, p. 242.
[2] See Allan H. Gilbert (ed.), *Literary Criticism*, pp. 74 (Aristotle), 224 (Trissino (before 1563)), 252 (Giraldi (1543)), 513 (Guarini (1599)); Herrick, *Comic Theory*, pp. 130ff, 227ff (Robortello (1548)); Barrett H. Clark (ed.), *Theories of the Drama*, p. 59 (Minturno (1564)). *Cf* Sanesi, *Commedia*, vol. I, p. 225; Doran, *Endeavors of Art*, pp. 85–92; Weinberg, *Italian Renaissance*, pp. 101, 317, 441, 535ff, 741, 797–813; Cochrane, 'A Case in Point: the End of the Renaissance in Florence'.
[3] Scaliger, *Poetics* (1561), in Padelford (trans.), *Select Translations*, pp. 42–3; Castelvetro, *Poetica* (Basel, 1576), p. 61.
[4] Castiglione, *Book of the Courtier*, trans. Hoby, pp. 138ff; see above, p. 85.

much more with the taste of the audience and the atmosphere of the spectacle. In the eighteenth century, Goldoni said he was enchanted to find in *Mandragola* a 'comedy of character', and most subsequent critics would agree that *Mandragola* was the masterpiece, if not the only masterpiece, of Italian learned comedy. But in the mid-sixteenth century the play was criticised (by Girolamo Ruscelli) because Machiavelli concentrated on the character of Messer Nicia to such an extent that he produced a quiet and uneventful fourth act ('which certainly ought to be avoided as regards the plot of a comedy'), instead of finding opportunities to arouse suspense by means of a fresh intrigue.[1] It could be added that *Mandragola* pursues a single intrigue, whereas most dramatists and critics preferred a double plot, notwithstanding what Aristotle said. Giraldi explained, taking Terence's *Andrian* as his example, that a double plot showed 'diverse kinds of persons of the same station in life, as two lovers of different character, two old men of varied nature', and so on; he preferred Ariosto's *Cassaria* to his other plays for this reason (though others might prefer the *Suppositi*, overlooking the improbability of the servant's defiance of his old master).[2] Similarly, Giraldi preferred the intricate variety of *Orlando Furioso* to the uniformity recommended for a regular epic. Writing, like Ariosto before him, under the patronage of the court of Ferrara, where he was producing his own tragedies in the 1540s (the first tragedies in a modern language to reach the stage), Giraldi emphasised horror in tragedy, but he also advocated poetic justice and a happy ending. The qualities and status of the characters in fiction were to be fixed and static, the writer's business was to manipulate the imaginable events that could occur to them, so as to surprise, excite and reassure. He was to balance sententiousness with fantasy; the essential faculty of a poet was his capacity to invent marvels.[3]

In much the same way, the pragmatic Castelvetro, who rounded off the Italian theorising about the *Poetics* in 1571 by propounding the rule of unity of place in drama, was quite sure that the first principle of a play was not the imitation of an action, as Aristotle held, but the giving of pleasure to an audience within the commonsense limits of

---

[1] Girolamo Ruscelli (ed.), *Comedie Elette* (Venice, 1554), pp. 182–4.
[2] Giraldi, 'Discorso...intorno al Comporre delle Comedie' [1543] in *Discorsi* (Venice, 1554), pp. 214–15 (part translated in Allan H. Gilbert, *Literary Criticism*, p. 254). See Horne, *Tragedies of Giraldi*, pp. 36–9.
[3] Giraldi, 'On...Romances' (1549), in *Discorsi*, trans. Gilbert, *Literary Criticism*, p. 270.

visual illusion. Again, the dramatist's main task is the manipulation of imaginable events. 'The poet's function is to give a semblance of truth to the happenings that come upon men through fortune' – not to give any fresh insight into the qualities of men themselves – and it follows that the poet's work 'is not and ought not to be called directly or properly imitation', but rather his 'strife' with 'the disposition of fortune, or...the course of mundane things, in finding an incident of human conduct delightful to listen to and marvellous'. The marvellous is just as important as the probable, and an extra dimension in a play is the writer's skill in reconciling both.

As for unity of action (the only dramatic unity Aristotle had laid down), Castelvetro admits only two arguments in its favour. One, that the unity of time (the supposed credibility-limit of twelve hours for a play's events) and 'the limitation of the space in which it is acted' will not allow room for very much to happen; the other, that a dramatist will exhibit all the more 'judgment' and 'industry' if he can manage to sustain interest with the vicissitudes of a single plot. Otherwise, the psychology of the theatre is all in favour of multiplicity – 'for because of the number of actions, variety, novel happenings, and multitude of persons and peoples, the plot carries with it pleasure and greatness and magnificence'.[1] Most Italian comic dramatists had evidently thought the same; they promised their audiences two sets of 'jests' or practical jokes, or studied how to complicate their intrigue by interweaving plots from two or even more previous comedies or *novelle*.

It was this kind of technical virtuosity that attracted sixteenth-century audiences and changed the whole form of European drama, while the mere prestige-value of restoring a classical art by imitation could be disregarded or at least taken for granted. For instance, when Charles Etienne published his French translation of the anonymous Sienese comedy, *Gl'Ingannati*, as a modern equivalent of Terence, and dedicated his revised version of the translation to the Dauphin in 1552, it was the attraction of a well-managed plot that he emphasised; the writers of New Comedy, he says, delight the spectators by 'changing themes, introducing things unexpected and hidden, then disclosing them, leaving one matter to take up another, then returning to the first again, leading everything dextrously [and stylishly: *avecq' si grande dexterité & maniere*] to the conclusion'. He

---

[1] Castelvetro, *Poetica*, in Gilbert, *Literary Criticism*, pp. 307, 312, 318; see Weinberg, 'Castelvetro's Theory of Poetics'.

hoped the French would follow the Italians into New Comedy, 'not treating of other events than marriages, love-affairs, and similar things', in place of their satiric farces, which, like others, he compared to Old Comedy.[1] Etienne's first version of *Gl'Ingannati* had come out at Lyons in 1543, only six years after the first Italian edition and twelve years after the first performance; in 1548, the French court witnessed the first production in France of a *commedia erudita, La Calandria,* and Du Bellay, imbued with Italian ideas, was urging French poets and dramatists to embellish their own language by imitating the classics. Jodelle's *L'Eugène,* the first French 'regular' comedy, was acted in 1552.

Etienne's volume of 1543 had been the earliest foreign translation of an Italian play. It was followed by a series of translations or close adaptations of Italian comedies and *novelle* into French, Spanish and English during the generation before Shakespeare. The translators appear to have neglected the best Italian comedies, those of Machiavelli and Ruzzante, perhaps the only ones which now seem, on their own merits, of European stature; but Ruzzante had stuck to dialect, and Machiavelli was not a good selling name in the later sixteenth century. Although a number of comedies were translated, the favourites by far seem to have been *Gl'Ingannati*, and Ariosto's *Suppositi*. The latter found three French translators between 1545 and 1594; it was the first Italian comedy to be acted in Spain, being presented to the court at Valladolid in 1548, 'with such apparatus and scenery as are used at Rome';[2] and it was the play chosen by Gascoigne in 1566 for the first published English translation of an Italian comedy, his *Supposes*. The reputation of *Gl'Ingannati* was even greater. It was indebted to the *Menaechmi* and to *Calandria*, where Bibbiena had thought of the innovation of making one of the interchangeable twins a girl in masculine disguise; but the Sienese comedy was the first to exploit the romantic possibilities of this device. In 1554, the plot was turned into a *novella* by Bandello – an unusual procedure on his part – whence it was taken over successively by Montemayor, for the story of Felix and Felismena in his pastoral romance, *Diana* (*c.* 1559), and, in England, by Googe (in his *Eglogs,* 1563) and, by way of a French translation, for two of Barnabe Riche's stories in his *Farewell to Military Profession* in 1581.[3] On the stage, meanwhile, *Gl'Ingannati*

---

[1] Etienne, quoted Doran, *Endeavors of Art,* pp. 180, 425.

[2] Rennert, *Spanish Stage,* p. 21; Shergold, *History of the Spanish Stage,* p. 236n; see D'Ancona, *Origini,* vol. II, p. 171n; Jeffery, *French Renaissance Comedy,* pp. 21, 191.

[3] Rennert, *Spanish Pastoral Romances,* pp. 54–6; Purves (ed.), *Gl 'Ingannati,* pp. 7–8.

had been imitated in several Italian comedies, including Secchi's *Gl'Inganni* (1549), which John Manningham, the Elizabethan lawyer, compared to *Twelfth Night*.[1] It was known in England within a few years of Etienne's translation, by 1547, when a Latin version was acted at Cambridge; in 1565 John Jeffere borrowed a few scenes for *The Bugbears* (which was mainly an adaptation of another Italian comedy, by Grazzini); and by 1595, when a second Latin *Laelia* was acted, also at Queens' College, there were two fresh editions of Etienne's translation in French and two versions of the play in Spanish.[2] By this time Stephen Gosson had asserted that 'bawdy Comedies in Latin, French, Italian and Spanish have been thoroughly ransacked to furnish the Play houses in London', though only one sure example is known, Anthony Munday's *Two Italian Gentlemen* (*c.* 1584), from a comedy by Pasqualigo.

Shakespeare, therefore, was one of the first English dramatists to borrow from Italian learned comedy, but in borrowing from *Supposes* and, directly or indirectly, from *Gl'Ingannati*, he was following the lines prepared by the modern taste of the previous generation – just as he chose what was probably the most famous of modern love-stories as the subject of *Romeo and Juliet* in the same early phase of his career. And his borrowings from Plautus belonged to the same current of taste and ideas; from the time of the Italian revival of classical comedy, the *Menaechmi* was probably the best-known play in Europe.[3]

In spite of the changes he made in everything he borrowed for his comedies, Shakespeare's Italian, or Roman–Italian borrowings were decisive. Leaving his late romances out of account, he drew directly on New Comedy for five of the twelve comedies he wrote between about 1592 and 1604. He used Plautus in *The Comedy of Errors* and *The Merry Wives of Windsor*. He used the *Supposes* for the Lucentio–Bianca plot in *The Taming of the Shrew* and probably the same play helped to suggest the planning of *The Comedy of Errors* and *Two Gentlemen of Verona*. He was indebted to *Gl'Ingannati* indirectly, through Montemayor, for the story of Julia in *Two Gentlemen of Verona* and (probably) directly for the main plot of *Twelfth Night*. In all these plays he had a double plot, as the Italians interpreted it, and in *Twelfth Night* he followed the method of the Italians by going behind

[1] Herrick, *Italian Comedy*, pp. 126–30; Bullough, *Sources*, vol. II, pp. 269ff.
[2] Bond (ed.), *Early Plays*, p. lxx; F. P. Wilson, *English Drama, 1485–1585*, pp. 113–14.
[3] Salingar, 'Shakespeare's Romances', p. 15n.

Gl'Ingannati to the *Menaechmi* for the second strand in his main double plot, Sebastian's adventures. In *Love's Labour's Lost* and *A Midsummer Night's Dream* he seems to have invented the central entanglements but he was still applying the methods of the Italianate double plot, with its confusions of identity and crossed complications; and these two plays clearly illustrate his interest in the Renaissance tradition of comedy as a form of court entertainment. The main plot of *As You Like It* is taken from Lodge's *novella, Rosalynde* (1590), but the heroine's disguise in the play, as in its source, belongs to the tradition of Italian comedy. The main plots of Shakespeare's four other comedies represent a different kind of choice, but not a radical departure, since *All's Well, The Merchant of Venice, Much Ado* and *Measure for Measure* are based on Italian *novelle* (by Boccaccio and three of his successors, the late-fourteenth-century Giovanni Fiorentino and the Renaissance authors Bandello and Giraldi); and Shakespeare's elaboration of the stories he was using again follows the precedents of learned comedy – for instance, in bringing not one, but three married couples to Belmont, or in contriving to unloose the knot in *Measure for Measure* by introducing Mariana. Shakespeare's secondary plots or sub-plots of deception, such as the trickery against Benedick and Beatrice, and against Malvolio and Parolles, again appear to be his own inventions, but they follow the lines of the *beffe* in Italian stories and comedies, rather than the contrivances of the resourceful slaves in Plautus. Shakespeare imagines Italian cities as the main or occasional settings of half of his comedies. It is true that his Italy is a faintly exotic and romantic territory, especially at first, with little or nothing of that sense of an intimate town life that gives touches of realism to Italian comedies; Shakespeare borrows in his own way, belonging to a different generation, another kind of theatre and a different national tradition. But, paradoxically, the play in which he comes nearest to a wholesale adoption of Italian methods and an Italian manner is *The Merry Wives of Windsor*, his only comedy set in England.

As Shakespeare is such a complex author, even in his lightest comedies, it is impossible, or at least, artificial, to isolate one thread in the composition of his plays from the others. The richness of his mental world, the sense it gives of familiarity-together-with-strangeness, springs from his extraordinary power to bring out parallels and affinities between stories and dramatic devices from separate traditions. What the Italians had to give him was a familiarity with Plautus and Terence as contributors to the modern stage, a group of new dramatic motifs, such as that of the heroine in male disguise, and, above all, a taste for varied movement in a comedy and intricate plotting. Without the force of their example, his own broader and freer methods of dramatic composition would have lacked a basis.

THREE ITALIAN COMEDIES

The *Suppositi*, the *Calandria* and *Gl'Ingannati* are not the best or most original of Italian learned comedies, but it is no accident that they were so often copied or translated. They were typical of Renaissance comedy in their deft combination of carnival jokes and literary fantasy, of echoes from Boccaccio and imitations of Terence and Plautus.

A Renaissance comedy might be justified as a 'mirror of human life, wherein vices are attacked' and 'virtues praised', but it was essentially a 'carnival show',[1] an explosion of high spirits licensed and ratified by custom. The season – normally the only season in which plays were permitted – stretched from mid-January or even the Christmas holidays (corresponding to the special time of Misrule in England) to the last days before Lent. In popular custom[2] it was a time for release and mimic expiation, expressed through wooing games, mock-battles between Carnival and Lent (which Carnival usually won, until the age of the Counter-Reformation)[3] and through dances and processions led by animal- and devil-masks. In the celebrations organised for the princes, like the races at Rome or the processions of triumphal chariots bearing gods and demons singing carnival songs, introduced by Lorenzo de' Medici at Florence, popular custom was raised to a plane of ceremony, excitement and heightened fantasy. In these festivals at their best, says Burckhardt, the Italians of the Renaissance found 'the point of transition from real life into the world of art'.[4] And conversely it could be said that art of an improvised kind passed back into private life, in the shape of buffoonery and practical jokes, adventures and intrigues pursued under masquerade. As an example

---

[1] Leone di Somi, *Dialogues* trans. Nicoll, *Development of the Theatre*, pp. 241, 260.

[2] See Toschi, *Origini*, chs. 4–5 and article, 'Carnevale'; Apollonio, 'Carnevale'; Rademacher, 'Carnival'; *cf* Chambers, *The English Folk-Play*.

[3] Toschi, *Origini*, pp. 149ff; D'Ancona, *Origini*, vol. I, pp. 538–45; Lozinski (ed.), *La Bataille de Caresme et de Charnage*, pp. 104–20. See also Hollstein, *Dutch and Flemish Engravings*, vol. III, pp. 118, 137, 140, 309; vol. IX, p. 50 (I am grateful for this reference to Mr Eric Chamberlain, of the Fitzwilliam Museum, Cambridge).

[4] Burckhardt, *Renaissance*, p. 246.

of the 'kind of merry pranks when a man deceiveth himself' in the discussion of humour in *The Book of the Courtier*, Castiglione makes Bibbiena, the principal speaker, relate how during the last carnival his own fondness for practical jokes was turned against himself, because it was known to 'my Lord's Grace of Saint Peter ad Vincula' what 'a delight' Bibbiena had when he was 'in maskery to play merry pranks with Friars'; the joker found himself pelted with eggs as he galloped through the streets in masquerade, carrying behind him a supposed friar who turned out to be one of the bishop's stablemen, also in disguise.[1] The historian, William Thomas (who introduced the word *carnival* into English in 1549) relates how, 'in the shroving time', the 'ordinary pastime' of the Roman cardinals 'is to disguise them selves, to go laugh at the Courtesans' houses, and...to ride masking about with them, which is the occasion that Rome wanteth no jolly dames'; and how, at Venice, 'in their *Carnival* time (which we call shrovetide) you shall see maskers' – strangers in the city – 'disguise them selves in the Venetians' habit, and come unto their own noses in derision of their customs, their habit [*dress*], and misery [*stinginess*]'.[2] Presumably these mockers were simply exploiting the liberty of the season. But, also at Venice, in 1549, Sir Thomas Hoby, Castiglione's future translator, witnessed a day of carnival masquerading for a visiting nobleman, which began in 'great sport and merry pastime' with running at the ring in Turkish costumes and 'casting of eggs into the windows among the ladies', and ended in a brawl over a lady in a masked ball at night, which cost the nobleman his life.[3] Bandello tells how Romeo ventured into the Capulets' house in a Christmas masquerade; similarly, Giraldi uses carnival masquerade to give plausibility to two of his sensational *novelle*: in one, which ends with a suicide, a man adopts the same disguise as his friend in order to seduce the friend's wife.[4] And at the end of the century another English traveller in Italy, Fynes Moryson, observed carnival disguises with sarcastic disapproval, especially those of women in masculine dress:[5]

many times in the Cities (as at Padua) I have seen Courtesans (in plain English, whores) in the time of shroving, apparelled like men, in carnation or light coloured doublets and breeches, and so playing with the racket at

[1] Castiglione, *Courtier*, trans. Hoby, pp. 173–4.
[2] William Thomas, *The historie of Italie* (1549), pp. 39*v*, 84*v*, 85*r*.
[3] Welsford, *Court Masque*, pp. 101–2.
[4] Bandello, *Novelle* II.9; Giraldi, *Hecatommithi*, IX.6 and 7.
[5] Fynes Moryson, *Itinerary* [1617] (Glasgow, 1907), part IV, p. 222.

Tennis with young men, at which time of shroving, the Women no less than Men (and that honourable women in honourable company), go masked and apparelled like men in the afternoon about the streets, even from Christmas holidays to the first day in Lent.

Evidently, then, there was some basis in real life for the Italian stage convention of the heroine in male disguise. But art was one thing and life another, even – or especially – in a culture which delighted in blending them together; and certainly the moralists of the later sixteenth century were anxiously concerned about the impact of the theatrical arts on life. Even that 'open-minded friar' and enthusiastic journalist, Tommaso Garzoni (1549–89), who trumpeted the first immortal Isabellas and 'divine' Vittorias of the *commedia dell'arte*, had nothing but indignation for carnival masquerade and its defenders. Writing his *Piazza universale di tutte le professioni* (or survey of all professions) in 1584, he denounces masks as inventions of the devil and Carnival as a pagan relic of the Bacchanalia. Carnival masquerading is a ruinous expense for private families, he says, and it is a degrading exhibition when respectable citizens dress and behave like stage clowns:[1]

the actions are vain, the gestures absurd, the witticisms derisory, the language stupid, the laughter foolish, the devices mad, the speeches only fit for loafers, the whole conduct really crazy, as of men out of their minds. To see a sober gentleman dressed like Pedrolino making a thousand senseless capers, what can be more futile than that? a Lord dressed as Burattino holding forth as a mountebank, what can be more unseemly than that? an eminent Doctor doffing his gown and girding his shoulders with a sack to deliver a thousand quips fit for a buffoon, what can be more unbecoming than that?...where is order, where symmetry?

And the women in carnival are even more indecorous:

But is it not even worse to see the women dressed as men, and sometimes taken riding by their lovers, as you can see in some places? and all those harlots going in men's clothes with their stumpy legs sticking out like so many turtles?

Carnival masquerade, in short, is simply a provocation to idleness, gadding-about, debauchery, fraud and all sorts of crimes, even murder.

---

1 Tommaso Garzoni, *La Piazza universale di tutte le professioni del mondo* [1584] (Venice, 1616), Discorso LXXXIIII, pp. 278ᵥff; *cf* Discorso CIIII. See Toffanin, *Cinquecento*, p. 552; Taviani, *La Fascinazione del Teatro*, pp. 47–81.

The only concession Garzoni will allow to the custom – an argument significant of the age, and for Shakespeare's Duke of Vienna – is that it will give opportunity to

Princes, with greater safety and freedom, to go about at a certain time, and note with their own eyes the behaviour of their subjects, learn what opinion of them is spouted among the people, hear their praise or their blame, and so correct what is not right in themselves and their subjects.

Otherwise, the whole chapter might almost be taken from Philip Stubbes's contemporary denunciation of May-games in England. Yet at the end, Garzoni quotes a more ambiguous judgment –

that a Mask has four notable effects; it makes one bold, because his person is not known, it hides the poverty of those who are badly dressed, it teaches the shamefaced to speak, and it gives freedom to personages of gravity and respect.

This psychology of masquerade is important for Renaissance comedy in several ways.

The adherence or truth to life of 'learned' Italian comedy did not lie, therefore, in any tendency towards moral instruction – which the dramatists proclaimed much less than the critics – even though satire in the plays could sometimes be pungent, as with Machiavelli, or vociferous, with Aretino. Nor did it lie in the use of incidents from real life, which the dramatists sometimes advertised in their prologues.[1] As Nino Borsellino points out in the valuable introduction to his anthology, the 'realism' of comedy expressed the secular and 'hedonistic' interests of the courtly and bourgeois Italian public of the time.[2] The playwrights' working philosophy was the naturalism of the *Decameron*, reaffirmed with selective emphasis through the conventions of carnival. This emphasis meant on one side an urge towards fantasy or wish-fulfilment, which the formal imitation of classical New Comedy rather codified than restrained; on the other side, the dramatists' sense of the presence of carnival frequently led to a give-and-take between their awareness of the play as a fictional, festive performance and their awareness of it as a partial reflection of life outside the theatre – a form of juggling with the complicity of the

---

1 See Machiavelli, *Clizia* (*Literary Works*, p. 67); Annibal Caro, *Gli Straccioni* (ed. Borlenghi, *Commedie*, vol. I, p. 123; ed. Borsellino, *Commedie*, vol. II, pp. 199, 202); Cecchi, *L'Assiuolo* (ed. Borlenghi, *Commedie*, vol. I, p. 871; ed. Borsellino, *Commedie*, vol. I, p. 128).

2 Borsellino (ed.), *Commedie*, vol. I, p. xvii.

audience for which classical comedy had already furnished the precedents.[1] In this way, the Italians recaptured the ironic collective self-awareness which had distinguished classical comedy as a form of entertainment.

The dramatists frequently bring in carnival as the supposed as well as the real acting time of their plays. This is particularly noticeable in comedies based on the *Menaechmi*; for example, in the close adaptations by Firenzuola (*c.* 1540) and Trissino (1548) and in the freer adaptations in *Gl'Ingannati* (1531) and Cecchi's *La Moglie* (*The Wife*, 1543); in *Gl'Ingannati*, the servants plan a party for themselves during 'this last day' of Carnival (though they are willing to hold it in Lent, while their masters are 'wooing women at the sermon', if there is not time enough) and in *La Moglie*, the twin brother arriving at Florence unknown thinks it is due to the 'carnival pranks [*burle carnascialesche*]' of the Florentines that he is repeatedly mistaken for the resident twin. Probably the *Menaechmi* seemed a particularly 'festive invention', as Trissino called it,[2] and hence became the most popular classical play on Renaissance stages, precisely because it exploited the laughable consequences of a confusion of identities, which could be associated with carnival masquerade, more than any other Roman comedy. However, the dramatists introduce carnival into the fictitious time of plays from other sources as well. The two 'delightful practical jokes [*dolci burle*]' that constitute the action of Aretino's *Cortigiana* (1526–34) are forgiven by their principal victim at the end because 'in any case it is Carnival'. In Machiavelli's *Clizia* (1525) the old father tries to get his son – and rival in love – out of the way, with the pretext that 'on carnival days like this young men like you are out amusing themselves, looking at the costumes'; and his counterpart in Cecchi's *L'Assiuolo* (*The Owl, c.* 1549) constructs an elaborate ruse on the same foundation.[3] Donato Giannotti's *Il Vecchio amoroso* (or *Old Man in Love, c.* 1535) begins as an avowed imitation of the father-and-son rivalry in Plautus's *Merchant*; but the author declares that Plautus's ending is 'woven very simply', whereas he wants an ending which

1 See above, pp. 94ff, 99, 103, 113, 115, 118ff.
2 Trissino, *I Simillimi* (Venice, 1548), dedicatory letter to Cardinal Farnese; *cf* Act III (Biij*v*); Agnolo Firenzuola, *I Lucidi*, epilogue, p. 54; G-M. Cecchi, *La Moglie* (Venice, 1550), III.v (p. 23*r*), IV.ix (p. 32*r*) (= pp. 19*r*, 30*r* in the verse redaction, Venice, 1585); *Gl'Ingannati*, II.vi (trans. Bullough, *Sources*, vol. II, p. 307).
3 Aretino, *La Cortigiana*, V.xxv, in *Commedie*, ed. De Sanctis, p. 223; Machiavelli, *Clizia*, III.i, in *Literary Works*, p. 88; Cecchi, *L'Assiuolo*, II.vii (ed. Borlenghi, *Commedie*, vol. I, p. 900; ed. Borsellino, *Commedie*, vol. I, p. 153).

will be 'all the more lively' the more it is preceded by 'fears, suspicions and disorders [*turbamenti*]'; so he invents a new ending, in which the two young men of his play search the streets for the missing heroine under one set of carnival disguises and then carry her off from the house of one of their fathers under another.[1] This gives Giannotti the chance for an impressionistic street-scene of carnival manners (IV.iv) and later (v.iii) for a farcical invention outdoing Plautus. The two old men, Teodoro and his ally Arrigo, have hired two professional buffoons to entertain them in a clandestine banquet at Arrigo's house; when Arrigo's wife returns inopportunely from his farm, the buffoons – copying Plautus's *Mostellaria* – try to frighten her away by pretending that the house is haunted and improvising an exorcism; but they are ignominiously thrown out by flesh-and-blood 'devils', who are the young men in their second carnival disguise. Here the carnival situation gives rise to a fiction reacting upon a fiction, of the kind that the later, baroque theatre was to elaborate into the play-within-the-play.

Even when the plays do not specify carnival as their acting time, it is the spirit of the season, or of the carnival aspect of the *Decameron*, that governs their motifs and their choice and grouping of characters. The pretence for the tricks in Roman comedy had been strictly functional, to obtain possession of the heroine for the young lover, whatever secondary entertainment they had given rise to. In Italian comedy the *burle* or *beffe* are more elaborate and more nearly self-justifying in the eyes of the playwright. The whole plot of Aretino's *Marescalco* (*The Farrier*, 1526), for instance, consists of a practical joke planned by the Duke of Mantua (off-stage), who foists a bride – actually, a boy in disguise – on his unwilling, misogynistic and perhaps homosexual farrier (it was this plot which suggested that of Jonson's *Silent Woman*;[2] but Aretino's tone towards the Duke is not very different from that of Cervantes towards the Duke and Duchess who so painstakingly fool Don Quixote and Sancho Panza). In other plays, the principal episodes consist of the deception and mockery of a pretentious booby – such as the elderly bourgeois, Calandro (lifted from the *Decameron*) in Bibbiena's comedy, the crassly provincial Florentine lawyer, Messer Nicia, in *Mandragola*, or the upstart, Messer Maco, who hopes to become a courtier at Rome and then a cardinal, in

---

1 Donato Giannotti, *Il Vecchio amoroso*, ed. Borsellino, *Commedie*, vol. I. See Herrick, *Italian Comedy*, pp. 101–3.
2 See O. J. Campbell, 'The Relation of *Epicoene* to Aretino's *Il Marescalco*'.

Aretino's *Cortigiana* (or *Court Comedy*). In his *Candelaio* (1582), Giordano Bruno promises to show the fooling of three such dupes at once, 'the insipid lover, the sordid miser, the stupid pedant'.[1] Whatever other pretext is alleged for belabouring such elderly boobies, the chief one is their self-deception through what Castelvetro calls lack of 'common understanding' or 'ignorance of the arts and the sciences' or else over-estimate of one's own capacity,[2] and the chief pleasure offered by the dramatist is the humanist enjoyment of the intellect applied to action. At the same time, these dupes are usually made grotesque as husbands or would-be lovers, and the mockery directed against them is part of the carnival mockery of sexual deficiency or irregularity;[3] in this respect it resembles the skimmington rides in *Hudibras* and *The Mayor of Casterbridge*.

To these figures of ridicule the Italians added a gallery of types new to regular comedy, if not to literature since Boccaccio and Chaucer – notably bogus magicians, hypocrites in religion, and pedantic schoolmasters. Here again, humanistic motives are evident. Satire on corrupt friars, like Fra Timoteo in *Mandragola*, belongs to the pre-reforming phase of the Renaissance (in Counter-Reformation Florence it was thought objectionable),[4] and so does the ridicule of bawds who operate under cover of piety, whether amateurs like Lucrezia's mother in *Mandragola* or professionals like Alvigia in *La Cortigiana*. Similarly, the even more frequent comic episodes involving pretended exorcism or magic (as in *Mandragola* or Ariosto's *Necromancer*, 1520) convey the intellectuals' ridicule of that increasing supersitition and susceptibility to the weird and wonderful that accompanied the enlightenment of the age like a shadow.[5] And there is a similar humanist vein, the scorn for mechanical book-learning, in the ridicule of pedants, who seemed to Montaigne the typical butts of Italian comedy.[6] These Italian friars, magicians and pedants recall the

[1] Giordano Bruno, *Il Candelaio*, Argumento (ed. Borsellino, *Commedie*, vol. II, p. 296); trans. J. R. Hale, in Bentley (ed.), *Genius of the Italian Theater*, p. 199.

[2] See above, p. 86.

[3] See Claude Noirot, *L'Origine des Masques*, 1609 (quoted in Petit de Julleville, *Histoire du Théâtre en France: Les Comédiens*, pp. 207–9); Swain, *Fools and Folly*, p. 79.

[4] See Benedetto Varchi, Prologue to *La Suocera* (c. 1546), ed. Borlenghi, *Commedie*, vol. I, p. 1034; Sanesi, *Commedia*, vol. I, pp. 295–6.

[5] Bibbiena, *Calandria*; Aretino, *La Cortigiana*; Giannotti, *Il Vecchio amoroso*; Lorenzino de' Medici, *Aridosia* (ed. Borlenghi, *Commedie*, vol. I). See Bond, *Early Plays*, pp. xxxiff; Herrick, *Italian Comedy*, pp. 121, 136. 137, 152.

[6] Montaigne, *Essais* I.xxv (1580); see Bibbiena, *La Calandria*; Francesco Belo, *Il Pedante* (ed. Borsellino, *Commedie*, vol. II); *Gl'Ingannati*; Bond, *Early Plays*, p. xxix.

impostors of classical comedy, just as they point forward to the
pretenders in Ben Jonson. But they are not presented mainly for the
sake of satire, as in Jonson; they are incidental characters or agents
in a love-intrigue, and if the pedants are mocked for their sexual
double-talk, the corrupt friars and the pseudo-magicians are usually
helpers to the young lovers. They belong to the atmosphere of
sensuous excitement, willing illusion and gleeful derision appropriate
to carnival; their satiric function, at most, is to show up the credulity
of the older generation – they are not either moneyed or the spokesmen
of authority themselves, like the classical *alazones*. Likewise, the braggart warrior, who now reappears on the stage (in *Gl'Ingannati*) from one
of the Spanish armies of occupation – with a long career ahead of him
in the *commedia dell'arte* – has lost the status he once held as the young
lover's principal antagonist. Except in the plays of Ruzzante, who
shows the grimly absurd impact of war on the peasant, the swash-
buckler is little more than an incidental comic butt.[1] Or he joins the
group of pompous and ridiculous lovers (sometimes Neapolitans)
spouting hackneyed Petrarchan phrases.[2]

In some plays, the pimps and parasites from Roman comedy
reappear, but Ariosto and his successors increasingly took their minor
comic figures from the bustle of Italian streets – inn-keepers, street-
vendors, policemen, thieves, even a pair of locally known eccentrics
(in Annibal Caro's *Straccioni* – or *Tatterdemalions* – 1544). And there
are more domestic servants, young and mature, male and female,
than in Roman comedy, with more varied dramatic functions. Many
of them are still the traditional manipulators of their masters' love-
intrigues, often with even more complicated tasks than before –
like Fessenio, who opens *La Calandria* with a monologue describing
some of the cross-intrigues of the plot and his own burdens therein:

I have to do the impossible single-handed. No one can serve two people and
I have to serve three: the husband, the wife, and my own master; so that I
never have a moment's rest.

But Italian comic servants may also swindle their masters entirely

---

[1] Ruzzante, *Ruzzante Returns from the Wars* (trans. Angela Ingold and Theodore
Hoffman, in Bentley (ed.), *Classic Theatre*); *La Moscheta* (ed. Zorzi, *Ruzante*;
ed. Borlenghi, *Commedie*, vol. II; French trans., Mortier, *Ruzzante*); see also
Boughner, *The Braggart*.

[2] E.g. Signor Parabolano in Aretino, *La Cortigiana*; Ligdonio in Piccolomini, *L'Amor
costante* (ed. Borlenghi, *Commedie*, vol. I; ed. Borsellino, *Commedie*, vol. II). See
Nicoll, *Masks*, pp. 246ff.

for their own ends. Or they may be stupid instead of clever; or nothing more to the play than messengers, or voices in a kind of informal chorus, grumbling or jeering. They are related to the fools – the moral simpletons – of late-medieval satire – and in their sexual directness and their appetites for food and drink they are direct representatives of Carnival; as one modern scholar writes, there is 'a whole programme' of entertainment in such servants' names as Scrocca (Shark), Sguazza (Guzzler), Trappola (Pitfall) or Panzana (Humbug).[1]

What may be called the carnival pattern of mocking dismissal of last year's sins and exuberant welcome to the coming year affects the central love-intrigues of Italian comedy strongly as well. Plautus and Terence had shown old men blocking their sons' desires, or even rivals to their sons in love. In Italian comedy, such old men are even more prominent; miserly fathers, wealthy but decrepit suitors, superannuated husbands or interfering amorous dotards feature in at least half of the sixty or more examples of 'learned' comedy that Marvin T. Herrick outlines in his survey of the subject.[2] In some of these plays there are hints of bitterness over political failure. Machiavelli suggests a contrast between modern Florence and ancient Rome when in *Mandragola* he gives the name of Lucrezia to the wife who surrenders to her lover coming from Paris after she finds she has been betrayed by her husband, her mother and her confessor together;[3] and Giannotti, also a Florentine diplomat, writing his *Vecchio amoroso* within a few years of the fall of the Republic, makes one of his young men justify their rebellion against their fathers because the old 'have ruined this fine province of Tuscany with their ambitious and wretched management' (IV.v). In other plays, there is some social criticism: in *La Lena* (1528) Ariosto shows the mean collusions enforced by poverty, and in *La Cortigiana*, Aretino, while flattering Venice, denounces the court of Rome and the prevailing moral corruption ('since wars and plagues and famine and the times. . .have bewhored the whole of Italy' (II.x)). And there are outbursts in the comedies against arranged matches, as in *La Calandria* (II.x), where Fulvia exclaims, 'See what a lovely husband my brothers gave me! It makes me sick to look at him.' But complaints like this derive from Boccaccio, together with the compensation the *mal maritata* will exact; and in general the comic playwrights coarsen the subtle and varied picture Boccaccio had given of the interaction between the

---

[1] Bocci, 'Un Teatro aulico', p. 124.   [2] Herrick, *Italian Comedy*, chs. 3–4.
[3] Croce, *Poesia popolare*, p. 246; *cf* Borsellino, *Commedie*, vol. I, pp. 4, 62.

sexes and the generations, and concentrate on the broad contrast between effete or grotesque lovers and the passionate and virile, paying little attention to social comment. Or, at most, the dramatists appeal to a sense of social fitness, as through the words of the friend of the infatuated father in Giannotti's play (II.ii):

do you want to compete with your son in a case like this, and deprive him of those pleasures which are not unseemly for the young, when they take them moderately?

Whereas a kind of pathos, a limited pathos, is allowed to the young lover's perplexities or those of the sexually frustrated wife, the love of an older man (perhaps with the single and not disinterested exception of Machiavelli's *Clizia*) is entirely a subject for caricature, a mocking tribute to Eros. In Greco-Roman comedy, the family had been the vital social factor, and the young men's love had served to renew the family, even though they might defy their fathers for a while. In Italian comedy there are fortunate adulteries (which would have been unthinkable for Terence and Plautus, but are now laughable when elderly husbands are the victims), and wives who pull the wool over the eyes of their errant but suspicious husbands. And the stage conflict between young and old has little to do with the hidden genius of the family, even though the Italians often resurrect the convention of a surprise dénouement which makes the young man's marriage acceptable. Love is now, as in Boccaccio, an independent natural force, thrusting aside the legal conventions of society. A carnival mood governs most of the plays.

At the same time, although they refer to Petrarch in humour rather than earnest, the Italian comic playwrights keep a strain of courtly love, which is new to the stage. There is something of the romantic side of the *novella*, for instance, in the ardours and the expedients of the hero of *Mandragola*, Callimaco, who has come back to Florence in quest of Lucrezia, inflamed by the praise of her 'beauty and sweetness of nature' that he had heard amid talk of ladies in Paris. And, in spite of the theoretical objection to the presence of respectable young women on the comic stage – that is, the street – Italian dramatists gave much more prominence to the heroine than before, especially the heroine who, again in the manner of romances and *novelle*, could palliate her misfortunes with a masculine disguise.[1] The woman who can suffer

---

[1] See Sanesi, *Commedia*, vol. I, pp. 219–21, 331; Freeburg, *Disguise Plots*, pp. 39–47; Bocci, 'Un Teatro aulico', pp. 110–22; p. 44 above.

and undertake as much as a man for the sake of love comes, again, from medieval literature, but is new to 'regular' comedy. These heroes and heroines from the Italian bourgeoisie have their own wit and their own resourcefulness, in the tradition of Boccaccio, and are not, therefore, so dependent on their servants as the classical *adulescentes*. On the other side, their self-reliance is tried to the uttermost by the pangs of love and the malice of Fortune. In the second half of the sixteenth century Italian dramatists wrote comedies approaching tragi-comedy in tone, with sentimental conflicts between love and honour or friendship, plots involving an apparent danger of incest or death, and situations in the manner of hellenistic romances, where husbands and wives preserve against odds their honour and their constancy, believing each other dead. Perhaps the earliest of the comedies in hellenistic style was Alessandro Piccolomini's *Amor costante* (1536),[1] though it was the complication of hidden identities that interested Piccolomini as much as the sentiment.

The conventions taken over from New Comedy plots extend and develop and finally transform the carnival motifs fundamental to Italian comedy. They serve to sustain a practical joke or to diversify a deception or the confusion of identities in a sort of masquerade, with refinements of ingenuity. And they serve to develop the romantic possibilities in a story in such a way that the audience can share the pathos and the suspense, appreciate the ironies, and anticipate the form of the solution within the framework of a two- or three-hour performance. For the enjoyment of irony and suspense alike, a recognition of conventions governing and framing the plot was essential, and theorists justified imitation of the Roman five-act system on psychological as well as academic grounds; as it was described by Leone di Somi, a man of the theatre rather than an academic, it prepared the audience for two waves of suspense and anticipation:[2]

the first act of a well-constructed comedy should contain the argument and exposition, in the second we should see various disturbances and hindrances, in the third some adjustment must be made, ruin and disaster must threaten in the fourth, while in the fifth a solution is to be reached, bearing all to a joyous and happy ending.

But this linear rhythm was not enough; like most Italian commentators,

---

[1] See above, p. 36.
[2] Leone di Somi, *Dialogues*, trans. Nicoll, *Development of the Theatre*, p. 248; *cf* Herrick, *Comic Theory*, ch. 4.

di Somi also wants what he calls a double, not a single, plot:[1]

> By an entire theme I mean that which contains a double plot, since comedies with but a single development or of simple plot were little esteemed among the ancients and by us are regarded as of slight value. The reason is that double plots well harmonized together seize more powerfully on the imagination of an audience and avoid monotony by the variety of action introduced. Hence those comedies are worthy of greatest praise which cheat spectators into the belief that one action must end in a particular way and then conclude in another, for every one derives greater pleasure from witnessing a fresh and unexpected termination of events.

Giraldi had already said that a double plot had the interest of bringing in two or more characters of the same status. Towards the end of the century, Guarini was to analyse the classical model of the double plot, *The Andrian*, more precisely by pointing out that in Terence's play there are two pairs of lovers, whose affairs are so interlocked that the moves affecting one couple first bar and then release the hopes of the other; if there had only been the leading plot, Guarini adds – the secret marriage of Pamphilus and his father's forgiveness – it 'might indeed have been pathetic and have displayed character'; but then 'how insipid the story would have been!' And Italian authors had seized the principle of two plots running in contact or, better still, interlocking, in the first days of learned comedy. A double plot allowed for a balance of moods, the ribald against the pathetic, as in Bibbiena's *Calandria*. And a double plot with a well-marked temporal rhythm and a pattern that could be recognised, either from experience of the theatre or by reference to a classical model, offered the dramatist two other kinds of advantage. By alternating his lines of interest and by providing for the unexpected, he could suggest an aspect of reality in which the men of Machiavelli's generation were keenly interested, intent as they were upon gauging the limits of the calculable and the force of the unpredictable in human affairs, in a time of discoveries and disasters ('if there was ever an age in which wonders and dissimilar things were seen', wrote Bandello, 'I believe that our age is such, in which occasions for amazement, compassion and censure happen much more than in any other').[2] But in the theatre a dramatist could also afford his audience an emotional release by means of a

---

[1] Leone di Somi, *Dialogues*, trans. Nicoll, *Development of the Theatre*, p. 245; Guarini, *Compendium of Tragicomic Poetry* (1599), trans. Alan H. Gilbert (ed.), *Literary Criticism*, pp. 528–9. *Cf* pp. 185–8, above.

[2] See Griffith, *Bandello's Fiction*, pp. 43, 124; Felix Gilbert, *Machiavelli and Guicciardini*.

classical double plot, with its contrived impression of the accidents in life, all the more because he had brushed against reality and had satisfied or amused his audience with a kind of logic of the unexpected in the circumstances affecting his characters. In this respect, there must have been congruity of mood between the acted plays and their imposing architectural settings. Like the stage-designers, the dramatists aimed at a skilful transition from an illusion of reality to a harmonising fantasy.

There is very little of the splendid and fantastic invention of Ariosto's poetry to be found in the *Suppositi*, but the play has something of his sober realism, his enjoyment of varied incidents and his sense of balance. Erostrato has come from Sicily to Ferrara to study, has fallen in love with Polynesta, and has gained access to her by changing names with his servant, Dulippo, and taking employment in her father's house. The first scene – out-of-doors, Roman fashion – shows Polynesta confiding in their go-between, her nurse, who her lover, the supposed servant, really is, and how (in the words of Gascoigne's translation)

even at his first arrival [he] met me in the street, fell enamoured of me, and of such vehement force were the passions he suffered, that immediately he cast aside both long gown and books, and determined on me only to apply his study.

The hero's disguise as a servant (the 'ground of all the supposes' in the play, as Gascoigne's marginal note says), is borrowed from the lover's disguise in Terence's *Eunuch*; but this encounter and the story of Erostrato's prolonged service, over two years, and of his secret meetings with his mistress in the danger of her father's house, are much more in the style of a *novella*. The first half of the play blends this romantic tone with the realistic tone of a *novella* and the tone of carnival farce. There is a rival suitor, the lawyer, Doctor Cleander ('the old dotard', as Gascoigne describes him), who has a parasite, like the braggart soldier in *The Eunuch*; Cleander is bleary-eyed, senile, pedantic, miserly and vain, but he wants to marry for a family and causes Erostrato anxiety because he is wealthy and the heroine's father listens to him. To fend him off, the real servant, Dulippo, who has been studying under his master's name, has also pretended to be a suitor for Polynesta; but a crisis has been reached, leading the fictitious suitor, as he tells his master (II.i), to offer as big a dowry

as Cleander, alleging that his father is on his way to Ferrara, ready
to confirm the offer. How will that help, asks the real lover, since his
real father is in Sicily; 'and though he come, how may I any way hope
of his consent?' But the resourceful servant has been equal to the
occasion, with the help of chance:

harken a while then: this morning I took my horse and rode into the fields to
solace myself, and as I passed the ford beyond Saint Anthony's gate, I met at
the foot of the hill a gentleman riding with two or three men: and as me
thought by his habit and his looks he should be none of the wisest.

The stranger is a Sienese, on his way home through Ferrara after a
month's stay in Venice; and Dulippo, or Erostrato, as he calls himself,
has not found it difficult to persuade him that the Duke of Ferrara
is furious with the Sienese because of a diplomatic incident (invented
on the spur of the moment), and that his best course of safety in
passing through the town is to stay with Erostrato – a friend to all
Sienese – and pass himself off as Erostrato's father from Sicily; after
which the servant reckons it should not be hard, before the newcomer
finds out the truth about the diplomatic quarrel, to persuade him to
carry through the masquerade all the way. All this related to the
impatient listener with circumstantial detail (Gascoigne omits one or
two local references), in an admirably leisured narrative, a realistic
anecdote in the *novella* tradition. It leads on to a pointed reference to
the classical wheel of Fortune, when the real Erostrato has time to
reflect in a monologue (III.ii):

This amorous cause that hangeth in controversy between *Domine doctor* and
me, may be compared to them that play at primero...O how often have I
thought my self sure of the upper hand herein? but I triumphed before the
victory...Thus have I been tossed now over, now under, even as fortune list
to whirl the wheel, neither sure to win nor certain to lose the wager. And this
practice that now my servant hath devised, although hitherto it hath not
succeeded amiss, yet can I not count my self assured of it: for I fear still that
one mischance or other will come and turn it topsy turvy. But look where my
master cometh.

As the story moves here from a recall of the miscellaneous chances
conceivable in real life to a recall of a well-defined literary pattern,
the audience know what to anticipate: that the wheel will turn for
Erostrato, but that the first blow, at least, will come from a quarter
he does not suspect. And so it is. His master, Damon, who now
comes on, has heard of the lovers' intrigue through a servants'

quarrel, and orders three of his other men to lock the supposed Dulippo 'into the dungeon under the stairs' (III.iii). For the moment, however, the play's tone is still realistic, with an infusion of moral seriousness (which Gascoigne's translation increases). Damon curses 'spiteful fortune', but he blames the old nurse ('for we see by common proof', Gascoigne makes him say, 'that these old women be either peevish, or pitiful: either easily inclined to evil, or quickly corrupted with bribes and rewards' – a characterisation Shakespeare may have remembered when he came to *Romeo and Juliet*). And Damon laments the loss of his wife and dilates on his own mistakes over marrying off his daughter, and on his present dilemma. Death is the only satis-factory revenge against his servant, but 'in such cases it is not lawful for a man to be his own carver. The laws are ordained, and officers appointed to minister justice for the redress of wrongs'; on the other hand, 'if to the potestates I complain me, I shall publish mine own reproach to the world'.

This is the point where Fortune's wheel should begin to turn yet again, but first there is a fresh 'disturbance' in the plot, a half-anticipated distraction: Philogano, the real father of the real Erostrato, has arrived unannounced, coming all the way from Sicily – and enduring the officiousness of the customs – 'only to see [his] son', whom he has missed so much since his departure 'as from that day to this I have passed few nights without tears' (IV.iii). There are now two pathetic fathers in the play, besides two comic seniors, the Sienese and Cleander. And Erostrato's difficulties look like being solved, perhaps after some parental scolding. But at first the play-wright diverts attention to his father: at Erostrato's lodging, Philogano is confronted by the Sienese, who has usurped his identity (IV.iv) and by Dulippo, who has not only usurped his son's identity, but can produce local witness in his favour (IV.vii). Philogano, too, thinks of recourse to the law, and consults Cleander; whereupon it turns out, as client and lawyer discuss the case, that Philogano's family servant, Dulippo, from Sicily, is really Cleander's long-lost son, carried off by the Turks in a raid on Otranto, rescued by an Italian ship, and bought from the crew by Philogano (v.v). Seeing Cleander is satisfied by the recovery of his son, the way is clear for the lovers' marriage.

Ariosto has turned a *novella* situation into a classical comedy, combining motifs from several Roman plays to form a smooth dramatic narrative, neatly balanced. The interest shifts from the younger to the older players; from the lovers' plight (seen from the daughter's point of view) to the problem of providing a substitute father for the hero, back again, when he is locked up, to the lovers' plight (seen from her father's point of view) and then to the perplexity of the hero's real father. And this apparent displacement of interest is the means by which the playwright brings about the revolution of Fortune's wheel. Although Giraldi did not notice it, Ariosto here devises what others, di Somi and Guarini, for instance, would have recognised as a classical double plot. In Guarini's terms the story might have been 'pathetic and have displayed character' if it had consisted solely of Erostrato's secret love affair crowned by forgiveness, but it would have been 'insipid'. But there are two pairs of characters involved, the lovers on one side and Cleander and his son; and the concealed interaction of the two consequent lines of motivation turns the wheel round. Cleander interferes with the lovers' hopes because he wants to replace his lost son; his unknown son counters by inventing a father; which drives the real father to consult Cleander; which leads to a double resolution. The seeming disaster for Erostrato of being locked up when his father arrives is necessary for the resolution of the second plot, or part of the plot; and, that being so, Dulippo's consternation and effrontery towards his old master are necessary for the resolution of the main plot. But Ariosto makes it seem, plausibly enough, that new, unexpected contingencies have arisen, hiding the all-too-regular movement of Fortune's wheel. To make the recognition scene affect the servant instead of the heroine was a new move in the old game. It entails some inconsistency of character (since Cleander becomes more sympathetic at the end of the play than at the beginning), but that might be considered a small sacrifice for the sake of a technical success. The *persona ex machina* in *The Andrian* had been entirely a stranger to the other speaking characters in the play; in Ariosto's play, his coming is prepared for. And by the time Ariosto has introduced the conventional image of Fortune (in Erostrato's soliloquy), he has accustomed the audience to a semi-realistic impression of the comings-and-goings of ordinary town life (there are more minor characters, for instance, than in a classical play). The play seems to illustrate, not character, but the way everyday chance and poetic Fortune both affect people from the outside. It is not easy to distinguish the two.

Here I should like to anticipate the subject of a later section of this chapter, by digressing to part of Shakespeare's technical debt to

Supposes. T. W. Baldwin has suggested that in *The Comedy of Errors* Shakespeare borrowed a detail from *Supposes*, the circumstance of the war between Ephesus and Syracuse which reacts upon Egeon.[1] In both plays a father (from Sicily) is travelling to find a beloved son; in both he is blocked by the consequences of a political dispute, genuine or feigned; and in both, his knowledge of his own family is confuted by a local witness (the Duke vouches for Antipholus of Ephesus, as the father's guide in Ferrara vouches for the pretended Erostrato). But I believe the hints Shakespeare gathered from *Supposes* went much further than this. No doubt he took the story of Egeon and his wife and children from medieval romance, and obviously he took the central plot mainly from the *Menaechmi*. But he turned his material from the *Menaechmi* into a double plot in the Italian manner by bringing in Luciana and making Antipholus of Syracuse woo her, suddenly and dangerously, in his brother's house. Meanwhile, his namesake, with a real claim to enter, is kept outside, somewhat like Erostrato's namesake in *Supposes*, with his fictitious claim to woo the heroine respectably. The scene (III.i) where Antipholus of Ephesus first comes on the stage, to be shut out of his own house, is largely borrowed from *Amphitryon*, but the indirect way it arises recalls the scene of doubled identities where the father is refused admission to his son's lodging in *Supposes*. Up to this point in *The Comedy of Errors*, Adriana and her brother-in-law have both been seeking the same man. The wooing scene (III.ii) turns Shakespeare's complication into a double plot, with an obvious prospect of solution, but first what may be called the original plot reasserts itself, and the traveller begins to suffer from his brother's connections and acquaintances: he is frightened because his own Dromio has been mistaken by the kitchen-wench (III.ii), he is delayed by the Courtesan (IV.iii) and he is threatened because of his brother's debt to Angelo the goldsmith (V.i). In the *Menaechmi*, the traveller's slave had rescued the resident twin and brought about the recognition, as if the family likeness between the twins had simply been allowed to come to the surface. In *The Comedy*, as in *Supposes*, several characters are intent on their legal rights or their fears from the law, there are scenes of imprisonment or arrest, and it is recourse to the law, the public institution apparently untouched by the vagaries of chance, that brings about the dénouement: Antipholus of Syracuse runs into the priory for sanctuary, and later the Abbess appeals to the Duke

---

[1] Baldwin, *Five-Act Structure*, pp. 665, 674, 685.

on his behalf, thereby unloosing the whole tangle of knots. As in *Supposes*, too, the timing of this resolution depends on the father's arrival at the city, painful to himself and only indirectly connected with the central business of the plot.

Baldwin argues that in constructing *The Comedy of Errors* Shakespeare followed contemporary text-book teaching based on *The Andrian*. But the text-book teaching dwelt on the Roman five-act structure, not on the principle of the double plot, which the Italians had elaborated, and which Shakespeare carries even further than Ariosto. He was to use both the *Menaechmi* and *Supposes* again, but it seems very probable that it was the latter, as an influential modern play, that suggested the choice of *Errors* as his title and stimulated him to construct a more than classically complicated and yet neatly coherent plot. With its bustle of citizen characters and its criss-crossing of the action, *The Comedy* is as much Italian as Roman in spirit. And Shakespeare was evidently aware of several aspects of the Italian stage tradition, not merely *Supposes*, at the beginning of his career; he mentions the pantaloon, from the *commedia dell'arte*, in *The Taming of the Shrew* and the zany in *Love's Labour's Lost*. It has been pointed out that the role of the two Dromios in *The Comedy*, partly domestic buffoons and partly messengers who miscarry and get beaten, is much more like that of the Zanni in the *commedia dell'arte* than that of their nominal counterparts, the slaves in Roman comedy.[1]

Bibbiena's *Calandria* soon acquired the reputation in Italy of the first 'true vernacular comedy worthy of the name';[2] after the original production at Urbino in 1513, it was performed again for the courts of Rome and Mantua, at Venice, and for the French and the Bavarian courts; and it was printed twenty times before the end of the century. The reputation throws a hard light on sixteenth-century taste, since most of the humour in the play consists of cold-blooded mockery. However, Bibbiena exploits more fully than Ariosto the range of tones possible to Renaissance as distinct from classical comedy. At one extreme, the belly-laughter of Carnival, more self-consciously sought for than the farcical tricks in Plautus; at the other extreme, a pathos

[1] Lea, *Italian Popular Comedy*, vol. II, p. 438.
[2] See Sanesi, *Commedia*, vol. I, pp. 222, 233, 376, 404; Ruscelli (ed.), *Comedie Elette*, p. 166; Leone di Somi, *Dialogues*, trans. Nicoll, *Development of the Theatre*, p. 244; Riccoboni, *Histoire du théâtre italien*, vol. II, pp. 147ff; Borsellino *Commedie*, vol. II, p. 11.

more elaborate than that of Roman comedy, supported by the precepts and the cultivated sentiment derived from the tradition of courtly love. At the two extremes, the gross and the idyllic, there is a negative attitude towards everyday bourgeois life, or a sense of release from ordinary constraints. Between these extremes comes the enjoyment of the wit or resourcefulness the dramatist gives to some of his characters, and of his own ingenuity in manipulating the incidents.

The play is a dramatised *novella*, rounded off by borrowings from the *Menaechmi*. Most of it is taken up with the middle-aged woman, Fulvia (who has a son of marriageable age), her grotesque husband, Calandro, and their unconsciously competitive pursuit of a young stranger in Rome, Lidio, who has unwittingly inflamed the husband's desires by adopting a female disguise so as to facilitate his intrigue with the wife. The principal among several wire-pullers is Lidio's servant, Fessenio, who has taken service with Calandro so as to help the young lover and who mocks Lidio's tutor in an early scene (I.ii) when the latter tries pedantically to dissuade his pupil from love. Calandro is patently copied from the famous booby in the *Decameron* (VIII.3 and 6; IX.3 and 5); he is so asinine that he can be delighted by Fessenio's description (I.iv) of his pretended errand as a go-between:

When I saw her just now, she was – just a moment! sitting with her hand to her chin; and, listening intently as I spoke about you, she had her eyes and her mouth wide open, with a bit of her little tongue hanging out, like this.

Under Fessenio's instructions, Calandro learns how to kiss, to die and revive, is carried towards his mistress in a trunk, so that he is tumbled into a ditch (III.ii), and tries again in a porter's disguise, whereupon he is caught by his wife (III.xii). On her side, Fulvia behaves like a cat on hot bricks, repeatedly despatching her maid – who finds her own satisfaction more easily – on love-errands, employing an ignorant adventurer who passes as a magician, and running after her lover in male disguise. She conceals this folly, however, by catching her husband, and fools him a second time at the end, when he believes he has found her with her lover in the house.

There are dozens of short scenes consisting of staccato intriguing or mockery. They are punctuated by more elevated 'sentences', often in soliloquy, taken from Boccaccio. For example, Lidio replies to his tutor's reproaches (I.ii) with a maxim –

Polinico, there is nothing in the world which puts up with advice or opposition less than love; whose nature is such that it will sooner be consumed of its own accord than be removed by the warnings of others.

– thus echoing the introduction to one of Boccaccio's tales (IV.8), where the long periodic sentence begins:

And because in the whole of nature there is nothing which puts up less with advice or opposition than love, whose nature is such that it will sooner be consumed of itself than be removed by any admonition, it occurs to me to tell you a story.

Fulvia echoes several tales from the *Decameron* (III.5 and 6, for instance) when she bewails the misfortunes of her sex (III.v):

Oh, what miserable luck women have, and how badly their love is often gratified in their lovers!...There's no pain like that of a woman who finds she has wasted her youth.

And, after she has plucked up the courage to sally out in disguise, and returned rampant with her baffled husband in tow, Fessenio lifts his admiring commentary (III.xiii) out of another tale (VII.4):

O Love, how great your power is! What poet, what doctor, what philosopher could ever point out the expedients and the guile that you teach those who follow your banner? All the wisdom, all the learning of anyone else is sluggish when compared with yours. Without love, who else would have found the expedient to escape from such a tight corner as she has? I never saw such an artful dodge.

Altogether, modern editions of *Calandria* draw attention to such echoes from a score of different tales in the *Decameron*.[1] Boccaccio supplies the Renaissance playwright with the whole groundwork of his comedy, the contrast between witty love and inept love, and the contest of Love and Wit with Fortune.

The novelty in the play consists in taking from Plautus an additional complication which is also the means to a resolution. In the second prologue, or Argument, to the play, it is explained that Lidio and his twin sister, Santilla, have escaped separately to Rome after their birthplace, Modone, was sacked by the Turks; and as Santilla has adopted her brother's appearance and name – just as her brother has adopted hers – she and her servant-adviser can weave in and out of the main intrigues at the dramatist's will, until we reach the twice-postponed recognition scene. This device both doubles the carnival

---

[1] See *Calandria*, ed. Borlenghi, *Commedie*, vol. I, and Borsellino, vol. II; *cf* Giraldi, 'Discorso intorno al Comporre de i Romanzi' in *Discorsi* (Venice, 1554), p. 179.

sex-disguises and compensates for the harsh if conventional sexual naturalism of the farce by means of an indulgent irony. The dramatic image of Fortune's tricks frames and distances the cat-and-dog fight in a bourgeois household, and Santilla balances Fulvia, as a more sympathetic heroine, representing courage in adversity. Not that Santilla is altogether edifying (she agrees that it would be clever to blackmail Fulvia, for instance), but she has the romantic excuse of pure misfortune behind her contrivances. She begins the line of Renaissance stage heroines in male disguise, a character-type from a *novella*[1] set in a pattern of events from Plautus.

Gl'Ingannati, the play which confirmed the romantic status of such heroines in comedy, was written by an unidentified member of the Sienese Academy of the Intronati for the carnival of 1531. The Academy had been founded in 1525, the year of the French catas-trophe at Pavia which delivered Italy to the power of Charles V. It was one of a series of literary clubs in Siena, but it soon became famous as the first one in Italy, perhaps in Europe, to adopt an *impresa*, a symbolic title and a constitution. Its *impresa* was a *zucca* (a peasant salt-box made from a gourd), with crossed pestles and an Ovidian motto implying hidden mental virtues ('*meliora latent*'); its title was also ambiguous, since *intronati* could mean both 'thunder-struck' or 'astonished with some rattling noise' and 'enthroned'.[2] The Articles, dating from 1532 (after the sack of Rome, the Pope's submission to Charles V and the collapse of the Florentine republic), set out the Academy's purpose extensively:[3]

At the time when the armies of the barbarians, summoned by the discord between our princes from the furthest parts of the west and entered into the sacred house of God, had expelled not only from Tuscany but from all parts of Italy every thought save that of war,...some noble spirits excelling in divers accomplishments of learning joined together in our city...to found a society in which, quitting...all tedious and troublesome thoughts and all other worldly cares, they would betake themselves exclusively and with a firm purpose to literary exercises as well in Italian as in Greek and Latin, reading, discussing,...writing...and studying,...not only in philosophy but in the humanities...and all liberal and noble arts, giving liberty to everyone in the

---

[1] See p. 200, n. 1, above.
[2] See Maylender, *Accademie d'Italia*, vol. III, pp. 350ff; Iacometti, 'L'Accademia degli Intronati', pp. 190ff. *Cf* John Florio, *A Worlde of Wordes, or Most Copious and Exact Dictionarie in Italian and English* (1598); G. Torriano, *A Dictionary Italian and English* (1659).   [3] Iacometti, 'L'Accademia degli Intronati', p. 191.

said society for the more especial exercitation of his wit to propound problems, jests, cant words, emblems, new forms of speech [*conclusioni, motti, gerghi, imprese, nuove lingue*] and any other kind of invention connected with literary studies. And from their firm resolution to feign not to understand or heed anything else in the world, they are pleased to adopt the name of *Intronati*.

Behind all this solemnly Pickwickian joking there may have been another concealment, since the meetings of the Academy were involved in or suspected of heresy and propaganda for reform of the Church in the course of the next thirty years.[1] But officially their principal public object was to flatter and amuse the ladies of Siena. One of the early members, a kinsman of two of the founders of the Academy, was Alessandro Piccolomini (1508–78), comic playwright, populariser of Aristotle and, ultimately, archbishop;[2] in his comedies for the Intronati (in the prologue to *Amor costante* in 1536, for instance) he dwells on this programme of courtly jesting:[3]

their [the academicians'] precepts can be listed briefly: always to seek to know how to make the best of the world; and to be the slaves, the devoted and languishing servants of these ladies and on occasion, for their love, to give a comedy or something similar to show them our zeal.

Fiddling while Rome burns shows depraved insensibility; but to fiddle after the sack of Rome may have been a means of consolation.

In 1531 the Intronati offered the ladies of Siena two linked entertainments. The first, on Twelfth Night, was a mock-ceremony called the Sacrifice. The show began with a song in which the singer, accompanying himself on a lyre, addressed the 'charming Ladies' on behalf of the Intronati: having wasted 'the flower of their years' in 'the prison of amorous sufferings' for the ladies of Siena, but finding themselves repulsed and disdained, the Intronati are now coming one by one to burn their dearest love-tokens on 'this altar' and thus free their hearts from 'error', while the ladies will be punished by remorse and loss of 'fame'.[4] Then a presiding Priest prayed to the gods, especially to

[1] See Borsellino, 'Rozzi et Intronati', pp. 157–8; Maria Rossi, 'Le opere letterarie di Alessandro Piccolomini', *Bullettino Senese di Storia Patria*, XVII (1910), 310–11; Cantimori, 'Italy and the Papacy', p. 264.

[2] See Maria Rossi, 'Alessandro Piccolomini'; Pirotti, 'Aristotelian Philosophy'; Iacometti, 'L'Accademia degli Intronati', p. 196.

[3] See Piccolomini, Prologues to *L'Amor costante* (1536), *L'Ortensio* (1560) (ed. Borlenghi, *Commedie*, vol. I, pp. 280, 1044) and *L'Alessandro* (*c.* 1544) (quoted, Maria Rossi, 'Alessandro Piccolomini').

[4] *Il Sacrificio de Gl'Intronati* (Venice, 1553: bound in with Ruscelli (ed.), *Comedie Elette*), pp. 3–9. See Luce (ed.), *Twelfth Night*; Purves (ed.), *Gl'Ingannati*, p. 7.

Minerva, to accept the coming sacrifices and release the celebrants from love:

Those wings that Heaven had given them, and that lofty wit [*altero ingegno*] and the other gifts which could make them eternal and fly living into Heaven, they have spent in serving these proud, these harsh, pitiless and reluctant foes [*queste superbe,/Queste crude nemiche empie,/e ritrose*]; nor were their studies turned to any other end than praising and exalting them everywhere, both in speech and with ornate pen [*con l'ornato stile*].

This is the tone of Petrarchan and mock-Petrarchan devotion that was to become familiar to Donne and to Shakespeare:

> I cannot breathe one other sigh to move,
> Nor can entreat one other tear to fall,
> And all my treasure, which should purchase thee,
> Sighs, tears, and oaths, and letters, I have spent;

or Viola's imagined *canzoni* for Olivia:

> Make me a willow cabin at your gate,
> And call upon my soul within the house;
> Write loyal cantons of contemned love
> And sing them loud even in the dead of night;
> Halloo your name to the reverberate hills,
> And make the babbling gossip of the air
> Cry out 'Olivia'! –

or Orsino's reproaches, violent but still Petrarchan, to the same 'cruel', 'perverse', 'uncivil lady', his 'marble-breasted tyrant',

> To whose ingrate and unauspicious altars
> My soul the faithfull'st off'rings hath breath'd out
> That e'er devotion tender'd!

Orsino's lines, in particular, suggest that Shakespeare had read the text of *Il Sacrificio* (which was printed with *Gl'Ingannati* in some editions and provided the first title).[1]

After the Priest's invocation, thirty members of the Intronati advanced in turn, under their club names, such as Lo Stordito (Dizzy) – this was Alessandro Piccolomini[2] – Il Caroso (Moth-eaten), Lo Sdegnoso (Indignant) or Il Soppiatone ('privy whisperer', according to Florio's dictionary). Reciting appropriate verses, each committed

---

[1] *Cf* Bullough, *Sources*, vol. II, pp. 271–3.
[2] *Il Sacrificio de Gl'Ingannati* (in Ruscelli (ed.), *Comedie Elette*), p. 11; *cf* Iacometti, 'L'Accademia degli Intronati', p. 196.

a love-token to the sacrificial urn – a handkerchief 'bathed in tears', a 'broken faith', a mirror, a book of poems in his lady's honour, her glove, her 'image', her veil, a heart, a dove, an ornamental pen. It was a carnival ceremony of precisely the type that Savonarola had tried to treat in earnest, a burning of the vanities. One of the sacrificers, whom Shakespeare may well have noticed,[1] the only one to use what looks like a genuine name, was Messer Agnol Malevolti, who deposited 'a carved Cupid, a gift from his lady' and recited a poem in retaliation for his disillusionment:

Love, what reward, what happiness you once promised me! That you turned my desires to follow you, you know; and I, what you gave me, Love, in torment, treated as jest [*à gioco*]; but then, when your fire in me was already spent, with what deceit [*inganno*] – the truth grates on me – how strange the thought is, you caused the heartless Lady to give me yourself [the Cupid], with her promises of grace in pawn! You are surely not worth calling a God any longer, and now your infinite faults will be punished. And if it delights you so to see the wretched undone in fire, grain by grain, now you can taste a little how sweet and gentle is the flame.

The ceremony ended with the Priest ordering the sacrificers to throw the ashes of their burnt pledges over their shoulders and leave, heart-free, while the lyre-player sang to the ladies in the audience, warning them to consecrate their youth to love, or else they would be despised, instead of praised, for their hard hearts. But in the final stanza he assured them that if they would relent, the Intronati, too, would return 'more ready to love than ever'.

As if to fulfil this assurance a few weeks later, the second part of the carnival entertainment, the comedy of *The Deceived*, addressed particularly to the ladies through the spokesmanship of the Prologue, was an *amende honorable*, a kind of *Legend of Good Women*. It shows how the young heroine, Lelia, takes risks for the sake of love and wins her truant admirer, Flamminio, by her devotion. Lelia's family has been scattered by the sack of Rome, four years earlier. Her father has retired to his remaining house at Modena and has recently placed her for safety in a convent near the city while he is away on business. Before that, they had received many visits from Flamminio Carandini ('being of our political party and a close friend of my father's'), who covertly gave the girl many an 'amorous sign', which filled her with happiness. In this she was evidently the first in the play to be deceived,

---

[1] *Il Sacrificio de Gl'Ingannati*, p. 25. See Luce (ed.), *Twelfth Night*, p. 180 (but also Hotson, *First Night of 'Twelfth Night'*, p. 108).

for over the months he has forgotten her and begun to pay court to Isabella Foiana. Now, however, just before her father's return, 'hearing nothing but love talked about by those reverend Mothers', she has learned through their help that Flamminio wants a page, and, egged on by one of the Sisters, has left the convent in a boy's disguise and entered Flamminio's service, where she finds herself favoured but given the odious trust of carrying his messages to Isabella. 'O what a fate is mine!' she exclaims in her first scene (I.iii):[1]

I love a man who hates me, who always scorns me; I serve one who does not know me; and to make things worse I help him in his love for another (though, if it should become known, nobody surely could believe it); all without any hope other than of feasting my longing eyes by seeing him all day as I please.

On the other hand, she is far from passive; Isabella has fallen passionately in love with her in her page's disguise, 'and I pretend not to wish to love her until she makes Flamminio cease paying court to her' (I.iii). As Flamminio's page, she slyly reminds him of his former love, herself, and tells him he is only getting what he deserves if Isabella now is cold to him – 'for if you have a mistress whom you do not appreciate, it is only reasonable [*ragionevol*] that others will not appreciate you' (II.i); meanwhile, as Isabella's desired lover, she responds at last to Isabella's kisses with both feigned and genuine reluctance (II.vi):

On the one hand I am having fun at the expense of her who believes me a man, on the other I should like to get out of this scrape, and I don't know what to do.

When in the next scene she hears Flamminio attribute Isabella's coldness to the fact that he once courted Lelia Bellenzini – but does not hear him say how attached he feels to his new page – her self-pity boils up ('Rejected, dismissed, fled from, hated! Why do I still pursue him who flees me?') and she decides to run to her old nurse, Clemenzia, whom she has already taken into her confidence.

She has little to do in the middle scenes of the play, but when Flamminio learns that his page has been deceiving him he reacts with the same kind of fury that Orsino was to express towards Viola at a similar point in *Twelfth Night* ('I shall cut off his lips and ears, and dig out one of his eyes' (IV.viii). His fury takes him to Clemenzia's

---

1 *Gl'Ingannati*, trans. Bullough, *Sources*, vol. II, p. 292.

house, where however the old woman calms him down: 'You young men take every misfortune well, for you are the most ungrateful people on earth' (v.ii). As if to prove a general point, she tells him Lelia's story, without the names, glossing over the provocation to Isabella and stressing how the girl had 'imperilled her own honour' and devotedly taken 'service with her beloved'. Flamminio, of course, is duly impressed by the exemplary case – 'Did this really happen in Modena?...Why has such a thing not happened to me?' – and swears that marriage could be the only 'reward' for such a paragon:

I would nevermore show my face among gentlemen and knights, my peers, if I did not prefer her as a wife,...rather than the daughter of the Duke of Ferrara.

Once the moral trap is sprung, Clemenzia can produce her charge, in woman's dress (v.iii) and Flamminio gladly confirms his oath:

I truly believe it is God's will, who has had pity on this virtuous maid, and on my soul that it may not go down into perdition.

All this has gone to show, if the audience have recalled the Prologue,

how great is the power of chance and good fortune in affairs of love; and how great too in them is the value of long-enduring patience accompanied by good counsel.

Yet Lelia's part in the comedy has a shade more dignity than that. It is based on folk-tale motifs of the rejected bride, the clever wench and the pledge fulfilled, but it is treated with the realism of a *novella*. The Modenese place-names and some of the family names belonged to real life.[1] The beginning of Lelia's love is related with circumstantial detail; Clemenzia's horror when she learns of Lelia's temerity is realistic, and so is Lelia's failure of nerve. At the same time, the story hails from romance, with the heroine's disguise and her reversal of the traditional roles of the sexes in love-service. And the conclusion has the elevated tone of a *novella* used as moral example, both in Clemenzia's way of telling Lelia's story and in Flamminio's reaction; the code of reason, justice and honour, which Flamminio acknowledges at the end, is that of Boccaccio's courtly tales, as with Giletta of Narbonne. Boccaccio had already restated the knightly principle of binding honour in terms of the bourgeois code of fair or reasonable

---

[1] See Borsellino, *Commedie*, vol. I, notes to pp. 208, 211, 215, 235, 244, 258.

exchange of services and the merchant's pledged word.[1] The Sienese comedy surrounds the ideal motives of romance with even more of the atmosphere of modern bourgeois life (Lelia is even allowed a little sharp practice, and yet *virtù* is rewarded). Nevertheless, Lelia's story preserves a balance between courtly idealism and Renaissance scepticism;[2] she is the first seriously romantic heroine on the Renaissance stage. And, apart from the plays of Machiavelli and Ruzzante, with their utterly different tone, this is perhaps the first modern comedy in which characters are shown to follow a credible purpose, see the consequences of their actions, waver, develop and change.

The realism shades off into carnival farce. When Clemenzia demands, 'aren't you ashamed to be seen like that?' of Lelia in her boy's clothes, Lelia can reply (I.iii):

As if I were the first! I have seen hundreds in Rome dressed like this; and in Modena there must be many every night who go about on their private affairs in this disguise.

Similarly, her father, Virginio, because he has lost much of his wealth, is willing to marry her off to Isabella's father, Gherardo, a widower, who is the grotesque elderly suitor typical of carnival comedies. The two elderly men boast of their virility, but Clemenzia calls the suitor a 'musty, oafish, rancid, snivelling fellow' (I.iv), and his efforts to live up to his part bear her out. His servant, Spela, describes his master's 'frenzy of love' (I.v):[3]

He's shaving himself bald, combing himself, mincing about like a woman. He goes out at night to sword-parties, and he carols all day long in a wheezy, raucous voice to a big lute more out of tune than himself. And now to cap it all he's given himself over to making pizzles [epistles]...and songets and whimsies [*capogirli*: for *capitoli*] and stringmaroles [*strenfiotti*/*strambotti*] and materials [madrigals] and a thousand other comedies, enough to make the donkeys burst with laughing, let alone the dogs. And now he wants to use civet.

But the civet is beyond the old lover's reach; the perfumier tells Spela, so he reports (II.v), that his master must have meant itch-ointment. A second absurd would-be lover is the Spanish soldier, who appears in three scenes unconnected with the main plot. He has designs on

---

[1] Branca, *Boccaccio Medievale*, pp. 80ff.
[2] *Cf* Croce, *Poesia popolare*, pp. 263–6; Bocci, 'Un Teatro antico', pp. 111, 117–19.
[3] See Borsellino, *Commedie*, vol. I, p. 224n.

Isabella, but he cannot speak Italian and is thoroughly fooled by Isabella's maid.

The complementary carnival strain in the play, the celebration of youthful sensuality and the enjoyment of masquerade, comes out in the second division of the main plot, which is taken from the *Menaechmi*, and which enables the author – to quote Etienne's preface to his translation again – to '[change] themes, introducing things unexpected and hidden', before 'leading everything dextrously... to the conclusion'. Lelia's long-lost twin brother, Fabrizio, arrives unannounced at Modena, in the company of his solemn tutor and his greedy servant, just when his sister's affairs have reached a crisis, at the beginning of Act III. There is first a comic genre scene with faintly satiric overtones, in which the travellers are invited to choose between staying at the Mirror and staying at the Madman, and plump for the second, more popular inn. Then Fabrizio wanders about the town, so that his father and Gherardo mistake him for Lelia, disgracefully at large in masculine dress, and insist on locking him into Gherardo's house with Isabella (III.vii). The result is entirely satisfactory to Isabella (IV.v); but when her father finds out, there is a comic street-fight between the two old men and their followers (IV.ix–v.i) before the twins can be distinguished and everyone pacified. Here the borrowing from Plautus is much more neatly used to form a double plot than in *La Calandria*. And there is a steady gradation of comic tones in the play, from Lelia's romantic marriage to the unpremeditated match between Fabrizio and Isabella – purely the result of 'chance and good fortune' – on to the mockery of the old men and would-be lovers and the carnival appetites of the various servants. The French translator was justified in singling out *Gl'Ingannati*, not because it was the best Italian play he could have chosen, but because in it the author or authors found a genuinely modern equivalent for classical New Comedy, in the tradition of the *novella* and in the spirit of carnival masquerade.

DOUBLE PLOTS IN SHAKESPEARE

When in Terence's *Eunuch* the young scapegrace Chaerea relates how he had gained access to the women's apartment in Thais's house under cover of his disguise, he excuses his act of rape by reference to a picture he saw there (III.v; 584). It is one of those passages in New Comedy that recall the older fashion of mythological burlesque:

that picture was there, showing how Jupiter once sent a shower of gold into Danae's lap. As I began to look at it, it encouraged me immensely to think how he once played the same game, changing himself from a god to a man and coming stealing over the tiles on another man's roof for the sake of a false turn with a woman.

No such mythologies cross the mind of Erostrato, Chaerea's counterpart in *Supposes*. But when in *The Taming of the Shrew*, Lucentio, whose role is adapted from Erostrato's, arrives at Padua to study with his servant (of the Plautine name of Tranio) and sees and falls in love with Bianca, literary and classical allusions come thick and fast. Erostrato's servant had teased him by reminding him, 'the books that you toss now-a-days, treat of small science' (*Supposes*, II.i); in *The Shrew* (I.i), Tranio makes a flourish over a similar theme:

> *Mi perdonato*, gentle master mine...
> Only, good master, while we do admire
> This virtue and this moral discipline,
> Let's be no Stoics nor no stocks, I pray,
> Or so devote to Aristotle's checks
> As Ovid be an outcast quite abjured.

A moment or two later, having seen Bianca in the street, Lucentio bursts into literature, comparing himself incongruously with Dido, and then recalling another of the divine metamorphoses:

> I saw sweet beauty in her face,
> Such as the daughter of Agenor had,
> That made great Jove to humble him to her hand,
> When with his knees he kiss'd the Cretan strand.

This is from Ovid, right enough; so is the passage in the previous scene in *The Shrew*, in the Induction, where the Lord's servants offer to delight Christopher Sly with provocative 'pictures' of Adonis, Io, or Daphne sought after by enamoured gods; and possibly the 'pictures' reminded Shakespeare of Terence as well, since in the dialogue with Lucentio, Tranio quotes in Latin from a grammar-book variant of a line from another scene in *The Eunuch*.[1] Unlike Ariosto, then, Shakespeare embroiders his episode of the student falling in love with classical reminiscences. The very fact that they are scattered reminiscences and the way they are introduced suggest a generalised reference to school-learning in Shakespeare's mind and a deliberate

[1] Ovid, *Metamorphoses* I.452ff, 588ff; II.846ff; X.520ff. See Hibbard (ed.), *The Taming of the Shrew*, pp. 173–4, 184–5.

comparison between romantic love and acquired culture, which is completely different from the unadvertised recall of the *novella* tradition in the love-story in the *Supposes*. Shakespeare had already inserted a similarly generalised reference to Ovidian metamorphoses in *The Comedy of Errors*, in the scene (III.ii) where Antipholus of Syracuse tries to woo Luciana:

> Are you a god? Would you create me new?
> Transform me, then, and to your pow'r I'll yield...
> O, train me not, sweet mermaid, with thy note,
> To drown me in thy sister's flood of tears.
> Sing, siren, for thyself, and I will dote;
> Spread o'er the silver waves thy golden hairs,
> And as a bed I'll take them, and there lie;
> And in that glorious supposition think
> He gains by death that hath such means to die.
> Let Love, being light, be drowned if she sink.

The situation here may have been adapted from Ariosto or Gascoigne (*supposition*, incidentally, is not a common word with Shakespeare), but not the style.

Contrasts of this sort between Shakespeare and the Italians could easily be multiplied. However closely the Italians follow Roman New Comedy plots, however candidly they acknowledge such borrowing in the prologues to their comedies, they make it a point of honour to treat their dialogue realistically – allowance made for stylistic echoes from Boccaccio, – to confine it to the matter in hand and to make their characters speak like typical educated contemporaries, except for occasional passages of caricature. Shakespeare does nothing of the kind. The stuff of his dialogue is much richer and more varied than the Italians'; it is also, on the surface, more anachronistic and more literary. Not only are his characters, unlike those of the Italians, presented to their first spectators as foreigners from distant, semi-fictitious countries, but their minds are full of foreign literature, especially the literature of a vanished epoch, learned at school. And unlike most of the Italian authors of comedy, Shakespeare uses verse as his principal medium – not, most of the time, the medieval stanza-forms still current in early Elizabethan interludes, or the Tudor fourteener or even the rhyming quatrains such as Antipholus of Syracuse employs for a passionate harangue, but the blank verse metre which Marlowe had popularised as the form suited to heroic actions, and which Surrey had introduced for his translation of Virgil.

Paradoxically, Shakespeare's comedies are more obviously classical than the Italians'.

In part, the historical explanation of this paradox could be that the revival of classical culture was less mature in Shakespeare's England than in Ariosto's Italy. The Elizabethans had not assimilated it as throughly to their own manner of life and thought; they were still fascinated by the verbal rhetoric of classical poetry and its narrative substance, and had not yet reached the stage of abstracting from it a generalised theoretical concept of artistic form.[1] On this view, Shakespeare, by comparison with Ariosto, is a medieval playwright advancing towards the classics. Yet this explanation, though probably valid as far as it goes, would be incomplete. A great deal of water had flowed under the bridges since Ariosto's day; and in any case, it was impossible for an Englishman to approach ancient Roman culture in the same spirit of self-identification as an Italian, especially in a century of growing national pride. For Shakespeare, Roman New Comedy was a product of a foreign though fascinating culture, not the most obvious model of expression for his own. And similarly with the modern versions of Roman comedy in Italian. Hence the typical sequence of events in an ancient or a renaissance New Comedy was something more than, and different from, a scenario for a carnival entertainment; it was still attached to a festive, holiday mood, but it was also the pattern for something more distant from common practical life, for experiences connected with books and the imagination. A play, for Shakespeare, could not take place as a seasonal diversion in the context of ordinary social life, in exactly the same way as it could for the early sixteenth-century Italians or for the Romans and Athenians before them, if only because he was a professional actor–playwright, belonging to almost the first genera-tion in Europe of a predominantly commercial theatre.

The scheme of social experience in which Shakespeare places his characters for the sake of the comedy is also different in many ways from the scheme adopted by playwrights like Ariosto. For instance, Shakespeare does not begin his stage action at a point where Anti-pholus or Lucentio is already in love; he shows them falling in love instead, while they have been aiming at something else. And if, in this respect, they resemble young men in some *novelle* or knights in medieval romances, their expression of love is not continuous with the rest of their social code, as in *novelle* or as with the language of

---

[1] *Cf* Panofsky, *Renaissance and Renascences in Western Art.*

amour courtois in knighthood. They feel themselves 'transformed' and they take a literary language remote from their daily lives (or the daily lives of their audience) to say so. They quote, in effect, from the highest secular literature inculcated by Tudor schoolmasters, but the imagery they draw upon still has an alien colouring. And it is dramatically appropriate for this very reason. For Shakespeare's characters are not merely capable of being surprised by what happens to them, dismayed or delighted, like the people in Italian comedies; they can be carried out of their normal selves, 'transformed', observe themselves passing into a new phase of experience, so strange that it seems like illusion. This is only part, indeed, of a more fundamental innovation which in its general effect distinguishes Shakespeare's plays from all previous comedies, that he gives his people the quality of an inner life. Their inner life, with their capacity for introspection, changes the whole bearing of the incidents that make up a traditional comic plot. It is as if Shakespeare separates the events that compose the plot from the centres of consciousness in his leading characters, so that the plot-machinery operates on a different plane, the plane where the characters are being 'transformed'. To the irony of events considered whether as accidents or probabilities, Shakespeare adds an ironic interplay between situations and personalities. Nevertheless, Shakespeare needs and uses the machinery of the double plot as elaborated by the Italians. He needs it precisely to bring into relief his own kind of psychological irony.

There are three marriages by the end of *The Taming of the Shrew* and a fourth at the beginning, if we count Christopher Sly's pretended spouse, the page who sounds the *leitmotif* for what is to follow:

> My husband and my lord, my lord and husband;
> I am your wife in all obedience.

The main action deals with the taming of Kate and the wooing of her sister, Bianca, in nearly equal proportions; if anything, more of the dialogue hinges on the wooing of Bianca. Here Shakespeare borrows liberally from *Supposes*, but his treatment illustrates his independence from his sources. Erostrato had been unaware of a crucial fact, Damon's discovery of his intrigue, but secure in his emotional ties with Polynesta; Lucentio, on the other side, is completely successful on the level of action, but misjudges Bianca's character. His infatuation is bookish and adolescent, he fails to notice any danger-signal when she flirtatiously enters his game of deception but keeps her own counsel (III.i), he has to be hurried off to his opportunely-contrived wedding by his waggish page, Biondello (IV.iv), and he bets much too confidently on his bride's obedience. Shakespeare treats the assumptions behind this romantic or novellistic wooing with irony. And he links the two plots concerning the sisters together by methods which are typical of the Elizabethan theatre but, in large part, at least, different from the Italian. In an Italian double plot, the events in each plot are so arranged as to interfere causally with those in the other, and the actions shown on the stage follow a strictly temporal sequence, so that each plot can react on the other at exactly the right moment. The stage timing of Fabrizio's arrival is important in *Gl'Ingannati*, for instance, and it is vital to the effect of *Supposes* that the father, Phylogano, should arrive exactly when he does. Italian learned comedy is one of the first artistic expressions of a civilisation regulated by clocks.[1] But Shakespeare adopts this principle of plot-interaction more loosely and intermittently, alongside of another principle which could be described as thematic alternation, whereby scenes from one part of his total plot react on scenes from another by way of latent psychological parallels or repetitions of imagery, without any strict temporal or causal connexion. Kate's wedding, for instance, leaves the road clear for Bianca's but does not affect its circumstances; the relation between the two episodes (III.ii and IV.iv) is simply that the first ceremony is grotesque but above-board, whereas the second is decorous but deceitful. Again, Shakespeare retains from *Supposes* the episode of the attempted deception of the father – in his play, Vincentio – when he comes to visit his son. In *The Shrew*, this episode at Padua (V.i) is no longer essential to the mechanism of the plot; but Shakespeare makes it serve the comic idea in his play, and makes it serve twice over, by bringing Vincentio into an earlier game of misattributed identities, in the scene (IV.v) where Kate seals her partnership with Petruchio by pretending to mistake the old man for a 'young budding virgin'. The second, borrowed scene provides the only occasion in the play where Petruchio is temporarily deluded, when he believes Vincentio is lying and tells him (V.i.30), 'Why, this is flat knavery to take upon you another man's name'; and this, in turn, is a hint that Petruchio has finished with his own play-acting.

The network of deceptions and self-deceptions is even more

---

[1] *Cf* Hale, *Renaissance Europe, 1480–1530*, pp. 11–14.

intricate in *The Shrew* than in *Supposes*. Bianca has an extra suitor, and each of her three genuine wooers deceives himself while thinking he is deceiving others: old Gremio, by presenting Lucentio to her father as a supposed tutor, Hortensio by coming disguised as a music-teacher, and Lucentio himself by winning her hand. Hortensio had been the first to think of getting Kate out of the way by using Petruchio (I.ii) and Hortensio is the first to be disillusioned with Bianca, when with Tranio he watches her 'kiss and court' with the pretended tutor (IV.i); but he is deceived even in his disillusionment, as he accepts at its face value Tranio's 'unfeigned oath, | Never to marry' Bianca, and abruptly remembers the 'wealthy widow', of whose affection to himself he feels entirely confident:

> Kindness in women, not their beauteous looks,
> Shall win my love; and so I take my leave,
> In resolution as I swore before.

He does not learn very much, even from his attendance at Petruchio's 'taming-school'. In contrast, the girls' father, who is apparently deceived by nearly everyone else in the play, loses nothing at all through his gullibility; while Petruchio has his way by exploiting fictions and pretences with psychological understanding. Shakespeare, in other words, has enlarged the scope of Ariosto's 'supposes', shifting them towards the plane of psychological relationships.

At the same time, he has shaped both of his own main plots, and linked them with each other and with the added Induction precisely by extending the principle of 'supposes' he has borrowed from Ariosto.[1] Moreover, he has taken other hints from Italian comedy. Gremio is an 'old pantaloon' (III.i.36), though less absurd than Italian seniors; Biondello is a cheeky page in the Italian tradition (like the 'crack-halter' or 'slipstring', Crapino, in *Supposes*; Shakespeare could conceivably have taken his name from another early translation from Italian, *The Bugbears*);[2] and the mock-bride, who does not figure in the source-anecdote for the Lord's trick on Christopher Sly, could have been suggested by Aretino (whose *Marescalco* and other comedies were printed in London in 1588).[3] And Shakespeare amuses himself, like Italian playwrights, with phrases from a foreign language – for instance, Italian, which Grumio, like a zany, mistakes

---

[1] See Seronsy, ' "Supposes" as the Unifying Theme in *The Shrew*'.
[2] Bond (ed.), *Early Plays*, p. 274.
[3] Radcliff–Umstead, *Birth of Modern Comedy*, p. 240; Bullough, *Sources*, vol. I, pp. 109–10; *cf* p. 196, n. 2, above.

for Latin (I.ii.28). Above all, he applies the lesson of the balanced and inter-connected double plot, which he is more likely to have learned from *Supposes* than anywhere else. In his first act, the marriage of Kate is introduced only as a means to another end, the release of Bianca, and the rivalry over Bianca occupies most of the dialogue, although Shakespeare ensures the momentum of his double plot by interesting the audience more in Kate. He maintains the latent contrast between the two halves of his plot by devising scenes dealing with the pretended tutoring of Bianca before he comes to Petruchio's 'schooling' of Kate in Act IV. He then links the two plots causally together, first by making Hortensio and his real or pretended rivals join in offering Petruchio inducements to 'break the ice' for them (I.ii.263) by wedding the elder sister, and then by making Tranio point out to Lucentio 'our vantage in this business' in the midst of Kate's marriage-scene (III.ii.140), before he brings the two marriages together (with Hortensio's added) for comparison in the final scene. This is not mere imitation of New Comedy or Italian plots, but the application of Italian methods to new purposes.

The Two Gentlemen of Verona is a student play akin to *Supposes* and the Lucentio plot in *The Shrew*: Valentine and Proteus travel to Milan to complete their formation at the court as gentlemen, and each receives his *éducation sentimentale*. The triangle plot of their rivalry for Silvia belongs to the atmosphere of Lyly's educational fable, *Euphues* (1578), and its successors.[1] But Valentine's ill-fated stratagem with the rope ladder recalls that other Veronese lover, Romeo; the loutish official suitor, Thurio, comes from the scheme of things in Italian comedy; so do the episodes of stage business with letters and Proteus's intrigues – Shakespeare could have found a precedent for fickle cross-wooings, for instance, in Munday's *Fedele, or Two Italian Gentlemen* (c. 1584), adapted from a recent comedy by Pasqualigo;[2] and even Shakespeare's outlaws, cardboard though they are, suggest some knowledge about contemporary Italy.[3] And the complementary part of Shakespeare's double plot, Julia's disguise, comes from *Gl'Ingannati*, by way of Montemayor.[4] Whether Shakespeare already

---

[1] Bullough, *Sources*, vol. I, pp. 203ff.

[2] (Munday), *Fedele and Fortunio. The Two Italian Gentlemen.* See Shapiro, 'Shakespeare and Mundy'; Herrick, *Italian Comedy*, p. 152; Bullough, *Sources*, vol. I, pp. 208, 256ff.

[3] See Kamen, *The Iron Century, 1560–1660*, pp. 341ff.

[4] Rennert, *Spanish Pastoral Romances*, pp. 54–6.

knew the original source or not, he brings Julia's duet with her maid Lucetta (I.ii) and her scene with the Host (IV.ii) closer to Italian comedy than the corresponding passages in Montemayor's pastoral romance.[1] And he interweaves Julia's scenes with the others for ironic effect. Her second scene, her scamped parting from Proteus (II.ii), follows the scene at Milan in which one of the gentlemen, Valentine, shows he has already changed his principles by courting Silvia; when the audience next see Julia, determining to run after Proteus in disguise as 'a true-devoted pilgrim' (II.vii), they have just heard him 'forswear' her for Silvia's sake; and conversely, in her next two scenes, when she overhears Proteus's serenade (IV.ii) and delivers his message to Silvia (IV.iv), they already know that, in spite of Proteus, 'the banished Valentine' has found allies in the greenwood (IV.i) and that Silvia plans to follow him (IV.iii). The rhythm of the whole action is marked by the two men on their travels and then the two girls in flight. In spite of its weaknesses, this is something more than apprentice work on Shakespeare's part. He has not tried simply to dramatise Monemayor's pastoral narrative; he has taken what he wants from it to fit a well-balanced comic structure.

Shakespeare's next two comedies in probable order of composition are both connected with *The Taming of the Shrew* and *Two Gentlemen of Verona*. *Love's Labour's Lost* is linked with them by way of the academic motif, the character-types resembling the *commedia dell'arte* ('the pedant, the braggart, the hedge-priest, the fool and the boy'), and the business of the crossed letters; and *A Midsummer Night's Dream*, by way of the taming of Titania, the escape to the woods, and the more general theme of reason and constancy in love. Shakespeare seems to have invented the main stories in both; the multiple plot of the *Dream* is a triumph in the adaptation of Italian techniques. No doubt what can be called the central situation derives from Chaucer's *Knight's Tale* – the appeal to Theseus just before the celebration of his marriage to Hippolyta, the rivalry between Demetrius and Lysander for Hermia and their duel in the woods. But Shakespeare turns this nucleus into a classical double plot by adding Helena and inventing his amatory criss-cross of pursuers and pursued. Oberon's flower is the same 'love in idleness' (II.i.168) whose 'effect' in *The Shrew* (I.i.146) had been to cause Lucentio to fall

---

[1] Extracts from *Diana* in Bullough, *Sources*, vol. I, pp. 230-5.

suddenly in love, without benefit of magic; Demetrius and Lysander switch devotions, like Proteus or Flamminio, his predecessor in *Gl'Ingannati*; Helena finds herself, much like Lelia in the Italian comedy, adored by a lover she rejects while she is scorned by the lover she has tried to win back and serve. All four Athenians seem to have taken 'a sup of the cup of error' which Barnabe Riche describes to his readers in *Apolonius and Silla*, his story derived indirectly from *Gl'Ingannati*:[1]

for to love them that hate us, to follow them that fly from us, to curry favour with them that disdain us, to be glad to please them that care not how they offend us, who will not confess this to be an erroneous love, neither grounded upon wit nor reason?

As in the *Menaechmi* and Italian comedies, their entanglement is made worse by an accidental meeting with characters from another part of the action, accompanied by a mistake of identities; and the resolution comes for them from the same external source. Their love is a product of 'fantasy' (i.i.32), a matter of 'thoughts and dreams', 'poor Fancy's followers' (i.i.154): Lysander claims 'reason' when he is least the master of his own feelings (ii.ii.115f); but Bottom is sagely aware that 'to say the truth, reason and love keep little company together now-a-days' (iii.i.131). There is dramatic point, therefore, not mere stage convention, in the fact that the young Athenians are rescued by accident, not by means of their own intelligence. They are saved by something outside themselves, in a way they do not recognise or understand. Although Fortune's wheel is not mentioned in this comedy, it is virtually that that saves them; or rather, what is behind Fortune's wheel, the mythology of the cycle of Nature. When in the morning Theseus finds them in the wood, he imagines 'they rose up early to observe | The rite of May' (iv.i.129); and the whole comedy is presented as a dream appropriate to Midsummer Night,[2] one of the principal turning-points in the year, the magic moment of wheels of fire and of the fern-seed that produces invisibility, of revelations as to future brides and bridegrooms and of encounters with the fairies – the fairies whom Shakespeare here elevates into Ovidian weather-gods. Not content with this, and with assimilating Puck to a Roman

---

[1] Riche, *Apolonius and Silla*, ed. Spencer, *Elizabethan Love Stories*, p. 97.
[2] *Cf* Schanzer, '*A Midsummer Night's Dream*'; Brand, *Popular Antiquities of Great Britain* (ed. Ellis), vol. I, pp. 298ff; Chambers, *Mediaeval Stage*, vol. I, p. 126; vol. II, p. 165; Baskervill, 'Dramatic Aspects of Medieval Folk Festivals in England', pp. 51–2; *cf* Frigout, 'La Fête Populaire', pp. 268ff.

comic servant, he transforms Bottom by lifting the ass's head from Apuleius's tale of witchcraft. Like the lovers, Bottom believes he has lived through a 'dream', while the audience have been privileged to observe the conjuncture of accidents that have brought their illusions about, as in Italian comedy. And, as in Italian comedy, Puck can make a mistake; while, in relation to Oberon, it is no more than a timely chance that brings Bottom to the wood. There is a cycle in the chain of being in *A Midsummer Night's Dream*, as well as in the sequence of events.

A Midsummer Night's Dream marks the end of the first phase in Shakespeare's writing of comedies, when one of his main interests is to devise an intricate plot. In most of his later comedies mere intricacy of plot is less important, though of course it is still present, and Shakespeare still applies the Italian principle of the double plot, as for instance in *Much Ado*, where he carefully interweaves his borrowed intrigue, the slander of Hero, with his invented intrigue, the deception of Beatrice. But *The Merry Wives of Windsor* shows how thoroughly he had absorbed the methods of classical and Italian comedy, and how readily he could fall back on them as his principal standby when – as seems very likely in this case – he was more than usually pressed for time. It has less psychological or poetic substance and is more simply a lively stage entertainment than any other of his mature comedies, so that there is no strong reason to doubt the eighteenth-century legend that he wrote it in about a fortnight, to obey the Queen's wish that he should show Falstaff in love. In view of the last Act, it can be called a fairy play, like *A Midsummer Night's Dream*; and it looks as if it was written for a first performance at Windsor, to celebrate an installation of knights of the Garter,[1] just as the *Dream* looks as if it was written for a first performance at a noble wedding. In any case, the play has, with good reason, remained a favourite on the stage, and if Shakespeare did in fact compose it in a fortnight, it is, as Gildon said, 'a prodigious thing, when all is so well contrived, and carried on without the least confusion'.[2] It is a brilliant example of the more mechanical side of Shakespeare's art as a comic playwright.

In one respect it is quite different from Italian Renaissance comedy,

---

[1] See William Green (ed.), *Merry Wives*, in *Complete Signet Classic Shakespeare*, ed. Barnet, pp. 962–6.
[2] Charles Gildon [1710] (quoted, Bullough, *Sources*, vol. II, p. 3).

in that it depends on exploiting the reputation of characters Shakespeare had created and made popular himself. Although Falstaff has lost most of his irony and his resourcefulness, his reputation with the public can be taken for granted, so that his mean shifts can be taken in at once as evidence that he is falling off from his previous glory, to a caricatural antithesis to everything the Order of the Garter stands for, while his dismal failure even in trickery gains in comic effect because the audience can co-operate by remembering him as cleverer than, on the showing of the present action, he really is. Similarly, the audience must have been prompt to welcome a familiar figure of fun in Justice Shallow; and so too with Pistol, Bardolph, Nym and Mrs Quickly – although the latter does not appear to be the hostess already known to the public, but a similar person of the same name. Shakespeare had either already used or was soon to use again the device of reintroducing Falstaff and associated characters of his own invention into the historical sequels to *1 Henry IV*; and this device was no doubt one of the primary reasons for the theatrical success of *The Merry Wives* – it makes a kind of greeting from the playwright to his public. Even a new character in this play, Fenton, can be placed by a passing allusion to *Henry IV*: 'The gentleman is of no having: he kept company with the wild Prince and Poins' (*Merry Wives*, III.ii.62).

The device of exploiting known characters depends on an established intimacy between dramatist and public. Shallow and Pistol and the rest are stock types, but something more as well. They have mannerisms which can be exploited because the audience already know something about them, can partly anticipate their reactions, and can be pleased to find their expectations a little exceeded – as when Falstaff is brought on to bluff his way through charges of poaching and robbery, or Nym declares, 'I will keep the haviour of reputation' (I.iii.74), or, in the opening scene, Shallow boasts of the coat of arms he has borne, 'any time these three hundred years', threatens to bring Falstaff before the Star Chamber for 'riot' and then, in the next breath, exclaims, 'Ha! o' my life, if I were young again, the sword should end it' (I.i.36). Here, surely, the actor is to take advantage of the spectator's previous knowledge about him and his readiness to project a shadowy personal history from another play. And Shakespeare also exploits the discovery he uses to great effect in *Henry IV*, the invention of a personal biography for fictitious as well as historical characters, the attribution to fictitious people of a personal memory including off-stage events and acquaintances as well as details of their own past. Thus Shallow here says, in 'character', 'if I were young again', and later (II.iii.40), in the cadence of *2 Henry IV*:

Bodykins, Master Page, though I now be old, and of the peace, if I see a sword out, my finger itches to make one. Though we are justices, and doctors, and churchmen, Master Page, we have some salt of our youth in us; we are the sons of women, Master Page.

This comes as a response to Page's presumably ironic reference to Shallow's fighting days, in keeping with his biography in *2 Henry IV*. The same device is carried over to Shallow's new stage companion, his nephew, Slender, who boasts to Anne Page, in the family manner, how he has 'bruis'd [his] shin' with a fencing-master and how he has 'seen [the bear] Sackerson loose twenty times, and [has] taken him by the chain', notwithstanding the shrieks of the ladies present (I.i.258ff). Slender's great stroke as a suitor imbued with family pride is, 'Pray you, uncle, tell Mistress Anne the jest how my father stole two geese out of a pen, good uncle' (III.iv.39) (he had, of course, been complaining with Shallow in the first scene, of being robbed by Falstaff's crew). Better still in a similar vein is Mrs Quickly's character-sketch of Dr Caius's servant – 'An honest, willing, kind fellow . . . ; his worst fault is that he is given to prayer; he is something peevish that way; but nobody but has his fault' (I.iv.9). This is the kind of superfluous detail where Shakespeare could be described as at his most Dickensian. Yet these touches, which are commonest in the actors connected with *Henry IV*, certainly do not amount here to characterisation in depth. Nor are they 'humours', psychological deviations, in Jonson's sense, though Nym is fond of the word; there is no general satire behind them. Nym's catchword, 'humour', or Slender's repeated sigh, 'Ah, sweet Anne Page!' are no more than comic personal tags, like 'Barkis is willin'', and Shakespeare uses them to create nothing more than 'character' parts of the mechanical sort that Strindberg was to decry in his preface to *Miss Julie*. At most, *The Merry Wives* marks a fresh step in the creation of such 'character' parts, since the amusement it arouses is like the amusement people share over known personal kinks within an intimate social group.

The purely verbal humour in the play has a similar effect. Falstaff's wit is still there, but at a low ebb. Sir Hugh Evans's Welsh English, Dr Caius's French English, Pistol's bombast and the Host's cosmopolitan and military-sounding epithets belong to the general farce tradition of linguistic extravaganza that Shakespeare also uses, to better effect, in the Fluellen scenes in *Henry V*. There is a slight suggestion that command of English English should go with mental superiority, so that Falstaff is brought down an extra peg when he realises at the end that one of his tormentors is 'that Welsh fairy', 'one that makes fritters of English'; but that is all. For the most part, the dialogue has very little of the inner richness and significance of Shakespeare's other mature comedies; it simply adds zest to the entertainment of the intrigue. The play as a whole would make poor supporting evidence for Coleridge's opinion that Shakespeare always preferred character to plot.

On the contrary, *The Merry Wives* fits easily into the fashion of the late 1590s for rapid and complicated intrigues, as in the first comedies of Chapman and Jonson. And it seems most probable that, like Chapman and Jonson, Shakespeare turned back to Roman comedy for the suggestion for his principal plot. If he was indeed faced with a commission to write a court play at short notice about the fat knight in love, the most promising model to consider would have been Plautus's *Braggart Soldier*.[1] Possibly Shakespeare had remembered Plautus's comedy previously, in the Ephesian setting of his *Comedy of Errors*;[2] in any case, it could now have given him the essentials for the scenario he needed – the boaster, inordinately vain about his sexual charm, who is lured into an intrigue with a married woman (a pretended married woman in Plautus), steals into his neighbour's house, is soundly thrashed and is terrified into avowing his fault. Pyrgopolynices, already wealthy, had been actuated simply by sexual vanity, whereas Falstaff is in search of funds, but this hardly affects the scenario. Plautus, like Shakespeare after him, harps on the craft of women; and (as I have suggested in Chapter 3) the 'good-natured' bachelor, the *bon viveur* in *The Braggart Soldier* could have furnished other elements in Falstaff's character and also the character of his Host, who takes a friendly share in a young lover's intrigue; while the Host's far-fetched military jargon (for which there is no strong reason in Shakespeare's scheme) could have been prompted by the exotic names used to describe the victories of Plautus's warrior. In general structure, too, Plautus's play anticipated the main lines of Shakespeare's: there is a static opening scene showing off the role of Pyrgopolynices, then comes the first of the two intrigues against him,

---

[1] *Cf* Reinhardstoettner, *Plautus*, pp. 595ff; Boughner, *The Braggart*, pp. 10ff.
[2] Baldwin, *Five-Act Structure*, pp. 665, 684; and see above, pp. 115–17.

the intrigue involving the invention of a double identity for the heroine, who is in his clutches for the time being, and whom he will agree in the course of the second intrigue to release so as to pursue his new supposed innamorata, while the heroine is led off by her real lover in disguise. *The Merry Wives* also begins with a scene exhibiting Falstaff's character, reputation and exploits, with no direct consequences for the main intrigue. Then much of the first two Acts is taken up with the rivalries over Anne Page, which are due to end in a manner not unlike *The Braggart Soldier*.

It has been suggested also that Shakespeare borrowed from Plautus's *Casina*, where husband and wife are at odds over a girl's marriage, like Anne's parents, and where Shakespeare could have found hints for the way Dr Caius and Slender are hoaxed into marrying two boys in disguise, as well as for the scene where Falstaff receives a drubbing in the garments of 'the fat woman of Brainford'.[1] At the same time, crossed wooings and sex-disguises were also part of the Italian comic tradition, and Shakespeare elaborates them in the Italian manner. The details of Falstaff's misadventures, for instance, cannot be traced to any particular source but belong to a broad renaissance tradition. Professor Bullough discusses three or four possible sources,[2] including a tale by Ser Giovanni Fiorentino, whose book (published in Italy in 1558) had certainly provided Shakespeare's main source for *The Merchant of Venice* and could have suggested the buck-basket episode in *The Merry Wives*. Another tale, based on an Italian model, comes from *Tarlton's News out of Purgatory* (1590), and a third, in the same tradition of farcical *novelle*, comes from Riche's *Farewell to Military Profession*; it contains a beating episode involving a Soldier, a Doctor and a Lawyer, three lovers of the same married woman. Tales of wives who outwit either their husbands or their lovers can be traced back, as Bullough points out, to the *Decameron*; and they form the common stock of Italian carnival plays like *La Calandria*. Shakespeare's cast and his repertoire of situations in *The Merry Wives* come from this joint narrative and stage tradition. In Munday's *Two Italian Gentlemen*, for instance, there are cross-wooings, letters and misleading messages, a braggart soldier, a comic pedant, a witch who is also a go-between, transferred disguises, a scene where a lover has been lured into a woman's bedroom, a street-fight and a scene of incantations and nocturnal mock-terrors in a graveyard. Shakespeare has absurd elderly wooers (Falstaff and Dr Caius) and an absurd young wooer

---

[1] Bullough, *Sources*, vol. II, p. 9.   [2] *Ibid*. pp. 4ff.

(Slender); in addition to his braggart soldier, he provides a pantaloon, a comic doctor, a comic clergyman–pedant, a female go-between, a supposed witch or fortune-teller (Falstaff as the fat woman) and a climax in a nocturnal scene of magic which is not genuine but feigned.

A common feature in the *novelle* Professor Bullough discusses is the pattern of the duper duped. Thus, in Riche's story, the Doctor and the Lawyer hope to trick the wife but are tricked themselves; in Ser Giovanni's tale and in *Tarlton's News*, the lover, a youth, confides in an older man without knowing that his adviser is his mistress's husband, the husband pretends to counsel the lover and tries to trap him with his wife, and after each of the first two escapades – there are three altogether in each tale, as with Falstaff – the lover unwittingly relates to the husband how the wife had hidden him or spirited him away in the nick of time. Although the upshot in Shakespeare's comedy is different, this pattern evidently underlies the sub-plot wherein Ford visits Falstaff disguised as 'Brook' and hears enough to keep his causeless jealousy boiling.

Moreover, Shakespeare carries this principle further. The theme of the duper duped is common in farces like *Maître Pathelin*: possibly it expresses at bottom the revenge of native shrewdness against acquired cunning, of the layman against the clerk. But in Italian comedies on the lines of *Supposes* and *Calandria* it becomes an extended pattern, with duplicated or antithetical situations in a balanced symmetry. Similarly, *The Merry Wives* becomes a network of 'supposes'. Not only does Falstaff imagine he is deceiving both wives and husbands in one plot, while Ford believes he is outreaching his wife and Falstaff, whereas in fact the two wives are outwitting both men; but the link between the Falstaff plot and the wooing plot is precisely that Mr and Mrs Page, who are impregnable against Falstaff, both blunder over their daughter's marriage becase they attempt to use trickery against her and against each other. Similarly with the efflorescent sub-plots: Falstaff thinks he can reduce Pistol and Nym to mere messengers and they turn against him; when Dr Caius challenges Sir Hugh because the latter is helping Slender's suit, and the Host prides himself on having tricked the doctor and parson out of their duel, both league against the Host in reprisal, swindling him out of his horses – which in turn provokes the Host to help Fenton snatch the bride away from both of his scheming rivals. Meanwhile, Mrs Quickly encourages all three of Anne's suitors, tries to make them – and herself – believe she is indispensable, and accomplishes nothing for herself or any of them. In a sense, her bustling about is quite superfluous to the plot and a less talkative go-between would have served equally well. But Mrs Quickly helps to complete the pattern; imagining she is deceiving those around her, but chiefly fooling herself, she is a counterpart to Falstaff. Moreover, it is part of Shakespeare's joke that the audience cannot be quite sure which way some of the intrigues are tending; one sleight-of-hand serves to camouflage another.

At the same time, the two main plots are antithetical in moral substance and parallel in progression. One action deals with attempted adultery, the other with match-making; in one, lust is the cover for money, in the other, love triumphs over mercenary concerns. Falstaff, or 'bully Hercules' as the Host calls him (i.iii.6), is notable for his cowardice – which provides the fun of the discovery scenes at Ford's house. The other action is filled at first with the bellicose words of men of peace, the doctor, the parson and Justice Shallow (who, like Mrs Quickly, contributes to the pattern of characters over and above the intrigue). Some scenes, about a third of the play, deal with both actions in close proximity, while the rest alternate between one action or its sub-plots and the other, until both are tied together in the episode of the fairies' dance around Herne's oak. But meanwhile the two actions appear to move in opposite directions. In one, Falstaff, the central actor, begins the action, although his schemes recoil on himself; he is trying to gain something from the other characters. In the second, Anne, who is passive, is the central figure in the sense that she is the magnet who draws the others. It is plain from the outset what Falstaff's story will be like, or at latest it is plain from the moment when the two wives compare his letters (ii.i), and the comic interest can only spring from variations on a declared theme. The theme of Anne and her rival suitors is no less familiar, and is heralded in the opening scene, but the form it will take is partly camouflaged by the sub-plot concerning the doctor's duel with the parson and their joint revenge on the Host. This sub-plot is sustained from i.iv to iv.v, while the *tertius gaudens*, Fenton, who has also been introduced early (i.iv), remains in the background, not meeting Anne on the stage until iii.iv, the scene following the buck-basket episode, when the farcical interest of the first main plot has begun to quicken. Even then, the lovers' dialogue is soon interrupted, and it is not until iv.iv, in the scene at Ford's house where the dominant interest is the reconciliation between Ford and his wife and the hatching of another, general scheme against the fat knight, that the audience are given a hint of the form the conclusion of Anne's story will take, by means of a couple of short asides, from Page and his wife (IV.iv.72, 83).

A few details in Shakespeare's plan, in the horse-stealing business, for instance, may have been made to seem unduly cryptic because of a bad text. But there is no call for editorial theories of revision or the mangling of topical allusions. As it stands, the camouflage device is highly effective. In the first place, it allows the characters to meet at Ford's or Page's house, at Falstaff's inn, or in the street or the fields outside Windsor, without making it too obvious that they are propelled by the machinery of the plot. Such accidental-seeming encounters are part of the realistic scheme of Italian city comedies. Lyly had attempted something similar in the Rochester of *Mother Bombie*, but with more patent artifice; in several plays close in date to *The Merry Wives*, like *Every Man in his Humour*, this impression of everyday movement in the streets was evidently a sought-after dramatic effect.

Secondly, the camouflage provides for some suspense and gives the audience the pleasure of discovering a new spurt in the action just when it appears that the conclusion can be foreseen. This is precisely one of the main technical objects of an Italian double plot; and Shakespeare contributes to this result further by the way he manipulates Anne's three suitors. Caius blusters, but does not meet her directly; Slender woos her like a nincompoop; while Fenton at first seems to be relying on help from Mrs Quickly and does not show his hand to the audience (by approaching the Host for help) until late in the game (IV.vi). By this time we know that Anne's parents have each begun their own plots, so that they seem to be helping Fenton against their will. And since Anne herself seems to make no move at all – an unusual passivity for a comic heroine in Shakespeare – her marriage when announced has the appearance (as Ford, now for once a consoler, soothingly tells her parents), of guidance from 'the heavens themselves' (v.v.219). In relation to her parents' scheming, it results in rounding off the pattern of the dupers duped. And this incidentally brings a grain of consolation to Falstaff, in the final release of forgiveness.

Shakespeare habitually works towards a finale much grander than in Roman or Italian comedies. In this case, he evidently wanted a closing device which would serve two purposes at once, to complete the gulling and punishment of Falstaff in public, and to cover the last moves in the wooing of Anne; at once an exorcism and a celebration. Hence, it would seem, his choice of the wives' third trick against Falstaff, with the knight wearing a stag's head as Herne the hunter – an implicit mockery of his effort to cuckold others – and the other actors in disguise as tormenting fairies dancing round him. But for the substance of the wives' trick Shakespeare turned back to the legend of Actaeon in one of his favourite books, Ovid's *Metamorphoses*, which he evidently knew well, in Latin and in Arthur Golding's translation (1567), and used extensively in his poems and again and again in his plays.[1] In the *Metamorphoses* (III.138–252), Actaeon, while hunting, accidentally comes upon Diana bathing, surrounded by her nymphs; the offended goddess changes him into a stag; and the poor mortal is torn to pieces by his own hounds. Shakespeare uses this legend several times. In *A Midsummer Night's Dream* it may have supplied some of Hippolyta's recollections (IV.i.109) of hunting with Cadmus (Actaeon's grandfather) with 'hounds of Sparta' in 'a wood of Crete', and the Latin text (III, 173) provided the name of Titania, an unusual alternative for Diana. In the *Dream*, Shakespeare also salutes the legend by inverting it, making the wood-enclosed goddess pursue the mortal and transforming the mortal into an ass. He probably recalls it again in *As You Like It*, through the First Lord's literary description (II.i) of the 'poor sequest'red stag' whose tears fall, like Actaeon's, into a brook; and he alludes to it more directly in *Twelfth Night* (I.i), when Orsino's attendant invites him to hunt 'the hart', and the duke punningly replies:

> Why, so I do, the noblest that I have.
> O, when mine eyes did see Olivia first,
> Methought she purg'd the air of pestilence!
> That instant was I turn'd into a hart,
> And my desires, like fell and cruel hounds,
> E'er since pursue me.

Orsino's image of the hunter hunted is in line with the medieval and Renaissance tradition of Ovid moralised, and in *The Merry Wives* Shakespeare uses the legend in a similar way. Actaeon is mentioned twice in the course of the play (II.i.106 and III.ii.34) as the emblem of a cuckold; but the idea behind Falstaff's masquerade as the hunter wearing a stag's head could have been taken from Golding's

---

[1] Highet, *Classical Tradition*, pp. 116, 203–7; Whitaker, *Shakespeare's Use of Learning*, pp. 26, 64, 101, 104; *cf* Bullough, *Sources*, vol. I, pp. 161, 179, 371, 373; vol. II, p. 17; vol. VI, pp. 12, 88.

moralistic interpretation of the legend, in his Epistle to Leicester:[1]

> All such as doo in flattring freaks, and hawks, and hownds delyght,
> And dyce, and cards, and for to spend the tyme both day and nyght
> In foule excesse of chamberworke, or too much meate and drink:
> Uppon the piteous storie of Acteon ought to think.
> For theis and theyr adherents usde, excessive are indeed[;]
> The dogs that dayly doo devour[,]theyr followers[-]on with speede.

'Fie on sinful fantasy', the Windsor fairies sing as they pinch and burn Falstaff; Ford mocks him by asking where the horns are now; and Falstaff is compelled 'to perceive that [he has] been made' – like Bottom – 'an ass'. Shakespeare conceals his borrowing from the Actaeon legend behind Mrs Page's narration (iv.iv) of a local 'old tale' – apparently invented; but then at the beginning of the final scene, he makes Falstaff refer to other amatory metamorphoses, as if in compensation to Ovid:

Now the hot-blooded gods assist me! Remember, Jove, thou wast a bull for thy Europa; love set on thy horns. O powerful love! that in some respects makes a beast a man; in some other a man a beast. You were also, Jupiter, a swan, for the love of Leda. O omnipotent love! how near the god drew to the complexion of a goose! A fault done first in the form of a beast – O Jove, a beastly fault! – and then another fault in the semblance of a fowl – think on't, Jove, a foul fault! When gods have hot backs what shall poor men do? For me, I am here a Windsor stag; and the fattest, I think, i' th' forest. Send me a cool rut-time, Jove, or who can blame me to piss my tallow?

This is very much the style of Chaerea, in *The Eunuch*, and the first divine disguise Falstaff calls to mind is taken from the same legend of Europa ('the daughter of Agenor') that Lucentio had quoted in *The Shrew*. Here again, Shakespeare's ranges freely across Ovid's poetry, not for separate details but to link together a whole chain of images and ideas. And again the principle that unites the chain is the theme of the psychological transformation caused by love. Ovid enables Shakespeare to turn his action into something at once richer and stranger than any Italian comedy. On the other hand, he introduces the invented folklore of *The Merry Wives* with the same amused scepticism that the Italians reserved for stage magic; when Mrs Page has described the terrors inspired by Herne the Hunter, 'Sometime a keeper here in Windsor Forest', she adds,

---

[1] Golding (trans.), *Ovid's Metamorphoses*, *Epistle*, lines 97ff, ed. Nims, p. 408.

> You have heard of such a spirit, and well you know
> The superstitious idle-headed eld
> Receiv'd, and did deliver to our age,
> This tale of Herne the Hunter for a truth;

on which her husband comments,

> Why yet there want not many that do fear
> In deep of night to walk by this Herne's oak.
> But what of this?

'This', the first audiences would have been prompted to notice, was going to be magic of quite a different sort from that in *A Midsummer Night's Dream.*

During an Italian court entertainment Ovid's mythology would have figured separately in the *intermezzi*, not inside the comedy. The motif of transformation in *A Midsummer Night's Dream* and *The Merry Wives* typifies both the poetic and the theatrical divergences between Shakespeare and the earlier Renaissance playwrights. Shakespeare's art is even more self-conscious than the Italians'; he is not following their tradition but using it. Otherwise, however, the *Dream* and *The Merry Wives* show him exploiting the methods of the Italian double plot to the uttermost, with stories which he can be said to have invented. And in both plays he goes to the centre of the Italian tradition of comedy and the classical tradition behind it. In the *Dream* the happy ending is due principally to Fortune, in *The Merry Wives*, to trickery. But both plays are festival masquerades. And in both, the consequence of illusions is to restore what seems to be the right or natural course for love and domestic harmony. The masquerade changes the characters.

Shakespeare sums up this major phase of his early comedy-writing in *Twelfth Night, or What You Will* (c. 1600). It is possible that Shakespeare's interest in *Gl'Ingannati* was aroused or re-aroused as an indirect result of the performance of the second Anglo-Latin adaptation, *Laelia*, at Queens' College in 1595. No less a person than Essex came to Cambridge to watch it; and in 1599 a Queens' man, John Weever, published a volume of *Epigrams in the Oldest Cut and Newest Fashion*, in the fourth 'week' or section of which he celebrates two Fellows of his College and their success as entertainers 'with far-famed *Laelia*' (iv.19). Two pages later come tributes to Shakespeare and to the actor, Edward Alleyn. The former, *Ad Gulielmum Shakespeare* (iv.22) is a sonnet which begins:

> Honie-tong'd *Shakespeare* when I saw thine issue
> I swore *Apollo* got them and none other,

and continues, after mentioning Venus, Lucrece and Tarquin,

> *Romea* [*sic*] *Richard*; more whose names I know not,
> Their sugred tongues, and power attractive beuty
> Say they are Saints althogh that Sts they shew not
> For thousands vowes to them subjective dutie:
> They burn in love thy children *Shakespear* het them [heated them]
> Go, wo[o] thy Muse more Nymphish brood beget them.

This was neither good poetry nor the first printed eulogy Shakespeare could have read.[1] Nevertheless, published notices, especially of mere playwrights, were not so common that even Shakespeare is likely to have ignored it; and, if so, it is quite likely that he glanced at Weever's other epigrams as well.

In any case, *Twelfth Night* clearly takes the main road of Renaissance comedy. The title proclaims an affinity with the season of Christmas and Carnival. The main plot combines what was probably the most influential of Italian comedies in the sixteenth century with what was certainly the most popular of its classical antecedents. It is typical of the mature Shakespeare that he makes the initial deadlock spring from posing or self-dramatisation on the part of both Orsino and Olivia, but that on the other hand he makes Viola enter Orsino's service by accident, not by design, as Lelia serves Flamminio. It is typical also that Viola's disguise breaks the deadlock, as it enables her to stir Olivia with a vicarious declaration of love more 'clamorous' (evidently) than anything she has heard from Orsino (I.v) and brings the two women close together (III.i) in a kind of fascinated curiosity:

> – I prithee tell me what thou think'st of me.
> – That you do think you are not what you are.
> – If I think so, I think the same of you.
> – Then think you right: I am not what I am.

Shakespeare ignores Lelia's scheming against the second heroine, the 'good counsel' that helps her, and the explicit sense of justice, in the tradition of the *Decameron*, that wins Flamminio over. Instead, he

---

[1] Weever, *Epigrammes* (ed. McKerrow), p. 75. See Boas, *University Drama in the Tudor Age*, pp. 289–97; Chambers and Williams, *Short Life of Shakespeare*, app. II (contemporary allusions).

concentrates for his own heroine on 'the value of long-enduring patience' and makes Viola pin her hopes on 'time'. Accordingly, it is Fortune that completes what disguise began in *Twelfth Night*, since, unlike the dénouement in *Gl'Ingannati*, it is the discovery or half-disclosure of Sebastian's marriage to Olivia that precipitates Orsino's marriage to Viola. This makes a fresh application by Shakespeare of the interlocking double-plot technique. But Sebastian explains his own surprising share in the recognition scene to Olivia by saying,

> So comes it, lady, you have been mistook;
> But nature to her bias drew in that;

and at the end of the same scene, Feste dismisses Malvolio with, 'thus the whirligig of time brings in his revenges'.

As the play advances, psychological mistakes dissolve into 'errors' of identity; Time and Nature, assuming the guise of Fortune, are stronger than the characters' 'reason', their conscious will. Although the actors have been given some of the depth and self-awareness of individuals in real life, they are caught up in a situation that evidently belongs less and less to real life and increasingly to the stage. As we have seen, actors in Roman and Italian plays sometimes exclaim, with an air of transparent pseudo-realism, that the situation they are in is like a comedy;[1] and Shakespeare picks up this kind of internal comparison between the present play and the conventions it springs from, and makes it one of the shaping factors in *Twelfth Night*. He not merely takes over the elements from the *Menaechmi* already incorporated in *Gl'Ingannati*, but he rearranges them by going back directly to Plautus for the second part of his main double plot. This first becomes apparent in the otherwise meaningless geography of Sebastian's second speech, where he tells Antonio (II.i.10ff), just before mentioning the loss of his twin sister, 'my determinate voyage is mere extravagancy' (that is, he has no plans except to wander about) and, 'you must know of me then,...my father was that Sebastian of Messaline whom I know you have heard of'. But Antonio could only have 'heard of' 'Messaline' if he carried a verbal memory of the corresponding scene in the *Menaechmi* (II.i; 233ff), where the travelling brother's servant (Messenio) complains of the endlessness of their journey in search of the missing twin (my italics):

> Nam quid modi futurum est illum quarere?
> His annus sextust, postquam ei rei operam damus.

[1] See pp. 118–21, 171 above.

Histros, Hispanos, *Massiliensis, Hilurios,*
Mare superum omne Graeciamque exoticam
Orasque Italicas omnis, qua adgreditur mare,
Sumus circumuecti. Si acum, credo, quaereres,
Acum inuenisses, si appareret, iam diu.
Hominem inter uiuos quaeritamus mortuum;
Nam inuenissemus iam diu, si uiueret.

['Why then let's even as long as wee live seeke your brother: six yeeres now
have (we) roamde about thus, Istria, Hispania, *Massylia, Ilyria,* all the upper
sea, all high Greece, all Haven Towns in Italy, I think if we had sought a
needle all this time, we must needs have found it, had it bene above ground.
It cannot be that he is alive; and to seek a dead man thus among the living,
what folly is it?']¹

Shakespeare himself may have remembered this passage so well that
he did not trouble to look back at the text or think about the modern
name for Massilia; and thereafter he makes Sebastian meet in turn
(IV.i) with Feste, Sir Toby and Olivia – which is much more like the
sequence of encounters between the travelling Menaechmus and the
cook, his brother's mistress and the parasite (*Menaechmi* II.ii, II.iii,
III.ii) than the adventures of Fabrizio in *Gl'Ingannati*. It is significant,
too, that Illyria follows Massilia in the list of place-names from
Plautus. Whatever else Illyria meant to Shakespeare (such as a haven
for the 'notable pirates' and 'salt-water thieves' with whom the duke
identifies Antonio), it was the region of Epidamnus and hence the
setting for the *Menaechmi*, the prime example for the Renaissance of
'festive' masquerade. It was the typical land of comedy. And that this
tacit allusion to the classical tradition was sufficiently plain for some
at least of Shakespeare's first spectators appears from the diary of the
Middle Temple lawyer, John Manningham, in one of the rare notes
to be preserved of early Shakespearean performances:

At our feast [for Candlemas, February 2, 1602] wee had a play called 'Twelve
Night, or What You Will', much like the *Commedy of Errores,* or *Menechmi*
in Plautus, but most like and neere to that in Italian called *Inganni.*

The lawyer may not have spotted Shakespeare's principal source right
away, but he knew exactly where to look.

If the emphasis of Shakespeare's borrowed or adapted main plot in
Twelfth Night falls on Fortune, that of the invented sub-plot falls on

¹ *Menaechmi,* trans. W. Warner (1595), ed. Bullough, *Sources,* vol. I, p. 17. See
Salingar, 'Design of *Twelfth Night*', pp. 128, 137–9.

the other aspect of the renaissance tradition, trickery. The 'good practise', as Manningham calls it, against Malvolio belongs to the vein of Italian gulling comedies like the deception of the upstart courtiers in Aretino's *Cortigiana* and of English improvised plays of Christmas 'merriment' directed against unpopular individuals.[1] But one of the threads connecting it with the main plot is that the cause of quarrel between Malvolio and Sir Toby is the misrule in Olivia's household: 'have you no wit, manners, nor honesty', demands the steward (I.iii.84), 'but to gabble like tinkers at this time of night?... Is there no respect of place, persons, nor time, in you?' By way of contrast, it is precisely the ability to

> observe their mood on whom he jests,
> The quality of persons, and the time

that Viola admires in the professional merry-maker, Feste (III.i.59); and it is the professional to whom Shakespeare gives the epilogue, with his song about the passage of time. *Twelfth Night* is the summing-up of a major phase in Shakespeare's writing, the last romantic play at the end of a decade, because it deals with the psychological value of revelry and its limits as well; it is a comedy about comedy. It illustrates at once his fundamental debt to the earlier Renaissance tradition of comic playwriting and his abiding sense of detachment from it.

---

[1] *Cf* Hotson, *First Night of 'Twelfth Night'*, ch. 5; Sisson, *Lost Plays of Shakespeare's Age*; Barber, *Shakespeare's Festive Comedy*, ch. 3; Baskervill, *The Elizabethan Jig*.

6

AN ELIZABETHAN PLAYWRIGHT

I must have wanton Poets, pleasant wits,
Musicians, that with touching of a string
May draw the pliant king which way I please:
Music and poetry is his delight,
Therefore I'll have Italian masks by night,
Sweet speeches, comedies, and pleasing shows.

Marlowe (*c.* 1592)

The best actors in the world, either for tragedy, comedy, history, pastoral, pastoral-comical, historical-pastoral, tragical-historical, tragical-comical-historical-pastoral, scene individable, or poem unlimited. Seneca cannot be too heavy, nor Plautus too light. *Hamlet* (*c.* 1601)

Player is like a garment which the tailor maketh at the direction of the owner; so they frame their action at the disposing of the poet: so that in truth they are reciprocal helps to one another; for the one writes for money, and the other plays for money, and the spectator pays his money.

'T. G.' (1616)

The young lovers in Shakespeare's three earliest comedies – Antipholus of Syracuse, Lucentio, and Valentine and Proteus – all have this in common, that they are swept off their feet shortly after arriving at a strange city. They are all 'transformed' by love in unfamiliar surroundings. It does not seem far-fetched to read into these plays, with the intimately known bourgeois settings in the first two and the vaguely descried court in the third, something of the author's inner struggle for adjustment, as a young provincial trying his fortunes in London. And possibly there are projections from a more intimate part of Shakespeare's experience in Antipholus's encounter at Ephesus with the neglected but possessive wife of his other self. There may be something of the same kind in the way the more mature Petruchio, as contrasted with Lucentio, employs his talents as an actor to shape his wife to his liking.

However, there are no more hints of this kind of *dépaysement* in

Shakespeare's comedies. Love is no longer a bewildering sequel to a distant journey. Even the tender Viola has recourse to her 'wit' immediately after a shipwreck, while Sebastian, though melancholy for a while, is 'most provident in peril', and bobs up like a cork. There are hardly any strange travel-adventures in the old style of romance. Petruchio has come a-wooing with an eye to money; and, though suitors flock 'from the four corners of the earth' as to a 'shrine' to win Portia, the heiress of Belmont is wealthy as well as beautiful and wise. Otherwise, none of Shakespeare's men cross land or sea because of a lady's fair name, until he refurbishes 'that mouldy tale', *Pericles*, and brings in that other late and significant exception, Iachimo.

From *The Two Gentlemen of Verona* onwards, romantic love in the comedies is courtly love in the terms of renaissance literature and – by no means the same thing, however - Elizabethan society. It can still overwhelm and transform the lover, but on the surface it is no stranger than a lively, cultivated game, the rules of which both players believe they understand. It is the hidden prize at stake in 'a skirmish of wit'.

'Wit' becomes a key-word in *Two Gentlemen* and even more in *Love's Labour's Lost*, about two years later, where the term occurs more than forty times. The quick-witted speakers in *Love's Labour's Lost* are like privileged guests after 'a great feast of languages', who can laugh at those who have merely 'stolen the scraps'. From one point of view, this distinct emphasis on verbal sophistication and speed of thought no doubt reflects Shakespeare's growing awareness of, and delight in, his own literary powers; from another point of view, it probably denotes his enlarged social experience and enhanced self-confidence (shown also, in the years just before the play, by his two dedications of *Venus and Adonis* and *The Rape of Lucrece* to his young patron, the Earl of Southampton, and the tone of respectful intimacy apparent in the second). The courtiers in *Love's Labour's Lost* are drawn with admiration, irony and freedom. And they are not merely witty lovers, they are lovers who are also wits. As wits in this special sense, as brilliant and self-conscious talkers, they are probably the first full representatives of their type on the English stage. Meanwhile, Shakespeare has also carried further another change from the original scheme of his comedies, by making the ladies in *Love's Labour's Lost* even sharper-witted than the lords:

> The tongues of mocking wenches are as keen
> As is the razor's edge invisible,

> Cutting a smaller hair than may be seen;
> > Above the sense of sense; so sensible
> Seemeth their conference; their conceits have wings
> Fleeter than arrows, bullets, wind, thought, swifter things.

And more is implied here than a tribute to female intuitiveness. Emotionally, it is now the women who are given the decisive role in the romantic comedies, who carry the major share of daring, understanding and decision in love, from Julia in *Two Gentlemen* to Helena in *All's Well*. They are essentially heroines in the tradition of Boccaccio.

Shakespeare's conception of wit makes for a self-inspection of language and stage dialogue of a new kind, however, which only Lyly, perhaps, had foreshadowed among his predecessors, but which Lyly had not treated seriously. And it changes the comic pattern of the Italians, based on the antithesis between witty love and boorishness or dotage. After Gremio and Thurio and Don Armado in his early plays, all secondary figures, there are no more elderly or grotesque would-be lovers in Shakespeare's comedies, except when he returns very directly to the Italian manner in *The Merry Wives*, with Dr Caius and Master Slender, and *Twelfth Night*, with Malvolio and Sir Andrew. The main battleground for wit in his comedies lies between the sexes and also within the characters of the lovers themselves. The 'mocking wenches' have the last word in *Love's Labour's Lost*. And already, in the opening dialogue of *The Two Gentlemen*, Valentine had informed Proteus that love was

> but a folly bought with wit,
> Or else a wit by folly vanquished.

This is much more like the pedantic tutors in Italian comedy than the typical young men; though Valentine himself is soon to learn that there is more to his own maxim than he realises. But meanwhile, he has introduced a theme on which Shakespeare was to write many variations. 'Better a witty fool than a foolish wit', says Feste, grounding himself on the authority of his invented sage, 'Quinapalus'.

The contrast that governs Shakespeare's comic dialogue is no longer a one-way antithesis between wit in love and ignorance or ineptitude, but a two-way antithesis between earnest and jesting, learning and nature and, in sum, Wit and Folly. From *The Comedy of Errors* onwards, he brings in family jesters, sagacious dullards and voluble or impudent servingmen who present a running fire of comment on their masters' love affairs and are apt to hold up 'some necessary question of the play' with their comic patter, in the fashion Hamlet was to disapprove of. And after his professional association with the actor, Robert Armin, who specialised in fools natural and occupational, began, Shakespeare created the parts of professional Fools as wise men under camouflage, in Touchstone, Feste and the Fool in *Lear*. These clowns – to use the modern general term; until 1600, the word meant 'peasants'; one of those words that encapsulate social destinies – these Shakespearean clowns no longer, as a rule, advise their masters and manipulate the intrigue, like the trickster-slaves in Roman comedy, because wit, in the sense of resourcefulness and *savoir faire*, has been up-graded since Boccaccio: yet their presence and their patter are evidently needed to make the comedy complete.

In a broad sense, Shakespeare was following here the general European tradition of the late Middle Ages and the early Renaissance; as Rabelais makes Pantagruel point out, the prestige of Fools was such that[1]

the son of Picus, King of the Latins, the great soothsayer Faunus, was called Fatuus by the witless rabble of the common people [*du vulgue impérit*]. The like we daily see practised amongst the comic players [*jongleurs*], whose dramatic rolls, in distribution of the personages, appoint the acting of the fool [*du Sot et du Badin*] to him who is the wisest [*le plus périt*] of the troop.

But this passage (from *Le Tiers Livre*, ch. 37, published in 1546) springs from a more specifically north-European tradition, which is not the same as that of the equally popular buffoon-mimic of the Italian Renaissance. Pantagruel is advising his servant, Panurge (who, he is certain, will be cuckolded in the end), to consult a Fool among his oracles on the agonising question, whether or not to marry, because, as he says, the ability 'to presage events to come by divine inspiration' is proper to those whose 'neglects of sublunary things are vulgarly imputed folly' (in contrast to the man 'who narrowly takes heed to what concerns the dextrous management of his private affairs', who 'is called a worldly wise man, though perhaps in the second judgment of the intelligences which are above, he be esteemed a fool'). In similar spirit, Feste says that 'there is no true cuckold but calamity' in the course of his demonstration to his 'madonna' that she is a 'fool' to pretend to espouse a single life for the sake of her brother's memory (*Twelfth Night*, I.v); although later (III.i) he tells Viola that

[1] Rabelais, *Oeuvres* (ed. Scheler), p. 484; trans. Urquhart (1693), vol. II, p. 32.

'the Lady Olivia has no folly' and 'will keep no fool, sir, till she be married'. Especially where marriage is concerned, men and women are enveloped in folly. Shakespeare may well be taking hints from Rabelais here (Celia mentions Gargantua in *As You Like It* [III.ii], and there is a strong family resemblance between Feste's pseudo-erudition and the Frenchman's learned nonsense), but in any case there stands Erasmus, with his *Praise of Folly*, behind Rabelais and Shakespeare alike. In her mock-sermon, or mock-oration of self-eulogy, Erasmus makes Folly identify herself with natural instinct, as opposed to the pretensions of kings and monks, the proud, the learned and the self-satisfied, before she ironically shifts her ground to the evangelical wisdom of religion, as opposed to formal theology and superstition. And this, in essentials, is what Rabelais and Shakespeare also make of Folly, except that Shakespeare couples Folly in specific antithesis to Wit, and not merely to learning or socialised self-esteem in general. In early Tudor England, where Erasmus thought of his seminal discourse, a satirist was not unduly troubled by the pretensions of Wit. Nevertheless, in the line that runs from Erasmus to Shakespeare's comedies, there is already a faint adumbration of that contrast Matthew Arnold was to dwell on between the hebraic and the hellenic strains in English culture.

Shakespeare's 'mocking wenches' are well aware of the pitfalls of folly in love. The ladies in *Love's Labour's Lost* insist on making sure, by means of a year's penance, that the lords are in earnest, or else they will consider their overtures as no more than

> courtship, pleasant jest, and courtesy,
> As bombast and as lining to the time

of their diplomatic reception. Beatrice warns her cousin to please herself, not merely her father, before she commits herself to the social dance of wooing and wedding (*Much Ado*, II.i):

For hear me, Hero: wooing, wedding, and repenting is as a Scotch jig, a measure, and a cinquepace. The first suit is hot and hasty like a Scotch jig (and full as fantastical); the wedding, mannerly modest, as a measure, full of state and ancientry; and then comes Repentance and with his bad legs falls into the cinquepace [*sink apace*] faster and faster till he sink into his grave.

And even Rosalind, head-over-heels in love, is quick to guard against illusions, especially the literary illusions that Valentine, in his sage precocity, had already detected in 'some shallow story of deep love' like Marlowe's story of Leander:

The poor world is almost six thousand years old, and in all this time there was not any man died in his own person, videlicet, in a love cause. Troilus had his brains dashed out with a Grecian club...Leander...went but forth to wash him in the Hellespont, and being taken with the cramp, was drowned; and the foolish chroniclers of that age found it was 'Hero of Sestos'. But these are all lies. Men have died from time to time, and worms have eaten them, but not for love.

Romantic adoration, to these stage heroines, seems a lure and a trap. Similarly, Olivia admits, 'Nor wit nor reason can my passion hide', when her reserve breaks before the sex-disguised Viola; wit would have saved her from indiscretion.

> 'Tis not all spirit, pure and brave,

Donne makes the lover say to his mistress in *The Dream*,

> If mixture it of fear, shame, honour have;

but, as the poet implies clearly enough, it was precisely this 'mixture' that distinguished the reality from the fiction.

For Shakespeare's women, wit is partly a defensive reaction in courtship (though it is not only that, of course) because it is associated with the ideal of a free choice in love as the sole basis for marriage, which ran counter to the established practice of marriage by arrangement, under the authority of a woman's parents; *Romeo and Juliet* became the classical love-story of the sixteenth century because it dramatised the clash between the age's ideal for marriage and the prevailing custom. But wit is one of several considerations opposed to love for Shakespeare's men as well. The literary code of love-service as a chivalric training in high courtesy had virtually died out in England by the Reformation (the Bible in English, says a reforming pamphlet of 1539, is now in every man's hand, 'instead of the old fabulous and fantastical books of the Table Round, Launcelot du Lac &c., and such other, whose unpure filth and vain fabulosity the light of God has abolished utterly').[1] And attempts to replace the old tales of knighthood with modern literature from Italy met for a long time

---

[1] *A Summary Declaration of the Faith...in England* [1539] (quoted, Sweeting, *Early Tudor Criticism*, p. 39); see also: Lord Berners, Preface to *Arthur, c.* 1520 (quoted Berdan, *Early Tudor Poetry*, p. 370); Juan Luis Vives, *De Institutione Feminae Christianae*, 1523 (Eng. trans., 1529, in Nugent (ed.), *Anthology of Tudor Prose*, p. 78); Hammond (ed.), *English Verse*, p. 14. *Cf* Berdan, *Early Tudor Poetry*, p. 498; Nugent, *Anthology of Tudor Prose*, p. 566.

with sharp hostility from reformers and influential humanists. One of the first translators from the Italian, Henry Parker, Baron Morley (a member of Wyatt's circle) thought it necessary to defend his version (*c.* 1550) of Petrarch's *Triumph of Love* by reference to the 'theological secrets declared' therein; and in 1562, Arthur Brooke thought it appropriate or else discreet to preface his version of Bandello's *Romeus and Juliet* (which Shakespeare used later) with the admonition[1] that

> to this ende (good Reader) is this tragicall matter written, to describe unto thee a coople of unfortunate lovers, thralling themselves to unhonest desire, neglecting the authoritie and advise of parents and frendes, conferring their principall counsels with dronken gossyppes, and superstitious friers (the naturally fitte instrumentes of unchastitie) attemptyng all adventures of peryll, for th'attaynyng of their wished lust, usyng auriculer confession (the kay of whoredom, and treason) for furtheraunce of theyr purpose, abusyng the honorable name of lawfull mariage.

Even such prudent disavowals of intention to corrupt would not, however, have satisfied men like Roger Ascham (1515–68), who had been Elizabeth's tutor while she was a princess, and who, distinguished humanist though he was, denounced the translators from Italian in the 1560s as a Papist fifth column, undermining the morals and religion of young Englishmen even more with their books than the examples of 'open mans-slaughter and bold bawdry' in the old tales of chivalry:[2]

> Ten Sermons at Paul's Cross do not so much good for moving men to true doctrine, as one of these books do harm, with enticing men to ill living.

In the 1570s, George Gascoigne (*c.* 1539–78) fell foul of authority for a time when trying to use his knowledge of Italian poetry and *novelle* to forward his career; and when John Lyly (*c.* 1554–1606) succeeded with a similar enterprise in 1578, it was by adopting almost the opposite procedure. His elegantly tricked out fable purported to show the foolhardiness of dalliance with love for an able but conceited gentleman-graduate.[3] Lyly took the hero's name and much of the scheme of his *Euphues, or The Anatomy of Wit* from Ascham's *Schoolmaster* (published in 1570), where Ascham is concerned with the 'true notes of a good wit' for education, and applies the name, Euphues,

---

[1] Hammond (ed.), *English Verse*, p. 387; Bullough, *Sources*, vol. I, p. 285; see Mason, *Shakespeare's Tragedies*, p. 5.
[2] Roger Ascham, *The Schoolmaster*, in *English Works*, pp. 229–31.
[3] See Prouty, *Gascoigne*; Hunter, *Lyly*.

to his first type, the young man who is apt for learning by 'goodness of wit' and 'readiness of will', though subject to corruption if not checked in time by 'wise fathers' and 'wise magistrates'. The hostility of men like Ascham to the modern literature of courtly love stemmed from their determination to use humanism to form a Protestant aristocracy for the public service.

The pressure of this attitude can be felt even in Elizabethan love poetry. For example, Sir Philip Sidney worries over the reproaches he himself or his friends can level against his Petrarchan sonnets of devotion to Stella:

> My youth doth waste, my knowledge brings forth toys,
> My wit doth strive those passions to defend
> Which, for reward, spoil it with vain annoys   (Sonnet XVIII)

or:

> Your words (my friend), right healthful caustics, blame
> My young mind marred, whom Love doth windlass so,
> That mine own writings, like bad servants, show
> My wits quick in vain thoughts, in virtue lame;
> That Plato I read for nought but if he tame
> Such coltish years; that to my birth I owe
> Nobler desires, lest else that friendly foe,
> Great expectation, wear a train of shame.   (XXI)

There was a sense of tension, then, for Sidney between courtly love and courtly wit. And, in what was already a new literary climate, Donne likewise could still feel the pull of counter-amatory temptations in the midst of his most vehement love poems:

> Let sea-discoverers to new worlds have gone,
> Let maps to other, worlds on worlds have shown;
> Let us possess one world, each hath one, and is one;

or, to someone who can be imagined offering 'healthful caustics', like Sidney's 'friend':

> For God's sake hold your tongue, and let me love,
>   Or chide my palsy, or my gout,
> My five gray hairs, or ruined fortune flout;
>   With wealth your state, your mind with arts improve,
>   Take you a course, get you a place,
>   Observe his honour, or his grace,

> Or the king's real, or his stamped face
> Contemplate; what you will, approve,
> So you will let me love.

Donne here, speaking as a lover, takes nearly the same ironic tone as Erasmus, speaking in the name of Folly. He knows very well that much of the official culture and opinion of his time is against him.

Shakespeare exhibits a similar tension of ideas. Falling in love, especially in his early comedies, is a deviation from a man's normal (English) self, and a lover is laughed at, not because he is dissipated, like a youth in Roman comedy, but because he is supposed to have adopted a fashion of behaviour which is exotic and affected. Egeus has an angry sneer at Lysander's 'feigning' verses; Jaques thinks Orlando 'mars' the forest with his. Speed knows infallibly that Valentine has been 'metamorphised with a mistress', by 'these special marks' – that he has 'learned' to 'wreathe [his] arms, like a malcontent', 'to relish a love song', to walk alone, to sigh, and 'to speak puling, like a beggar at Hallowmas', and that he has lost his spirit and his appetite. Moth ridicules Armado by asking him if he intends to 'win [his] love with a French brawl' (punning on the name of a dance) – that is, with jerky dance movements, 'with turning up your eyelids', with singing alternately through his throat and his nose, and similar preposterous manifestations:

with your arms crossed on your thin-belly doublet like a rabbit on a spit, or your hands in your pocket like a man after the old painting; and keep not too long in one tune, but a snip and away. These are complements [*accomplishments*], these are humours, these betray nice wenches (that would be betrayed without these) and make them men of note – do you note me? – that most are affected to these.

And Benedick has much the same to say about Claudio:

I do much wonder that one man, seeing how much another man is a fool when he dedicates his behaviours to love, will, after he hath laugh'd at such shallow follies in others, become the argument of his own scorn by falling in love; and such a man is Claudio. I have known when there was no music with him but the drum and the fife, and now had he rather hear the tabor and the pipe; I have known when he would have walk'd ten mile afoot to see a good armour, and now will he lie ten nights awake carving the fashion of a new doublet. He was wont to speak plain and to the purpose, like an honest man and a soldier, and now is he turn'd orthography; his words are a very fantastical banquet, just so many strange dishes.

In Italian comedy, jokes about such capers had been reserved for the ignoramus or the old man in his second childhood who 'dedicates his behaviours to love', not for otherwise typical members of their class and age-group like Valentine or Claudio. The jesters associate love with faked accomplishment, not true courtship, with the bearing of a 'malcontent', not 'an honest man and a soldier'. Valentine and the lords in *Love's Labour's Lost* imagine their destiny as renaissance courtiers is to renounce love in favour of learning; and the lords are driven from one affectation to another. Shakespeare gives expression to much the same oblique view of love in his tragedies, with characters as different from each other as Mercutio and Iago. And some of the main complications in his mature comedies arise from the tension between the idea of love and the position of an Elizabethan gentleman or courtier. Benedick has set himself up as a bachelor-philanderer who 'challeng'd Cupid'; he comes of 'a noble strain', but he depends on royal patronage, and to commit himself to marriage would undermine his position as a courtier as well as a wit. Claudio (in *Much Ado*) is also a courtier by birth and career, who aims at a conventional marriage, subject to his prince's approval and arrangement;[1] he is much quicker to respond to his sense of honour as a gentleman than to his love for Hero when she is slandered. Bertram in *All's Well* is even more touchily conscious of his rank, and it is easy for Parolles to persuade him to run away to the glories of war from an unwanted marriage. Angelo is a puritan by temperament, whose sexual repression is connected with his image of himself as a high officer of state, and who has also – it appears – broken off with Mariana when her dowry was not forthcoming. There is no equivalent for these social complications in a typical Roman or Italian comedy. For Shakespeare, the interplay between Wit and Folly in love affects the whole comedy in depth, not merely the surface of the dialogue.

With this change goes a more obvious departure from classical tradition, in that Shakespeare brings princes on to the comic stage. As against the classical rule or convention that comedy should deal entirely with citizens or people of low rank, he has a ruler in nearly every comedy. (The only exceptions are *The Shrew*, where he has a Lord, and *The Merry Wives*, where there is talk of the court's 'grand affair' at Windsor, and where Fenton has been a companion of Prince Hal.) In most of his comedies, and again in his late romances, Shakespeare either makes princes leading characters, or at least brings

---

[1] Prouty, *Sources of 'Much Ado'*, pp. 41–7.

them close to the centre of the intrigue; and when he borrows the outline of his story, he either raises the rank of a leading character (Orsino in *Twelfth Night*, as compared with Flamminio, in *Gl'Ingannati*), or introduces a ruler where there was none before (the Doge at the trial scene in *The Merchant of Venice*), or gives the prince a much more active and prominent part, as with Don Pedro in *Much Ado*, the French King in *All's Well* and the Duke in *Measure for Measure*. The prince's authority is represented as the ultimate sanction for a gentleman's marriage; and the idea of education as training for the prince's service conditions the attitude of Shakespeare's gentlemen towards love and wit. And where the plan of his comedies differs most markedly from classical tradition, the prince's role is usually involved. The action in *Love's Labour's Lost* takes place in a park or the open country because of the King's caprice, on which the plot hinges; and in *Two Gentlemen*, *A Midsummer Night's Dream* and *As You Like It*, the lovers take to the greenwood to escape from their prince's rule. Geographically and socially, Shakespeare's comedies take a wider scope than those of the Italians, with the prince's role at the centre. The prince's will, or his sense of duty, causes an initial complication, as with Solinus in the first scene of *The Comedy of Errors*, the Duke in *Two Gentlemen*, or Theseus. And it is the prince's status, or the status of a character near the prince, that brings together the numerous characters in Shakespeare's comedies and governs the secondary actions which are added to the complications he had learned from the Italian double plot. Fairies and mechanicals meet in the *Dream* because both plan to honour Theseus's wedding. Jaques comes into the scheme of *As You Like It* as a companion of the exiled Duke. In *Much Ado*, Shakespeare changes the motive for slander from jealousy in love to political resentment, and links his invented plot with his borrowed plot by way of the prince's pleasure in matchmaking, while Dogberry and the constables impinge on the main plot because they are 'to present the Prince's own person'. The subplots of Malvolio and Parolles hinge on the status of Olivia and of Bertram; *Measure for Measure* opens and continues as a play about 'government', involving men and women from almost every rank in Vienna.

The prince's ideal role, or his influence on the other characters, usually affects the rhythm of the whole action, as in a kind of ebb and flow, a recoil from his authority and then a return. In *Love's Labour's Lost*, for instance, the King himself abandons his serious or ideal role at the beginning of the play and prepares to go back to it by the end. The usurper and the rightful duke change places in the course of *As You Like It*. In other plays, there is a reaction of some kind against the prince early in the plot, and then a large cast of actors are assembled under his authority at the end. The prince presides over the recognition scene in nearly every one of Shakespeare's comedies, and, as if for this purpose, the dramatist assembles a throng of the prince's subjects in the last act (there are thirteen speaking parts, as well as supers, in the last scene of *The Comedy of Errors*, for example, as compared with three actors in the *Menaechmi* and six speakers with two or three mutes in *Supposes*). The prince's role provokes the decisive comic problem either for himself or, more usually, for the other characters, and the happy ending can only be complete with his approval.

For the first ten years or so of his career, Shakespeare was writing comedies in alternation with national history plays, the new dramatic form of which he was largely the creator, not with tragedies affiliated to the classical tradition. And his comedies are related in form to his chronicles of the national monarchy; taken altogether, they include a panorama of the public aspects of national life. Off-stage wars, for example, affect the action in several comedies, from *The Comedy of Errors* onwards; there are battle scenes in *Cymbeline*; and in *All's Well* the disgracing of Parolles turns on something close to the modern notion of regimental honour.[1] *Love's Labour's Lost* is nominally about a treaty. There is the wrestling-match in *As You Like It*, comic duels in several plays, and more dignified habits of the aristocracy are represented in the hunting episodes shown or discussed in several others. Men of the church are brought into more than half the comedies, not usually to be satirised, even when they are friars. The social arts of peace are represented in two or three plays by dialogues about education and in all of the comedies by some form of entertainment, from the patter or repartee of domestic jesters to songs and serenades, masques and masked dances, banquets or wedding ceremonies in the course of the play, improvised practical jokes in the Italian manner, or shows specially prepared to honour a lord or a king. The love-intrigues are worked out amid the ceremonies of an organised community. On the other hand, there are the characters, from the fairies at Athens down to the layabout, Christopher Sly, whose very existence on the stage illustrates or hints at the limits of

---

[1] *Cf* Hale, 'Armies', pp. 183ff.

a rational, human social order – the outlaws in *Two Gentlemen*, the exiles in *As You Like It*, who 'live like the old Robin Hood of England', the professional entertainers of uncertain status, the thieves at Windsor and the riff-raff of Vienna, not forgetting the constables in *Love's Labour's Lost*, *Much Ado* and *Measure for Measure* who bring out the weaknesses of public authority by their comic ineptitude. But, in sharp contrast to these glances at the margins of organised social life, there are scenes or episodes in every comedy referring to the power or the machinery of the law: regular trial scenes and scenes of public accusation, episodes of arrest or imprisonment, lawsuits and threats of lawsuits. If Shakespeare is very much an Elizabethan in his sense of national history and regal ceremony, he is equally a man of his time and country in his persistent legalism.[1]

Whereas classical and Italian comedies pictured the life of a city, Shakespeare very nearly pictured the life of a whole nation. In the two parts of *Henry IV*, he conjured up an image of the varied ranks and regions of Britain, such as no one had seriously attempted since Chaucer – an image that was to influence fiction, from Scott onwards, profoundly. Nevertheless, there are some striking omissions from his comedies. Although he refers repeatedly to the countryside, he shows little or nothing on the stage of the life of yeomen or farm-workers, which he must have known well. He shows none of the interest in the condition of the peasants as a subject for drama that appears in the writings of Ruzzante or Lope de Vega; he is a national playwright, but he looks towards London. And even in his urban scenes, he shows little or nothing of the working life of the craftsman or apprentice or the ordinary shopkeeper in staple trades, by comparison with a contemporary like Dekker; he shows bourgeois householders and tradesmen, but his merchants deal in luxury goods like the goldsmith in *The Comedy of Errors*, or they are the moneylender and the patrician venturer of Venice. His stage world gravitates towards the great house or the court. He depicts the gentry from outside, but they stand at the centre.

Secondly, his comic vision remains very largely a vision of the stage. To quote Bernard Shaw again, he shows us ourselves, but not our problems; or rather, he has none of the ambition that actuated writers of Shaw's time to represent people struggling to solve their problems rationally, under lifelike conditions. On the contrary, even in his most serious comedies, he reverts to the ancient conventions of

---

[1] Ives, 'The Law and the Lawyers'.

Fortune and trickery; even the earnest and privileged Duke of Vienna corrects the vices of his government by subterfuges more devious than those of a slave in Plautus. In part, Shakespeare's reliance on the ancient conventions of comedy sprang from realistic if not unavoidable assumptions, however; he could expect much less than men like Shaw from rationality in human affairs because his society was much more fragile than theirs, living closer to the starvation-line, much more exposed to the pressures of Nature. And in part, Shakespeare's attitude seems to reflect a conscious bias or choice. His people live through their emotional problems in comedy precisely by being transformed or disguised, by coming into contact with the special conditions of the stage. Shakespeare does not, as a rule, invite his audience to escape from normal psychological conditions by forgetting what they are like, but he invites them to contemplate special conditions, which are not presented as typical of life in general, but are contra-distinguished from everyday life outside the theatre by devices carried over from the comic tradition. The theme of the place of comedy itself in social life is usually latent in Shakespeare's plays and often comes near the surface.

Shakespeare's preoccupation with the real influence of the monarch, even in comedy, and, at the other extreme, his preoccupation with the idea of play-acting, set him apart from all but his immediate predecessors. They reflect his historically novel situation, as a professional playwright in a mainly commercial theatre, writing for, and even in a sense creating, a national public, but depending first and last on aristocratic and royal favour. At one pole of his comic world is the actor–poet, at the other, his ultimate patron, the prince.

THE PLAYER IN THE PLAY

Although professional entertainers of all sorts – acrobats, minstrels, mimes, *jongleurs* – can be traced far back through the Middle Ages, they were not necessarily performers of plays, and their share in the plays acted about the beginning of the sixteenth century was minor and occasional.[1] By far the greatest share in dramatic productions and semi-dramatic shows or pastimes, everywhere in Europe, fell to part-time actors, amateurs: in local folk-plays; in the vast biblical plays and miracles organised by guilds or cities, which called for stage-

[1] Chambers, *Mediaeval Stage*, vol. I, chs. 1–4; Nicoll, *Masks*, ch. 4.

hands and actors from every rank of society, including clerics and even noblemen; in civic pageants; in the moral allegories produced by *chambres de rhétorique* in France and the Netherlands; in the humanistic stage exercises of schoolboys or students; in festive productions like the bourgeois carnival shows at Nuremberg, or the carnival *sotties* which had grown out of the burlesque Feast of Fools among the law-clerks and bourgeois of France, or the masques and 'disguisings' of the early Tudor court. Especially when the civic religious plays, with their many scores of participants, are taken into account, there must have been very many more people engaged in occasional performances of drama in western Europe about 1500 than were engaged in regular productions of professional drama 100 years later.

The development of this multiform religious and festive drama, as part of the normal annual round of towns and villages, was checked by local and central governments, and partly by churchmen, in the new conditions that accompanied the Reformation, just when an independent, secular literary drama, the 'learned' drama of the Renaissance, was beginning to emerge. But meanwhile the new form was acquiring its own momentum: for example, Ariosto was complaining, by the end of his career, that texts of his plays had been printed without his permission, and had been stolen from him by the actors.[1] Angelo Beolco and his colleagues were gentlemen and part-time actors, but they performed regularly together in Venice and elsewhere in northern Italy during the 1520s, and their author–manager was known by the name of the part he created and often played, Ruzzante.[2] On the continent, the records of full-time actors playing together in organised companies begin towards the mid-century – in Spain, about 1540, with the company of the actor-playwright, Lope de Rueda; in Italy, from 1545 onwards, with the first practitioners of what was to be called professional comedy, *commedia dell'arte*; in France, by 1552, when a contract is recorded between several musicians and a director who is described as a 'joueur d'histoires et moralités'.[3] The terms, *comedia, commediante, comédien,* which first come into use at this time, indicate a general sense of a new form of entertainment or a new type of occupation.

---

[1] Ariosto, letters to the Marquis of Mantua and Prince Guidobaldo Feltrio della Rovere (1532), in *Opere minori*, pp. 836–9.

[2] Zorzi (ed.), *Ruzante*, pp. xxiii–xxiv.

[3] Shergold, *Spanish Stage*, pp. 151ff; Petit de Julleville, *Les Comédiens*, pp. 1–14, 338; Wiley, *Early Public Theatre in France*, ch. 2; *cf* above, pp. 177–8.

In England, the records of small companies of *histriones* or *lusores* or 'players of interludes', travelling together under royal or noble patronage and acting for payment, go back to the last quarter of the fifteenth century.[1] They visited castles, abbeys and towns; an early morality play like *Mankind* (*c.* 1470), requiring half-a-dozen actors and no heavy portable properties, could have been taken into their repertory. For a long time, however, such companies were few, and took only a small share of the seasonal or occasional payments for entertainment recorded by local authorities. In Kent, for example, where surviving municipal records are unusually full in this respect, a company of Lord Arundel's men are recorded as early as 1478; but until about 1540, paid visits to the Kentish towns by such companies of lords' 'men' were much less frequent than paid visits by groups of minstrels or by companies of part-time actors from neighbouring towns.[2] After 1540, however, the situation in Kent changed: thirty-eight patronage companies are recorded over the next thirty years, as against only twelve for the thirty years before; their share of the towns' outlay for official entertainment increases; and by 1570 payments to minstrels and to companies of semi-amateur town players have come to an end. From the published records available, much the same seems to be true for the country as a whole. There was a general increase in the number of companies travelling under the protection of lords or even mere gentlemen, and in the middle decades of the century they seem to have visited more provincial towns, and visited them more frequently. The records seem to show a distinct fall in their activities during the troubled reign of Edward VI (1547–53) and thereafter a steady rise, which becomes very rapid after the accession of Elizabeth I in 1558. The company under the patronage of Elizabeth's favourite, Leicester, which flourished from about 1559 until his death in 1588, is the first whose history and personality can be reconstructed in any detail.[3] Altogether, there were perhaps twice as many companies (some forty, all told) visiting the provincial towns during the first decade of Elizabeth's reign as in the previous decade, and their visits seem to have been about three times as frequent; places not too far from London, such as Norwich (where

1 Chambers, *Mediaeval Stage*, vol. II, p. 186; Wickham, *Early English Stages*, vol. I, pp. 266–9.
2 See Dawson (ed.), *Players in Kent, 1450 to 1642*; Salingar, Harrison and Cochrane, 'Les Comédiens en Angleterre', pp. 531, 576.
3 Chambers, *Elizabethan Stage*, vol. II, pp. 85–91; Bradbrook, *Rise of the Common Player*, chs. 2 and 6.

Robert Greene grew up), Bristol, Canterbury (Marlowe's birthplace), Gloucester, Coventry or Stratford were beginning to receive one or two visits every year.

The government's action in putting a stop to the old mystery plays in towns like York and Chester after the Rising of the North in 1569 removed one source of competition; and although the Act against Vagabonds in 1572 deprived strolling players of the right to legal protection by anyone under the rank of a baron, it was not completely observed, and the fall in the number of recorded companies under the patronage of knights or mere gentlemen in the years that followed it was more than compensated by an increase in those patronised by noblemen.[1] Professional acting continued to increase in the 1580s and 1590s, when it seems to have reached its peak in the provinces, with slightly fewer companies active than in the previous twenty years, but perhaps three visits on average for every two before. At London, meanwhile, during the 1570s the principal adult companies were gradually overtaking their rivals, the companies of trained school- and choir-boys, on the coveted ground of performances at court. And in 1576, the leading spirit in Leicester's men, James Burbage, a joiner by origin, built the Theatre, just outside the administrative limit of the City – the first permanent playhouse in England, and the first functional building of its kind in modern Europe, not designed by architects with prestige and ideal town-scapes in mind, like the court theatres of Italy, but built by actors, for acting.[2] Burbage's example was soon followed by others. Some forty years later, just after Shakespeare's death, the traveller, Fynes Moryson, was to remark that in London by this time there were regularly 'four or five companies of players with their peculiar theatres capable of many thousands, wherein they all play every day in the week except Sunday', so that, although he knew France and Italy and other parts of the continent well, 'there be in my opinion more plays in London than in all the world I have seen'.[3] When Shakespeare had begun acting this growth of the profession was just approaching its climax.

[1] Salingar, Harrison and Cochrane, 'Les Comédiens en Angleterre', pp. 531–2; *cf* Chambers, *Elizabethan Stage*, vol. I, p. 279; vol. IV, p. 270; Wickham, *Early English Stages*, vol. II, p. 107; Gardiner, *Mysteries' End*.

[2] Chambers, *Elizabethan Stage*, vol. II, pp. 305ff, 384ff; Bradbrook, *Rise of the Common Player*, pp. 56–7; *cf* Leclerc, 'La Scène d'illusion', p. 582.

[3] Fynes Moryson, *Shakespeare's Europe*, p. 476 (quoted, G. E. Bentley, *Profession of Dramatist in Shakespeare's Time*, p. 15n).

More performances meant, of course, a demand for new plays, some of which reached print.[1] From 1520 to 1539, 14 plays in English were printed; in the next twenty years, the number fell to 8; but from 1560 to 1579, it rose again to 35, 16 of which were 'offered for acting' (printed with cast-lists grouped so as to show that they could be acted by small companies of travelling players). In the 1580s, while Lyly was giving his plays at court, with boy actors, the men's companies began to buy or commission plays by other university poets, including Marlowe, Peele and Greene, in addition to those the actors wrote themselves. Before 1590, only a few printed texts had carried any details about their performance, those that had been acted at the Inns of Court, or before the Queen; but in that year came out the two parts of *Tamburlaine*, with the notice on the title-page, 'as they were sundry times shewed upon Stages in the City of London. By the right honourable the Lord Admiral, his servants.' It was the sign of a new epoch. Between 1590 and the closing of the theatres in 1642, there may have been, on Professor Gerald Bentley's reckoning, some 2,000 new plays in London, of which 1,200 are known by both title (at least) and author's name; of these, some 265 plays can be allocated to as many as 200 writers whom he describes as amateur playwrights, but the great majority were the work of 44 men writing for money, 22 of whom accounted for 'perhaps half' of the plays of known authorship in the whole period.[2] By 1590, then, when Shakespeare began his career, it is possible to speak of professional playwrights as well as professional players. On the other hand, it was not until 1594, when Marlowe's *Edward II* and three plays by Greene and Lodge were printed, that any title-pages of plays given by the men's companies carried an author's name as well – and by that year, Greene (1558–92) and Marlowe (1564–93) were both dead. The manuscript of a play was the actors' property, not the poet's; they were chary of printing it as a rule in case a rival company could use it; and when they did sell to a printer, they were evidently indifferent about advertising the writer's name without some special reason. In his *Groats-worth of Wit, bought with a Million of Repentance*, the pamphlet written in the last year of his life, Greene complains bitterly of exploitation by his ill-educated employers, warning three fellow-graduates (presumably Marlowe, Nashe and Peele) to profit from his example before it was

---

[1] Chambers, *Elizabethan Stage*, vol. III, pp. 157ff; vol. IV, pp. 379ff; *cf* Harbage and Schoenbaum, *Annals of English Drama*.
[2] See G. E. Bentley, *Profession of Dramatist*, ch. 2.

too late, and attacking the actor–playwright, the 'upstart Crow, beautified with our feathers', who 'supposes he is as well able to bombast out a blank verse as the best of you' and 'is in his own conceit the only Shake-scene in a country'.

Greene's accusation of literary theft was not altogether wild, but the material advantage the young Shakespeare evidently enjoyed was that he was an actor (and sharer) in his company, as well as a dramatist. Even so, his name did not appear on a title-page of a play until 1598, when *Love's Labour's Lost* was printed ('As it was presented before her Highness this last Christmas'), although seven other plays of his had appeared in quarto – with or without his company's consent – since 1594, and the quarto of *1 Henry IV*, also of 1598, carried the significant additional description to its title, 'with the humorous conceits of Sir John Falstaff', instead of naming the author. By this date, however, the poet of *Venus and Adonis* and the creator of Romeo was already well known. Henry Chettle had published a reply to Greene, defending Shakespeare's 'civil' 'demeanour' and his 'facetious grace in writing', as well as his excellency 'in the quality that he professes' (as an actor) as early as 1592, and in 1598 the literary gossip, Francis Meres, singled him out as 'the most excellent' of English playwrights as well as the reincarnation of 'the sweet witty soul of Ovid' in his poems. Meres's tribute marks the beginnning of the explicit recognition of the actor–dramatist by university men. Already in 1596 Shakespeare had applied for a coat of arms and in 1597 he had begun to purchase New Place.

Nevertheless, in his professional life Shakespeare was first of all an actor; and throughout his lifetime 'the quality he professed' was still new and officially unwelcome in society. A man playing for his livelihood had no rank or function in the recognised scheme of things; unless he was censored, he might spread heresy or sedition; even if his plays were neither dangerous nor indecent in themselves, they drew congregations away from church; and even if his hours of playing were regulated, he attracted servants and prentices away from work, tempted the very poor to part with pennies they could barely spare and brought together crowds with the attendant dangers of crime, riot and infection from plague in overcrowded and insufficiently policed cities. In Catholic and Protestant Europe alike, therefore, the new profession was apt to be regarded with suspicion. In 1564, for example, Edmund Grindal, Bishop of London, wrote to Cecil about 'some politic orders to be devised against Infection':[1]

> By search I do perceive, that there is no one thing of late is more like to have renewed this contagion, than the practice of an idle sort of people, which have been infamous in all good commonweals: I mean these *Histriones*, common players; who now daily, but specially on holydays, set up bills, whereunto the youth resorteth excessively, and there taketh infection: besides that God's word by their impure mouths is profaned, and turned into scoffs.

Besides the danger of plague, which was very pressing, Grindal was complaining of a spiritual offence (though it is characteristic of his time that he was not referring to irreligion as such, but to the bringing together of 'God's word' and buffoonery); and he was offended by the temerity of 'an idle sort of people' to exhibit themselves 'daily', with their disturbing effect on 'the youth'. Idleness again – their inability to justify themselves in terms of property, status or work, in a society increasingly troubled by economic displacement and vagabondage – accounts for the inclusion of 'common players in interludes' in the regulations of the Act of 1572, whereby, unless they can satisfy two Justices in the shire where they are found that they 'belong' to a nobleman, they are liable to be gaoled, whipped and even 'burnt through the gristle of the right ear with a hot iron of the compass of an inch about'. For this savage humiliation, they are classified not merely with bearwards and minstrels but with 'jugglers, pedlars, tinkers and petty chapmen' and all other persons who, 'being whole and mighty in body and able to labour', nevertheless 'having not land or master, nor any lawful merchandise craft or mystery...can give no reckoning how he or she doth lawfully get his or her living'; they are relegated, in short, to the category of 'Rogues Vagabonds and Sturdy Beggars'.[2]

Even with the vital safety-clause for those who could legally pass as a nobleman's servants – as members of his household, nominally employed for his private entertainment but permitted by him to travel – the moral or theological offence of public exhibition remained; while the social offence grew worse, or potentially worse, especially at London, where from 1580 onwards, just as the actors were establishing their first playhouses on the fringes of the City Council's jurisdiction, the municipal and the central authorities were striving helplessly to cope with problems of immigration and over-

[1] Chambers, *Elizabethan Stage*, vol. IV, p. 266.   [2] *Ibid.* pp. 269–71.

crowding.[1] The spate of sermons and pamphlets against the play-houses began as soon as they were built; and the City kept up a steady pressure on the Privy Council to restrict the players' activity, if they could not suppress them altogether.[2] In 1580, for instance, the Lord Mayor calls them 'a very superfluous sort of men, and of such faculty as the laws have disallowed', in a letter to the Lord Chancellor; in another letter, to Burghley, he objects to the 'double peril', from infection ('God's wrath') and from 'the drawing of the people from the service of God and from honest exercises', entailed by 'the erecting and frequenting of houses very infamous for incontinent rule out of our liberties and jurisdiction'. Again, for example, in about 1584, when the Queen's men have petitioned for a relaxing of the restrictions on their playing in London so as to enable them to earn their livings and prepare themselves to entertain her majesty, the Corporation reply, first[3]

that it is not convenient that they present before her majesty such plays as have been before commonly played in open stages before all the basest assemblies in London and Middlesex, and therefore sufficient...that... they make their exercise of playing only in private houses;

and, second, that

where they pretend the matter of stay of their living:
It hath not been used nor thought meet heretofore that players have or should make their living on the art of playing, but men for their livings using other honest and lawful arts, or retained in honest services, have by companies learned some interludes for some increase to their profit by other men's pleasure in vacant time of recreation.

It is not play-acting as such that the Corporation object to officially, or payment to actors 'in vacant time of recreation' (or, as they say in their preamble, 'in private houses only at marriages or such like'). And they certainly do not pretend to interfere with the Queen's pleasures. What they find socially objectionable is that men should try to earn their whole living by acting as nearly as possible all the year round, on 'open stages' before the 'multitude'. Quite apart from the danger of infection, it was the publicity of the actor's 'quality' and indeed his professionalism as such that disturbed men in authority.

---

[1] See Salingar *et al.*, 'Les Comédiens en Angleterre', p. 547.
[2] Chambers, *Elizabethan Stage*, vol. I, chs. 8–9; vol. IV, pp. 197ff.
[3] *Ibid.*, vol. IV, pp. 279, 281, 300; *cf* Harbage, *Shakespeare's Audience*; Bradbrook, *Rise of the Common Player*, ch. 3.

And this sort of social objection carried weight where the extremes of theological denunciation were disregarded and perhaps – as Sidney's *Apology* implies – resented. It was repeatedly thought desirable to limit not merely what or when an actor could play, but where – before whom. As Chancellor of Oxford, for example, Leicester considered 'the Prohibition of common Stage Players' from the city 'very requisite', although he approved of 'Exercises of Learning in that kind' within the colleges,[1] and had been actively defending the privilege of his own men to perform in public elsewhere.

In what Chambers calls the struggle between Court and City over the right of the players to fix themselves in or near London, the trump card in the Privy Council was the argument that 'these poor men' had to be practised, in 'readiness with convenient matters for her highness' solace' at Christmas (that is, for the court holiday season, which stretched intermittently, like the Italian carnival season, from about Christmas to just before Lent).[2] Unlike Italian potentates and her father and her successor, Elizabeth did not regularly provide court or public shows herself. She paid for her entertainment through her Master of the Revels (who was also her censor), but she did not maintain or instruct her actors; she received them instead. The patrons who ensured that there would be skilled men to present to her were, above all, the great lords of her Council and household – like Leicester, Sussex, Pembroke (probably Shakespeare's master for a time), Charles Howard (the Lord Admiral) and the two Hunsdons, father and son, both Lords Chamberlain and Shakespeare's masters in succession from 1594 until the end of the reign. It does not appear that these grandees planned their actors' repertory in any way, but their indirect provision of plays at court was a form of tribute to their sovereign, an extension of the principle of entertaining her when on progress, much cheaper no doubt but possibly for that very reason, more competitive. The intervention of Leicester must have been decisive in gaining his men a foothold at London just before they built their Theatre,[3] and court protection (which was not the same thing as indiscriminate favour) remained decisive in keeping a place for the acting profession at London against the opposition of the City Council. And in the provinces, which, even for the leading companies, still

---

[1] Leicester, letter of 1584, quoted, Boas, *University Drama*, p. 192; *cf* Bradbrook, *Rise of the Common Player*, p. 59.

[2] Chambers, *Elizabethan Stage*, vol. I, pp. 213, 237; vol. IV, p. 283.

[3] Bradbrook, *Rise of the Common Player*, ch. 2.

provided an appreciable share of the actors' income and at least a reserve public when London was closed to them by the plague, the lords' protection was no less valuable. Referring to Gloucester and other cities in the expansive days for provincial acting about the 1570s, Shakespeare's contemporary R. Willis recalls that

the manner is...that when Players of Interludes come to town, they first attend the Mayor, to inform him what nobleman's servants they are, and so to get licence for their public playing; and if the Mayor like the Actors, or would shew respect to their Lord and Master, he appoints them to play their first play before himself, and the Aldermen and common Council of the City; and that is called the Mayor's play, where everyone that will comes in without money, the Mayor giving the players a reward as he thinks fit, to shew respect unto them.[1]

Provincial gentlemen welcomed players themselves and sometimes noblemen expressly asked mayors to show a company favour;[2] while from the point of view of the town council, it was important to keep a great lord's goodwill. An incident reported from Maldon in 1590 indicates how this consideration might conflict with others; in that year, a former Bailiff of the town, John Morrys, was indicted by his successors for protesting to them on behalf of

the misdemeanors of disordered, unrulie, and contemptuous persons in their evell behaviour; as when certain players played on the Lord's day in the nyght, contrarie to both the erle of Essex' lettre [Essex was High Steward of Maldon] and Mr Baylieffs' commaundement, and Mr Baylieffs rebuking them for the same, Mr Morrys spoke openlie in the [town] hall that – Before tyme noble-men's menn hadd such entertaynement when they came to the towne that the towne hadd the favour of noble-men, but now noble-men's menn hadd such entertaynement that the towne was brought into contempt with noble-men. And when Mr Morrys was gonne out of the hall into the streete, he spake thes woordes alowde – A sort of precisians and Brownists!

This little explosion was a foretaste of difficulties soon to come for the actors, as provincial councils began to tire of their frequent visits.[3] Meanwhile, it illustrates how the actors under Elizabeth evaded the worst consequences of the law and social hostility – by attaching

---

[1] Chambers, *Elizabethan Stage*, vol. I, p. 333; Salingar *et al.*, 'Les Comédiens en Angleterre', pp. 526–7.

[2] J. T. Murray, *English Dramatic Companies, 1558–1642*, vol. II, p. 234; Rowse, *England of Elizabeth*, pp. 165–6; Boas, *University Drama*, p. 222; *cf* Neale, *Elizabethan House of Commons*.

[3] A. Clark (ed.), *Shirburn Ballads*, p. 48; see Salingar *et al.*, 'Les Comédiens en Angleterre', pp. 560ff.

themselves to the semi-official system of patronage, which was a growing system in many departments of late sixteenth-century life, especially politics and appointments affecting the public service.[1] On the other hand, they could never escape completely from the sense that they were misfits in the social order. In 1580, for example, a pamphleteer (probably Munday) attacked the lords for their show of patronage:

Since the retaining of these caterpillars, the credit of noblemen hath decayed, and they are thought to be covetous by permitting their servants, which cannot live of themselves, and whom for nearness they will not maintain, to live at the devotion of alms of other men, passing from country to country, from one Gentleman's house to another, offering their service, which is a kind of beggary.[2]

Conversely, some poets, or their friends, like Francis Meres, complained that noblemen did not show the players patronage enough. Or it was denied that nominal patronage really dignified the actor's calling at all: 'howsoever he pretends to have a royal Master or Mistress, his wages and dependance prove him to be the servant of the people'. The satirist (J. Cocke) delivered this snub to the actor's commercialism in 1615, at the end of Shakespeare's lifetime, when for more than ten years the patronage of companies had been reserved to James I and the members of his family.

Ultimately the outstandingly successful members of the profession, like Alleyn and Shakespeare himself, could demonstrate their respectability. Meanwhile, writers interested in the stage could point in their defence to the antiquity of acting, and could argue – like Whetstone and Sidney and Lodge and Nashe – that plays did, or, with some literary reform, could, provide public lessons in patriotism and morality. Or, at least, that men needed times of recreation. Towards 1612, Thomas Heywood could add the telling point that the theatres had contributed to the tourist attractions of London, and the more interesting though less demonstrable proposition that 'within these 60 years' play-acting had enormously refined the 'euphony and

---

1 See Neale, 'The Elizabethan Political Scene'; Hurstfield, 'Social Structure, Office-Holding and Politics'.

2 Munday (?): see Chambers, *Elizabethan Stage*, vol. IV, p. 210; Bradbrook, *Rise of the Common Player*, p. 75. *Cf* Francis Meres, *Palladis Tamia* (1598), ed. Gregory Smith, *Elizabethan Critical Essays*, vol. II, p. 313; J. Cocke, in Chambers, *Elizabethan Stage*, vol. IV, p. 256; 'T. G.', *The Rich Cabinet* (1616) in John Dover Wilson (ed.), *Life in Shakespeare's England*.

eloquence' of the language.[1] Yet these were no more than debating arguments. They did not convey an intimate assurance that acting was justified by its own nature or distinctive function. What professional actors needed in the sixteenth century was not simply a theory about their 'quality', but something more like an ideology – or rather, a cultural pedigree and an emblem. And Heywood points to the pedigree they found in the verse preface to his *Apology for Actors*, which begins with a famous commonplace, supported by a marginal reference to the Church Fathers:

> The world's a theatre, the earth a stage,
> Which God and nature doth with actors fill:
> Kings have their entrance in due equipage,
> And some their parts play well, and others ill...
> All men have parts, and each man acts his own.

The actor–playwright continues:

> Some citizens, some soldiers, born to adventer,
> Shepherds, and seamen. Then our play's begun
> When we are born, and to the world first enter,
> And all find exits when their parts are done,

with the conclusion –

> He that denies then theatres should be,
> He may as well deny a world to me.

It was from this ancient commonplace that actors or professional dramatists drew their social justification; while they found the equivalent of a professional emblem in the novel theatrical device of inserting a play within the play.

The device of a play within the play could take several forms. An early and interesting example comes from the Dutch miracle, *Mary of Nimmegen*, which was printed at Antwerp about 1518 (and was translated into an English chapbook story). Mary is seduced by a devil and lives with him for seven years under the name of Emma; until one day, returning to Nijmegen and prompted by her love of poetry, she watches the annual pageant-play of the debate over God's mercy between a devil and our Lady, which stirs her to repentance. Here the play-within-the-play is praised because it catches the

[1] Thomas Heywood, *An Apology for Actors*, 1612 (ed. Shakespeare Society), p. 52.

conscience of a spectator, and it even helps her to win back her baptismal name.[1]

In England, the idea behind the presentation of the Nijmegen pageant-play was a bit of theatrical folklore, familiar to others besides Shakespeare.[2] But English dramatists also experimented with other ways of presenting two different planes of dramatic illusion.[3] In *Fulgens and Lucrece* (*c.* 1497), which can be called the first English humanist comedy, Medwall makes two servants discuss the plot of the play that is to be shown, and then take part in it. Much later, the court play, *The Rare Triumphs of Love and Fortune* (1582) shows the two disputing goddesses of the title manipulating the actions of the mortals in the main play each in turn from above, until Jupiter sends Mercury to reconcile them. Possibly the notion of this mythological framing action was adapted from Italian *intermezzi* (as the word *Triumphs* suggests); and the theme of a supreme arbiter was appropriate to a show offered to the Queen, as in Peele's contemporary masque-like play (*c.* 1581), *The Arraignment of Paris*. At the end of *The Rare Triumphs*, Fortune blesses the audience and prays for the Queen.[4] In *The Spanish Tragedy* (*c.* 1587), one of the favourites of the London public theatres, Kyd makes much more varied use of internal staging devices. His framing dialogues between the Ghost of Don Andrea and the figure of Revenge have dramatic force because Don Andrea is keenly interested in the main stage action, but unable to influence it. Early in the main action, old Hieronymo presents and expounds a military pageant at the Spanish court. He discovers his murdered son as in a 'spectacle' or tableau, and there are several other tableau-like scenes in which characters spy, observe and comment on each other's strange behaviour, as when Hieronymo runs mad on meeting 'the lively image of [his] grief' in another helplessly bereaved father. Although he is a Justice himself, he cannot obtain justice from the King against Prince Lorenzo and Don Balthazar, and therefore determines on an indirect revenge, pretending reconciliation with his enemies and agreeing to give another court show with their help. He gives a tragedy in which he 'fits' his ally and his two intended victims and himself with appropriate parts; and when he has told the

---

1 *Mary of Nimmegen*, trans. Ayres. *Cf* Nugent (ed.), *Anthology of Tudor Prose*, p. 657; see Weevers, *Poetry of the Netherlands*, pp. 57ff.

2 See *Hamlet*, II.ii.500; *A Warning for Fair Women* (1599), II.1076ff (ed. R. Simpson, *School of Shakespere*, vol. I, p. 311); Heywood, *Apology for Actors*, p. 58.

3 Righter, *Shakespeare and the Idea of the Play*, pp. 35ff, 69ff.

4 See above, p. 37.

King that the stage murders that have just been acted are not 'fabulously counterfeit', he draws a curtain for another 'spectacle' of his murdered son.

It is not strange that this melodrama was so popular, for Kyd shows a remarkable sense of the theatre. This comes out in his fondness for surprise effects, in his use of different physical levels of his stage simultaneously, and in the way he makes spectators within the play, actors within the play and characters apparently following their own purposes interact and exchange roles. At the same time, he combines this theatrical sleight-of-hand with the emotive theme of Hieronymo's 'unrest':

> Thus therefore will I rest me in unrest,
> Dissembling quiet in unquietness. (III.xiii.29)

At least in the dramatist's evident intention, the shifting planes of illusion on the stage correspond to a quality of illusion in life.

Greene also liked to experiment with the play within the play. In his morality, *A Looking Glass for London* (written in collaboration with Lodge), he makes the prophet Oseas comment on the stage sins of Nineveh in a manner recalling a medieval play-presenter. In his romance of *James IV*, he invents an exchange of shows between Oberon, king of fairies and the Scot, Bohan, who has withdrawn from court and country. To justify his misanthropy, Bohan shows Oberon the main play, with its treachery towards the heroine, Queen Dorothea. At the end of the first Act, Oberon admits that Bohan's play has 'means to paint the world's inconstant ways'; but meanwhile, as well as trying to please his host with fairy dances and showing him consolatory symbolic dumb-shows, Oberon has promised his favour to Bohan's two sons, who thereupon enter the main action as court servants. One, the dwarf, helps to save Dorothea; the other, the clown, is rescued from hanging by the fairies. The original story (borrowed from Giraldi) changes as it is enacted; Greene juggles with the stage performance as moral allegory, as pseudo-history, as pastime or consolation, and as a harmless demonstration of magic. He gives a similar demonstration of theatrical magic in *Friar Bacon and Friar Bungay*, especially in the scene (II.iii) where Bacon and Prince Edward, from Oxford, with the help of the magician's 'glass prospective', watch and then interfere in the 'comedy' of Lord Lacy's wooing at Fressingfield.

In Greene's plays and in *The Spanish Tragedy* there is a strong suggestion that a theatrical fiction reacts upon reality as well as reflecting or symbolising it. A kind of apologia for the professional stage poet is implicit in this suggestion. Another view of contemporary playing comes out in *Histrio-mastix, or The Player Whipt,* which was evidently touched up by Marston, but in its original form and main outlines was probably written about 1590, close in time to Greene's plays; and the author shared Greene's view of the mere uneducated player. The show unfolds in three sections. Each of the six Acts is introduced by a group of allegorical speakers, whose leader governs the following scenes – first Peace and her companions, the liberal arts; then Plenty and her company; then Pride, Envy, War; and finally Poverty, who completes the cycle by restoring Peace and the desire to work; whereupon Peace gives place to Queen Elizabeth, as Astraea, goddess of justice, presiding over a new golden age. This allegory of the cycle of prosperity, or Fortune, resembles a renowned civic pageant from the mercantile capital, Antwerp;[1] there are similar cyclic allegories in *Summer's Last Will* (1592), by Nashe, and in Dekker's *Old Fortunatus* (1599). The second section of *Histrio-mastix* concerns a number of lords and citizens, who obey the influence of the presiding deities Act by Act; and thirdly, there is a group of ignorant rogues, a beard-maker, a fiddle-string maker, a pedlar and a tap-room poet, who form themselves into a company of players under the patronage, not of a lord, but allegedly of a knight, Sir Oliver Owlet. In the Act governed by Plenty, these strollers act for Lord Mavortius, despising the 'Town-play' and the Mayor's 'reward'; but they put on such doggerel nonsense, vamped up by their own poet, that an Italian lord present as a guest 'blushes' for his English host. Then they think of employing the scholarly poet, Chrisoganus, but refuse him his fee, the ideal sum of £10, under the influence of Pride. When Envy reigns, they quarrel among themselves; in the time of War, they are pressed; the press-money is their 'reward', and the recruiting Officer brushes aside their plea that they only fight on the stage while their audience fights for them in the field. Under Poverty, they are stripped of their stage finery by the Soldiers, who jeer that they are the 'sharers' now, and the players 'the hired men'. In a sense, this play reverses the method used by Kyd and Greene, since it

---

1 *Histrio-mastix*, in Marston, *Plays*, vol. III, ed. Wood; *cf* Sheila Williams, 'Les Ommegangs d'Anvers', pp. 349ff, 386–8; Jacquot, 'Le Répertoire des Compagnies d'Enfants à Londres, 1600–1610', in Jacquot (ed.), *Dramaturgie et Société*, pp. 731ff, 782; Chew, 'Time and Fortune', p. 102.

shows social reality breaking in on a stage fiction; but reality is in fact represented by a pageant-like allegory, and ostensibly the satire is not turned against actors as such, but against parasites posing as actors, 'Proud Statute Rogues'. However, the satire illustrates a self-consciousness or professional self-questioning that must have been unavoidable for men working in the theatre at the time when Shakespeare was beginning his career.

The Induction to *The Taming of the Shrew* could be taken as a reply to *Histrio-mastix*. Christopher Sly is a drunken rogue of the same stamp as the would-be actors, Belch, Gutt and Incle, the pedlar. He too has been within reach of the Act against Vagabonds, as a pedlar, cardmaker (for the wool-trade), 'by transmutation a bearherd', and now 'by present profession a tinker', threatened with the stocks when the play opens for not paying his shot. But he protests that his family 'came in with Richard Conqueror' – he is a sort of Durbeyfield in advance – and in his imagination the cycle is completed for him when he appears to become a lord. He has vaguely heard of *The Spanish Tragedy* – he misquotes, 'Go, by Saint Jeronimy' – but he is ignorant about the stage ('Is not a comontie a Christmas gambold or a tumbling trick?', he asks).[1] On the other side, the Lord, unlike the principal lord in *Histrio-mastix*, is a cultivated man, who has sage reflections on drunkenness although he possesses 'wanton pictures', can improvise a 'pastime' with Sly as soon as he finds him, and warns his servants to 'husband' it with 'modesty' so as not to spoil the joke. He understands play-acting. He sees that Sly's transformation will seem to him when he wakes up like 'a flatt'ring dream or worthless fancy', a confusion between fantasy and actuality, which the members of the Lord's household can appreciate as spectators as well as actors, but which with respect to Sly is an appropriate consequence to his wilfully befuddled state. And on the timely arrival of the players who 'offer service' to him, he greets them with courtesy and discrimination. In particular, he remembers the actor who 'wooed the gentlewoman so well', because the 'part | Was aptly fitted and naturally performed'; and he sends them to the buttery before they play. He has not been at all put out when he sees that his visitors are only players, and not 'some noble gentleman', as he had thought on hearing their trumpet.

The Players, apparently, are worthy of the Lord's mistake. They have very little to say in the first scene, where the emphasis is on

---

[1] Righter, *Shakespeare and the Idea of the Play*, p. 94; cf above, p. 8.

their patron. But clearly they are fitting guests for such a host, and far above the capacity of Sly, who goes to sleep after watching their first scene. (In *The Taming of a Shrew*, the comedy with a puzzling relation to Shakespeare's, Sly remains attentive and draws a moral at the end from what he has seen. Many editors believe that Shakespeare's text must have contained a like scene at the end. But in *A Shrew*, Sly knows what a 'comedy' is and it is the Players who blunder; whereas Shakespeare's point seems to be precisely that *his* Players are not the men for spectators like Sly.)[1] Certainly, the Players can improve on the Lord's improvised, witty but amateur play with a more sustained performance. And, whereas the Lord's 'pastime' only contains a brief amusement, a 'flatt'ring dream' of lordship and marriage for Sly, which cannot be developed far and is bound to come to an awakening, the professional play shows a development of character, which can be imagined as lasting and which, farcical though it is, can be pictured as a reality by comparison with what happens to Sly. As the total comedy advances from the Induction to the play proper, one kind of fictional entertainment displaces the other. And one figure, Petruchio, presumably the player who had 'wooed the gentlewoman so well' in a previous play, dominates the occasion because he understands how to use his acting. In the last scene, which echoes the hunting language the Lord had used at the beginning, it is Petruchio who is the 'lord and husband'. Hortensio receives the answer that he must have 'some goodly jest in hand' when he sends for his wife; and Lucentio, who had taken the opposite course to Sly by willingly disguising himself as a servant, finds in effect that he has involved himself in a similar 'worthless fancy'. (An intimation of the respect due to good players like that in *The Shrew* is given also in *Sir Thomas More* (*c.* 1595), in which Shakespeare had a hand.)

In both *Love's Labour's Lost* and *A Midsummer Night's Dream* Shakespeare elaborates further on the motif of a play, or show, introduced within the play as an 'offering of service' to a lord; and in both, the motif has a bearing on the author's profession. Indeed, there are virtually two such shows in each play – the lords' masque precedes the pageant of the Nine Worthies as a show of welcome for the Princess of France, and at Theseus's wedding there is the fairies' dance as well as the play by the mechanicals. Revels to celebrate a

---

[1] On Sly in *A Shrew* and *The Shrew*, see Hibbard (ed.), *The Shrew*, pp. 41–4; and Bullough, *Sources*, vol. I, pp. 58ff; Righter, pp. 95–6; Heilman (ed.), *The Shrew*, in *Complete Signet Classic Shakespeare*, ed. Barnet, pp. 321ff.

royal occasion form the governing action in each comedy; in other words, instead of writing a comedy for inclusion in a court festival, like his Italian predecessors, Shakespeare includes the court festival within his comedy. Whoever the first audience were for either play, it is written to be performed anywhere, treating the court, in the spirit of Elizabeth's reign, as a spectacle for the whole people. And Shakespeare's professional interest in acting and its social context appears in the way he first takes his audience behind the scenes, to show preparations or rehearsals, and then shows the reactions of his stage spectators. On the surface, both comedies reveal a professional's irony at the expense of untrained amateurs, since the cultivated stage spectators are merely amused by the blundering efforts of the performers in the pageant and in *Pyramus and Thisbe*. But the irony does not stop there; at another level, the dramatist is interested in the relation between the actor and his role, and the relation between the stage play and the spectators' imagination. An implicit justification of the professional drama runs even deeper through these plays than in *The Shrew*.

Because the King of Navarre and his lords have forsaken the usual occupations of royalty to devote themselves to 'a little Academe', (in a manner recalling the Sienese Intronati, with their feigned indifference to 'the world'), they disappoint the Princess of the reception she has a right to expect for her embassy, lodging and greeting her in the King's park (II.i):

– Fair princess, welcome to the court of Navarre.
– Fair I give you back again; and welcome I have not yet: the roof of this court is too high to be yours, and welcome to the wide fields too base to be mine.

It is true that the Princess is given the pleasure of a 'shoot' (IV.i) (like Elizabeth in Leicester's famous entertainment at Kenilworth);[1] but the King has not accompanied her, being busy with composing a love-poem to her instead; and it is not until he and his lords have agreed that love has made them 'forsworn' that they decide (like the Intronati, offering the ladies a carnival comedy after their *Sacrifice*) to furnish 'revels' suitable to the occasion. And even then, although they have professed 'plain-dealing' among themselves (IV.iii.366), they intend to use their masque of welcome for a covert wooing. When the ladies get wind of their intention, they decide to give 'mock

[1] Chambers, *Elizabethan Stage*, vol. I, p. 123 and ch. 4, *passim*.

for mock' (v.ii.140), encouraging Boyet to spoil Moth's speech as the masquers' presenter by his interruptions, then frustrating the lords' wooing by changing masks themselves, and mocking the lords afterwards when they come back again, no longer disguised as far-travelling Muscovites. The ladies oppose their own improvised 'sport' to their wooers' contrived 'revels'; and they are the better actors. When Berowne guesses that Boyet has spoiled the lords' game, he compares him with the clown in Italian improvised comedy, 'some carrytale, ...some slight zany' (v.ii.463); a moment before, he has been comparing the ladies' overthrow of the masque to an English Christmas entertainment:

> I see the trick on't: here was a consent,
> Knowing aforehand of our merriment,
> To dash it like a Christmas comedy.

It is like the carnival trick against himself that Bibbiena had described in *The Courtier*;[1] Berowne may be thinking generally of Christmas 'pastime' in England but probably he is thinking more particularly of the Gray's Inn revels of Christmas 1594–5, when the master of ceremonies pretended that he must forgo some formalities because he was exhausted after a 'visit' to Russia, and the climax to one evening's 'sports' (after 'the Lord Ambassador and his Train [from the Inner Temple] thought that they were not so kindly entertained, as was before expected') was 'Dancing and Revelling with Gentlewomen', followed by a performance of Shakespeare's *Comedy of Errors*. The mock-chronicle of Gray's Inn (*Gesta Grayorum*) pretended that 'that Night was begun, and continued to the end, in nothing but Confusion and Errors', which 'had gained to us Discredit, and itself a Nickname of Errors'. The dramatist turns a fiction elaborated from a real festive performance into a new fiction for his own stage, where the 'Confusion' is incorporated into the 'comedy'.

The Nine Worthies were mainly associated with civic pageants.[2] In *Promos and Cassandra*, published in 1578, Whetstone represents such a pageant being prepared in order to welcome the king (of Hungary) on a royal entry to his town of Giulio. The dishonest town official, Phallax, is shown giving orders to a carpenter:

[1] See p. 192, above.
[2] See Venezky, *Pageantry on the Shakespearean Stage*; Wickham, *Early English Stages*, vol. I, p. 80; Anglo, *Spectacle Pageantry*, pp. 54, 157, 329; Nevinson, 'A Show of the Nine Worthies'.

> Dispatch Dowson, up with the frame [*stage*] quickly,
> So space your rooms, as the Nine Worthies may
> Be so installed as best may please the eye.   (Part II, I.iv)

Another stage, for the town waits, is to be set up at 'Saint Anne's Cross' and the Four Virtues are to be stationed 'on Jesus gate'. Phallax also tells the Merchant Taylors where to place their pageant of Hercules conquering monsters and giants, and gives instructions to 'two men, apparelled like Green Men at the Mayor's feast, with clubs of fire-work', who are 'to keep a passage clear' for 'the King and his train'; Whetstone was obviously thinking of English pageants, with their street tableaux and colourful processions, bearing messages of civic propaganda and loyalty to the throne. Since there are verbal echoes from *Promos and Cassandra*, particularly this passage, in *Love's Labour's Lost*, it seems certain that Shakespeare was taking hints for his own pageant from Whetstone.[1] And, as in Whetstone, his pageant miscarries, though for very different reasons.

Holofernes suggests the subject of the Nine Worthies in the scene after the lords have made their own plan for 'revels', when Armado informs him (v.i) 'that the king would have me present the princess, sweet chuck, with some delightful ostentation, or show, or pageant, or antic, or fire-work'; as the local man of learning, Holofernes knows at once what will suit. He distributes the parts for this 'excellent device' among Armado and the others – though the quick-witted Moth is sceptical – and leads his company off the stage with an exuberant *'allons!'*, echoing Berowne's *'allons!'* at the same point in the previous scene (IV.iii.379; v.i.132). The pageant is next heard of (v.ii.485) when Costard comes to ask the King for permission to present it while the lords are smarting from the discomfiture of their own masque; and artistically, it is just as much a failure. The King is reluctant at first to allow what he knows will be an incompetent performance, only permitting it after Berowne has pointed out that ' 'tis some policy | To have one show worse than the king's and his company' and the Princess has added, 'That sport best pleases that doth least know how'. So that when Costard comes on to speak his lines as Pompey 'the Big' or 'Great', Sir Nathaniel the curate as Alexander, Holofernes as Judas Maccabaeus (also presenting the page-boy Moth as the infant Hercules), and Don Armado, the self-styled 'soldier', as Hector, it is easy for the lords of Navarre and Boyet

[1] See David (ed.), *Love's Labour's Lost*, notes to v.i.113, 141, 500, 753.

275

to trip up the players' lumbering, old-fashioned verse with punning catcalls, mock their appearance and ruin the show. Seeing the absurdities of the would-be performers, the real audience in the theatre can share the merriment and be prepared for the final changes of mood on the stage, as the lords regain their self-esteem and move towards an alliance in laughter with their guests.

But there is still a difference to be resolved between the two groups of stage spectators. The lords of Navarre want to put Holofernes and the rest 'out of countenance' for their own sakes, but the Princess, equally critical of the performance, receives the intention behind it more generously; and in the same spirit, Rosaline reminds Berowne at the end (v.ii.849) that

> A jest's prosperity lies in the ear
> Of him that hears it; never in the tongue
> Of him that makes it.

In this sense, the ladies are taking sides with the crestfallen amateur actors. Holofernes has already protested to his exultant mockers, 'This is not generous, not gentle, not humble' (v.ii.621), and Armado as Hector has rebuked them with unexpected dignity (v.ii.652):

The sweet war-man is dead and rotten; sweet chucks, beat not the bones of the buried; when he breathed, he was a man.

Here, as again in the *Midsummer Night's Dream*, Shakespeare speaks for the actor's need of a sympathetic hearing; without an understanding audience, no play is complete. And, conversely, he insists, here as elsewhere,[1] on the actor's (or jester's) need of a sense of timing, an appreciation of the occasion and the mood of his listener. Much of the ridicule in *Love's Labour's Lost* is directed against clever men's self-conceit.

Along with this goes his equally professional interest in the relation between the actor as a real man and the role he assumes. The lords first speak of 'Costard the swain' and Armado, with his 'high-born', 'fire-new words' as if these two will unwittingly afford 'recreation' from the rigours of study (i.i.159–78); but the clowns parody the wits as the play develops, even more than they provide them with 'sport'. The King, announcing his scheme of study at the outset, invites his companions to join him in winning 'fame', as the 'heirs of all eternity', as 'brave conquerors', prepared to

---

[1] *Comedy of Errors*, I.ii.68, II.ii.32; *Twelfth Night*, III.i.59; *Hamlet*, III.ii.36.

war against your own affections
And the huge army of the world's desires.

And the three lords agree, in spite of Berowne's warning that for them the project is not 'in season'. But the clowns' project at the end to 'pursent', or even 'parfect', each of the Nine Worthies is a similar ambition, with a similar flaw. As Costard says when Sir Nathaniel stumbles hopelessly in his part (v.ii.569),

O, sir, you have overthrown Alisander the conqueror!...A conqueror and afeard to speak! Run away for shame, Alisander;

and, to the lords who have put the curate out,

There, an't shall please you, a foolish mild man; an honest man, look you, and soon dash'd. He is a marvellous good neighbour, faith, and a very good bowler; but for Alisander – alas! you see how 'tis – a little o'erparted.

This is a corollary to the Lord's compliment in *The Shrew* to the professional actor whose 'part' had been 'aptly fitted and naturally performed'. And Costard distinguishes, as the witty spectators of the pageant fail to distinguish, between an incompetent performance, the performer as a man, and the imaginative dignity of the part he represents.

Pyramus and Thisbe is an even more hilarious disaster than the pageant of the Nine Worthies. But here, too, Shakespeare is concerned with more than romping satire at the expense of 'homespun' town players, the now out-dated rivals of the professionals. He is concerned again with the attitude of well-informed aristocratic spectators, and with the way his inserted piece, exaggeratedly theatrical through its very blunders, reflects back on the stage spectators themselves and their experience in the main action. As a tale of lovers escaping from their parents, a tale well-known even to ballad-mongers, the subject of *Pyramus and Thisbe* hints broadly at a conceivable tragic outcome for Hermia and Lysander in the woods – in Henry James's term, a 'possible other case'; now, however, that possible tragic outcome may safely be relegated to farce. But the naïve presumption of Bottom's company that they are really acting at the wedding is no more wide of the mark than the protestations of Demetrius and Lysander in the quarrel scene in the woods and the supposition of Helena and Hermia that the others are acting when they are not:

– Ay, do! Persever, counterfeit sad looks...
– Do you not jest?...

– Fie, fie! You counterfeit, you puppet, you!

And, before he pretends to die on the stage in the presence of Moon-shine, Bottom has already echoed Demetrius's opinion that the scenes in the moonlit wood have been merely a 'dream'. The courtiers and the mechanicals are alike in that they do not know for sure when they are genuine, self-determining characters and when they are no more than actors or 'shadows'.

Again, too, as in *Love's Labour's Lost*, Shakespeare takes up through Theseus and Hippolyta the question of the nobleman's generous reception of well-meant 'service' from actors, and the question of the spectator's co-operation with the players (v.i):

– The best in this kind [says Theseus] are but shadows; and the worst are no worse, if imagination amend them.
– It must be your imagination then, and not theirs.
– If we imagine no worse of them than they of themselves, they may pass for excellent men.

This contains a disarming apology for other players besides Bottom and Flute. But Shakespeare's emphasis on *imagination* in this scene also marks a new step in his awareness of himself as a dramatic poet. Previously, he had used the word only in passing ('Beyond imagina-tion is the wrong' done to Antipholus of Ephesus), or to denote mere images in the mind ('unfelt imaginations', the 'bare imagination of a feast');[1] now, for the first time, Shakespeare emphasises the mental faculty, in the discussion of the lovers' story between Hippolyta and Theseus that opens this scene:

> – 'Tis strange, my Theseus, that these lovers speak of.
> – More strange than true. I never may believe
> These antique fables, nor these fairy toys.
> Lovers and madmen have such seething brains,
> Such shaping fantasies, that apprehend
> More than cool reason ever comprehends...
>
> Such tricks hath strong imagination,
> That, if it would but apprehend some joy,
> It comprehends some bringer of that joy;
> Or in the night, imagining some fear,
> How easy is a bush supposed a bear!

Theseus expresses the rationalistic mistrust of imagination which was

[1] *Comedy of Errors*, V.i.201; *Richard III*, I.iv.80; *Richard II*, I.iii.297.

normal in the sixteenth century (before the word had acquired the general literary prestige the Romantics were to give it). It was subject to sense-impressions and irresponsible desires, a 'passion of the mind' that 'corrupteth the understanding' if yielded to;[1] it was identified with childishness, hallucination, neurosis or witchcraft. The same general sense comes out in *1 Henry IV* (I.iii.198), in Northumberland's comment on Hotspur's irrelevancies:

> Imagination of some great exploit
> Drives him beyond the bounds of patience;

to which Worcester subjoins,

> He apprehends a world of figures [*mental images*] here,
> But not the form of what he should attend.

In the Athenian dialogue, however, Hippolyta has a tentative reply to Theseus:

> But all the story of the night told over,
> And all their minds transfigured so together,
> More witnesseth than fancy's images,
> And grows to something of great constancy;
> But howsoever, strange and admirable.

('Fancy' here, as usually in Shakespeare, refers to the imagination of lovers in particular; 'admirable' means remarkable, to be wondered at.) In other words, Hippolyta refers to what the spectators have already seen, to delusions they can account for. Theseus thinks of 'fairy toys' in the scoffing spirit of Mercutio's Queen Mab speech. In *The Comedy of Errors* Shakespeare had repeatedly connected the 'fallacies' of people in comedy with the thought of madness (as when Antipholus of Syracuse finds himself claimed as husband by Andriana:

> What, was I married to her in my dream?...
> Am I in earth, in heaven, or in hell?
> Sleeping or waking, mad or well-advised?
> Known unto these, and to myself disguised?).

In the Athenian comedy, Shakespeare now associates the stage manifestation of 'fairy toys', of self-disguise, of apparent madness or dream, with the imagination. Moreover, in Theseus's most famous

---

[1] Thomas Wright, *The Passions of the Minde* (1604), pp. 7, 45, 48–57. *Cf* Montaigne, *Essais*, I.xxi; Thorndike, *History of Magic and Experimental Science*, vol. v, pp. 100ff, 485; vol. vi, pp. 132, 235–7, 477ff, 531.

lines (which I omitted from his speech a moment ago), he associates them specifically with the *poet's* imagination. These lines take up and develop a number of ideas already present in *Love's Labour's Lost*. As Dover Wilson has shown, from the printing of the Quarto, they were almost certainly added by Shakespeare to the manuscript the printer was working from, as an afterthought;[1] they represent a kind of critical appreciation by the poet of his own play.

In the earlier play, Shakespeare had dwelt on the speed of 'wit' and the remoteness of the materials it brings together, as in Rosaline's tribute to Berowne –

> His eye begets occasion for his wit;
> For every object that the one doth catch
> The other turns to a mirth-moving jest,
> Which his fair tongue (conceit's expositor)
> Delivers.

But this praise of wit is not altogether unambiguous, since the Princess has just spoken of 'such short-lived wits' (with a faint echo from Ascham or *Euphues*), while Katherine has just voiced some doubts about Dumaine, in that 'he hath wit to make an ill shape good' (II.i); and this ambiguity or doubt about verbal inventiveness comes out again in the mock-modest self-praise Shakespeare gives to Holofernes (IV.ii):

This is a gift that I have, simple; a foolish extravagant spirit full of forms, figures, shapes, objects, ideas, apprehensions, motions, revolutions. These are begot in the ventricle of memory, nourished in the womb of *pia mater*, and delivered upon the mellowing of occasion.

The 'mellowing of occasion' in the pageant of the Nine Worthies is due to expose this 'foolish extravagant spirit' in the schoolmaster; but meanwhile,

the gift is good in those in whom it is acute, and I am thankful for it.

And in the last scene of *Love's Labour's Lost*, following the logic of the play, Berowne attributes the like extravagancy, not to wit, but to love, which has 'deformed' him and his friends (v.ii.741f; some modern editions read '*strange* shapes' in place of 'straying'):

> As love is full of unbefitting strains,
> All wanton as a child, skipping and vain,
> Formed by the eye and therefore, like the eye,

---

[1] John Dover Wilson (ed.), *Midsummer Night's Dream*, pp. 80–6.

Full of straying shapes, of habits and of forms,
Varying in subjects as the eye doth roll
To every varied object in his glance;
Which parti-coated presence of loose love
Put on by us,

[if we behaved, that is, like fools in motley],

    if, in your heavenly eyes,
Have misbecomed our oaths and gravities,
Those heavenly eyes that look into these faults
Suggested [*tempted*] us to make...

All these themes of stage metamorphosis, aberration of mind, love
and rapid invention are brought together in Theseus's speech about
the poet and his imagination:

  The lunatic, the lover, and the poet
  Are of imagination all compact.
  One sees more devils than vast hell can hold,
  That is the madman. The lover, all as frantic,
  Sees Helen's beauty in a brow of Egypt.
  The poet's eye, in a fine frenzy rolling,
  Doth glance from heaven to earth, from earth to heaven;
  And as imagination bodies forth
  The forms of things unknown, the poet's pen
  Turns them to shapes, and gives to airy nothing
  A local habitation and a name.

Theseus's reference to 'a brow of Egypt' is another link with *Love's
Labour's Lost* and the joking there about Rosaline's 'black...brows'
(IV.iii). It seems very likely that the repeated talk in *Love's Labour's
Lost* about study and stars, love and eyes, had been prompted by
Giordano Bruno's *De gli eroici furori* [*Heroic Raptures*], which had been
published at London in 1585, with a dedication to Sir Philip Sidney;[1]
and if so, there may well be a further echo here from Bruno's effusion,
which attempted to disjoin poetic rapture from love and unite it with
philosophical speculation. Theseus stresses the cosmic sweep of the
poet's eye, his 'fine frenzy' and the contact of his imagination with
'things unknown'. His words are still tinged with scepticism, but the
dramatic context shows that his scepticism is misplaced. The poet in
this play may not have arrived at an ultimate truth such as Giordano
Bruno was striving for, but he has employed 'antique' (or 'antic')

[1] Yates, *A Study of 'Love's Labour's Lost'*, chs. 5–6; *cf* Mazzeo, 'Metaphysical Poetry'.

'fables' and 'fairy toys' to a new purpose, and has given them 'shapes' and 'a local habitation and a name' without betraying their invisibility, their quality of 'airy nothing'. 'Shapes' often refers in Shakespeare to actors or their disguises (as in Berowne's reference to the lords' masque);[1] and soon Theseus is to bring in the synonymous term, 'shadows', with reference to the players' roles and the onlooker's 'imagination'. Elsewhere in this play, it is love (according to Lysander) that is 'Swift as a shadow, short as any dream' (I.i.144), but also Puck applies it to the fairies: excusing his misapplication of the magic flower to Lysander instead of Demetrius as a mistake due to their common 'Athenian garments' and not one of his own usual 'knaveries', he conciliates Oberon with the title, 'king of shadows' (III.ii.347). When Puck comes to his epilogue – 'If we shadows have offended' – the word stretches from the fairies to the whole acting company, but still with an immediate reference to those decisive helpers, shaped, named and localised by the poet from airy nothing, whom the other actors, except for Bottom, have never seen. The same word applies to the would-be impersonators Theseus laughs at and the agents of fortune he is unaware of. They have already been set in parallel by the design of the play, since both groups have been intending to honour the royal wedding.

While from the first Shakespeare had connected the effects of love in comedy with the metamorphoses described by Ovid, he now connects them directly with the imagination of the dramatic poet. The changes of identity the lovers encounter on the stage are the property of 'shadows', unreal and real at the same time. From *Love's Labour's Lost* and the *Dream*, it appears to be necessary for the lovers to act out their fantasies, and to meet living images or parodies of themselves, before they can rid themselves of their affectations or impulsive mistakes. In the former play, the wits come as a result to a position of self-criticism. Shakespeare denies this degree of conscious awareness to the lovers in the *Dream*, but on the other hand he confers it on the audience, who see the theatrical causes of all their delusions. He does not seem to be claiming, as against Theseus, that what the poet's imagination finds is true, but that it has a special function in the theatre. It projects shadows, illusions, not mirror-images of reality. But, provided those illusions can be recognised for what they

---

[1] *1 Henry VI*, V.iii.35; *2 Henry VI*, III.i.79; *3 Henry VI*, III.ii.192; *Richard III*, II.ii.27; *Two Gentlemen*, IV.ii.126; *Love's Labour's Lost*, V.ii.287, 751. See Ure (ed.), *Richard II*, p. 141; Righter, *Shakespeare and the Idea of the Play*, pp. 86ff.

are, he seems to be saying, they represent faithfully those influences, whether psychological or social, which change people's feelings from outside of their conscious minds and wills, influences which they need to undergo before their vision of themselves can change. Shakespeare's central characters are led through a passage of illusion, as in a rite of initiation. To convey something like this through the medium of the play itself, moreover, was to suggest a social function for the theatre.

When Thomas Heywood mentioned the Church Fathers as the authorities for his metaphor, 'The world's a theatre, the earth a stage', he could have gone much further back in history, to Plato, or even earlier, to Democritus.[1] In the age of Athenian New Comedy and the Cynic and Stoic philosophers, the idea became a moralist's commonplace, as in the lay sermon by Teles comparing Fortune to a playwright, instancing roles in life, such as those of 'the ship-wrecked man, the poor man, the exile, the king, the beggar', as if they were temporary or external to the essential self, and urging that 'what the good man has to do is to play well any part with which Fortune may invest him'; and this, or Plato's conception of the gods as stage-managers and spectators of mankind, was passed on to Christian moralists like St John Chrysostom, St Augustine and Boethius, to be revived in force at the Renaissance by writers with humanist training such as Ficino, Erasmus, Vives and even Luther and Calvin. By Shakespeare's time, it was a well-known commonplace for poets to use and for dramatists to take as the starting-point for complex stage devices. In 1599, it furnished the motto (*'Totus mundus agit histrionem'*) to Shakespeare's company's new theatre, The Globe; to be echoed next year in the name of the principal rival playhouse, The Fortune. Originally, of course, such a metaphor could only have been coined and passed into general use in a civilisation where the theatre was an established, prominent feature of life. Yet no Greek or Roman playwrights seem to have thought it part of their business to lay any stress on the idea. And during the Renaissance, it does not seem to have been uttered in connection with an acted play until after the emergence of commercial drama, in the second half of the sixteenth century.

Two passages are worth quoting here at some length to illustrate Shakespeare's certain or probable acquaintance with literary

[1] See Jacquot, ' "Le Théâtre du Monde" '; Curtius, *European Literature*, pp. 138–44; Righter, *Shakespeare and the Idea of the Play*, ch. 3. *Cf* above, pp. 153–7.

statements of the theme. The first and more impressive comes from Erasmus's *Praise of Folly*. After describing her own appearance and mythological origins, Folly begins, like some heraldic orator, to claim for herself an extensive empire. Sexual pleasure and therefore life itself, childhood, old age, the behaviour attributed to the gods, marriage and friendship, the ambitions of kings, the bonds of political association and the pretensions of solitary thinkers, the artist's thirst for fame and the moralist's desire to benefit from experience – all would be unthinkable without Folly's influence. True wisdom, she maintains, using a Socratic image, is 'like the figures of Silenus' with 'two completely opposite faces, so that what is death at first sight, as they say, is life if you look within, and vice versa, life is death'. And then[1] –

What's the point of this, someone will say. Hear how we'll develop the argument. If anyone tries to take the masks off the actors when they're playing a scene on the stage and show their true natural faces to the audience, he'll certainly spoil the whole play and deserve to be stoned and thrown out of the theatre for a maniac. For a new situation will suddenly arise in which a woman on the stage turns into a man, a youth is now old, and the king of a moment ago is suddenly Dama, the slave, while a god is shown up as a common little man. To destroy the illusion [*errorem tollere*] is to destroy the whole play, for it's really the characterization and make-up [*figmentum et fucus*] which hold the audience's eye. Now, what else is the whole life of man but a sort of play [*fabula*]? Actors come on wearing their different masks and all play their parts until the producer [*choregus*] orders them off the stage, and he can often tell the same man to appear in different costume, so that now he plays a king in purple and now a humble slave in rags. It's all a sort of pretence but it's the only way to act out this farce. [*Adumbrata quidem omnia, sed haec fabula non aliter agitur*].

Coming where it does, this extended metaphor touches on the problem of the gap between men's official standpoints and their actions or real motives (between 'profession' and 'policy', as Marlowe was to express it) – a problem which was to trouble the sixteenth century deeply after Machiavelli had exposed the difference between morality and statecraft and the Reformation had brought about a distinction between obedience and faith; 'we are all (in effect) become comedians in religion', Sir Walter Raleigh was to say.[2] But the base of Erasmus's metaphor is the theme of Fortune connected

[1] *The Praise of Folly*, XXIX (trans. Radice, p. 103).
[2] *Cf* Raleigh, *History of the World* (1614), Preface (*Works*, vol. II, pp. xxxi–xxxii).

specifically with the theatre since the period of New Comedy.

There is a similar application of the idea of life as a play, with an explicit reference to Fortune (or 'Chaunce') in a passage Shakespeare must have known from *The Zodiac of Life*, an encyclopedic verse treatise dealing with astronomy and morals, published in Italy about 1535 by an obscure author known as Palingenius. The Latin text was used in England as a school-book, and it was translated by Barnabe Googe in the 1560s. Palingenius brings in the theme (Googe replacing the original 'play', *fabula*, with 'pageant' in his translation) in the course of a discussion of the vanity of life, especially of honours and ambition:

> Wherefore if thou dost well discerne, thou shalt behold and see
> This mortall lyfe that here you leade, a Pageant for to bee.
> The divers partes therein declarde, the chaunging world doth showe,
> The maskers are eche one of them with lively breath that blowe.
> For almost every man now is disguised from his kinde [*nature*]
> And underneth a false pretence they sely soules do blinde.
> So move they Goddes above to laugh wyth toyes and trifles vayne,
> Which here in Pageants fond they passe while they do life retayne.
> Fame, Glorie Praise, and eke Renowne are dreames, and profitlesse:
> Bicause with *Chaunce* they are obtaynd, and not by *Vertuousnesse*.

It seems certain that Shakespeare remembered this passage in his dialogue about the world as a stage in *As You Like It*, because he goes straight on, like Palingenius, to the vanities of the successive ages of man's life.[1]

Although Erasmus had been interested in all forms of the theatre, and defended *The Praise of Folly* by reference to popular farces,[2] Folly takes her extended metaphor from the literary remains of classical drama, without trying to apply it to the contemporary stage. What appears to be the earliest literary application of the commonplace to a play in performance dates, by a coincidence, from the year of Shakespeare's birth. In the carnival of 1564, *La belle Genièvre* was acted for the French court at Fontainebleau. The play has disappeared, but the epilogue which Ronsard wrote for it can still be read. The poet moralises in traditional manner on the vanities due to Fortune, touching also on the allied commonplace that life is a dream, but this

---

[1] Palingenius, *The Zodiake of Life*, trans. Googe (ed. Tuve), p. 99. See Baldwin, *Shakespere's Small Latine*, vol. I, pp. 652ff; Whitaker, *Shakespeare's Use of Learning*, pp. 22–4.
[2] *Cf* above, p. 178.

time he attaches the thought to a justification of the living theatre:[1]

> Ici la Comédie apparaît un exemple
> Où chacun de son fait les actions contemple:
> Le monde est le théâtre, et les hommes acteurs,
> La Fortune qui est maîtresse de la scène,
> Apprête les habits, et de la vie humaine
> Les Cieux et les destins en sont les spectateurs.
> En gestes différents, en différents langages,
> Rois, Princes et Bergers jouent leurs personnages
> Devant les yeux de tous, sur l'échafaud commun,
> Et, quoi que l'homme essaye à vouloir contrefaire
> Sa nature et sa vie, il ne saurait tant faire
> Qu'il ne soit, ce qu'il est, remarqué d'un chacun.
> L'un vit comme un pasteur, l'un est roi des provinces,
> L'autre fait le marchand, l'autre s'égale aux Princes,
> L'autre se feint content, l'autre poursuit du bien;
> Cependant le souci de sa lime nous ronge,
> Qui fait que notre vie est seulement un songe,
> Et que tous nos desseins ne finissent en rien...
> Il ne faut espérer être parfait au monde,
> Ce n'est que vent, fumée, une onde qui suit l'onde;
> Ce qui était hier ne se voit aujourd'hui.
> Heureux, trois fois heureux, qui au temps ne s'oblige,
> Qui suit son naturel, et qui sage corrige
> Ses fautes en vivant par les fautes d'autrui.

Ronsard elegantly turns the old commonplace round about, so that it is now precisely the artificiality, the patent illusion of the stage that gives it moral value, as an example applicable to life. He was writing for a play at court (apparently founded on an episode from *Orlando Furioso*), at a time when everywhere in western Europe drama was assuming new, secular and socially problematic forms. The courtly and academic type of drama which Ronsard and his friends wanted to establish in France in place of the dying medieval theatre was directly borrowed from Italy; meanwhile the new profession of acting had already emerged far enough to come under attack.

It seems that an English audience could have heard a similar utterance in the theatre about a year after the performance at

---

[1] Ronsard, 'Vers Récités à la Fin de la Comédie représentée à Fontainebleau', in *Poésies Choisies*, ed. de Nolhac, p. 251. See Prouty, *Sources of 'Much Ado'*, pp. 14, 20; Lebègue, 'Les Représentations Dramatiques à la Cour des Valois'.

Fontainebleau. In Richard Edwardes's *Damon and Pithias*, as the hero arrives at Syracuse he tells his servant:[1]

> we will here
> As men that come to see the soil and manners of all men of every degree.
> Pythagoras said that this world was like a stage,
> Whereon many play their parts; the lookers-on, the sage
> Philosophers are, saith he, whose part is to learn
> The manners of all nations, and the good from the bad to discern.

Again, the thought of Fortune is implied, especially as *Damon and Pithias* deals with life at court. The image of the court as the nation's supreme stage was to fascinate English poets and dramatists down to 'that memorable scene' of Charles I. And Edwardes (*c.* 1523–66) was writing for the court, like Ronsard. But as Master of the Children of the Chapel Royal, providing music and poetry for the Queen's revels, he was interested in drama from a professional point of view. The text of *Damon and Pithias* published in 1571 contains a prologue 'somewhat altered for the proper use of them that hereafter shall have occasion to play it, either in Private, or open Audience', where Edwardes uses and defends the term 'tragical comedy' and, quoting Horace, states the doctrine of comic *decorum* for the first time in English:

> In comedies the greatest skill is this: rightly to touch
> All things to the quick, and eke to frame each person so
> That by his common talk you may his nature rightly know.

Edwardes's interest in the rhetorical image of the world as stage goes with his practical interest in modern, or modernised, forms of comedy.

The metaphor of the world as stage referred primarily to the world as portrayed in New Comedy – to the present, Fortune-dominated, iron age, not the mythical golden age that Aristophanes had pretended to resuscitate. Shakespeare's principal reference to the theme comes in the pastoral setting of *As You Like It* (1599). But Shakespeare does not merely discuss it, he dramatises it as well.

Pastoral literature played with the daydream of an escape to a golden world. The shepherds in Montemayor's *Diana*, for instance, lead a life untroubled except by the pangs of love; in the chorus of Tasso's *Aminta* (1573) the shepherds long for the golden age, when love

---

[1] *Damon and Pithias*, ed. Adams, in *Chief Pre-Shakespearean Dramas*. See Righter, *Shakespeare and the Idea of the Play*, p. 67; F. P. Wilson, *English Drama*, pp. 111–12.

was uninhibited. In Shakespeare's narrative source, Lodge's *Rosalynde*; *Euphues' Golden Legacy* (1590), the contrast between the shepherds' life and the court recalls the contrast between the golden and the iron age:[1]

Here (Mistress) shall not Fortune thwart you, but in mean misfortunes, as the loss of a few sheep; which, as it breeds no beggary, so it can be no extreme prejudice...Envy stirs not us, we covet not to climb, our desires mount not above our degrees, nor our thoughts above our fortunes. Care cannot harbour in our cottages, nor do our homely couches know broken slumbers: as we exceed not in our diet, so we have enough to satisfy: and Mistress I have so much Latin, *Satis est quod sufficit.*

Much of the dialogue in *As You Like It* is taken up, similarly, with antitheses beween court and country, Fortune and Nature, the present world and the golden age. But Shakespeare is not repeating a pastoral myth; the New Comedy myth of the world as a stage comes nearer to the fictional life of his characters. This is the main theme shared by Jaques and Touchstone, the two outstanding figures Shakespeare has added to Lodge's story. Nevertheless, moralising in this vein is clearly not the main drift of the play as a whole. In the person of Rosalind, Love laughs at moralists, and Rosalind's gaiety enables her to act her part on the stage set by Fortune. She does not pretend to restore any golden age, but paradoxically she approaches the wonder-working buffoons of Aristophanes through the sense of happiness she communicates, because she knows and the audience know when she is in earnest and when she is acting.

Shakespeare introduces the motif of the golden age deliberately near the beginning of his play, when he first mentions the exiled Duke and his friends, who 'fleet the time carelessly, as they did in the golden world' (I.i); this comes in Oliver's dialogue with the wrestler, showing Oliver's envy towards his brother. Again, Le Beau, warning Orlando to escape from Duke Frederick's malice at court, hopes they may meet again, 'Hereafter in a better world than this' (I.ii.263). In the first of these two speeches (I.i.106), Shakespeare couples the golden life of the exiles in the Forest of Arden with that of 'the old Robin Hood of England', as if he knew or guessed one of Lodge's main sources (the *Tale of Gamelyn*), and was using it to compare his own story with the subject of a favourite traditional summer folk-play.[2]

[1] Lodge, *Rosalynde*, ed. Bullough, *Sources*, vol. II, p. 188.
[2] Bullough, *Sources*, vol. II, pp. 143ff; *cf* Barber, *Shakespeare's Festive Comedy*, pp. 7, 18.

But he was evidently thinking mainly of the description of the ages of the world and the ages of man in the first and last books of Ovid's *Metamorphoses*, or in Golding's translation. Palingenius, whom he drew upon for the discussion of life as a stage-play, would have led him back to these passages in Ovid (and apparently the passage from Ovid's last book was in his mind again a few months later, when writing *Julius Caesar*).[1]

The golden age, as described in Ovid's first Book (lines 89–112), was the time immediately after the creation of the world, when (in Golding's words) 'There was no feare of punishment, there was no threatning lawe.' There was no need for trade or armies; men lived in simplicity, leisure and plenty, on what the earth freely produced, such as 'the acornes dropt on ground, from Jove's brode tree in fielde'. It was a time of everlasting spring. The silver age brought the division of the year into seasons, including winter's 'icicles', and men needed to live in forest shelters and learned to plough (113–24). The bronze age (125–7) introduced warfare. And the iron age (127–50) brought in human wickedness, 'Craft, Treason, Violence, Envie, Pride and wicked Lust'; then fathers feared sons-in-law, friend turned against friend, and brother against brother. This was the age of property-divisions, commerce and mining for iron and gold. The iron age led to the rebellion of the giants, and the punishment of Jupiter's flood (245–312), so that mankind would have been wiped out but for the one just couple, Deucalion and Pyrrha.

Ovid concludes the vast catalogue of his *Metamorphoses* by returning to the same theme, through an exposition of the teachings of Pythagoras, the sage who went into voluntary exile 'for the hate he had | To Lordlynesse and Tyranny'. Pythagoras starts with vegetarianism; the golden age of freedom for beasts and men alike was brought to an end, he explains, when men sinfully began to kill animals for food (xv.60–142). There is a consolation, however: men need not fear death, because their souls migrate perpetually to other men and to and from beasts as well (142–75); 'All things doo chaunge. But nothing sure dooth perish' – which compensates for the tabu on eating meat. Pythagoras is now launched on the sublime theme behind Ovid's whole book, the perpetuity of change:

In all the world there is not that that standeth at a stay.

[1] See Baldwin, *Shakspere's Small Latine*, vol. I, pp. 657–77; Whitaker, *Shakespeare's Use of Learning*, pp. 8, 26, 225; *cf* Lovejoy and Boas, *Primitivism in Antiquity*, pp. 43ff, 59ff; above, pp. 137ff.

Things eb and flow: and every shape is made to passe away.
The tyme itself continually is fleeting like a brooke.

Time changes repeatedly, and the seasons of the year succeed one
another like the ages of man (176–236); the four elements displace
and replace one another (237–51). Nothing in Nature keeps the same
form for ever, but nothing in Nature is lost (252–61):

> And though that varyably
> Things passe perchaunce from place to place: yit all from whence they came
> Returning, do unperrisshed continew still the same.
> But as for in one shape, bee sure that nothing long can last.
> Even so the ages of the world from gold to Iron past.

And Pythagoras, or the Roman sage, King Numa, who is speaking
for him here, goes on at length to describe the changes that can take
place on the surface of the earth, in the condition of rivers, the forms
of animals, the fortunes of nations and cities; he concludes (431–78)
by reminding his listeners that the fall of Troy meant the birth
of Rome, and by warning them once again against the sin of killing
their 'brothers' the animals for their food. This same mythology of
change is the subject of Spenser's *Mutability Cantos*.

Several speeches in *As You Like It* sound like casual allusions to
these two Books of Ovid. Rosalind, finding Orlando's verses in the
forest, says, 'I was never so berimed since Pythagoras' time, that I
was an Irish rat'; and when Celia tells her she has seen Orlando himself 'under a tree, like a dropp'd acorn', she retorts, 'It may well be
called Jove's tree, when it drops forth such fruit' (III.ii.163, 220).
And Touchstone names the Roman poet, to impress Audrey (III.iii.5).
But when we first hear the old Duke and his friends in their golden
world of Arden, Ovid's mythology is the principal theme. The Duke
consoles himself and his companions for 'the stubbornness of fortune'
(II.i.1):

> Now, my co-mates and brothers in exile,
> Hath not old custom made this life more sweet
> Than that of painted pomp? Are not these woods
> More free from peril than the envious court?
> Here feel we not the penalty of Adam,
> The seasons' difference; as the icy fang
> And churlish chiding of the winter's wind,
> Which when it bites and blows upon my body,
> Even till I shrink with cold, I smile and say

'This is no flattery; these are counsellors
That feelingly persuade me what I am'.
Sweet are the uses of adversity . . .

When the Duke speaks of 'old custom' he could mean that he and
his friends have got used to roughing it by now, but he surely means,
beyond that, that they have returned to the simplicity of Ovid's
first two ages. The condition of the silver age, 'the seasons' difference',
is certainly present, but, by contrast with the iron age at court, the
Duke does not 'feel' the cold and is mentally back, living with Nature,
in the golden age. Many of Shakespeare's editors prefer 'but' to
the Folio's reading, 'not', in the Duke's fifth line ('Here feel we not the
penalty of Adam'), arguing that since the Duke must suffer from the
Fall, like everyone else, he can only be saying that he is happy now
to have no more than Adam's penalty to put up with; and, in favour
of 'but', one editor (J. W. Holme) remarks that 'it is perhaps over-
refinement on Whiter's part to suggest that "the seasons' difference"
is not specifically mentioned in Genesis as part of Adam's penalty; it
was surely a natural corollary of the curse'. According to Golding,
however, in his interpretative Epistle to Leicester, Ovid's cosmology
must have been taken from *Genesis*, and hence the seasons' difference
as described by Ovid was not merely a natural corollary to the loss of
Paradise, but a direct consequence:[1]

Moreover by the golden age what other thing is ment,
Than Adam's time in Paradyse, who being innocent
Did lead a blist and happy lyfe untill that thurrough sin
He fell from God? From which tyme foorth all sorrow did begin.
The earth accursed for his sake; did never after more
Yeeld foode without great toyle. Both heate and cold did vexe him sore.
Disease of body, care of mynd, with hunger, thirst and neede,
Feare, hope, joy, greefe, and trouble, fell on him and on his seede.
And this is termd the silver age.

Golding is too zealous, and his gloss on the silver age partly contradicts his translation. But the seasons' difference is certainly the
main topic of the few lines he and Ovid devote to that era; and the
Duke's point in Shakespeare is (as the Folio says) that he does *not*
feel even the penalty of the silver age, because he has returned in
spirit to the golden age's innocence.

   A difficulty occurs, however. The Duke wants to hunt; which
brings him up against Pythagoras:

[1] Golding (ed. Nims), *Epistle*, lines 338ff, 469ff.

> Come, shall we go and kill us venison?
> And yet it irks me the poor dappled fools,
> Being native burghers of this desert city,
> Should in their own confines with forked heads
> Have their round haunches gored.

The Duke cannot live consistently in the 'old custom' of the golden age. To rub the point home, the First Lord quotes Jaques, 'moralizing the spectacle' of the wounded and 'sequest'red' stag. The Lord's report of Jaques's view begins and ends by comparing the exiled Duke with the usurper:

> Thus most invectively he pierceth through
> The body of the country, city, court,
> Yea, and of this our life, swearing that we
> Are mere usurpers, tyrants, and what's worse,
> To fright the animals and to kill them up
> In their assign'd and native dwelling-place.

Jaques is no Pythagorean; he is more like a Cynic philosopher in his attacks on all forms of social convention (like Diogenes, for instance, as represented in Lyly's play, *Alexander, Campaspe and Diogenes*, or in the literary satire of the 1590s). He is what Lovejoy and Boas would call a hard primitivist, not a soft one like Ovid.[1] But he brings out right away a contradiction in the Duke's position.

A similar contradiction to the dream of living in the golden age again comes out in what – after a quick flash-back to Duke Frederick at court – is nearly an immediate sequel, the scene (II.iii) between Orlando and Adam. As Adam (whose name Shakespeare has retained from Lodge) warns his young master to escape in time, he exclaims,

> O what a world is this, when what is comely
> Envenoms him that bears it!

The old man is at pains to point out that he has kept his health thanks to temperate living when he offers to accompany Orlando; and Orlando praises him as a survivor from some feudalised golden age:

> O good old man, how well in thee appears
> The constant service of the antique world,
> When service sweat for duty, not for meed!

---

[1] See O. J. Campbell, *Comicall Satyre*; Lecocq, *La Satire en Angleterre de 1588 à 1603*, pp. 291ff; *cf* Lovejoy and Boas, *Primitivism in Antiquity*, ch. 4.

But what he is grateful to Adam for is the offer of his 'gold', his 'thrifty' life-savings, appurtenances of the age of iron.

Potential contradictions of this sort have begun even earlier, in the first scene, where Orlando has complained of his treatment by Oliver:

call you that keeping for a gentleman of my birth, that differs not from the stalling of an ox?... [He] mines my gentility with my education... You have train'd me like a peasant, obscuring and hiding from me all gentleman-like qualities.

In his character, Orlando illustrates Lodge's pastoral argument that Nature, 'ingrafted in the heart', will be stronger than nurture in the end;[1] but in his speeches, he appeals from Nature to breeding and 'the courtesy of nations'. On the other hand, when the two princesses appear in the next scene, the devoted Celia suggests, to cheer up her cousin, that they should

sit and mock the good housewife Fortune from her wheel, that her gifts may henceforth be bestowed equally.

This speech opens a second series of antitheses in the dialogue, Nature against Fortune. Since it is Fortune and courtly malice that have started the plot moving, some of the antitheses that now come up in the course of the play can be aligned together – Court/Country, Fortune/Nature, this world/the golden age. But other contrasts brought out in the course of the dialogue cut across this neat opposition of terms – breeding/Nature and Wit/Folly, for instance. Again, there are the antitheses of prose and poetry, satire and love or charity, the genuine and the 'counterfeit', a 'holiday humour' and the acknowledgment of Time. They all revolve around the central situation, without forming a straightforward or continuous debate.

Nevertheless, *As You Like It* comes nearer in form to a discussion play or a symposium than any other of Shakespeare's comedies. Not only is the action punctuated by songs; there is much reporting of meetings and conversations, and the comparatively uneventful plot marks time while the actors talk. On the other hand, although there is no formal play within the play, there are several tableau scenes such as those Kyd and Greene had used and Shakespeare himself had used with Puck, where some characters are watching others as spectators, and then step forward and interfere. In the wrestling scene

---

[1] Lodge, *Rosalynde*, in Bullough, *Sources*, vol. II, p. 164.

(I.ii), for instance, interest is divided between contestants and spectators; Rosalind and Celia are twice onlookers of the 'pageant' of Silvius's love (II.iv, III.iv–v), and the second time Rosalind determines, like Puck, to 'prove a busy actor in their play'; Jaques watches Touchstone's wooing of Audrey, and interferes (III.iii); the final wedding masque is contrived by Rosalind's theatrical 'magic'. And there is a dramatic movement of give-and-take between episodes consisting mainly of dialogue or song.

The discussion scene between the Duke and Jaques (II.vii) illustrates this movement. It has a kind of prologue, in the Duke's first scene, where Jaques has merely been reported (II.i); and it almost forms a miniature drama in five acts. At first (1–7), the Duke is looking for Jaques, whom he calls 'a beast' for avoiding company (an ironic echo of Jaques's sympathy for the isolated stag); he is surprised to hear he has been 'merry', and to meet him in the same mood. When they meet, there are two long character-sketches (8–87), Jaques describing Touchstone and then, with the Duke's comments, describing his own '[ambition] for a motley coat'. He has been delighted that a mere 'fool', a 'motley fool', could 'rail' on the 'miserable world' and Lady Fortune 'in good set terms', while he 'laid him down and bask'd him in the sun'; and he has been impressed by Touchstone's 'lack-lustre' contemplation of his watch –

> 'And so, from hour to hour, we ripe and ripe,
> And then, from hour to hour, we rot and rot;
> And thereby hangs a tale.'

But what attracts Jaques (much like that other talkative gentleman, Gratiano, in *The Merchant of Venice*) to the idea of playing the fool on the world's stage is not merely his patronising sympathy with the jester's sour wisdom, but his desire for a jester's 'liberty', his irresponsibility (and, by implication, his indifference to the passage of time). He expects the world 'patiently' to 'receive [his] medicine'; and when the Duke observes that he would be an insincere 'libertine', trying to 'disgorge' his own remorse on others, Jaques has the evasive but rhetorically effective reply that moral satire or denunciation is universal, not personal. Between the optimist and the pessimist, the honours are fairly even.

Here Orlando interrupts, 'with his sword drawn', demanding food for 'necessity' (88–135). Jaques greets him with sarcasm, the Duke with courtesy. But Orlando's appeal to sentiment undercuts the

Duke's former complacency as well as the asperity of Jaques; it upsets the dream of a 'golden world', where men can 'fleet the time carelessly':

> whate'er you are
> That in this desert inaccessible,
> Under the shade of melancholy boughs,
> Lose and neglect the creeping hours of time;
> If ever you have look'd on better days,
> If ever been where bells have knoll'd to church,
> If ever sat at any good man's feast,
> If ever from your eyelids wiped a tear
> And know what 'tis to pity and be pitied,
> Let gentleness my strong enforcement be:
> In the which hope I blush and hide my sword.

Although this contradicts the Duke's views about the world outside of Arden, he responds, and Orlando goes to fetch Adam, 'like a doe,...to find my fawn | And give it food' – an unconscious reply to Jaques's theory of animal psychology. Orlando had said at first,

> I thought that all things had been savage here;
> And therefore put I on the countenance
> Of stern commandment.

Now the Duke picks up the thought of the masks imposed by Fortune, at the same time resuming his dialogue with Jaques:

> Thou seest we are not all alone unhappy:
> This wide and universal theatre
> Presents more woeful pageants than the scene
> Wherein we play in.

His lines have a neat general or allegorical application: he is an exile, who was once a prince; he is an actor in the Globe, where other plays have been and will be given; he is a man in the real world.[1] But he is also answering Jaques's wish to declaim at 'liberty' against the pride universal in others – 'we are not all alone unhappy'. The Duke's sense of charity counters the bitterness of the satirist, and his solitude. And, seeing that we are 'all' actors, the Duke poses again the question of Jaques's sincerity.

Jaques responds with the well-known commonplace (from Palingenius, no doubt):

[1] Jacquot, ' "Le Théâtre du Monde" ', p. 345.

> All the world's a stage,
> And all the men and women merely players:
> They have their exits and their entrances;
> And one man in his time plays many parts,
> His acts being seven ages...

All of Jaques's ages are incarnations of human vanity, looking before or after, and pining for what is not; only the fifth age shows satisfaction, and that is really complacency:

> And then the justice
> In fair round belly with good capon lined,
> With eyes severe and beard of formal cut,
> Full of wise saws and modern instances;
> And so he plays his part.

Whereafter man returns to the ages of 'youthful hose, well saved, a world too wide | For his shrunk shank', and of 'second childishness'. If this is Palingenius's wisdom, it is also Touchstone's; but Jaques has apparently forgotten Erasmus's version of the lessons of Folly, which the Duke has remembered: 'if anyone tries to take the masks off the actors...he'll certainly spoil the whole play and deserve to be ...thrown out of the theatre'. And, as he and the Duke have been commenting on Orlando's stage action, now Orlando's action reflects on Jaques; he comes back, supporting his 'venerable burden', Adam. This gives a different picture of the cycle of the ages; and although Adam qualifies for Jaques's 'last scene of all' in years, 'second childishness and mere oblivion' is not how the audience have seen him. Then, as Amiens sings a song which partly restores the euphoric mood of the golden world –

> Blow, blow, thou winter wind,
> Thou art not so unkind
> As man's ingratitude –

and partly echoes the 'merry' misanthrope of Jaques –

> Most friendship is feigning, most loving mere folly:
> Then, heigh-ho, the holly!
> This life is most jolly –

the Duke belies the song's statements (but chimes with its feeling) by asking Orlando sympathetically about his 'fortune'. The play prepares to move forward, in spite of Jaques's objection that it is only a play.

When Jaques next appears (III.ii), he comes on with Orlando, complaining of Orlando's love-poems and asking him either to leave him to himself or to join him in railing 'against our mistress the world'; to which the lover replies, in the manner of the Duke, 'I will chide no breather in the world but myself, against whom I know most faults.' As Orlando strikes the note of sincerity, he is met by Rosalind – who has been watching them – assuming a part:

I will speak to him like a saucy lackey, and under that habit play the knave with him.

This is not the same part she had assumed at first with her male disguise ('a swashing and a martial outside'), and in a few moments she is offering to assume yet another part, that of Rosalind herself. Here Shakespeare embroiders on Lodge's story. Unlike Lodge's heroine, Shakespeare's Rosalind pretends to have played a similar part before, and pretends to undertake it again so as to 'cure' Orlando of love.[1] And, in contrast to Jaques's 'medicine' of satire, her 'cure' is to be homoeopathic; she and Orlando are to pretend to woo.

In contrast, again, to Jaques, Rosalind maintains that Time is relative; it 'travels in divers paces with divers persons'. She cannot keep up this position when Orlando is late for an appointment, just as she cannot keep up her 'counterfeit' when she hears he has been injured. But her play-acting enables her to keep Orlando near her, to marry him in pretence, to 'cure' the deadlock between Silvius and Phoebe and to prepare the wedding-masque with pretended magic when (after the fashion of an Italian double plot) her real marriage is hurried forward by Celia's. Her 'cure' has the effect of dispelling the fantasies of courtship in jokes, like the frightening but harmless adventures of the Athenian lovers in the wood. In effect, it is an application of the lesson of the two faces of Silenus in Erasmus's sermon of Folly.

One modern commentator on *As You Like It* thinks Rosalind is merely playful: 'in her scenes with Orlando, [she] is in no danger; thus her original reason for pretending to be a man does not apply. Yet she does pretend, and it is only her disguise that prevents their immediate marriage.'[2] This, surely, is to overlook a cardinal social

[1] Bullough, *Sources*, vol. II, p. 211; *cf* Muir, *Shakespeare's Sources*, vol. I, p. 60.
[2] Albert Gilman (ed.), *As You Like It*, in *Complete Signet Classic Shakespeare*, ed. Barnet, p. 839.

assumption in the play (which would have been obvious to a dramatist like Marivaux, as well as to Shakespeare's first audiences) – that Rosalind is a princess, while Orlando is no more than a gentleman. But for the misfortune of her father's exile, they might not have met in sympathy as at first; but for the second misfortune of her own exile, as well as his, they could not have met in apparent equality in the Forest. She can hardly marry him 'immediately', after two minutes of stage talk, without appearing a simpleton like Audrey. As in Lodge's story, it is 'the good housewife Fortune' who unexpectedly makes their courtship and marriage possible. But Shakespeare's Rosalind is not merely carried round on the wheel. He shows her acting – in both senses of the word – as well. Her first disguise is imposed by Fortune; but he shows her deciding on a further part after two phases of discussion in the play – the discussion which shows that living in the golden world, as an escape from Fortune, is an unrealisable dream, and the discussion of the consequences of recognising that all the world's a stage. In the background action of the play, 'feigning' corrupts a humane society; Rosalind's 'counterfeiting' restores it. Shakespeare uses the moralists' commonplace of the world as a stage, not to insist on the vanity of life, but to recapture the original, primary purpose of comedy.

MARRIAGES AND MAGISTRATES

Scholars investigating Shakespeare's narrative sources (as distinct from the sources of poetic images) usually give the impression, intentionally or not, that he must have looked about for fresh material nearly every time he had to write a new play. On the face of it, this seems unlikely. It seems most unlikely that during the early and middle years of his career there were no stories in his head, waiting to be staged; or that when he came across a new story that interested him, he did not think about resemblances and connections with other stories that he knew already. On the one hand, all the evidence of his poetic imagery points to continuity in his imagination across the years, as well as far-reaching, unexpected and no doubt intimately personal ramifications. On the other hand, the evidence of his treatment of source material in his English and Roman history plays points to purposeful research, though not with the scholarly purposes of Ben Jonson. I believe that something similar holds good of his comedies: that they can be grouped (though not strictly into separate genres, since Shakespeare's interests evidently crossed theoretical boundaries, even those between comedy and tragedy), and that the grouping of his comedies by mood and structure corresponds to a grouping in the literary or theatrical sources he made use of. Some of this grouping of his comedies in tune with their sources was provided beforehand, by history. But in some respects I believe it was Shakespeare's personal choice, conscious and deliberate.

In *As You Like It*, the lovers and other leading characters take to the greenwood to escape from the reigning prince, and there the difficulties which originated at the court are resolved. The lovers are united, the exiled Duke finds his daughter again, and he can prepare to return to his throne without the need for a battle, as in Lodge, because it is reported that the usurper has been converted by 'an old religious man' as soon as he and his army have reached 'the skirts of this wild wood'. There is a similar flight from power, and a similar general reconciliation brought about in the greenwood, in *Two Gentlemen of Verona* and *A Midsummer Night's Dream*; and *Love's Labour's Lost* can be grouped with these three plays, in so far as the action takes place in a park and woodland; the King and his friends are there because the King himself wishes to evade his regal responsibilities, and the countryside is the scene where the lords find love and rid themselves of affectation.

Since Lodge's *Rosalynde* was published before *Two Gentlemen*, the earliest of these four comedies, was written, it could possibly have provided Shakespeare with his leading idea for all four. In any case, the structural idea was prominent in pastoral romances Shakespeare read or could have known about early in his career, such as Montemayor's *Diana* and Sidney's *Arcadia*. And, more important than the strictly pastoral theme, with its hellenistic antecedents, the pattern of a narrative alternating between court and the 'wild wood' was prominent in medieval romances, such as the *Tale of Gamelyn*, which Lodge transposed into the terms of a Renaissance love story in *Rosalynde*, or Chaucer's *Knight's Tale*, which Shakespeare used in *A Midsummer Night's Dream* (and again, much later, in *Two Noble Kinsmen*). Moreover, such a pattern had been common in stage romances since Chaucer's time, both in plays dealing with chivalric lovers and in plays dealing with the motifs that attracted Shakespeare, the trials of a father who has lost his rights or his family, and the sufferings of a calumniated wife. In *Two Gentlemen*, Silvia's choice of a champion to protect her in her escape, Sir Eglamour, harks back to such a verse romance, which had been dramatised in England in the fifteenth century.[1] Plays on these lines (as I have tried to show in chapter 2) must have been among the earliest that Shakespeare saw. And he returns to this cluster of motifs from Renaissance pastoral literature and late medieval or Tudor dramatised romance in his last comedies, from *Pericles* onwards.

Among the twelve comedies which occupied about half his writing time until *Measure for Measure*, when there is a gap in this section of his work, followed by a change of mood and style, four others are mainly derived from classical or Italian learned comedies: *Errors*, *The Shrew*, *The Merry Wives* and *Twelfth Night*. From Shakespeare's point of view, the classical tradition, whether in Roman or Italian guise, was more modern than the plays he must have seen as a boy; and he applies the structural devices of the Renaissance double plot and the fundamental classical notion of comedy as a matter of 'errors' due to trickery, disguise or Fortune to the plays of broadly pastoral and medieval inspiration, where he invents the details of the plot himself (*Two Gentlemen*, *Love's Labour's Lost* and the *Dream*), as well as enlarging on these structural principles in his play from Lodge's *Rosalynde*, where they were already present. For Shakespeare, these principles, with the latent awareness they carry of play-acting within the play, mark the distinctive feature of comedy in general, the difference between comedy and romance.

Nevertheless, the four plays borrowed largely from pre-existing classical comedies have certain features as a group. Three of them can be called farces, and in *Twelfth Night* farcical elements in the plot modify the emotional tone of romance in the leading actors. All four turn on transformations of identity, as do the woodland plays, but in the plays of classical origin the transformations are carried forward purely by deception or tricks due to chance; except for the woodland scene in *The Merry Wives*, which arises from trickery, they are entirely urban or courtly, like their prototypes. There are no episodes of magic in them, except what is supposed to be delusory; like classical comedies, they mainly represent the capacity of ordinary citizens, helped, at most, by Fortune, to sort out their private affairs without needing to escape to the greenwood from the overmastering authority of the prince. Two of them have no princely characters. Solinus, in *The Comedy of Errors*, springs from Shakespeare's medieval antecedents, and Shakespeare keeps him on the margin of the main plot. In *Twelfth*

Night, we see something of Orsino's role as a prince, but this is secondary to his role as lover, and only affects his actions indirectly; it makes very little difference that Shakespeare has shifted part of his borrowed plot to the court from the city.

One important set of devices, related to Shakespeare's position as an Elizabethan playwright, links two of these urban comedies and three of the woodland plays: the devices Charles Barber has analysed in his book on *Shakespeare's Festive Comedies*. There are passages of jester's patter or moments of song interspersed through the action in all eight of the comedies I have been mentioning; but with *Love's Labour's Lost*, Shakespeare began to incorporate episodes of revelry or pageantry or pastime in the action of his comedies. Moreover, in *Love's Labour's Lost*, the *Dream*, *As You Like It*, and in *The Merry Wives* and *Twelfth Night*, such episodes are either made crucial to the unfolding of the plot, or set the tone of a large part of the play, or both. As a series of variations on the theme of the play within the play, these structural devices illustrate Shakespeare's interest in his own professional medium; at the same time, they illustrate his concern with the place of revels, pastime and comedy as such in the national life.

There are, however, four of his comedies to which these considerations do not apply, or do not apply in the same way: *The Merchant of Venice*, *Much Ado*, *All's Well* and *Measure for Measure*. They were all written after *A Midsummer Night's Dream* and *Romeo and Juliet*, between 1596 (probably) and 1604, towards the middle of the dramatist's career; they were contemporary at first with his *Henry IV* plays and *Henry V*, and then with the beginning of his dominant interest in tragedy. The main plots of all four come directly or indirectly from a common type of literary source, Italian *novelle:* *The Merchant of Venice* from Ser Giovanni Fiorentino, the Hero and Claudio plot in *Much Ado* from Bandello (like *Romeo and Juliet*), *All's Well* from Boccaccio (like much of the central plot, the wager story, in *Cymbeline* later), and *Measure for Measure* from Giraldi (like Shakespeare's next play, *Othello*). And these four comedies are distinguished in mood and structure from Shakespeare's other comedies, even those he was writing about the same time. There are scenes of revelry in *The Merchant of Venice* (1596) and *Much Ado* (1598), but they are marginal to the main plot, not central; while in *All's Well* (*c.* 1602) and *Measure for Measure* (1604) there are no such scenes at all. The tone of these comedies is more serious than usual with

Shakespeare; they are sometimes tense or sombre, bordering on the tragic. *All's Well* and *Measure for Measure* are often described as 'problem' plays, and I shall use this term as a convenient label to denote characteristics common to all four, distinguishing them as a group. All four bring in trickery or disguise, as usual, and as usual Fortune (coincidence) comes to the aid of the heroine or her friends. But the heroine or her friends now have a serious, deliberate opponent to deal with at the centre of the intrigue: Shylock, Don John, Bertram, Angelo. And this opposition can no longer be fought out by trickery or trickery and luck alone; there has to be recourse to the law. One prominent feature common to all four of these plays is that each has one or more trial scenes, or scenes approximating to a trial (the accusation of Hero in the church, for instance). In *The Merchant* and *Measure for Measure*, a trial scene was a datum from the original story; in *Much Ado* and *All's Well*, Shakespeare invents it. What Bandello and Boccaccio provided for these two plays were problems arising from a nobleman's sense of his honour, with a prince's authority in the background; what Shakespeare does here is to bring the prince forward, just as he introduces the Doge into *The Merchant of Venice* and greatly enlarges the ruler's part in *Measure for Measure*. However, justice as the ruler's prime responsibility, the prince as the supreme earthly judge, are twin Renaissance themes close to the centre of all four plots Shakespeare has borrowed or adapted. Like his classical comedies, these four are predominantly urban; in *The Merchant*, the earliest of them, there is a difference between the commercial atmosphere of Venice and the serenity of Belmont, but even so, there is no escape into the woodland. But they are like the woodland comedies in that their plots revolve round the authority of the prince, except that there is something in the spirit of these encounters with the law that can fairly be called problematic rather than romantic.

Secondly, another striking feature links these four comedies and sets them apart from the others. Normally, Shakespeare's comedies lead up to a wedding celebration at the end (in *The Shrew*, there are ceremonies mid-way, but the real celebration is postponed to the last scene). In the four problem comedies something very different happens; either a wedding is legalised or about to be celebrated, or a union is consummated, early or in the middle of the play, but then the completion of the marriage is abruptly interrupted, and the heroine or her allies must perform a difficult task or resolve a quandary connected with the law before there can be a sense of celebration on the stage.

Immediately after their wedding ceremony, and before their marriage can be consummated, Portia hurries Bassanio away from Belmont to save Antonio, and follows him secretly to Venice; 'this looks not like a nuptial', as Benedick says in the church scene in *Much Ado*; Bertram weds Helena under duress, but refuses to bed her; for Claudio's secret union in *Measure for Measure*, he is under sentence of death. They are all stories of broken nuptials.

It is true that it is partly Shakespeare who has made them so: in Ser Giovanni, for instance, the Lady of Belmonte and Giannetto have been living together for some time before the husband, immersed in happiness, recalls his foster-father's deadly bond; and in Giraldi's story and its variants prior to *Measure to Measure*, the heroine's brother is sentenced for rape, not for an ecclesiastically faulty but legally binding marriage. Shakespeare, therefore, was looking for such dramatic possibilities, not merely finding them. Nevertheless, the four *novelle* contained what he was looking for. And it is striking that Shakespeare's other three leading plots derived from *novella* sources, in *Romeo and Juliet*, *Othello* and the wager story in *Cymbeline*, are all likewise centred on broken nuptials. Evidently, Shakespeare turned to Italian *novelle* for a particular type of plot.

That Shakespeare should have used Italian *novelle* in some way is not unusual at all. Ever since – to Roger Ascham's indignation – Brooke, Painter and others had been translating them in the 1560s, these stories had provided the most modern and interesting kind of fiction available to Elizabethan readers,[1] and they were frequently used by dramatists in England, especially after 1580, just as they were used by their Spanish contemporaries. But most of the later Elizabethan plays founded largely or mainly on Italian fiction fall broadly into two types. They are either farces of domestic intrigue, as represented in *The Merry Wives of Windsor*, or bloodthirsty tragedies of state, like *The Duchess of Malfi*. It is noticeable, however, that Shakespeare prefers to draw his tragedies of state from sources in Roman or British history (if *Hamlet* may be included among the latter) and that his two tragedies from Italian sources are mainly domestic. Unfortunately no Elizabethan comedy based on an Italian *novella* earlier than *The Merchant of Venice* has survived, except for Whetsone's *Promos and Cassandra* (which may not have been acted) although as early as 1582 Gosson mentions Painter's *Palace of Pleasure* in his list of sources

---

[1] See Pruvost, *Bandello*; Schlauch, *Antecedents of the English Novel*. Cf above, ch. 2, p. 72.

'ransackt to furnish the Play houses in London'. But though Shakespeare had predecessors in using Italian prose fiction for comedy, he was still making his own selection from the stories by Bandello, Giraldi or Boccaccio made current at the time in England,[1] a selection which expresses a distinct personal taste. The quandaries in his problem comedies, like the freeing of Antonio from his bond, came ultimately from folk-tales.[2] But Boccaccio and his successors had been noteworthy for their skill in surrounding such tales with modern circumstances and giving them an air of truth to reality; and this may well have attracted the dramatist. More particularly, Shakespeare was evidently interested in stories for dramatic material with two strong elements together, broken nuptials and a crisis involving the law. And he used such stories both for tragedy and comedy.

Of the seven *novelle* in all that Shakespeare used for leading dramatic plots, six had been translated or closely copied in English or in French before the dates of his plays,[3] but since Ser Giovanni's book does not appear to have been translated, he may have read that and even others in Italian (that Shakespeare knew more of Ser Giovanni's book than one tale seems quite probable from *The Merry Wives*). Whetstone had dramatised Giraldi's story of Epitia in *Promos and Cassandra*, which Shakespeare knew by 1595, when he was writing *Love's Labour's Lost*,[4] and which probably suggested some of the secondary action as well as the choice of subject for the main plot in *Measure for Measure*; but apart from that, and Brooke's reference to a lost play on Romeo and Juliet, which must have been acted about 1561, before Shakespeare was born, there is no clear evidence of any English play in Shakespeare's time which could have led him directly to his choice of *novelle*. He may possibly have read a lost manuscript translation of Ser Giovanni, as he evidently read Bartholomew Yonge's translation of *Diana* before it was printed. And we should not leave out of account the possibility that Shakespeare heard one or more of his source-stories told in detail by a friend (the convention of oral narrative is so firmly established in fiction, from Boccaccio and Chaucer to Bandello and Marguerite of Navarre, and Sidney and Cervantes, that it must have had a basis in social custom; and writers of Shakespeare's time were even more likely to pay attention to after-dinner anecdotes than a modern story-teller like Henry James).[5] In one way or another,

---

[1] Pruvost, *Bandello*, pp. 214ff.   [2] Lawrence, *Shakespeare's Problem Comedies*.
[3] See Bullough, *Sources*.   [4] See p. 275, n. 1, above.
[5] *Cf* Bennett, *English Books and Readers, 1558 to 1603*, pp. 10ff.

his reception of any Italian story he used may have been coloured by other minds besides the first author's.

What is important here, however, is the kind of story he selected, in the light of the use he made of it. The evidence of his choice of Italian plots, as compared with his contemporaries' choice, seems to show either that he specially noted, and even looked out for, stories of a special type, or else, equally likely, that he was only interested in using a selection from the Italian stories he knew. His interest in stories combining broken nuptials and a legal crisis must have grown from the beginning of his career, and his recognition of the attraction Italian *novelle* held for him must have crystallised towards 1595, when, after five or six years in which he had written five English history plays, one Roman melodrama, and four comedies (including *Love's Labour's Lost*), he produced *Romeo and Juliet*, his first play based on an Italian story. I believe there is strong internal evidence also that he knew three, possibly all four, of the stories behind his problem comedies about this time, although the writing of them was spread over nearly ten years; and that, as he planned them, he thought of each of the problem comedies, together with *Romeo and Juliet*, as belonging to a connected group.

This evidence points towards central issues in his comedies. Shakespeare often laughs at Justices of the Peace and constables, the amateur administrators of the law, but he treats professional lawyers and judges and, above all, the law itself, with almost unvarying respect. The morality plays he could have seen as a young man were full of appeals to the magistrate to stamp out vice and disorder, or, more earnestly, to carry out his high calling with integrity; their influence is apparent in semi-allegorical plays from narrative sources, like *Appius and Virginia* (*c.* 1564) and *Promos and Cassandra*, with its sub-plot of legal corruption and redress. And Kyd's *Spanish Tragedy* is the tragedy of a judge. Shakespeare's early history plays are focused on the same general question of law and order. In *1 Henry VI*, for example, he invents or popularises the legend, that the Wars of the Roses took their origin from a quarrel between noblemen in the Temple Garden (II.iv). The disputants are evidently members of one of the Inns of Court, as aristocrats of Shakespeare's time could well be, but he shows them over-riding the law with baronial arrogance:

> Faith, I have been a truant in the law

> And never yet could frame my will to it;
> And therefore frame the law unto my will.

Conversely, when depicting Cade's rebellion in *2 Henry VI*, he departs from his immediate sources and inserts material dealing with the Peasants' Revolt, so as to show that a principal motive with the rebels was blind hatred of the law. And in *Richard II* he insists on the obligation of the king himself to observe the law, enlarging Holinshed's statement (that Richard's seizure of Herford's 'lawful inheritance' after his father's death increased the people's 'hatred' towards the king) into a vehement and prophetic plea by the Duke of York (II.i):

> Take Herford's rights away, and take from time
> His charters and his customary rights;
> Let not tomorrow then ensue today:
> Be not thyself. For how art thou a king
> But by fair sequence and succession?

The same legalism comes out again in Shakespeare's treatment of the Lord Chief Justice's part in *2 Henry IV*.

In some of the comedies (*Two Gentlemen* and *As You Like It*), it is the ruler's will that affects the plot, not the law as such. In others – *Love's Labour's Lost* and *Much Ado* (which have several points of contact) – a prince trips over his own mistaken attitude to the law: thus, even before the King of Navarre meets the Princess who will upset his vow, the clown, Costard, can quibble with him (I.i) over 'hearing' (or 'marking') his proclamation against being 'taken' with a 'damsel' (or 'wench'); and in *Much Ado* (v.i) Dogberry produces Borachio as a witness against Don John, just when Don Pedro and Claudio, John's dupes, have been preening themselves on their wit – 'What your wisdoms could not discover, these shallow fools have brought to light.' But in at least six of the comedies there is a complex of narrative images connected with the law which carry a much stronger emotional charge. It can be described as the complex of the judge and the nun. Typically, it is like this: a man is legally condemned, though morally blameless; his judge is divided between law and mercy. If the judge has the man executed, he will also compel a woman to enter a convent, or stay there. If the woman can leave the convent, the man will be saved. This situation may very well represent a personal tension fundamental to Shakespeare's comedies.

The complex appears in the earliest of them in the romantic

framing plot of *The Comedy of Errors*. Egeon is morally innocent, but
has been arrested and condemned to death in accordance with
Ephesian law, as a citizen from the enemy state of Syracuse, who is
unable to pay his ransom. At the beginning of the first scene, Solinus
has evidently been overruling the merchant's plea for mercy:

> Merchant of Syracusa, plead no more;
> I am not partial to infringe our laws.
> The enmity and discord which of late
> Sprung from the rancorous outrage of your duke
> To merchants, our well-dealing countrymen,
> Who, wanting guilders to redeem their lives,
> Have seal'd his rigorous statutes with their bloods,
> Excludes all pity from our threat'ning looks.

This sounds like a revenge situation from Shakespeare's Wars of the
Roses, except that where the duke of Syracuse has apparently made
his will the law, the duke of Ephesus claims to obey the law, nothing
else. By the end of the scene, when Egeon has described how he has
been searching for his family, the ruler softens a little:

> Now, trust me, were it not against our laws,
> Against my crown, my oath, my dignity,
> Which princes, would they, may not disannul,
> My soul should sue as advocate for thee.

He is a constitutional monarch, not a despot; but the most he can
allow his prisoner is a day's respite. At the end of the day, however,
when the duke returns to the stage in procession with Egeon and the
headsman, Adriana pleads to him for 'justice' against the Abbess who
has sheltered Antipholus (supposedly Adriana's husband), and the
Abbess comes out again from her priory – to be revealed as Egeon's
lost wife, Emilia, and to bring about the recognition scene, in which
the duke pardons Egeon without even accepting the ransom money
from his Ephesian son. Now, the long-lost wife who reappears
providentially from a convent had figured in antecedent romances
(like *Apollonius of Tyre*), and so had the episode of a family recognition
bringing a last-minute reprieve from execution (a hellenistic motif
reproduced in Barnabe Riche's story of Sappho, Duke of Mantona).[1]
But Shakespeare has linked the two motifs independently, at the same
time bringing in the motif of the enmity between cities from *Supposes*

[1] See p. 65, above.

and heightening it to give emotional force to the idea of the rigour of the law. By the end of his play, after other legal incidents of arrest for debt, it appears as if the handy-pandy of comic mistakes of identity has had the consequence, and even, in part, the emotional function, of providing a way out from the law's logic. This sets the pattern for Shakespeare's later comedies. It is significant that he has put together fragments from a variety of sources so as to produce this result.

In *The Comedy of Errors* the connection between the judge and the nun does not come out until the end; in *A Midsummer Night's Dream*, it is stressed at the beginning. In a tone of solemnity, Hermia appeals to Theseus from her father's opposition:

> I do entreat your Grace to pardon me.
> I know not by what power I am made bold,
> Nor how it may concern my modesty
> In such a presence here to plead my thoughts;
> But I beseech your Grace that I may know
> The worst that may befall me in this case,
> If I refuse to wed Demetrius;

and Theseus, with a regal disregard for anachronism, replies:

> Either to die the death, or to abjure
> For ever the society of men.
> Therefore, fair Hermia, question your desires,
> Know of your youth, examine well your blood,
> Whether, if you yield not to your father's choice,
> You can endure the livery of a nun,
> For aye to be in shady cloister mew'd,
> To live a barren sister all your life,
> Chanting faint hymns to the cold fruitless moon.
> Thrice-blessed they that master so their blood
> To undergo such maiden pilgrimage;
> But earthlier happy is the rose distill'd
> Than that which withering on the virgin thorn
> Grows, lives, and dies, in single blessedness.

Like Solinus, Theseus is reluctant to impose the law, and gives Hermia a reprieve until 'the next new moon'; but then the law must take its course:

> Upon that day either prepare to die
> For disobedience to your father's will,
> Or else to wed Demetrius, as he would,

Or on Diana's altar to protest
For aye austerity and single life.

It is noticeable that the second alternative, the nunnery, is superfluous
to the plot, and that in addition Theseus has digressed to talk about
the Reformation. But the chastity motif, shadowed as it is by a father's
authority, backed by the stern law, gives emotional force and depth
to the main intrigue. And Theseus's digression softens any offence
to the Virgin Queen, Oberon's 'fair vestal, thronèd by the west', the
'imperial vot'ress', 'in maiden meditation, fancy-free' – who was apt to
interfere resentfully in the marriages of her courtiers. Here, the
threat of execution is directed against a woman, not a man, but the
connexion with *The Comedy of Errors* is obvious (and Lucina, the lost
wife in *Apollonius*, had become at Ephesus a priestess of Diana). In
this first scene, Theseus contents himself with admonishing Hermia
in front of her father, as constitutionally – it seems – he must, while
admitting, *en bon prince*, that he has overlooked his courtiers' affairs
because of his own, and hinting that he hopes to use his influence to
work a reconciliation:

> But, Demetrius, come;
> And come, Egeus; you shall go with me;
> I have some private schooling for you both.
> For you, fair Hermia, look you arm yourself
> To fit your fancies to your father's will,
> Or else the law of Athens yields you up –
> Which by no means we may extenuate –
> To death, or to a vow of single life.

What persuasion he could have used with Demetrius and Egeon we
are not allowed to know, because the lovers run away; but again, as
in *The Comedy of Errors*, a series of mistakes of identity absolves the
prince of the dilemma of choosing between mercy and the law, so that
when Demetrius waives his claim to Hermia, Egeon's angry demand
for 'the law upon his [Lysander's] head' (IV.i.152) – which takes us
back towards the situation in the earlier comedy – is inoperative.

In *A Midsummer Night's Dream*, what I have called the complex of
the judge and the nun is explicit, and determines the plot emotionally,
if not logically. In *The Merchant of Venice*, it is latent, but Shakespeare
has put it there. Portia goes to Venice to save Antonio from death,
in a trial where the judge hopes for mercy but is tied by the law;
this is merely a slight extension of the original story. But in Ser

Giovanni, the Lady of Belmonte is an independent princess, a kind of Circe, who lures adventurers to stake their wealth on the hope of satisfying her in bed, and defrauds them by means of drugs. Shakespeare censors this part of the story, substituting the parable of the caskets from the *Gesta Romanorum*, but introducing the parable material by way of the additional motif of Portia's father's testament. According to this motif, Portia says (with a possible double meaning in the last word of her sentence), 'If I live to be as old as Sibylla, I will die as chaste as Diana, unless I be obtained by the manner of my father's will' (I.ii.95). And, on her way to Venice, she pretends to lodge at a monastery in fulfilment of 'a secret vow' (III.iv.27). In effect, therefore, Shakespeare links the woman who saves the man from execution with a convent.

There is a faint echo, again, of the motif from *The Comedy of Errors* in *Twelfth Night*, at points where Shakespeare has departed from his sources. In the first scene, we learn that Olivia has vowed to live like a nun, not in obedience to her father's will, but as an aristocratic gesture of respect for her brother's memory:

> The element itself, till seven years' heat,
> Shall not behold her face at ample view;
> But like a cloistress she will veilèd walk,
> And water once a day her chamber round
> With eye-offending brine; all this to season
> A brother's dead love, which she would keep fresh
> And lasting in her sad remembrance.

This speech follows Orsino's comparison of himself to Actaeon, which implicity sets Olivia beside Diana. Interviewed by Viola, Olivia lifts her veil (I.v.218). And the revelation of her secret marriage to Sebastian in the last scene has the incidental result of freeing Antonio from bondage. This 'salt-water thief' has been at the 'mercies' of his 'enemies' before Orsino, who thus appears for the first time in his capacity of prince; and Antonio's role, as the merchant who risks his life for the love of a younger man, recalls Egeon as well as the other Antonio, in *The Merchant of Venice*. Shakespeare has added him to his original plot.

There is a variant of the theme of the judge and the nun in *Much Ado*, which perhaps should be added to the other six examples: once Don John's guilt has been exposed, Hero can be restored from her pretended burial, with a 'solemn hymn' addressed to Diana. In the church scene (IV.i), Claudio had told Hero,

> You seem to me as Dian in her orb,
> As chaste as is the bud ere it be blown;
> But you are more intemperate in your blood
> Than Venus, or those pamp'red animals
> That rage in savage sensuality;

and the Friar had considered the possibility of her taking the veil (IV.i.24); now, however (V.iii), Claudio reads by the monument,

> Done to death by slanderous tongues
> Was the Hero that here lies,

and the hymn follows, to music,

> Pardon, goddess of the night,
> Those that slew thy virgin knight;

in this case, therefore, justice releases Diana's votaress.

In the trial scene in *All's Well* (v.iii.275f), the reverse happens: in the cause of justice, Diana – the character named so by Shakespeare – releases Bertram and restores Helena to her husband just when Bertram is under sentence of death. Not only Diana's name, but this whole scene is of Shakespeare's devising. And in *Measure for Measure*, his complex of the judge and the nun takes over the whole story. His is the first version of the story of 'the monstrous ransom', or the unjust judge, the condemned brother and the maiden, in which the sister is a novice, about to enter a nunnery. Here the tensions between sexuality and authority, justice and mercy are crucial as never before. And Shakespeare places the solution of the dilemma in the hands of the supreme judge, the Duke, and makes him offer marriage to Isabella at the end, having previously given him the disguise of a friar. Shakespeare's friars are not, as Brooke had called them in his Preface to *Romeus and Juliet*, 'the naturally fitte instrumentes of unchastitie', but the disinterested friends of love-matches and justice. And in *Measure for Measure*, the friar-judge introduces and rescues another frustrated wife, added to the plot by Shakespeare, the 'dejected Mariana', 'forsworn' and abandoned to her 'moated grange'.

It seems, then, that the complex of the judge and the nun represents feelings that were strong in Shakespeare, from the first comedy to the last that he produced in a more or less continuous series. Again and again, he adds it to his given main plot; when it is incidental, it still indicates his emotional reading of the main situation;

in his first comedy of the series, it is the key to his added framing plot, in the last it is dominant. Whatever may have been the origins of the complex in psychology, religion or folklore, it represents a conflict in his mind over the claims of love and the claims of law in Elizabethan society.

Shakespeare can hardly be said to resolve this conflict completely, but his dramatic treatment of it varies and his emphasis changes after the writing of *Romeo and Juliet*. In *Two Gentlemen* and again in *As You Like It*, the lovers escape from a prince's decision to the woodland, where they find happiness and reconciliation after leading the life of outlaws. Something similar happens in *The Comedy of Errors* and *A Midsummer Night's Dream*, where it is the law itself, and not merely the prince's will, that constitutes the threat to love. In *The Merchant of Venice*, however, he takes a plot where the threat from the law is crucial, but where it is removed by the heroine's ingenuity, not by escape or chance. And in three of the six comedies that follow, the three others from Italian *novelle*, he shows variants of the same crisis and the same solution: in *All's Well* it is the heroine herself who removes a bar against marriage, in *Measure for Measure*, the heroine with the help of her ally, the Duke. In *Much Ado*, it is folly, not wit, that carries out the task of love and justice, by virtue of Shakespeare's departure from his source; but at the same time he adds a second heroine, the witty Beatrice, who vehemently defends her cousin's good name, and insists that Benedick should fight a duel to champion it. One new feature, then, is the purposeful role assigned to the heroine, as in Boccaccio and his followers.

At the same time, the tone of these four comedies is more realistic, less romantic than before. In other respects, too, *The Merchant of Venice* marks the beginnings of a new departure – thereafter, for instance, there are more vivid or powerful characters in Shakespeare's comedies, a more reflective attitude towards human experience in the dialogue and a stronger tendency towards prose. To call the four *novella* comedies problem plays is in one important sense a misnomer, since they raise burning moral questions only to solve them in what are still terms of theatrical ingenuity, instead of by systematic analysis or thorough discussion pointing to a general conclusion. Nevertheless, the problems are there, a weighty factor in the new development of Shakespeare's comic art. It seems difficult to avoid the inference that about 1595 or 1596 Shakespeare turned to the *novelle* behind his problem plays, stories of broken nuptials and rational solutions within the social limits of renaissance rationality, precisely because he was looking for a new way of working out dramatically the emotional tension behind the complex of the judge and the nun. This inference seems the stronger if, as I believe, this group of stories was known to the dramatist and connected in his mind from the outset.

As a preliminary to setting out the specific evidence for these statements, it may be useful to return for a moment to *A Midsummer Night's Dream*, where Theseus threatens Hermia with confinement to a nunnery or else death if she disobeys her father in marriage. Either threat alone would have served the needs of the plot sufficiently; the death penalty sounds horribly excessive. Where did this Athenian statute come from? It is not likely that Shakespeare found it in Plutarch or in Chaucer; but there is a very probable source in the comparable situation in Brooke's *Romeus and Juliet*, where old Capilet storms at his 'wofull', weeping, 'groveling' daughter as she begs to be excused from marrying Count Paris (lines 1945ff):

> The syre, whose swelling wroth her teares could not asswage,
> With fiery eyen, and skarlet cheekes, thus spake her in his rage,
> Whilst ruthfully stood by the maydens mother mylde,
> Listen (quoth he) unthankfull and thou disobedient childe;
> Hast thou so soone let slip out of thy mynde the woord,
> That thou so often times hast heard rehearsed at my boord?
> How much the Romayne youth of parentes stood in awe,
> And eke what powre upon theyr seede the fathers had by lawe?
> Whom they not onely might pledge, alienate, and sell,
> (When so they stoode in neede) but more, if children did rebell,
> The parentes had the power, of lyfe and sodayn death.
> What if those goodmen should agayne receave the livyng breth,
> In how straight bondes would they thy stubberne body bynde?
> What weapons would they seeke for thee? what tormentes would they fynde?
> To chasten (if they saw) the lewdnes of thy lyfe,
> Thy great unthankfulnes to me, and shamefull sturdy strife?

Painter's version of the story in 1567 (influenced, like Brooke's, by the French translation published by Pierre Boaistuau in 1559) repeats in substance, though more briefly, the old man's invocation of 'the puissance and authority our ancient Roman fathers had over their children', and, like Brooke, Painter makes him threaten to force Juliet to 'espouse and marry a prison' if she disobeys him. No such lecture on *patria potestas* swells the story in Bandello; it intrudes here from Elizabethan authoritarianism. Shakespeare himself omits it as an irrelevance in his own treatment of the scene in *Romeo and Juliet* (III.v), contenting himself with making the angry father exclaim, more appropriately,

> Hang thee, young baggage! disobedient wretch!
> I tell thee what: get thee to church o' Thursday,
> Or never after look me in the face:
> Speak not, reply not, do not answer me;
> My fingers itch.

But if the dramatist ignored Brooke's legal tirade here, he evidently kept it for *A Midsummer Night's Dream*, even making it a kind of springboard for his plot. The story of Romeo and Juliet brings a release through death to the conflict of emotions between love and authority, winning over the law to the side of the lovers and chastening the angry fathers at the end. It must have been in Shakespeare's mind for some time before he wrote the play, since a dozen Elizabethan writers he could have read by the time he was twenty refer to Romeo as a famous lover, whether lamenting him as a 'martyr' or condemning his secret marriage, several of them coupling his name and Juliet's with those of Pyramus and Thisbe;[1] and Shakespeare had already chosen Verona as a suitable birthplace for gentlemen destined to meet authoritative opposition in their loves. *A Midsummer Night's Dream* provides a happy resolution to the conflict of ideas in *Romeo*; but here Shakespeare's interest in the conflict evidently persisted, to give shape to the problem comedies as well.

It would be out of place here to try to discuss Shakespeare's treatment of his *novella* sources in the problem comedies at length. I shall concentrate now instead on the evidence for linking them together and with *Romeo and Juliet*. For each of the four comedies, I shall list a number of details where Shakespeare differs from the story he is mainly following, and where the material he substitutes can be attributed either to the writing of *Romeo and Juliet* or another of his own comedies in the same group, or else to his knowledge of another of the source-stories in the same group, even prior to his using the

---

1 See references in Pruvost, *Bandello*, to Elizabethan works of fiction published between 1562 and 1583 (page-numbers in italics refer to authors who link Pyramus with Romeo): pp. 13ff, 16ff, 44, *71–2*, 75, *84n*, 84, 85, *93–4*, 94 (three references, also one to Pyramus). *Cf* Vigorelli (ed.), *Bandello: Novelle*, p. 277; Bullough, *Sources*, vol. I, pp. 209, 374.

intrusive story in another play. Separately, some of these details are trifling or inconclusive; together, they seem to me convincing evidence of a linkage in the author's mind. It is noticeable that most of Shakespeare's alterations relate to the motif of broken nuptials, the emotional conflict between love and law. I give the items as nearly as I can in tabular form (references in square brackets refer to the translations of the *novelle* in Geoffrey Bullough's *Sources of Shakespeare*, vols. I and II):

1. *The Merchant of Venice*

(*a*) – The names Antonio and Lorenzo: not in Ser Giovanni; but in the story behind *Romeo*, old Capulet is called Anthony (by Painter); the Friar is called Lawrence.

– Jessica appears on a balcony (II.vi) before eloping with one of her father's enemies in a masque disguised as a 'torch-bearer'. No Jessica to elope in Ser Giovanni, but compare *Romeo and Juliet*.

(*b*) – When Portia leaves Belmont (III.iv), she commits 'the husbandry and manage of [her] house | Until [her] lord's return' to Lorenzo, and tells him (falsely) that she is on her way to 'a monastery', 'to live in prayer and contemplation', in fulfilment of 'a secret vow'. No evident practical need for this subterfuge; in Ser Giovanni, the Lady races to Venice, 'dressed like a lawyer', without ado [I.472]. But in Boccaccio's story of Giletta, the story behind *All's Well*, the heroine returns to her husband's estate after their marriage, where 'perceyving that through the Countes absence all thinges were spoiled and out of order, shee like a sage Ladye, with greate diligence and care, disposed his thinges in order againe' to his subjects' great satisfaction [II.392]; and when she receives the Count's humiliating letter, she summons 'the nobleste and chiefeste of her Countrie', tells them what she has done to win the Count's love, shews them the letter in which he refuses to see her, and announces that, to enable the Count to return when he wishes, she has 'determined to spende the reste of her time in Pilgrimages and devotion, for preservation of her Soule'. She leaves them 'to take the charge and governemente of the Countrie', going with her maid and one of her kinsmen, 'in the habite of a pilgrime'; only, instead of visiting any shrine, she goes straight to Florence, where her husband is and where, 'by fortune', she gains news of him. Shakespeare could have read this, in Painter's translation, at any time before 1596. When he changed Giletta into Helena, in *All's Well*, he omitted the sketch of the heroine as a *châtelaine*; he had used it already for Portia.

– After the trial at Venice, in Ser Giovanni, the Lady teases Giannetto on his return to Belmonte over the ring he had given to his 'lawyer': ' "I can swear", said the lady, "that you gave the ring to a woman" ' [1.475]. Portia makes much more of this: 'By heaven, I will ne'er come in your bed | Until I see the ring', and so on (v.i.190ff); she takes to her own use the story of the transfer of the ring between Beltramo and Giletta.

(*c*) – On her way to Venice, we hear that Portia has sent for 'notes and garments' to her cousin, Doctor Bellario of Padua, who recommends her to the Doge's court as 'a young and learned' lawyer (III.iv.47, IV.i.142). She impresses even Shylock by her legal knowledge. Ser Giovanni's Lady pretends to be 'a famous lawyer' from Bologna, but does not take advice from anyone [1.473]. However, Giraldi's heroine, Epitia, the forerunner of Isabella in *Measure for Measure*, has 'a sweet way of talking' when she pleads for her brother's life to the judge, and brings in moral considerations (which the Lady of Belmonte ignores), because she has been, 'with her brother, under the tutelage of an old man whom her father had kept in the house to teach them both Philosophy' [II.422]. Giraldi's story (*Hecatommithi*, VIII.5) had been published in 1565. If Shakespeare did not read it in Italian, he could have read it in Chappuy's French translation (1584). George Whetstone had dramatised the story in *Promos and Cassandra* and had summarised it again in prose, in his *Heptameron of Civil Discourses* (1582).[1] His Cassandra is eloquent, but her instructor is not mentioned. It looks as if Shakespeare had remembered Giraldi.

– Ser Giovanni's Lady provides Portia with the legal resource that disarms the Jew. But she says nothing to him about mercy. Portia's famous speech dilates on the subject.

> The quality of mercy is not strain'd;
> It droppeth as the gentle rain from heaven
> Upon the place beneath. It is twice blest:
> It blesseth him that gives and him that takes.
> 'Tis mightiest in the mightiest; it becomes
> The throned monarch better than his crown;
> His sceptre shows the force of temporal power,
> The attribute to awe and majesty,

[1] Whetstone, *The Story of Promos and Cassandra*, ed. Spencer, in *Elizabethan Love Stories*.

Wherein doth sit the dread and fear of kings;
But mercy is above this sceptred sway,
It is enthroned in the heart of kings,
It is an attribute to God himself;
And earthly power doth then show likest God's
When mercy seasons justice. Therefore, Jew,
Though justice be thy plea, consider this –
That in the course of justice none of us
Should see salvation; we do pray for mercy,
And that same prayer doth teach us all to render
The deeds of mercy.

A moving speech, theatrically very effective. But, on a prosaic level, what is this skilful pleader doing, directing these arguments, with their strong monarchist and Christian overtones, to a Jewish plaintiff, in the court of the proudest republic in Europe? Elsewhere in this play, Shakespeare pays some attention to details of local colour, but not here. However, in the story of Epitia, there are no less than four discussions of justice and mercy. Epitia pleads to the judge, Juriste, for mercy for her brother [II.422]; Juriste then replies that justice requires death for rape, but that he will save Epitia's brother if she will sleep with him [II.423]; she keeps the bargain, on condition that he marries her, but Juriste doubly breaks his word; and Epitia appeals to the Emperor Maximian. In strict justice for Juriste's two crimes, the Emperor orders him to marry Epitia first and then to be beheaded [II.428]; whereupon comes Epitia's second plea for mercy, this time on behalf of the man who is now her husband: 'It is, most sacred Majesty, no less praise for him who holds the government of the world as now your Majesty most worthily holds it, to exercise Clemency as to show Justice. For whereas Justice shows that vices are hateful and punishes them accordingly, Clemency makes a monarch most like to the immortal Gods' [II.429]. Shakespeare could have taken the substance of Portia's argument from many places, but this one seems the nost probable starting-point. And whatever it lacks, Giraldi's tale has a memorable schematic neatness. Whetstone's two versions of the story arrive at the dénouement differently.

2. Much Ado about Nothing

(*a*) – When Hero faints, Friar Francis advises her family to hide her, giving it out that she has died, and to place 'mournful epitaphs' on their 'family's old monument'; Leonato's first reaction has been to think her guilty. There is no friar in Bandello's tale of Fenicia, where Messer Lionato himself advises her to hide at his brother's villa [II.121]; but compare *Romeo and Juliet*. There is a family monument in Fenicia's story, but the way Shakespeare uses it at the end of *Much Ado* recalls *Romeo* again.

(*b*) – In Fenicia's story, there is nothing like a public denunciation in the church or legal procedure; but compare *The Merchant of Venice*.

(*c*) – When she can think of no other way to clear Hero's name, Beatrice urges Benedick, 'Kill Claudio'. In effect, she calls him a deceiving 'villain' (IV.i.303). In Bandello, the slanderous rival, overcome by remorse, begs Sir Timbreo (Claudio's predecessor) to kill him [II.124], but Fenicia's family have no thought of revenge against Sir Timbreo. However, there is a moment in Epitia's story [II.426] where Epitia is desperate and thinks of killing her 'deceiver'.

(*d*) – The first Quarto stage-direction shows that at one point Shakespeare must have thought of providing a wife for Leonato, named Innogen. He then decided not to use this character; but in *Cymbeline*, his later *novella* play about a calumniated wife, he marries an Imogen to a Posthumus Leonatus.

3. All's Well that Ends Well

(*a*) – Boccaccio does not name the Florentine girl who helps the heroine; Shakespeare calls her Diana Capilet, 'derivèd from the ancient Capilet' (V.iii.157).

(*b*) – When Helena has cured the King, he gives her 'power to choose' a husband from his court, 'by free election'; she goes up to three other lords on the stage in turn before naming Bertram (II.iii). In Boccaccio, Giletta has named Beltramo to the king as soon as she has cured him [II.391]; this scene in *All's Well* recalls the scene in *The Merchant* (I.ii) where Portia, complaining she is *not* free to choose, mentally passes her suitors in review. Again, there is nothing like the trial scene from this play in Boccaccio.

(*c*) – Helena is reported dead towards the end (V.iii.1), Bertram says he has 'lov'd' her since he had 'lost' her (54), then Diana and her mother enter (155), accusing Bertram; after some mystification, they produce Helena. None of this reported death or the rest in Boccaccio; but compare the Friar's advice to Hero after Claudio's insult to her in *Much Ado* (IV.i), his hopes from the effect of the report of her death on Claudio, and, in the final scene, after the business of detection, Hero's reappearance with Beatrice, both masked (Claudio's contrite promise to marry an unknown cousin of the dead girl derives from Bandello's story).

4. *Measure for Measure*

(*a*) – There are two important names new to this story, but familiar from Shakespeare himself: a second Juliet, secretly married, appears, and a second Claudio, whose 'headstrong' conduct in marrying without a dowry or a church ceremony ('the denunciation...of outward order', i.ii.140) makes him the exact opposite of the suspicious, conventional Claudio in *Much Ado*.

– There is no friar in Giraldi or Whetstone; the role of the duke as friar, comforting anguished lovers and arranging for sham deaths, comes from *Romeo*, again, and *Much Ado*.

– Another newcomer to this story is Escalus, who takes at least his name from the prince–magistrate in *Romeo and Juliet*.

(*b*) – There are no underworld characters in Giraldi. Very likely they were suggested by *Promos and Cassandra* (and *Henry IV*). But Elbow recalls Dogberry from *Much Ado* (also Dull in *Love's Labour's Lost*, where Shakespeare was already borrowing from *Promos and Cassandra*).

(*c*) – As has often been noted, the trick of the substituted mistress comes from *All's Well*. The complicated trial at the end, including Mariana as a veiled wife, recalls *All's Well* and *Much Ado*.

One or two other links between Shakespeare's plays founded on *novelle* are worth mentioning here. Don John is more like Iago than the slanderers in Bandello and other variants of the story behind *Much Ado*, who are actuated entirely by jealousy of a rival lover; this tends to confirm that Shakespeare knew Giraldi's book (*Othello* comes from *Hecatommithi*, III.7) well before 1604. In *Cymbeline*, Imogen's awakening from her drugged sleep and supposed death, to find what she thinks is the dead body of Posthumus beside her (IV.ii), and Posthumus's remorse for the supposed death of Imogen by his orders (V.i) clearly echo *Romeo* and *Much Ado*; there are no corresponding episodes in Boccaccio's story, Shakespeare's main source.

To sum up: the evidence of transposed details shows that Shakespeare drew from the stories of Giletta and Epitia while he was building up

Portia's role; it looks as if the other two stories were fresh in his mind at the time. A year or two earlier, he had been acquainted with Whetstone's play, drawn from Giraldi, as shown by *Love's Labour's Lost*. In the interval between *Love's Labour's Lost* and *The Merchant of Venice* – in a year or even less about 1595 – he had created *Romeo* and *A Midsummer Night's Dream*. He had been interested in the Romeo story for a few years at least; the *Dream* was to be his last comedy with a predominantly invented plot. With variations between high probability and a reasonable guess, we can say that he did not need to look for fresh stories as basic material for the seven comedies he was to write over the next eight or nine years; he knew them already. And in the case of the problem comedies beginning with *The Merchant*, his interest in them was connected with his interest in Romeo. *A Midsummer Night's Dream*, including the playlet of *Pyramus and Thisbe* translated into farce, represents one alternative to the fatal outcome of the lovers' story in *Romeo and Juliet*; the problem comedies, with their stories of broken nuptials repaired, represent another. They can be seen as successive experiments in responding to what was basically a continuing emotional pressure.

One role which stands out in four of Shakespeare's comedies connected with *Romeo and Juliet* is that of the forbidding or angry father of the heroine (the Duke in *Two Gentlemen of Verona*, Egeus at Athens, Portia's father and Jessica's father in the scenes of Shakespeare's devising in *The Merchant of Venice*, the change he makes in the attitude of Leonato in *Much Ado*). As if in counterpoise, Friar Laurence's sympathetic advice echoes through three of the four problem comedies (§§ 2(*a*), 3(*c*) and 4(*a*) above); while in the fourth, the disobedient daughter marries a Lorenzo.

Another dominant feature of each of the four problem comedies is its trial scene, or something very like one. Here Shakespeare was taking no more than suggestions, though vital suggestions, from the short stories he was utilising, and was evidently obeying his own sense of the theatre. It is the Elizabethan theatre, with the panoply of justice, not the private arbitrations he could have remembered from classical New Comedy. In *The Merchant of Venice*, the basic material for his trial scene was already provided, and it seems likely that Ser Giovanni's tale of the bond was exactly what drew him to the story. In the other problem comedies, where his share of invention in the legal circumstances is very much larger, he may be taking occasional hints from other Elizabethan plays, such as *Promos and Cassandra*. (In particular, he may have been influenced by *The Spanish Tragedy*, with its climax in a bloody play within the play, the sudden disclosure of another dead body, and the long harangue of self-justification by the frustrated and now murderous judge, Hieronymo, distracting the stage spectators' attention until his chosen moment for suicide – a climax which apparently stayed in Shakespeare's memory as late as the writing of *Othello*.) But the chief precedent for the complicated and surprising judicial climaxes in Shakespeare's problem comedies must have been the dénouement he had already devised himself for *The Comedy of Errors*. Here he had already invented his Chinese-box technique of disclosing successive identities in a judicial hearing, a technique he was to stretch to the limits of ingenuity at the end of *Cymbeline*. Now, the scene where Egeon's family are all assembled together in the presence of the Duke at the end of *The Comedy of Errors* pivots on the emotional theme of the judge and the nun. The judicial surprises and subterfuges whereby broken nuptials are mended in the problem comedies have virtually the same dramatic basis. In each sequence of episodes, a leading character is rescued from the threat of execution (or else, as with Hero, the appearance of death), and a ruler presides over dramatic reversals that save a wife's happiness and restore her to her husband. In each problem play, too, the threat to a marriage is connected in one way or another with the idea of legal or social authority on one side, and on the other, with the idea of a nunnery.

Shakespeare did not 'solve' the problems of moral justice he apparently set himself in his problem comedies. He did not even fully satisfy Chekhov's requirement, that the essential task for a writer is not to solve such problems, but to pose them correctly. There are too many disturbing questions left unanswered, or else disposed of by obstinately theatrical devices, even in the profound yet unequal comedy of *Measure for Measure*, which is the culmination of the series. With *Measure for Measure* and its predecessor, *All's Well*, the two plays habitually described as problem plays in modern criticism, one is sometimes left under the impression that the problem lies in the critics' difficulty of deciding what kind of plays they really are. Are they, for instance, intrigue comedies or tragi-comedies, allegories or romances? Except that it might only raise fresh arguments over literary definition, it seems to me that it would be most accurate to call them *novella* comedies, together with *The Merchant of Venice* and

Much Ado, from the nature of their sources. Even so, there would be fundamental critical questions to consider about them, as well as the question of nomenclature. The stories transmitted to Shakespeare by Boccaccio and his followers are remarkable, not so much for their air of reporting actualities (whatever their narrative substance), the air of telling 'news' that gives the genre its name, but for their internal balance and rationality, for the authors' skill in propounding a quandary in practical conduct and then showing its resolution by means of an exact system of moral equivalences, an exchange of gifts or actions or speeches which is symmetrical and at least logically satisfying. In Boccaccio such concern with ethical symmetry is a guiding artistic principle, in Bandello it is displaced somewhat by his pose of dispassionate reporter, in Giraldi it is overlaid with rhetoric, but it is present in all the stories that interested Shakespeare, and, together with the writers' sober attention to the realities of civic life, must have made the Italians' stories stand out from the other moralistic or ramblingly romantic fiction available to him. It is Shakespeare's response to these qualities in the Italian tales that makes his *novella* comedies problem plays in any operative sense of the term. Yet, transferred to his stage, these constructive qualities of mind become something entirely different, something much more strained, suggestive, explosive and perplexing. A Shylock or an Angelo, even a Bertram or a Claudio, will not stay content with filling out a neat demonstration of moral reciprocities. *A Midsummer Night's Dream*, *As You Like It* and *Twelfth Night* are more rounded and complete works of art than the problem plays, though they are also more limited. To some extent, the growing complexity of Shakespeare's mind and experience must account for the differences. But since his problem comedies overlapped in date with the plays he wrote in more or less continuous sequence stemming from older stage traditions, comic and romantic, it seems as if to some extent Shakespeare brought to the composition of the former a different side of his sensibility, of his mind and awareness of his age. To pass from *Twelfth Night* to *Measure for Measure* is somewhat like passing from the Renaissance to the Reformation.

The explosive force of the clash in Shakespeare's mind between the principle of sexuality and the principle of authority, which strains the construction of *Measure for Measure*, came out, a year or two later, in the most anarchic utterances he gave to King Lear. After *Measure for Measure*, there was a gap of four years or more in his production of comedies, for the first time in his busy career. The sequence of problem plays had evidently brought him to the limits of what he was prepared to write in comic form. Yet the new step they entailed was necessary and liberating, even if it meant breaking from or else warping the conventions of his stage. Otherwise there was a danger that the purely comic tradition, left to its own momentum, would end in the self-enclosed preoccupations of romance or else in the no less restrictive conventions that Ben Jonson was to create for satire. If Shakespeare's use of *novelle* did not bring about a wholly new dramatic constitution, with its own internal checks and balances, it gave a new dimension to comedy, a fresh feeling of open contact with modern life.

In this sense, Shakespeare brought to maturity in England a tendency which had been latent in Renaissance comedy from the outset, to deal with narratives of contemporary life on the stage, instead of (or more often, in addition to) repeating formulas inherited from the past. 'Our authour's plots', says Dr Johnson in his *Preface*, 'are generally borrowed from novels'; and though the statement is much too sweeping, it points to a vital factor in historical perspective. Once we take account of the antecedents of Elizabethan tragic plots, as well as Italian learned comedy, then the greatest creative writer whose influence can be felt widely diffused through Shakespeare's plays, however indirectly, is Boccaccio. Shakespeare stands with Cervantes at the end of that great development of late medieval or early modern European lay culture whose first potency appears with Boccaccio and Chaucer.

It would falsify historical perspective, however, to isolate Shakespeare's *novella* comedies from his others. 'He found the English stage', according to Dr Johnson again, 'in a state of the utmost rudeness; no essays either in tragedy or comedy had appeared, from which it could be discovered to what degree of delight either one or other might be carried.' This is another of Johnson's excessive statements that holds a solid chunk of truth. More than 200 years after Johnson's *Preface*, it is impossible to ignore the influence of the humanists in Tudor education and literature, or the influence of Lyly, Marlowe, Kyd, Greene and the other playwrights of Shakespeare's own day, as well as his more intangible, less documentable, debt to the preceding generations of common players and amateur performers alike, reaching back to Chaucer's time. Yet a study of Shakespeare's plays in relation to the known English drama of his early years only makes his innovations less obscure, not less impressive. No one, it seems safe to say, not even a critic as well informed about English practice and continental theory as Sir Philip Sidney, could have predicted before 1590 what an English history play would be like. And no one, not even Shakespeare, could have said with confidence what the form of a 'Shakespearean tragedy' would be much before 1600. No one could then have predicted, either, that anybody's tragedies would mark the peaks of achievement on the English stage; for a century, comedy had been, not of course the only form, but the typical and leading form of European drama. Comedy owed this pre-eminence to familiarity with Latin literatute as compared with Greek and to the spirit of Italian society at the time of the Renaissance. The Renaissance helped to destroy some of the stage traditions affecting comedy, but replaced them with a sense of intellectually coherent structure, in a new tradition, communicating with the classical past as well as open to the present. Yet, although a number of English writers before Shakespeare, chiefly writers for academic or court stages, had experimented in the new or classical tradition, no one before him in England seems to have 'discovered to what degree of delight' the old-new form 'might be carried'. No one before him seems to have realised fully the potentialities of adapting Plautus for the sake of rapid and coherent action, still less for a continuous dramatic image of changing aspects of personality and the ironies of Fortune. *The Comedy of Errors* was no less a landmark in Elizabethan play-writing than *Henry VI*. *Love's Labour's Lost*, similarly, was virtually the first Elizabethan play to represent a new intellectual type, the Renaissance courtier as wit. And, with this play, Shakespeare is no longer in his comedies merely a brilliant craftsman, but a professional poet reaching out towards a public of national scope, a new kind of presence in any modern theatre. He seems to have absorbed the technical lessons of Roman and Italian comedy as a professional; and as a professional with a wider and more varied public than his Italian predecessors, he not only took in their lessons but applied them. He was not following a single current of taste or obeying a fashion, but taking from a still relatively new and foreign set of conventions what he could use and what he could combine with more familiar, native traditions that he still found emotionally expressive. As an actor–poet earning his living in a commercial theatre, he found himself in a situation without precedent in the social history of drama, and his response, in his comedies, as in his history plays, shows him wide awake to the chances as well as the insecurities of his position. As an English playwright of the Renaissance, he was using the forms of New Comedy to reshape medieval romance. But in this he was doing more than naturalising New Comedy. He was creating comedies that seem aware of their place in the life of a nation, as perhaps no other comedies had been since the time of Aristophanes.

BIBLIOGRAPHY

PLAYS: EDITIONS AND TRANSLATIONS

Aristophanes: *Aristophane*, ed. and trans. V. Coulon and H. Van Daele, 5 vols. (Paris, 1954–8)

Duckworth, George E. (ed.), *The Complete Roman Drama*, 2 vols. (New York, 1942)

Edmonds, J. M. (ed. and trans.), *The Fragments of Attic Comedy*, vols. I and II (Leiden, 1957–9)

Euripides, *The Bacchae*, ed. E. R. Dodds (Oxford, 1944)

Menander: *Menander*, ed. and trans. Francis G. Allinson (Loeb Classical Library, 1930)

Il Misantropo [*Dyskolos*], ed. and trans. B. Marzullo (Turin, 1959)

Plays and Fragments, trans. Philip Vellacott (Penguin Classics, 1967)

Oates, Whitney J. and O'Neill, Eugene, jr (eds.), *The Complete Greek Drama*, 2 vols. (New York, 1938)

Page, D. L. (ed. and trans.), *Select Papyri III (Poetry)* (Loeb Classical Library, 1950)

Plautus: *Plaute*, ed. and trans. Alfred Ernout, 7 vols. (Paris, 1956–61)

Terence: *Térence*, ed. and trans. J. Marouzeau, 3 vols. (Paris, 1947–56)

Terentii...Comoediae [with Donatus's commentaries], ed. G. Stallbaum (Leipzig, 1831)

Ayres, Harry Morgan (trans.), *An Ingenious Play of Esmoreit*, intro. Adriaan J. Barnouw (The Hague, 1924)

A Marvellous History of Mary Nimmegen (The Hague, 1924)

D'Ancona, Alessandro (ed.), *Sacre rappresentazioni dei secoli XIV, XV e XVI*, 3 vols. (Florence, 1872)

Geyl, P. (trans.), *A Beautiful Play of Lancelot of Denmark* (The Hague, 1924)

Monmerqué, L. J. N. and Michel, F. (eds.), *Théâtre français au Moyen-Age* (Paris, 1839)

Paris, Gaston and Robert, Ulysse (eds.), *Miracles de Nostre Dame par personnages*, 8 vols. (Paris, 1876–93)

Roques, Mario (ed.), *L'Estoire de Griseldis en rimes et par personnages* (Geneva and Paris, 1957)

Schmidt, Léopold (ed.), *Le Théâtre populaire européen* (Paris, 1965)

Aretino, P., *Tutte le Commedie*, ed. G. B. De Sanctis (Milan, 1968)

Ariosto, *Commedie*, ed. M. Catilano, 2 vols. (Bologna, 1940)

Opere minori, ed. Cesare Segre (Milan and Naples, 1954)

I Suppositi, trans. see Gascoigne, *Supposes*

Bentley, Eric (ed.), *The Classic Theatre I: Six Italian Plays* (New York, 1958)

The Genius of the Italian Theater (New York, 1964)

Bibbiena, *La Calandria:* ed. Borlenghi, in *Commedie del Cinquecento*, vol. I

ed. Borsellino, in *Commedie del Cinquecento*, vol. II

trans. Oliver Evans, in Bentley (ed.), *Genius of the Italian Theater*

Borlenghi, Aldo (ed.), *Commedie del Cinquecento*, 2 vols. (Milan, 1959)

Borsellino, Nino (ed.), *Commedie del Cinquecento*, vols. I and II (Milan, 1962–7)

Bruno, Giordano, *Il Candelaio:* ed. Borsellino, in *Commedie del Cinquecento*, vol. II

trans. J. R. Hale, in Bentley (ed.), *Genius of the Italian Theater*

Cecchi, G-M., *La Moglie* [prose] (Venice, 1550)

La Moglie [verse] (Venice, 1585)

Cervantes, Miguel de, *Théâtre*, trans. Alphonse Reyer (Paris, 1862)

Firenzuola, A., *I Lucidi*, Biblioteca Classica Italiana: Secolo XVI, No. 7, Teatro Classico (Trieste, 1858)

Ingannati, Gl' (Anon.): *Il Sacrificio de Gl'Intronati. Celebrato nei Giochi d'un Carnevale in Siena. Et Gl'Ingannati, Comedia de i Medesimi* (Venice, 1553). See Ruscelli (ed.), *Delle Comedie Elette*

ed. Borlenghi, in *Commedie del Cinquecento*, vol. I

ed. Borsellino, in *Commedie del Cinquecento*, vol. I

see Purves

trans. Bullough, in *Narrative and Dramatic Sources of Shakespeare*, vol. II

Machiavelli, N., *Literary Works*, ed. and trans. J. R. Hale London, (1961)

Opere, ed. Mario Bonfantini (Milan and Naples, 1954)

Mortier, Alfred, *Un dramaturge populaire de la Renaissance italienne: Ruzzante*, 2 vols. (Paris, 1925–7)

Piccolomini, Alessandro, *L'Amor costante:* ed. Borlenghi, in *Commedie del Cinquecento*, vol. I

ed. Borsellino, in *Commedie del Cinquecento*, vol. I

Purves, J. (ed.), *Gl'Ingannati* (Edinburgh, 1943)

Ruscelli, Girolamo (ed.), *Delle Comedie Elette, Nuovamente Raccolte Insieme* (Venice, 1554). (Includes *Il Sacrificio:* see *Gl'Ingannati*)

Ruzzante: *Ruzante, Teatro*, ed. Ludovico Zorzi (with trans.) (Turin, 1967)

Secchi, N., *Gl'Inganni* (Venice, 1582)

Trissino, G. *I Simillimi* (Venice, 1548)

Adams, J. Q. (ed.), *Chief Pre-Shakespearean Dramas* (Cambridge, Mass., 1924)

Bond, R. Warwick (ed.), *Early Plays from the Italian* (Oxford, 1911)

Brooke, C. F. Tucker (ed.), *Common Conditions* (New Haven, 1915)

Dodsley, R. (ed.), *A Select Collection of Old Plays*, ed. W. C. Hazlitt, 15 vols. (London, 1874–6)

England, G. (ed.), *Towneley Plays* (E.E.T.S., 1897)

Furnivall, F. J. (ed.), *The Digby Mysteries* (New Shakspere Society, 1882)

Gascoigne, G., *Supposes* (trans. from Ariosto, *I Suppositi*), in Bond (ed.), *Early Plays from the Italian*

Greene, Robert, *Plays and Poems*, ed. J. Churton Collins, 2 vols. (Oxford, 1905)

Greg, W. W. (ed.), *Clyomon and Clamydes* (Malone Society, 1913)

Kyd, Thomas, *Works*, ed. F. S. Boas (Oxford, 1901)

Marston, John, *Plays*, ed. H. Harvey Wood, 3 vols. (Edinburgh, 1934–9)

Munday, A. (?), *Fedele and Fortunio. The Two Italian Gentlemen* (Malone Society, 1909)

Palsgrave, John, *Acolastus*, ed. P. L. Carver (E.E.T.S., 1937)

Shakespeare, W., *The Complete Works*, ed. Peter Alexander (London, 1951)
   The Complete Signet Classic Shakespeare, ed. Sylvan Barnet (New York, 1972)
   As You Like It, ed. J. W. Holme (Arden, 1914)
   The Comedy of Errors, ed. R. A. Foakes (New Arden, 1962)
   Cymbeline, ed. Edward Dowden (Arden, 1903)
   Cymbeline, ed. J. M. Nosworthy (New Arden, 1955)
   Love's Labour's Lost, ed. Richard David (New Arden, 1951)
   A Midsummer Night's Dream, ed. John Dover Wilson (Cambridge, 1924)
   Pericles, ed. F. D. Hoeniger (New Arden, 1963)
   Richard II, ed. Peter Ure (New Arden, 1956)
   The Taming of the Shrew, ed. G. R. Hibbard (New Penguin Shakespeare, 1968)
   The Tempest, ed. Frank Kermode (New Arden, 1954)
   Twelfth Night, ed. Morton Luce (Arden, 1906)
   The Winter's Tale, ed. J. H. P. Pafford (New Arden, 1963)

Simpson, Richard (ed.), *The School of Shakspere*, 2 vols. (London, 1878)

OTHER BOOKS AND ARTICLES

Aarne, A. and Thompson, Stith, *Types of the Folktale* (Helsinki, 1961)

Anderson, M. D., *Drama and Imagery in English Medieval Churches* (Cambridge, 1963)

Anglo, Sydney, *Spectacle Pageantry, and Early Tudor Policy* (Oxford, 1969)

Angus, C. F., 'Athens', in *Cambridge Ancient History*, vol. VII (Cambridge, 1928)

Apollonio, Mario, 'Carnevale', in D'Amico (ed.), *Enciclopedia dello Spettacolo*, vol. III
   Storia del teatro italiano, vols. I and II (Florence, 1938)

Arnaldi, F., *Da Plauto a Terenzio*, 2 vols. (Naples, 1946–7)

Ascham, Roger, *English Works*, ed. W. A. Wright (Cambridge, 1904)

Atkins, J. W. H., *Literary Criticism in Antiquity*, 2 vols. (Cambridge, 1934)

Baldry, H. C., 'Who Invented the Golden Age?', *Classical Quarterly*, n.s. II (1952)

Baldwin, T. W., *Shakspere's Five-Act Structure* (Urbana, 1947)
    Shakspere's Small Latine and Lesse Greek, 2 vols. (Urbana, 1944)
Bandello, M., *Novelle*, ed. G. Vigorelli (Garzanti, Italy, 1945)
Barber, C. L., *Shakespeare's Festive Comedy* (Princeton, 1959)
Baskervill, C. R., 'Dramatic Aspects of Medieval Folk Festivals in England',
    Studies in Philology, XVII (1920)
    'An Elizabethan Eglamour Play', *Modern Philology*, XIV (1917)
    The Elizabethan Jig and Related Song Drama (Chicago, 1929)
    'Some Evidence for Early Romantic Plays in England', *Modern Philology*,
    XIV (1916)
Beare, W., *The Roman Stage* (London, 1950)
Bédouin, J-L., *Les Masques* (Paris, 1961)
Bennett, H. S., *English Books and Readers, 1558 to 1603* (Cambridge, 1965)
Bentley, Gerald Eades, *The Profession of Dramatist in Shakespeare's Time* (Princeton,
    1971)
Berdan, J. M., *Early Tudor Poetry* (London, 1920)
Bernheimer, R., *Wild Men in the Middle Ages* (Cambridge, Mass., 1952)
Bevan, Edwyn, 'Hellenistic Popular Philosophy', in J. B. Bury (ed.), *The
    Hellenistic Age* (Cambridge, 1923)
Bevington, David M., *From 'Mankind' to Marlowe* (Cambridge, Mass., 1962)
Black, J. B., *The Reign of Elizabeth* (Oxford, 1936)
Boas, F. S., *University Drama in the Tudor Age* (Oxford, 1914)
Boccaccio, G., *Decameron*, ed. Vittore Branca, 2 vols. (Florence, 1960)
Bocci, Elena, 'Un Teatro aulico del Secolo XVI: l'Accademia degli Intronati
    a Siena', *Bullettino Senese di Storia Patria*, 3rd series, XII (1953)
Boethius, *The Consolation of Philosophy*, trans. 'I.T.' [1609] (Loeb Classical
    Library, 1918)
Bolgar, R. R., *The Classical Heritage and its Beneficiaries* (Cambridge, 1954)
Bonner, Campbell, 'Dionysiac Magic and the Greek Land of Cockaigne',
    Transactions of the American Philological Association, XLI (1910)
Bonner, Robert J., *Aspects of Athenian Democracy* (Berkeley, 1933)
Borsellino, Nino, 'Rozzi et Intronati. Pour une histoire de la comédie à Sienne
    au XVIe siècle', in Jacquot (ed.), *Dramaturgie et Société*
Boughner, Daniel, *The Braggart in Renaissance Comedy* (Minnesota, 1954)
Bowra, C. M., 'Songs of Dance and Carnival', in E. F. Jacob (ed.), *Italian
    Renaissance Studies* (London, 1960)
Bradbrook, M. C., *The Growth and Structure of Elizabethan Comedy* (London,
    1955)
    The Rise of the Common Player (London, 1962)
Bradbury, Malcolm and Palmer, David (eds.), *Shakespearian Comedy*, Stratford-
    upon-Avon Studies 14 (London, 1972)
Branca, Vittore, *Boccaccio medievale* (Florence, 1956)
Brand, J., *Popular Antiquities of Great Britain* [1795], ed. Sir Henry Ellis, 3 vols.
    (London, 1849)

Bréhier, Emile, *Histoire de la Philosophie,* vol. I (Paris, 1938)

Brockbank, P., 'History and Histrionics in *Cymbeline*' (*Shakespeare Survey 11,* 1958)

Brooke, C. F. Tucker, 'On the Source of *Common Conditions*', *Modern Language Notes,* XXXI (1916)

Brown, John Russell, 'The Interpretation of Shakespeare's Comedies: 1900–1953', *Shakespeare Survey 8* (1955)
 Shakespeare and his Comedies (London, 1957)

Brown, John Russell and Harris, Bernard (eds.), *Early Shakespeare,* Stratford-upon-Avon Studies 3 (London, 1961)
 Elizabethan Theatre, Stratford-upon-Avon Studies 9 (London, 1966)

Bruno, Giordano, *De Gli Eroici Furori:* in *Opere Italiane,* vol. II, ed. G. Gentile (Bari, 1927)
 trans. Paul Eugene Memmo, jr, *The Heroic Frenzies* (Ph.D. thesis, Columbia University, 1959)

Bullough, Geoffrey (ed.), *Narrative and Dramatic Sources of Shakespeare,* vols. I–VI (London, 1957–66)

Bundy, M. W., *The Theory of Imagination in Classical and Mediaeval Thought,* University of Illinois Studies in Language and Literature, vol. XII (1927)

Burckhardt, J., *The Civilization of the Renaissance in Italy,* trans. S. G. C. Middlemore (Phaidon Press, 1944)

Bury, J. B., 'The Age of Illumination', in *Cambridge Ancient History,* vol. V (Cambridge, 1927)

Caillois, R., *Les Jeux et les Hommes* (Paris, 1967)

Calderini, A., *Le Avventure di Cherea e Calliroe* (Turin, 1913)

Campbell, Lily B., *Scenes and Machines on the English Stage during the Renaissance* (Cambridge, 1923)

Campbell, O. J., *Comicall Satyre and Shakespeare's Troilus and Cressida* (San Marino, 1938)
 'The Relation of *Epicoene* to Aretino's *Il Marescalco*', *PMLA,* XLVI (1931)

Cantimori, Delio, 'Italy and the Papacy', in *New Cambridge Modern History,* vol. II (1965)

Castelvetro, Lodovico, *Poetica d'Aristotele vulgarizzata e sposta* [1571] (Basel, 1576)
 trans.: see Charlton; Gilbert (ed.), *Literary Criticism*

Castiglione, B., *The Book of the Courtier* [1528], trans. T. Hoby [1561] (Everyman's Library, n.d.)

Caxton, W., *The Golden Legend,* ed. F. S. Ellis, vol. VI (Temple Classics, 1900)

Chalmers, Walter R., 'Plautus and his Audience', in Dorey and Dudley (eds.), *Roman Drama*

Chambers, E. K., *The Elizabethan Stage,* 4 vols. (Oxford, 1923)
 The English Folk-Play (Oxford, 1933)
 The Mediaeval Stage, 2 vols. (Oxford, 1903)

Chambers, E. K. and Williams, Charles, *A Short Life of Shakespeare* (Oxford, 1933)

Charlton, H. B., *Castelvetro's Theory of Poetry* (Manchester, 1913)
Shakespearian Comedy (London, 1938)

Chastel, André, 'Le Lieu de la Fête', in Jacquot (ed.), *Les Fêtes de la Renaissance*, vol. I

Chew, S. C., 'Time and Fortune', *English Literary History*, VI (1939)

Childe, V. Gordon, *Man Makes Himself* (Thinker's Library, 1941)

Cioffari, V., *Fortune and Fate from Democritus to St Thomas Aquinas* (New York, 1935)

Clark, A. (ed.), *Shirburn Ballads, 1585–1616* (Oxford, 1907)

Clark, Barrett H. (ed.), *European Theories of the Drama* (New York, 1918)

Cloché, P., *La Démocratie athénienne* (Paris, 1951)

Cochrane, Eric, 'A Case in Point: the End of the Renaissance in Florence', in *The Late Italian Renaissance, 1525–1630*, ed. Cochrane (London, 1970)

Coghill, N., 'The Basis of Shakespearean Comedy', *Essays and Studies of the English Association*, n.s. III (1950)
'Six Points of Stagecraft in *The Winter's Tale*' (*Shakespeare Survey 11*, 1958)

Cohen, Gustave, 'Marie-Madeleine dans le Théâtre du Moyen-Age', in *Etudes d'Histoire du Théâtre en France* (Paris, 1956)

Coleman-Norton, P. R., 'The Conception of Fortune in Roman Drama', in *Classical Studies Presented to Edward Capps* (Princeton, 1936)

Coleridge, S. T., *Shakespearean Criticism*, ed. T. M. Raysor, 2 vols. (Everyman's Library, 1960)

Conacher, D. J., 'The Paradox of Euripides' *Ion*', *Transactions of the American Philological Association*, XC (1959)

Cooper, Lane, *An Aristotelian Theory of Comedy* (Oxford, 1924)

Cornford, F. M., *From Religion to Philosophy* [1912] (New York, 1957)
The Origin of Attic Comedy [1914], ed. Theodor H. Gaster (New York, 1961)

Costa, C. D. N., 'The Amphitryo Theme', in Dorey and Dudley (eds.), *Roman Drama*

Cox, Marian Rolfe, *Cinderella*, intro. Andrew Lang (London, 1893)

Craig, Hardin, *English Religious Drama of the Middle Ages* (Oxford, 1955)

Croce, B., *Poesia popolare e poesia d'arte* (Bari, 1933)

Curtius, E. R., *European Literature and the Latin Middle Ages*, trans. Willard R. Trask (New York, 1953)

D'Amico, Silvio (ed.), *Enciclopedia dello Spettacolo*, 9 vols. (Rome, 1954–62)
Storia del teatro italiano (Milan, 1936)

D'Ancona, Alessandro, *Origini del teatro italiano*, 2 vols. (Turin, 1891)

Dawson, Giles E. (ed.), *Records of Plays and Players in Kent, 1450 to 1642*, Malone Society Collections, VII (1965)

de L'Estoile, Pierre, *Journal d'un bourgeois de Paris sous Henri III*, ed. J-L. Flandrin (Paris, 1966) de Scudéry, Georges, preface to *Ibrahim* [1641], trans. Clara W. Crane, in Gilbert (ed.), *Literary Criticism: Plato to Dryden*

Diano, C., 'Edipo Figlio della Tyche', *Dioniso*, n.s. XV (1952)

Di Somi, Leone, *Dialogues on Stage Affairs* [1565?], trans. Nicoll, in *The Development of the Theatre*, App. B

Dodds, E. R., *The Greeks and the Irrational* (Boston, 1957)

Donaldson, I., *The World Upside-Down: Comedy from Jonson to Fielding* (Oxford, 1970)

Doran, Madeleine, *Endeavors of Art: a Study of Form in Elizabethan Drama* (Madison, 1954)

Dorey, T. A. and Dudley, Donald R. (eds.), *Roman Drama* (London, 1968)

Dover, K. J., 'Greek Comedy', in Platnauer (ed.), *Fifty Years of Classical Scholarship*

Duckworth, George E., *The Nature of Roman Comedy* (Princeton, 1952)

Dumur, Guy (ed.), *Histoire des Spectacles* (Paris, 1965)

Edwards, Philip, 'Shakespeare's Romances: 1900–1957' (*Shakespeare Survey 11*, 1958)

Ehrenberg, Victor, *The People of Aristophanes* (Oxford, 1951)
Sophocles and Pericles (Oxford, 1954)

Eliade, Mircea, 'Masks', in *Encyclopedia of World Art*, vol. IX (New York, 1964)
The Myth of the Eternal Return (Engl. trans., New York, 1954)

Erasmus, D., *Praise of Folly*, trans. Betty Radice, intro. A. H. T. Levi (Penguin Classics, 1971)

Evans, Bertrand, *Shakespeare's Comedies* (Oxford, 1960)

Evans, G. L., 'Shakespeare's Fools', in Bradbury and Palmer (eds.), *Shakespearian Comedy*

Farnham, W., *The Medieval Heritage of Elizabethan Tragedy* (Berkeley, 1936)

Ferguson, W. S., *Hellenistic Athens* (London, 1911)

Festugière, A. J., OP, *Epicurus and his Gods*, trans. C. W. Chilton (Oxford, 1955)

Finley, M. I., *The Ancient Greeks* (Penguin Books, 1963)

Flora, Francesco, *Storia della letteratura italiana* [13th edn, 1962], vols. II–III (Mondadori, 1967)

Florio, John, *A Worlde of Wordes, or Most Copious and Exact Dictionarie in Italian and English* (London, 1598)

Fraenkel, E., 'The Stars in the Prologue of *Rudens*', *Classical Quarterly*, XXXVI (1942)

Frank, Grace, *The Medieval French Drama* (Oxford, 1954)

Frank, Tenney, *Life and Literature in the Roman Republic* (Berkeley, 1957)

Frankfort, H. and H. A. (eds.), *Before Philosophy* (Penguin Books, 1949)

Frazer, J. G., *The Golden Bough, Part VI: The Scapegoat* (London, 1913)
The Golden Bough (abridged) (London, 1922)

Freeburg, V. O., *Disguise Plots in Elizabethan Drama* (New York, 1915)

Frigout, Arlette, 'La Fête Populaire', in Dumur (ed.), *Histoire des Spectacles*

Frye, Northrop, *Anatomy of Criticism* (Princeton, 1957)

    A Natural Perspective: the Development of Shakespearean Comedy and Romance (New York and London, 1965)

Furnivall, F. J. (ed.), *Robert Laneham's Letter* [1575] (London, 1907)

Gage, John, *Life in Italy at the Time of the Medici* (London, 1968)

Gardiner, H. C., SJ, *Mysteries' End* (New Haven, 1946)

Garin, Eugenio, *L'Educazione in Europa, 1400–1600* (Bari, 1957)

    Italian Humanism: philosophy and civic life in the Renaissance, trans. Peter Munz (Oxford, 1965)

    Medioevo e Rinascimento (Bari, 1954)

Garzoni, Tommaso, *La Piazza universale di tutte le professioni del mondo* [1584] (Venice, 1616)

Gaster, Theodor H., *Thespis: ritual, myth and drama in the ancient Near East* (New York, 1961)

Getto, G., *Vita di Forme e Forme di Vita nel 'Decameron'* (Turin, 1966)

Gilbert, Allan H. (ed.), *Literary Criticism: Plato to Dryden* (Detroit, 1962)

Gilbert, Felix, *Machiavelli and Guicciardini* (Princeton, 1965)

Gilmore, Myron P., *The World of Humanism, 1453–1517* (New York, 1952)

Giraldi Cinthio, G., *Discorsi intorno al Comporre de i Romanzi, delle Comedie e delle Tragedie, e di altre maniere di Poesie* (Venice, 1554)

    Discorsi, trans. (extracts), in Gilbert (ed.), *Literary Criticism*

    Hecatommithi [1565], Nuova Biblioteca Popolare, 3 vols. (Turin, 1853)

Glotz, G. and Cohen, R., *La Grèce au Ve siècle* (Paris, 1931)

Golding, Arthur (trans.), *Ovid's Metamorphoses* [1567], ed. John Frederick Nims (New York, 1965)

Gomme, A. W., 'Menander', in *Essays in Greek History and Literature* (Oxford, 1937)

Gower, John, *Confessio Amantis*, ed. Russell A. Peck (New York, 1968)

Grayson, C., 'Lorenzo, Machiavelli and the Italian Language', in E. F. Jacob (ed.), *Italian Renaissance Studies* (London, 1960)

Greene, William Chase, *Moira: Fate, Good and Evil, in Greek Thought* (Cambridge, Mass., 1944)

Grenier, A., *Le Génie romain* (Paris, 1925)

Griffith, T. Gwynfor, *Bandello's Fiction* (Oxford, 1955)

Grimal, P. (trans.), *Romans grecs et latins* (Paris, 1958)

Grossmann, F. (ed.), *Bruegel: the Paintings* (Phaidon Press, 1955)

Guarini, G., *Il Pastor Fido e il compendio della poesia tragicomica* [1601], ed. G. Brognoligo (Bari, 1914)

    The Compendium of Tragicomic Poetry, trans. (extracts) in Gilbert (ed.), *Literary Criticism*

Guthrie, W. K. C., *The Greeks and their Gods* (London, 1950)

    A History of Greek Philosophy, vols. I–III (Cambridge, 1962–9)

Hale, J. R., 'Armies, Navies and the Art of War', in *New Cambridge Modern History*, vol. III (Cambridge, 1968)

Renaissance Europe, 1480–1520 (Fontana Library, 1971)

Hall, Robert A., jr, 'The Significance of the Italian *Questione della Lingua*', *Studies in Philology*, XXXIX (1942)

Halliday, W. R., *Plutarch's 'Greek Questions'* (Oxford, 1928)

Hammond, Eleanor Prescott (ed.), *English Verse between Chaucer and Surrey* (Duke University Press, 1927)

Hanson, J. A. 'The Glorious Military', in Dorey and Dudley (eds.), *Roman Drama*

'Plautus as a Source Book for Roman Religion', *Transactions of the American Philological Association*, XC (1959)

'Scholarship on Plautus since 1950', *Classical World* (1965–6)

Harbage, A., *Shakespeare's Audience* (New York, 1941)

Harbage, A. and Schoenbaum, S. (eds.), *Annals of English Drama, 975–1700* (London, 1964)

Harrison, Jane, *Prolegomena to the Study of Greek Religion* (Cambridge, 1922)

Themis (Cambridge, 1927)

Harsh, P. W., 'The Intriguing Slave in Greek Comedy', *Transactions of the American Philological Association*, LXXXVI (1955)

Havelock, E. A., *The Liberal Temper in Greek Politics* (London, 1957)

Herodotus, *History*, trans. G. Rawlinson, 2 vols. (Everyman's Library, 1910)

Herrick, Marvin T., *Comic Theory in the Sixteenth Century* (Urbana, 1964)

Italian Comedy in the Renaissance (Urbana, 1960)

Tragicomedy: its Origin and Development in Italy, France and England (Urbana, 1955)

Heywood, Thomas, *An Apology for Actors* [1612] (Shakespeare Society, 1841)

Hibbard, Laura A. (Mrs Loomis), *Mediaeval Romance in England* (New York, 1963)

Highet, Gilbert, *The Classical Tradition* (London, 1967)

Hild, J. A., 'Fortuna', in C. Daremberg and E. Saglio (eds.), *Dictionnaire des Antiquités Grecques et Romaines* (Paris, 1896)

Hinks, Roger, *Myth and Allegory in Ancient Art* (London, 1939)

Hocart, A. M., *The Life-Giving Myth* (London, 1952)

Holinshed, R., *Chronicles of England* (London, 1587)

Hollstein, F. W. H., *Dutch and Flemish Etchings, Engravings and Woodcuts, 1450–1700*, vols. III and IX (Amsterdam, 1948)

Horne, R. R., *The Tragedies of Giambattista Cinthio Giraldi* (Oxford, 1962)

Hosley, R., 'The Formal Influence of Plautus and Terence', in Brown and Harris (eds.), *Elizabethan Theatre*

Hotson, Leslie, *The First Night of 'Twelfth Night'* (London, 1954)

Huizinga, J., *Homo Ludens: a Study of the Play-element in Culture*, trans. R. F. C. Hull (London, 1949)

Hunningher, Benjamin, *The Origin of the Theater* (New York, 1961)

Hunter, G. K., *John Lyly: the Humanist as Courtier* (London, 1962)

Hurstfield, J., 'Social Structure, Office-Holding and Politics, chiefly in Western Europe', in *New Cambridge Modern History*, vol. III (Cambridge, 1968)

Iacometti, F., 'L'Accademia degli Intronati', *Bullettino Senese di Storia Patria*, n.s. 12 (1941)

Ives, E. W., 'The Law and the Lawyers', *Shakespeare Survey 17* (1964)

Jacquot, Jean, ' "Le Théâtre du Monde" de Shakespeare à Calderón', *Revue de littérature comparée*, XXXI (1957)

(ed.) *Dramaturgie et Société, XVIe et XVIIe siècles*, 2 vols. (Paris, 1968)

(ed.) *Les Fêtes de la Renaissance*, 2 vols. (Paris, 1956–60)

Jeanmaire, H., *Dionysos: Histoire du culte de Bacchus* (Paris, 1951)

Jeffery, Brian, *French Renaissance Comedy, 1552–1630* (Oxford, 1969)

Johnson, Samuel: *Johnson on Shakespeare*, ed. Walter Raleigh (London, 1908)

Kamen, H., *The Iron Century: Social Change in Europe, 1560–1660* (London, 1971)

Kerényi, Karl, 'Uomo e maschera', *Dioniso*, n.s. XII (1949)

'The Trickster in Relation to Greek Mythology', in Radin, *The Trickster*

'Kind Kit', *Westward for Smelts* (1620)

Kirk, G. S., *Myth: its Meaning and Function in Ancient and Other Cultures* (Cambridge, 1970)

Kirk, G. S. and Raven, J. E., *The Presocratic Philosophers* (Cambridge, 1957)

Kitto, D. D. F., *The Greeks* (Penguin Books, 1951)

Greek Tragedy (London, 1939)

Klein, H. A. (ed.), *The Graphic Worlds of Peter Bruegel the Elder* (New York, 1963)

Knight, G. Wilson, *The Shakespearean Tempest* (London, 1932)

Krien-Kummrow, G., 'Maschera teatrale', in *Enciclopedia dell'Arte Antica*, vol. IV (Rome, 1961)

Laidlaw, W. A., 'Roman Drama', in Platnauer (ed.), *Fifty Years of Classical Scholarship*

Lancaster, H. C., *The French Tragi-Comedy from 1552 to 1628* (Baltimore, 1907)

Lattimore, Richard, *The Poetry of Greek Tragedy* (Baltimore, 1958)

Lawrence, W. W., *Shakespeare's Problem Comedies* (London, 1931)

Lawson, J. C., *Modern Greek Folklore* (Cambridge, 1910)

Lea, K. M., *Italian Popular Comedy*, 2 vols. (Oxford, 1934)

Leavis, F. R., *The Common Pursuit* (London, 1952)

Lebègue, Raymond, 'Persistance, altération, disparition des traditions dramatico-religieuses en France', in Jacquot (ed.), *Dramaturgie et Société*

'Quelques survivances de la mise en scène médiévale', in *Mélanges d'Histoire du Théâtre offerts à Gustave Cohen* (Paris, 1950)

'Les Représentations Dramatiques à la Cour des Valois', in Jacquot (ed.), *Les Fêtes de la Renaissance*, vol. I

Leclerc, Hélène, 'La Scène d'illusion', in Dumur (ed.), *Histoire des Spectacles*

Lecocq, Louis, *La Satire en Angleterre, de 1588 à 1603* (Paris, 1969)

Legrand, P. E., *The New Greek Comedy*, trans. J. Loeb (London, 1917)

Lenoble, R., *Histoire de l'idée de Nature* (Paris, 1969)

Lesky, A., *A History of Greek Literature*, trans. J. Willis and C. de Heer (London, 1966)

Lever, Katherine, *The Art of Greek Comedy* (London, 1956)

Lévi-Strauss, Claude, *Anthropologie structurale* (Paris, 1958)

Lope de Vega, *The New Art of Making Comedies* [1609], trans. Olga Marx Perlzweig, in Gilbert (ed.), *Literary Criticism*

Lovejoy, Arthur O. and Boas, George, *Primitivism and Related Ideas in Antiquity* (Baltimore, 1935)

Lozinski, G. (ed.), *La Bataille de Caresme et de Charnage* (Paris, 1933)

Lucas, D. W. (ed.), *Aristotle: Poetics* (Oxford, 1968)

McKeon, Richard, 'Literary Criticism and the Concept of Imitation in Antiquity', in R. S. Crane (ed.), *Critics and Criticism* (Chicago, 1952)

Manly, J. M., 'The Miracle Play in Mediaeval England', *Transactions of the Royal Society of Literature*, new series VII (1927)

Mason, H. A., *Humanism and Poetry in the Early Tudor Period* (London, 1959)
Shakespeare's Tragedies of Love (London, 1970)

Maylender, M., *Storia delle Accademie d'Italia*, vol. III (Bologna, 1929)

Mazon, Paul, 'La Farce dans Aristophane et les origines de la comédie en Grèce', *Revue d'Histoire du Théâtre*, III (1951)

Mazzeo, J. A., 'A Critique of Some Modern Theories of Metaphysical Poetry', *Modern Philology*, L (1952)

Micha, A., 'La Femme injustement accusée dans les Miracles de Notre-Dame', in *Mélanges d'Histoire du Théâtre offerts à Gustave Cohen* (Paris, 1950)

Montaigne, M., *Essais*, ed. Maurice Rat, 2 vols. (Paris, 1962)

Montemayor, Jorge de, *Diana*, trans. B. Young (1598)

Monteverdi, A., 'La Leggenda di S. Eustachio', *Studi Medievali*, III (1909)
'I Testi della Leggenda di S. Eustachio', *Studi Medievali*, III (1909)

Moryson, Fynes, *Itinerary* [1617] (Glasgow, 1907)
Shakespeare's Europe. Unpublished Chapters of Fynes Moryson's Itinerary, ed. Charles Hughes (London, 1903)

Muir, Kenneth, *Shakespeare's Sources*, vol. I (London, 1957)
(ed.), *Shakespeare: the Comedies* (Eaglewood Cliffs, N.J., 1965)

Mumford, I. C., 'Relationships between Italian Renaissance Literature and Elizabethan Literature, 1557–1603. A Bibliography', *Italian Studies*, IX (1954)

Murray, Gilbert, *Aristophanes* (Oxford, 1933)
'Excursus on the Ritual Forms Preserved in Greek Tragedy', in Harrison, *Themis*
Five Stages of Greek Religion (Thinker's Library, 1935)
'Ritual Elements in the New Comedy', *Classical Quarterly*, XXXVII (1943)

Murray, J. T., *English Dramatic Companies, 1558–1642*, 2 vols. (1910)

Musurillo, H., 'Fortune's Wheel: the Symbolism of Sophocles' *Women of*

Trachis', *Transactions of the American Philological Association,* XCII (1961)

Nagler, A. M., *Theatre Festivals of the Medici, 1539–1637* (New Haven, 1964)

(ed.), *A Source Book of Theatrical History* (New York, 1952)

Navarre, O., *Les Cavaliers d'Aristophane* (Paris, 1956)

Neale, J. E., *The Elizabethan House of Commons* (London, 1949)

'The Elizabethan Political Scene', in *The Age of Catherine de Medici* (London, 1958)

Nelson, J. C., *Renaissance Theories of Love: the Context of Giordano Bruno's 'Eroici Furori'* (New York, 1958)

Neri, Fernandino, *La Tragedia italiana del Cinquecento* (Florence, 1904)

Nevinson, John L., 'A Show of the Nine Worthies', *Shakespeare Quarterly,* XIV (1963)

Nicoll, Allardyce, *The Development of the Theatre* (London, 1958)

Masks, Mimes and Miracles (London, 1931)

Norwood, Gilbert, *Greek Comedy* (London, 1931)

Nugent, Elizabeth (ed.), *The Thought and Culture of the English Renaissance: an Anthology of Tudor Prose, 1481–1555* (Cambridge, 1956)

Pack, R. A., 'Tyche', in *Oxford Classical Dictionary*, ed. M. Cary (Oxford, 1949)

Palingenius, *The Zodiake of Life* [*c.* 1535], trans. Barnabe Googe [1576], ed. Rosemond Tuve (New York, 1947)

Panofsky, Erwin, *Renaissance and Renascences in Western Art* (Princeton, 1960)

Paris, Gaston, 'Le Cycle de la *Gageure*', *Romania,* XXXII (1903)

Patch, Howard H., *The Goddess Fortuna in Medieval Literature* (Cambridge, Mass., 1927)

The Tradition of Boethius (New York, 1935)

Perry, Ben Edwin, *The Ancient Romances* (Berkeley, 1967)

Petit de Julleville, L., *Histoire du Théâtre en France: Les Comédiens* (Paris, 1885)

Les Mystères, 2 vols. (Paris, 1880)

Pettet, E. C., *Shakespeare and the Romance Tradition* (London, 1949)

Pettie, George, *A Petite Pallace of Pettie his Pleasure* [1576], ed. I Gollancz, 2 vols. (1908)

Pickard-Cambridge, A. W., *Dithyramb, Tragedy and Comedy* (Oxford, 1927)

Pieters, J. Th. M. F., *Cratinus* (Leiden, 1946)

Pirotti, Umberto, 'Aristotelian Philosophy and the Popularization of Learning', in Eric Cochrane (ed.), *The Late Italian Renaissance, 1525–1630* (London, 1970)

Platnauer, M. (ed.), *Fifty Years of Classical Scholarship* (Oxford, 1954)

Post, L. A., *From Homer to Menander* (Berkeley, 1951)

Prouty, Charles T., *George Gascoigne* (New York, 1942)

The Sources of 'Much Ado about Nothing' (New Haven, 1950)

Pruvost, René, *Matteo Bandello and Elizabethan Fiction* (Paris, 1937)

Robert Greene et ses romans (Paris, 1938)

Pseudo-Xenophon, *The Constitution of Athens*, trans. H. Frisch (Copenhagen, 1942)

Rabelais, F., *Oeuvres Complètes*, ed. Lucien Scheler (Paris, 1955)
Gargantua and Pantagruel, trans. Sir T. Urquhart and P. Le Motteux, 2 vols. (Everyman's Library, 1929)

Radcliff–Umstead, D., *The Birth of Modern Comedy in Renaissance Italy* (Chicago, 1969)

Rademacher, C., 'Carnival', in J. Hastings (ed.), *Encyclopedia of Religion and Ethics*, vol. III (Edinburgh and New York, 1910)

Radin, Paul, *Primitive Religion* (London, 1938)
The Trickster: a Study in American Indian Mythology (London, 1956)
The World of Primitive Man (New York, 1953)

Raleigh, Sir Walter, *Works*, vol. II (Oxford, 1829)

Reinhardstoettner, K. von, *Plautus* (Leipzig, 1886)

Rennert, H. A., *The Spanish Pastoral Romances* (Philadelphia, 1912)
The Spanish Stage in the Time of Lope de Vega (Dover Books, New York, 1963)

Riche, Barnabe, *His Farewell to Military Profession* [1581] (Shakespeare Society, 1846)

Riccoboni, L., *Histoire du théâtre italien* (Paris, 1730)

Ridolfi, Roberto, *Life of Machiavelli*, trans. C. Grayson, (London, 1963)

Righter, Anne, *Shakespeare and the Idea of the Play* (Penguin Shakespeare Library, 1967)

Robinson, David M., 'The Wheel of Fortune', *Classical Philology*, XLI (1946)

Ronsard, P., *Poésies Choisies*, ed. P. de Nolhac (Paris, 1959)

Rossi, Maria, 'Le Opere Letterarie di Alessandro Piccolomini', *Bulletino Senese di Storia Patria*, XVII–XVIII (1910–11)

Rossi, Vittorio, *Il Quattrocento*, Storia Letteraria d'Italia (Milan, 1933)

Rowse, A. L., *The England of Elizabeth* (London, 1951)

Russell, Patricia, 'Romantic Narrative Plays: 1570–1590', in Brown and Harris (eds.), *Elizabethan Theatre*

Ryberg, I. S., 'Vergil's Golden Age', *Transactions of the American Philological Association*, LXXXIX (1958)

Saintsbury, G. (ed.), *Elizabethan and Jacobean Pamphlets* (London, 1892)

Saintyves, P., *Les Contes de Perrault et les récits parallèles: leurs origines (coutumes primitives et liturgies opulaires)* (Paris, 1923)

Salingar, L. G., 'The Design of *Twelfth Night*, *Shakespeare Quarterly*, IX (1958)
'Time and Art in Shakespeare's Romances', *Renaissance Drama*, IX (1966)

Salingar, L. G., Harrison, Gerald and Cochrane, Bruce, 'Les Comédiens et leur public en Angleterre de 1520 à 1640', in Jacquot (ed.), *Dramaturgie et Société*

Sanders, Norman, 'The Comedy of Greene and Shakespeare', in Brown and Harris (eds.), *Early Shakespeare*

Sanesi, Irenio, *La Commedia*, vol. I (Milan, 1911)

Scaglione, Aldo D., *Nature and Love in the Late Middle Ages* (Berkeley, 1963)

Scaliger, J. C.: *Select Translations from Scaliger's Poetics* [1561], trans. F. M. Padelford (New York, 1905)

Schanzer, Ernest, '*A Midsummer Night's Dream*', in Muir (ed.), *Shakespeare: the Comedies*

  The Problem Plays of Shakespeare (London, 1963)

Schlauch, Margaret, *Antecedents of the English Novel, 1400–1600* (Warsaw and London, 1963)

  Chaucer's Constance and Accused Queens (New York, 1927)

Segal, E., *Roman Laughter: the Comedy of Plautus* (Cambridge, Mass., 1968)

Seronsy, C. C., ' "Supposes" as the Unifying Theme in *The Shrew*', *Shakespeare Quarterly*, XIV (1963)

Shapiro, I. A., 'Shakespeare and Mundy', *Shakespeare Survey 14* (1961)

Shaw, G. B., *The Quintessence of Ibsenism* (3rd edn, London, 1922)

Shergold, N. D., *A History of the Spanish Stage...until the end of the 17th Century* (Oxford, 1967)

Simpson, Percy, 'Shakespeare's Use of Latin Authors', in *Studies in Elizabethan Drama* (Oxford, 1955)

Sisson, C. J., *Lost Plays of Shakespeare's Age* (Cambridge, 1936)

Smith, G. Gregory (ed.), *Elizabethan Critical Essays*, 2 vols. (Oxford, 1904)

Smyth, A. H., *Shakespeare's Pericles and Apollonius of Tyre* (Philadelphia, 1898)

Solmsen, Friedrich, *Hesiod and Aeschylus* (New York, 1949)

Spencer, T. J. B. (ed.), *Elizabethan Love Stories* (Penguin Shakespeare Library, 1968)

Spingarn, J. E., *A History of Literary Criticism in the Renaissance* (New York, 1908)

Spivack, Bernard, *Shakespeare and the Allegory of Evil* (New York, 1958)

Stegmann, André, 'Le rôle des Jésuites dans la dramaturgie française du début du XVIIe siècle', in Jacquot (ed.), *Dramaturgie et Société*

Stevenson, David Lloyd, *The Love-Game Comedy* (New York, 1946)

Stewart, Z., 'The *Amphitruo* of Plautus and Euripides' *Bacchae*', *Transactions of the American Philological Association*, LXXXIX (1958)

Stock, St George, 'Fortune (Greek)', in J. Hastings (ed.), *Encyclopedia of Religion and Ethics*, vol. VI (Edinburgh and New York, 1913),

Sumberg, Samuel L., *The Nuremberg Schembart Carnival* (New York, 1941)

Swain, Barbara, *Fools and Folly during the Middle Ages and the Renaissance* (New York, 1932)

Sweeting, Elizabeth J., *Early Tudor Criticism* (Oxford, 1940)

Tarn, W. W., *Hellenistic Civilization* (London, 1952)

Taviani, F., *La Commedia dell'Arte e la Società barocca: la fascinazione del teatro* (Rome, 1969)

Thomas, William, *The Historie of Italie* (1549)

Thompson, Stith, *Motif-Index of Folk Literature* (Bloomington, 1955)

Thomson, George, *Aeschylus and Athens* (London, 1941)

Thorndike, Lynn, *A History of Magic and Experimental Science*, vols. V and VI (New York, 1941)

Tierney, M., 'Aristotle and Menander', *Proceedings of the Royal Irish Academy*, XLIII (1936)

Todd, O. J., *Index Aristophaneus* (Cambridge, Mass., 1932)

Toffanin, G., *Il Cinquecento*, Storia Letteraria d'Italia (Milan, 1954)
'Il teatro del Rinascimento', in D'Amico (ed.), *Storia del teatro italiano*

Torriano, G., *A Dictionary Italian and English* (1659)

Toschi, Paolo, 'Carnevale', in *Enciclopedia Cattolica* (Rome, 1949)
Le Origini del teatro italiano (Turin, 1955)

Traversi, Derek, *Shakespeare: the Early Comedies* (London, 1960)

Trenkner, Sophie, *The Greek Novella* (Cambridge, 1958)

Trouillard, J., 'Le Néoplatonisme', in Brice Parain (ed.), *Histoire de la Philosophie*, vol. I (Paris, 1969)

Vandrik, Eric, *The Prometheus of Hesiod and Aeschylus* (Oslo, 1943)

Venezky, Alice, *Pageantry on the Shakespearean Stage* (New York, 1951)

Walker, E. M., 'The Periclean Democracy', in *Cambridge Ancient History*, vol. V (Cambridge, 1927)

Webster, T. B. L., *Art and Literature in Fourth Century Athens* (London, 1956)
Greek Art and Literature, 700–530 B.C. (London, 1959)
Greek Theatre Production (London, 1956)
Studies in Later Greek Comedy (Manchester, 1953)
Studies in Menander (Manchester, 1960)

Weever, John, *Epigrammes in the Oldest Cut & Newest Fashion* [1599], ed. R. B. McKerrow (Stratford-upon-Avon, 1922)

Weevers, Theodoor, *Poetry of the Netherlands* (London, 1960)

Weinberg, Bernard, 'Castelvetro's Theory of Poetics', in R. S. Crane (ed.), *Critics and Criticism* (Chicago, 1952)
A History of Literary Criticism in the Italian Renaissance, 2 vols. (Chicago, 1961)

Wells, J. W., *A Manual of Writings in Middle English, 1050–1400* (New Haven, 1916)

Welsford, Enid, *The Court Masque* (London, 1927)
The Fool (London, 1935)

Whitaker, Virgil K., *Shakespeare's Use of Learning* (Huntingdon Library, 1953)

Whitman, Cedric H., *Aristophanes and the Comic Hero* (Cambridge, Mass., 1964)

Wickham, Glynne, *Early English Stages, 1300 to 1660*, vol. I (London, 1959)

Wiley, W. L., *The Early Public Theatre in France* (Cambridge, Mass., 1960)

Willetts, R. F., *Blind Wealth and Aristophanes* (Birmingham, 1970)

Williams, Gordon, 'Some Aspects of Roman Marriage Ceremonies and Ideals', *Journal of Roman Studies*, XLVIII (1958)
'Some Problems in the Construction of Plautus' *Pseudolus*', *Hermes*, LXXXIV (1957)

Williams, Sheila, 'Les Ommegangs d'Anvers', in Jacquot (ed.), *Les Fêtes de la Renaissance*, vol. II

Wilson, F. P., *The English Drama, 1485–1585* (Oxford, 1969)

Wilson, John Dover, *Shakespeare's Happy Comedies* (London, 1962)

  (ed.), *Life in Shakespeare's England* (Cambridge, 1911)

Wilson, R. M., *The Lost Literature of Medieval England* (London, 1952)

Wolff, S. L., *The Greek Romances in Elizabethan Prose Fiction* (New York, 1912)

Wright, H. G., *Boccaccio in England* (London, 1957)

Wright, Louis B., *Middle-Class Culture in Elizabethan England* (Chapel Hill, 1935)

  'Social Aspects of Some Belated Moralities', *Anglia*, LIV (1930)

Wright, Thomas, *The Passions of the Mind* (1604)

Yates, Frances A., *The French Academies of the Sixteenth Century* (London, 1947)

  A Study of 'Love's Labour's Lost' (Cambridge, 1936)

INDEX OF PLAYS

GENERAL INDEX

(Analytic sub-entries are set successively according to the following scheme: (1) on a new line, (2) after a semi-colon, (3) after a comma. A number of separate headings are entered again under Shakespeare)

Actors, 47, 73, 92–4, 102, 113, 118, 120, 246, 284, 295, 323
  professional companies, growth of, 31, 71, 74, 177, 221, 238, 256–7, 270–8, 286, 324
agnoia, 149, 151, 161
alazones, 91–3, 101, 106–7, 109, 111, 116, 124, 161, 164, 168, 198
Apollonius of Tyre (Shakespearean source), 29, 62–6, 148, 307, 309
Aretino, Pietro (1492–1556), comedies, 194–7, 199
  possible influence on Shakespeare, 224, 242
Ariosto, Ludovico (1474–1553), comedies, 118–19, 121, 128, 175–80, 182, 186, 197–9, 203–6, 218–21, 233, 254, 257
  influence, 33, 188–91, 286; on Shakespeare, 78–9, 87–8, 173, 189, 206–8, 307–8 (*see also* Gascoigne)
Aristophanes (*c.* 448–*c.* 380 B.C.), comedies, 89–104, 108, 111–13, 121–3, 125–6, 130, 136–7, 140–5 (*see also* Old Comedy)
  comparative references, 1, 26, 44, 88, 105–7, 109–10, 114–17, 120, 128–9, 139, 152, 158, 160, 163–5, 170, 287–8, 325
Aristotle (384–322 B.C.), *Poetics*, 22, 89, 101–2, 105–6, 133, 145, 148–9, 154, 161, 219
  in renaissance critical theories, 77–8, 85, 87, 176, 184–7, 212 (*see also under* Renaissance),
'art' (of drama), *see* plot, construction
Ascham, Roger (1515–68), 2, 122, 249–50, 280, 303
Athens, 76, 89–90, 95, 97, 104–7, 122–5,

135–6, 139, 141–2, 150, 163, 181, 184–5, 313
Baldwin, T. W., 85, 207–8
Bandello, Matteo (1485–1561), 46, 188, 192, 202, 314, 322
  novelle as sources for Shakespeare, 190, 249, 301–2, 304, 318–9, 322
  see also Brooke; Romeo and Juliet (story)
Barber, C. L., 9, 14, 18, 301
Baskervill, C. R., 40–1, 46–7, 65, 67
Bibbiena, Bernardo Dovizi (1470–1520), 120–1, 179–80, 183–4, 188, 191–2, 196, 198–9, 208–11, 218, 232–3, 274
  influence, 208, 211
Boccaccio, Giovanni (1313–75), *Decameron*, 48, 216–17, 304, 322
  influence: on drama, 39, 323; on Italian comedy, 85, 87, 179–81, 184–5, 191, 197, 199–201, 209–10, 216–17, 220; on Shakespeare, 46, 55–7, 190, 232, 245–6, 301–2, 304, 312, 315–16, 318–19, 322–3 (*see also novella* tradition)
Boethius (*c.* 480–524), 30, 132, 149, 154–7, 283
Brooke, Arthur (d. 1563), translation of Romeo and Juliet story from Bandello, 249, 303–4, 311, 313–14
Bruegel, Pieter (*c.* 1525–69), 11, 41, 48
Bruno, Giordano (1548–1600), 197, 281
Bullough, Geoffrey, 232–3, 315

Cambridge, 32, 189, 238
Carnival
  acting season, 121, 176–7, 180, 183, 257, 264, 285
  renaissance customs, 11, 41, 121, 137,

347